HIGH SCORE!

the illustrated history of electronic games

Rusel DeMaria
Johnny L. Wilson

McGraw-Hill/Osborne

New York Chicago San Francisco

Lisbon London Madrid Mexico City

Milan New Delhi San Juan

Seoul Singapore Sydney Toronto

McGraw-Hill/Osborne
2600 Tenth Street
Berkeley, California 94710
U.S.A.

To arrange bulk purchase discounts
for sales promotions, premiums,
or fund-raisers, please contact
McGraw-Hill/Osborne at
the above address. For information
on translations or book distributors
outside the U.S.A., please see the
International Contact Information
page immediately following the
index of this book.

**High Score! The Illustrated
History of Electronic Games**

1234567890 WCT WCT 0198765432

ISBN 0-07-222428-2

Publisher	Brandon A. Nordin
Vice President & Associate Publisher	Scott Rogers
Editorial Director	Roger Stewart
Project Editors	Madhu Prasher and Monika Faltiss
Acquisitions Coordinator	Tana Diminyatz
Copy Editor	Judith Brown
Proofreader	Paul Tyler
Indexer	Claire Splan
Creative Direction	Dodie Shoemaker
Cover Design	Jeff Weeks
Book Design & Art Direction	Peter Grame
Permissions	Daniel Primeaux

This book was composed with QuarkXPress™.

Table of Contents

 Before the Beginning

A short tour of the prehistory of electronic games—including an homage to early pinball machines—and the key technological breakthroughs that made electronic gaming possible. Meet the earliest pioneers and experimenters who dreamed of using video screens for interactive entertainment.

 The 70s

Against the backdrop of a new era in social awareness and youth-oriented culture, the stage is set technologically for the birth of a new industry. Visionaries Ralph Baer and Nolan Bushnell lead the way, and Pong becomes a household word.

 The 80s

The electronic games industry is ready to rock and roll. While one hit follows another in the arcades, millions of homes across America are being invaded by Atari, Intellivision, and ColecoVision gaming systems. The personal computer and the floppy disk make it possible for *anyone* to become a game developer.

 The 90s

The CD-ROM, 3D graphics, and high-speed Internet access radically change the face of electronic gaming. New rivalries create rapidly escalating technologies, immersive realism, and a wide range of crossovers and tie-ins. Developmental budgets skyrocket, interactive games become *very* big business, and the companies themselves begin to merge and consolidate.

Acknowledgments

Literally hundreds of people contributed to *High Score!*, and we are going to try to thank every one of them here. This book represents a huge collaboration of the authors with a great many people.

Of particular note are a few people who gave exceptionally of their time and effort. At the top of the list is Matthew Henzel, who continually provided material whenever asked. Also of particular note is John Romero, who pulled an all-nighter with us, scanning from his extensive collection of old software, and whose nearly encyclopedic knowledge of game history came in handy on numerous occasions. Special thanks go to Michael Katz for knowing everybody in the business, or so it seemed, and for sharing generously of his time and knowledge. We also want to give special thanks to Ken and Roberta Williams. (They called from Mexico for about 3 hours on their bill!) Special thanks also to James Bright from www.quarterarcade.com for providing numerous arcade cabinet images and to Al Yarusso, who seemed to come up with everything we needed at the last minute.

Special thanks must also go to those people who opened their homes to us and let us dig through their histories: Trip Hawkins, Doug Carlston, Jim Levy, Richard Garriott, John Romero and Stevie Case, Al Alcorn, Rob Fulop, Ed Logg, Chris Crawford, Damon Slye, Jeff Tunnell, and Lyle Rains.

Finally, our gratitude to Ralph Baer, the Father of Video Games, for sharing his history with us, and taking us way back to the beginning.

Take a deep breath now. Other wonderful people in the electronic games industry who provided us with valuable assistance include Michael Abrash, Phil Adam, Ernest Adams, Scott Adams, Wilfredo Aguilar, Mike Albaugh, Dave Albert, Ed Annunziata, Minoru Arakawa, Mike Arkin, Steve Arnold, Tony Barnes, Doug Barnett, Jeronimo Barrera, Hal Barwood, Bob Bates, Michael Becker, Ellen Beeman, Adam Bellin, Scott Berfield, Mary Bihr, Joel Billings, Bob Bishop, Marc Blank, Don Bluth, Sue Bohle, Stewart Bonn, Bruno Bonnell, Hugh Bowen, David Bradley, Jeff Braun, Michael Bremer, Steve Bristow, Eric Bromley, Bill Budge, Roger Buoy, Nolan Bushnell, Paul Butler (Artech), Tom Byron, Billy Joe Cain, Doug Carlston, John Carmack, Louis Castle, Dr. Cat, Mark Cerny, Doug Church, Bob Clardy, Kevin Cloud, Pat Cook, Kraig Count, David Crane, Chris Crawford, Michael Crick, John Cutter, Don Daglow, Warren Davis (Q*Bert), Joe Decuir, Graeme Devine, Eddie Dombrower, Jerome Domurat, John Dondzila, Mike Dornberg, Diane Drosnes, Clint Dyer, Noah Falstein, Brian Fargo, Jamie Fenton, Andy Finkel, Gregory Fischbach, Kelly Flock, Nancy Fong, David Fox, Dean Fox, Jon Freeman, Brad Fregger, Ed Fries, Tom Frisina, John Garcia, Ron Gilbert, Ken Goldstein, Tony Goodman, Bing Gordon, Jim Gordon, Dan Gorlin, Paul Grace, Kirk Green, Andrew Greenberg, Arnold Greenberg, Clyde Grossman, Bill Grubb, James Hague, Holly Hartz, Gano Haine, Mike Halley, Cynthia Hamilton, John Hardy, Neil Harris, Will Harvey, Andy Heike, Bill Heineman, Guido Henkel, Richard Hicks, Rich Hilleman, Bill Hindorff, Larry Holland, Dave Holle, Todd Hollenshead, Andy Hoyos, Dan Illowsky, Brent Iverson, Bob Jacobs, Mark Jacobs, Dov Jacobson, Jane Jensen, Jerry Jewell, Greg Johnson, Mike Kalinske, Larry Kaplan, Arnie Katz, Bert Kerzsey, Ed Kilham, Gary Kitchen, Michael Kosaka, Stuart Kosoy, Cuck Kroegel, Ann Kronen, Bill Kunkel, Craig Lafferty, Rob Landeros, Lorne Lanning, Peter Leahy, Dave Lebling, Harvey Lee, Susan Lee Merrow, Dick Lehrberg, Ned Lerner, LevelLord, David Levine, Howard Lincoln, Bob Lindstrom, Peter Lipson, Starr Long, Gilman Louie, Al Lowe, David Lubar, Peter Main, John Manley, Susan Manley, Christy Marx, David Maynard, Kevin McGrath, Sherry McKenna,

Jordan Mechner, Dave Menconi, Sid Meier, Steve Meretzky, RJ Mical, Al Miller, John Miller, Rand Miller, Scott Miller, Shigeru Miyamoto, Peter Molyneux, Brian Moriarty, Richard Muldoon, David Mullich, Bob Nall, Dave Needle, P.S. Neeley, Paul Neurath, Al Nilsen, Alexey Pajitnov, Alan Pavilsh, Mark Pelczarski, Teri Perl, Dave Perry, Wallace Poulter, Philip Price, Kent Quirk, John Ray, Sherry Graner Ray, Wolfe Reichart, Paul Reiche III, Mark Rein, Bert Reiner, Steve Richie, David Riordan, Lane Roathe, Chris Roberts, Warren Robinett, Keith Robinson, Nicky Robinson, Henk Rogers, Bill Roper, Dave Rosen, Ed Rotberg, Howie Rubin, Jason Rubin, Peter S. Lanston, Jim Sachs, Louis Saekow, John Salwitz, George Alistair Sanger (The Fat Man), Keith Schaefer, Dan Scherlis, Roger Schiffman, Bert Schroeder, Joe Scirica, Jim Seifert, Jim Simmons, Norm Sirotek, Robert Sirotek, Tim Skelly, Tom Sloper, Chuck Sommerville, Damon Slye, John Smedley, Doug Smith, Jay Smith, Warren Spector, "Wild" Bill Stealey, Kevin Sullivan, Gregg Tavares, Chris Taylor, Doug TenNapel, Dave Theurer, Chris Thompson, Ray Tobey, Matt Toschlog, David Todd, Mark Tsai, Jeff Tunnell, Mark Turmell, Ronald Unrath, Jon Van Caneghem, Dan Van Elderen, Mark Voorsanger, Darlene Waddington, Gordon Walton, David Warhol, Silas Warner, Howard Scott Warshaw, CJ Welch, David Wessman, Anne Westfall, Bob Whitehead, Jay Wilbur, John Williams, Ken Williams, Roberta Williams, Ken Wirt, Jerry Wolosenko, Robert Woodhead, Steve Wozniak, Will Wright, Al Yarusso (www.atariage.com), and Joe Ybarra.

And then there are all the amazing people who provided support and/or material for the book: Chase (Sega), Fatslicky (www.fatbabies.com), Opi, SpooNMan (VideoGameObsession.com and spoonman.roarvgm.com), Sarinee Achavnuntakul (theunderdogs.org), Allen Adler (3DO), Eddie Adlum (RePlay Magazine), Haru Akenaga, Gale Alles (Infogrames), Matt Atwood (Capcom), Kevin Bachus (Microsoft), Rick Banks (Artech), Mike Beirne (Fujitsu), Dean Bender (Bender & Associates), Benjamin Bent (New World Computing), David Bergeaud, David Berk (Moby Games), Paul Berker, Jeff Blattner, Laura Bond (Williams), Jay Boor (Atari Games/Midway), Chris Brandkemp (Cyan), Mike Braun (Tandy), Reilly Brennan, James Bright (quarterarcade.com), Nance Brisco (Smithsonian Museum), Jeffery Brown (Electronic Arts), Ken Brown (*Computer Gaming World*), Lisa Bucek, Karen Busch (Sony Online), Nancy Bushkin (Infogrames), Nancy Bushnell, Paul Butler (Artech), Tracy Butler (Simutronics), Tony Byus (Taito), Michelle Caddell (assistant to Richard Garriott), Cathy Campos (Lionhead Studios), Chris Carro, Vickie Carson (National Park Service), Annette Carter (Acclaim), Jeff Castaneda (Rockstar Games), David Chen (Konami), Willy Chiu (IBM), John Chowenec (Cinemaware), Sarita Churchill (Dynamix), Rhonda Collette (Infogrames), Kevin Compton (AT&T), Philip Crews (Thumbs Plus), Florence De Martino, Brian Dear (PLATO), Chris Deering (Infogrames), Chris Dern,

Christopher DiSalvio (assistant to Doug Carlston), Marcelyn Ditter (Midway), Garrett Dockery, Evelyn Dubocq (The Learning Co.), Tim Eckel (arcade@home), Max Ehrman, Rob Ellis II (NearDeathstudios.com, Meridian 59), Margo Engel (Interplay), Eugene Evans (Infinite Ventures), Jon eXidy (arcade-classics.com), Amy Farris (Westwood), Sandie Fitzgerald (Electronic Arts), Nancy Fong (Electronic Arts), Chris Forman (www.yois.biz), David Foster, Beth Freeman (Sierra), Lars Fuhrken-Batista (the new Cinemaware, www.cinemaware.com), Mary Fujihara (Atari), Sue Garfield (Electronic Arts), Joe Garity (Origin History Museum), Mike Gedeon (videogameconnection.com), Christelle Gesler (Infogrames), Deborah Geyer (Midway), Kelley Gilmore (Firaxis Games), Michael Greene (Interplay), Heather Greer (Interplay), Jos Grupping (http://sim-flight.com/history/fsh/index.com), Lisa Guthridge (Electronic Arts), Lars Hannig (Atari-jaguar64.de), Tom Harlin (Nintendo), Dan Harnett, Kate Hedstrom (3DO), Laura Heeb (Enix), Kathy Helgason (Interplay), Dana Henry (Microsoft), Richard Hernandez (Apple), Steve Hildrew (gamesdomain.com), Conway Ho (Hana Ho games—HotRod: The Ultimate Joystick), Sheldon Hochheiser (AT&T), Kenn Hoekstra, Chris Hoffman (Working Designs), Mike Hogan (Turbine), Robin Holland (Totally Games), Darren Horwitz (Sony PlayStation), Carla Hosein (Oriental Institute, University of Chicago), Keita Iida (Atari Gaming Headquarters, www.atarihq.com), Amos Ip (Koei), Russ Jensen, Cathy Johnson (Oddworld), Dan Jonin, Bryan K. Youngblood, Perrin Kaplan (Nintendo), Cindy Keirstead (Bandai), Mika Kelly (Infogrames), Sean Kelly (Classic Games Expo), Brian Kemp (Microsoft), Steven Kent (author, *The First Quarter*, aka *The Ultimate History of Video Games*), Zachary Knolls, Jane Koropsak (Brookhaven), Chris Kramer (Konami), Bill Kunkel, Bill Lamphear (Epyx), Maryanne Lataif (Activision), Frank Laugh, Jeff Lee, Jim Leonard (Moby Games)**,** Sari Levy (for Sen. Joe Lieberman), Alan Lewis (Acclaim), Bill Linn (Linn PR), Lindsay Lowe, Alan Lundell, Kathryn Lynch (Infogrames), Anthony M. Pietrak (www.quarterarcade.com), Jenny Majalca (Sega), Gwen Marker (Sega), Jan Marsel (Activision), Peter Matisse (Infogrames), Michael McCart (Ensemble Studios), Scott McDaniel (Sony Online), Sun McNamee, Edmond Meinfelder, Alexis Mervin (LucasArts), Mike Meyers (3DO), Kathy Miller (Sierra), Kyoko Mitchell (Blue Planet Software), Melinda Mongeluzzo (Capcom), Rik Morgan, Becca Morn, Trudy Muller (EA), Masahiro Nakagawa (Sega Japan), James Namestka, Aaron Nanto (pcenginefx.com), Rae Nell Hicks (3DO), George Ngo, Michelle Nino (Activision), Janet O'Brien (Seattle Mariners), Masaaki Ohzuno (Taito), Chris Olmstead (Nintendo), Charlotte Oster (Infogrames), Jeff Oswalt (Cyan), Alyssa Padia (Infogrames), Charlotte Panther (Sony PlayStation), Del Penny, Steve Pereira, Tom Peters (Electronic Arts), Greg Peterson, Heather Philips (Interplay), Francoise Pietroforte (Infogrames), Bill Pitts (Stanford), Jonathan Poon (Cinemaware), Teresa Potts (Origin), Matt Pritchard (Ensemble Studios), Ocean Quigley

(Maxis), Brian Raffel (Raven), Keiko Randolph, Mary Resnick (Canon USA), Hugo Reyes (Namco), Tom Richardson (Infogrames), Linda Ripperger (assistant to Gilman Louie), Aaron Roberts (Digital Anvil), Robert Robinson (Apple Computer), Edward Rogers (Blue Planet Software), G.S. Sachdev, Gail Salamanca (Infogrames), Nicola Salmoria (M.A.M.E.), Mike Sandwick (Atari Football), Joe Santulli (Digital Press), Tom Sarris (LucasArts Entertainment), Sandy Schneider, Mychelle Seebach (Eidos), Carrie Seib, Jenny Shaheen (Oddworld), Robin Sherrer (assistant to Keith Schaefer), Gil Shif (Blizzard), Marjorie Simon (Electronic Arts), Mark Smotroff, Key Snodgress (RePlay Magazine), Stephanie Sonnleitner, Dawn Stanford (IBM), Andrew Stein, Marty Stratton (id Software), Tom Stratton (Nintendo), Topher Straus (assistant to Chris Roberts), Nathan Strum (M.A.M.E. images), Debbie Sue Wolfcale (Origin), Barbara Sweeney (AT&T), Jessica Switzer (Switzer Communications), David Swofford (Origin/Destination Games), Pete Takaichi (Atari), Eileen Tanner (Nintendo), Mike Teal (Shiny), Michael Thomasson (www.goodDealGames.com), Adam Trionfo (Astrocade), Ummagumma (www.emuunlim.com/doteaters/), Ronda Valenzuela (Electronic Arts), Mike Valgalder (Jaguar), Omar Vega, Cassie Vogel, Pam Wagner, Leighton Webb (AOL), Eric Wein (Microsoft), Laura Wheeler (Westwood), Gio Wiederhold (Stanford), David Winter (pong-story.com), Sean Wolff (Ensemble Studios), Jeane Wong (Electronic Arts), David Woolley (PLATO), Chris Wopat, Hideo Yotsuya (SQEA, Inc.), Jesse Young (Midway), and Bo Zimmerman (Commodore).

Extra special thanks to Viola Brumbaugh for being there throughout this project.

A lot of people at Osborne/McGraw-Hill spent hours at home and on weekends, in addition to their regular work hours, to complete this book and get it published. Special thanks must go to Scott Rogers for championing the book and for being a cool gamer, to Roger Stewart for putting up with us for a year and for being a great (and we do mean great) editor, and to Madhu Prasher and Monika Faltiss for handling endless editorial details and helping coordinate this huge task. Further thanks go to Dodie Shoemaker and Peter Grame for the design and layout, to Jeff Weeks for the cover, and to Kate Viotto for her tireless marketing efforts.

We also have to thank the creators of the Internet and the World Wide Web, which provided just about every obscure bit of information we needed. Special thanks go to Moby Games (www.mobygames.com), to the Killer List of Video Games (KLOV at www.klov.com), and to AtariAge (www.atariage.com).

And finally, more special thanks go to Canon USA for help with photographic equipment, and to Thumbs Plus—an amazing graphics organizer without which we are not sure we could have accomplished this project!

I recently read a *Sports Illustrated* book that attempted to name the greatest athletes of the 20th century. In their introduction, the authors talked about the impossibility of reducing their list to 25 of the greatest sports figures of the century. They listed many amazing performers who did not make the cut—superstars like Kareem Abdul-Jabbar and Jerry Rice, to name two—and only three whose inclusion could not be questioned: Muhammad Ali, Michael Jordan, and Babe Ruth.

It was refreshing to read such an honest and appropriate disclaimer, and I felt a kinship with those authors. In this book, Johnny and I have attempted to tell the story of electronic games, and we find ourselves thinking of those games or companies that do not appear in this book, or of those that received less coverage than they deserved.

Our goals when we started this project were to contact as many of the principal players in the development of the electronic games business as we could to get their firsthand accounts, and to obtain as many images as we could to create a visual journey through the games so many of us have enjoyed.

As the project evolved, we became fascinated with origins and inspirations: What inspired the creation of the games we remember best? How did the companies get started? What were the motivations of the pioneers and founders who made this history? We did not attempt to tell the whole story. If we had, we would have cut into the space for graphics; and the graphics were always a central focus of the book. We've told the part of the story that seemed most relevant historically, which is no more than the tip of the iceberg. Though we didn't have to narrow our field as much as our colleagues at *Sports Illustrated*, we simply ran out of pages before we ran out of pictures and stories.

We've also discovered that history belongs to those who tell it. This is the best account we could piece together after contacting hundreds of sources, realizing as we did so that there are thousands of other stories we did not get a chance to hear. Chronicling the origins and development of the electronic games industry has been an amazing journey—a jigsaw puzzle in some ways—and we offer the final result as a celebration of the entertainment medium that has fascinated each of us for more than 30 years.

As much as this book may fall short of perfection, it has been enriched by the collaboration of hundreds of people, the contribution of thousands of images, and our own unflagging enthusiasm for the medium of electronic games. It is our hope that in reading this you will catch some grins, find your fingers twitching on imaginary controllers, hum a game tune or two, and perhaps discover something you didn't know about your favorite games.

Most of all, we hope you enjoy it.

—Rusel DeMaria and Johnny L. Wilson

Before the Beginning

In this section, we very briefly turn back the clock to revisit some of the key events in the history of technology, without which there could have been no electronic games. In setting the stage we pay homage to pinball games, which in many ways paved the way for the electronic game revolution. We also look at the earliest known pioneers— the experimenters who first conceived and created entertainment on video screens and who, in some cases, helped inspire the generation of game designers that followed.

Prologue: Games People Played

Humankind has gamed throughout its history. Whether we look at the dice and primitive board games from King Tut's tomb or the graffiti representing game boards used by waiting patricians in the Roman forum, people have left artifacts indicating play as part of their legacy.

Is it any wonder that as our technology has changed, so has our capacity for play? Remarkably, it is now possible to play the hottest games of the year 2000—2000 B.C., that is. They can be found as shareware on the Internet.

You can download shareware versions of games from ancient history. Games like the Moorish Quirkat, Mayan Bul, Chinese Shap Luk Kon Tseung Kwon, and other games from ancient cultures ranging from those of the Egyptians to the Vikings. Each game comes with a lot of background and a guided tutorial, since you probably have never seen these games in your local toy store.

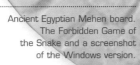

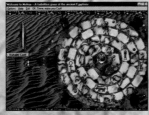

Ancient Egyptian Senet board and Windows version of Senet.

Ancient Egyptian Mehen board. The Forbidden Game of the Snake and a screenshot of the Windows version.

Top Left: Patolli
Top Right: Quirkat
Bottom Left: Bul
Bottom Right: Ur

Origins

Landmarks of Electronic Game Prehistory

1889

The Marufuku Company is established in Japan by Fusajiro Yamauchi to make Hanafuda playing cards, and by 1907 they expand to Western playing cards. In 1951, the company becomes the *Nintendo* Playing Card Company. Nintendo translates as "leave luck to heaven."
—see page 230

1891

In the Netherlands, Gerard Philips begins to manufacture incandescent lamps and other electrical products. Philips eventually becomes a world-wide conglomerate that owns electronics companies, music labels, and much more, including Magnavox, the company that produces the first home video game, the Odyssey. Philips also develops the audio-cassette and shares the honors with Sony for the development of the CD. Later, they also create the CDI system.
—see page 18

1918

The Matsushita Electric Housewares Manufacturing Works is established by Konosuke Matsushita. Matsushita is the parent company of Panasonic, who manufactures the first 3DO consoles and also has their own game development company in the 90s.
—see page 254

1932

Russian immigrant Maurice Greenberg starts the Connecticut Leather Company and creates leather products for shoes. Under the guidance of Leonard and Arnold Greenberg,

The original Connecticut Leather Company building.

Maurice's sons, the company expands into plastic swimming pools, home toys, and eventually games and game systems under the name Coleco.
—see pages 32 and 94

1945

Naming their picture frame business, Harold Matson and Elliot Handler combine their names and end up with Mattel. Using scraps left over from making the frames, Elliot begins making dollhouse furniture. Mattel ultimately creates a game division and manufactures the first hand-held games and, later, the Intellivision console. Still later, they find success with their line of games based on the Barbie franchise.
—see pages 30 and 70

1947

The Tokyo Telecommunications Engineering Company is founded by Akio Morita and Masaru Ibuka. They rise to prominence when they license transistor technology from Bell Labs and create the world's first pocket transistor radio. For world-wide marketing, they change their name to Sony, taken from the Latin word sonus, which means "sound." Ultimately, Sony becomes a giant in the world of electronics and introduces their PlayStation to the U.S. in 1995, establishing themselves as one of the most important game companies in the world.
—see page 283

1954

Service Games, created by Korean War vet David Rosen, is formed to export coin-operated amusement games to Japan. Later, deciding to create his own games in Japan, he purchases an old jukebox and slot-machine company. The name of the company becomes Sega, for SErvice GAmes. Sega produces many coin-operated arcade games and eventually becomes Nintendo's chief competitor in the home console business during the late 80s and early 90s.
—see page 232

Sega's founder, Dave Rosen in 1966

Sony's PlayStation

3

Homage to Pinball

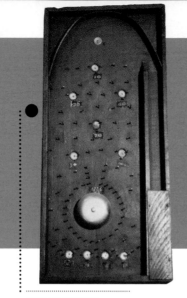

A full treatment of pinball games is beyond the scope of this book. Indeed, whole books have been written on that subject alone! We include this brief retrospective, however, because for many of us pinball was the precursor to our addiction to video and computer games.

1871 REDGRAVE PARLOR BAGATELLE
The first game to use a spring-loaded plunger.

1876 REDGRAVE ORIGINAL PARLOR BAGATELLE
Montague Redgrave's 1876 model.

1898 REDGRAVE "TWO BELL" PARLOR BAGATELLE
Note the slot in the spring-loaded shooter housing.

1932 THE PRESIDENT
Released in February 1933. It is nearly identical to the Mills official Pin Table which was released in July 1932.

1933 PACIFIC AMUSEMENTS CO. CONTACT
First game to use electricity instead of just gravity. First game to have an electrical ringing bell. First game to be designed by Harry Williams, who later founded Williams Pinball.

1936 BALLY BUMPER
The first game with scoring electric bumpers.

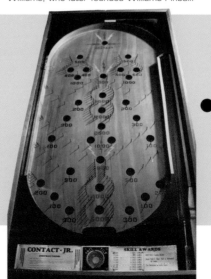

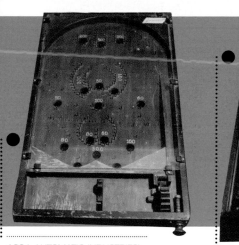

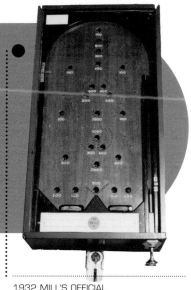

**1931 AUTOMATIC INDUSTRIES'
BABY WHIFFLE**
Generally regarded as the first
production "pin game."

1931 GOTTLIEB BAFFLE BALL
Gottlieb's first pin game. The game that
launched the entire pinball industry.

1932 BALLY BALLYHOO
The game that started
Bally Corporation.

1932 MILL'S OFFICIAL
First game to be advertised as "pinball."
The name has been used ever since.

**1947 GOTTLIEB
HUMPTY DUMPTY**
The first pinball game to use
flippers, forever altering the
direction of pinball games.

STAR SERIES
Early mechanical baseball
game from Williams.

U.S. MARSHALL
U.S. Marshall was produced by Mike Munves Company in the 1950's. It is
very similar to the ABT Challenger gun game series produced since the
1930's. The game shot small ball bearings at targets (detail to right).

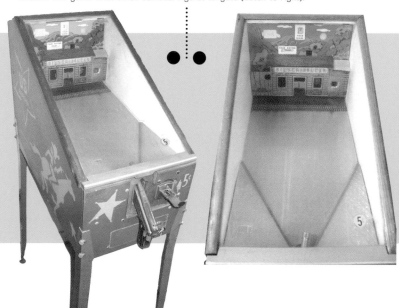

PHOTOGRAPHS ON THESE PAGES COURTESY OF WAYNE NAMEROW (WWW.PINBALLHISTORY.COM), MECHANICAL GAMES, THE PRESIDENT AND BALLY BUMPER COURTESY OF RICHARD GARRIOTT. (PHOTOS BY RUSEL DEMARIA).

5

Early Technology

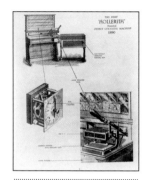

Herman Hollerith's census tabulating machine in 1890.

Advancement to the Information Age

While the concept of a computing device may not be as ancient as that of playing games, one of the earliest such devices, dating back to at least 300 B.C., was the counting board, later the abacus. This was a storage device used to help keep track of numbers. Not true calculating devices, these are still the earliest known aids to mathematical calculation.

Much, much later, but still as early as 1645, Blaise Pascal invented a mechanical adding machine, for which he received a patent from King Louis XIV. This could hardly be called a computer, but it was a calculating device and a very early step on the road to the computers of today.

Charles Babbage and Augusta Ada Byron

Back in the early days of the Industrial Revolution, the idea of a computer that could think intrigued a few intellectuals, but frightened most people who even bothered to consider the idea. One man who was particularly obsessed with the concept of computing machines was Charles Babbage, a British inventor, astronomer, and mathematician. As early as 1833, Babbage was working on the problem.

Babbage conceived of two mechanical computing devices, the "Analytical Engine" and the "Difference Engine," both of which were designed to automate mathematical calculations. Babbage was never able to build either one, but his colleague and patron, Augusta Ada Byron, wrote and published several papers describing Babbage's work. Byron, the future Lady Lovelace, was the daughter of Lord Byron, and arguably the first computer programmer. Even though the Analytical Engine was never built, Byron wrote instruction sets for the solving of mathematical problems.

Only Logical

In order for computers to evolve, many key concepts had to emerge. The idea that logic could be represented by machinery was one such concept. An expert on George Boole's work of the mid-1800s, American logician Charles Sanders Peirce was able to see that simple true/false calculations of Boolean algebra could be emulated by electrical circuitry, which could be switched between "on" or "off" states. By 1880, Peirce had devised a "switching circuit" that could be used to switch states and therefore emulate Boolean conditions of true/false, on/off. Up to this point, any attempts to make a computing device had relied entirely on mechanical components. Using electrical switches made possible smaller, faster, and somewhat quieter machines.

Charles Babbage and Augusta Ada Byron

Humble Beginnings

Hermann Hollerith's 1890 census tabulating machine may

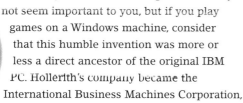

not seem important to you, but if you play games on a Windows machine, consider that this humble invention was more or less a direct ancestor of the original IBM PC. Hollerith's company became the International Business Machines Corporation, known more simply as IBM.

In the 1930s, IBM funded the development of an electromechanical computer known as the Mark I. By the time it was completed in 1944, however, it was already obsolete. Already, the speed of innovation was outstripping the speed of development.

General Purposes

Like Hollerith's census tabulation device, early computing machines were designed to accomplish a specific task. However, in the 1930s, British mathematician Alan Turing envisioned a machine whose entire function would be described by the instructions it was given. Instead of a machine dedicated to one purpose only, Turing's machine would be useful for multiple purposes. Turing's concepts bore fruit in the hands of another mathematician, John Von Neumann, who created the concept of the stored computer program.

Tubin'

While the Mark I was under construction, John Atanasoff and Clifford Berry were conceiving the first electronic computer, which used vacuum tubes in place of the mechanical relays used in previous devices. Their ABC, or Atanasoff-Berry Computer, "was the world's first electronic digital computer. It was built by John Vincent Atanasoff and Clifford Berry at Iowa State University during 1937-42. It incorporated

several major innovations in computing including the use of binary arithmetic, regenerative memory, parallel processing, and separation of memory and computing functions."*

For many years the patents and glory went to John Mauchley and J. Presper Eckert, the designers of the ENIAC, which for years was considered to be the first all-electronic computer. It wasn't until 1973 that a court ruled in favor of Atanasoff as creator of the first electronic computer.

ENIAC was impressive, however, if only for sheer size. Consisting of 30 separate units, it weighed in at more than 30 tons and contained 19,000 vacuum tubes, 1,500 relays, and hundreds of thousands of other pieces. Its electrical consumption was a whopping 200 kilowatts, and it required a forced-air cooling system.

Despite its monstrous size, ENIAC was a modern, pre–solid state computer, whose model for computer design is the basis for modern computers.

*Source: Iowa State University Web site at
http://www.cs.iastate.edu*

Above: Vacuum tubes from the ENIAC era.

IBM's original logo, c. 1924.

Left: 1946 photograph of ENIAC.

1947: A Tiny Breakthrough

Based on experiments in quantum physics, researchers became intrigued by the predicted behavior of certain crystals when electricity was run through them. These crystals behaved neither as conductors nor insulators, and came to be known as *semiconductors*. William Shockley headed one team of researchers that included Walter Brattain and John Bardeen. The trio of Shockley, Bardeen, and Brattain ultimately discovered how to run and modulate electricity through a semiconductor and created the first transistor.

The transistor was perhaps the single most important development in the history of electronics. Now electronic devices that once required a forklift to move could be held in the palm of your hand. They were more reliable and produced less heat. The electronics revolution truly began with the development of the transistor. In 1955, Shockley founded Shockley Semiconductor in Palo Alto, California, which ultimately set the stage for other semiconductor companies to move into the area. Because of its flourishing semiconductor industry, the area came to be called Silicon Valley.

The first transistor.

Shockley and his team at work.

Believe it or not, the monstrosity above is a transistorized calculator.

1958 Transistors and Printed Circuit Systems.
New, small, solid state transistors, accompanied with printed circuit techniques, permit greater speed and better reliability. Ferrite core technology replaces vacuum tubes for stored programs. Now two ten-digit numbers can be multiplied 100,000 times per second.

A Look at Nearly 30 Years of Integrated Circuits

The transistor led to the development of the integrated circuit, or IC, which combined several transistors on a wafer-like board, called a "chip." ICs became smaller and more complicated over the years. Originally intended for specific purposes, such as calculators, they evolved into fully programmable, highly miniaturized devices incorporating millions of transistors and very complex, almost invisible circuitry—the foundation of modern computers.

1985: Intel 80386
Clock speed: 16-33 MHz
275,000 transistors

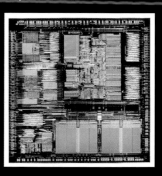

1971: Intel 4004
Clock speed: 108 kHz
2,300 transistors

1972: Intel 8008
Clock speed: 200 kHz
3,500 transistors

1974: Intel 8080
Clock speed: 2 MHz
6,000 transistors

1979: Intel 8088
Clock speed: 5 MHz
29,000 transistors

1982: Intel 80286
Clock speed: 6-12 MHz
134,000 transistors

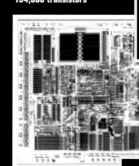

1997: Intel Pentium III
Clock speed: 450-600 MHz
9,500,000 transistors

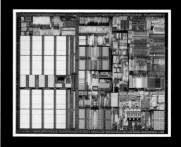

1993: Intel Pentium
Clock speed: 60-133 MHz
3,100,000 transistors

1989: Intel 80486
Clock speed: 25-50 MHz
1,200,000 transistors

1993: Intel Pentium Pro
Clock speed: 150-200 MHz
5,500,000 transistors

1997: Intel Pentium II
Clock speed: 233-300 MHz
7,500,000 transistors

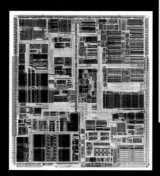

In the Background
2000: Intel Pentium IV
Clock speed: 400+ MHz
42,000,000 transistors

Tennis for Two:

The First Electronic Game?

Willy Higginbotham was a renowned physicist working at
Brookhaven National Laboratories in the 1950s. As a
designer of electronic circuits for the Manhattan Project
during World War II, Higginbotham came to Brookhaven
when it opened in 1947. In 1958, as head of instrumentation design, he decided to put some pop in the annual
visitor day by creating a little interactive game using an
oscilloscope, an analog computer, and some basic push
buttons. The result was a simple tennis game, more than a
decade before the advent of Pong. Willy Higginbotham's

"Tennis for Two" is the earliest known electronic game.

Tennis for Two was a big hit, and lines formed to get a
chance to play it. However, Higginbotham had no interest in
marketing the idea. For one thing, he later said that if he
had patented the idea, it would have been assigned to the
U.S. government and he would have made maybe ten dollars
on it. In any case, Tennis for Two remained operational for
two years and was finally dismantled in favor of an exhibit
that showed cosmic rays.

The whole thing would probably have been forgotten
except that teenager David Ahl saw it on a field trip to
Brookhaven. Ahl later founded *Creative Computing
Magazine*, the pioneer magazine of the electronic age,
and wrote of his experience with Higginbotham's game.

This is the setup at
Brookhaven with
several displays,
including Tennis
for Two (right).

HOW TO PLAY

BY WILLY HIGGINBOTHAM

The display showed a two-dimensional side view of a tennis court. A horizontal line, below center, represented the floor of the court. A shorter vertical line in the center represented the net. Before the start of play the ball was shown at a fixed position above one or the other end of the court. Each player had a small box, which he held in one hand. On the box were a knob to aim at the ball (up, down or level) and a push button. To start play, the person with the ball at his or her end of the court would select an angle and push the button, whereupon the ball would proceed over the net or hit the net and bounce back. If it went over the net, the other player would select an angle and attempt to return the ball. He could hit the ball as soon as it passed the net or after it bounced, or wait and see if it landed beyond the end of the court. There was some wind resistance, as some energy was lost in each bounce. The racquet was not shown and the strike velocity was pre-set. We had controls for velocity but judged that a player would have trouble operating an additional control.

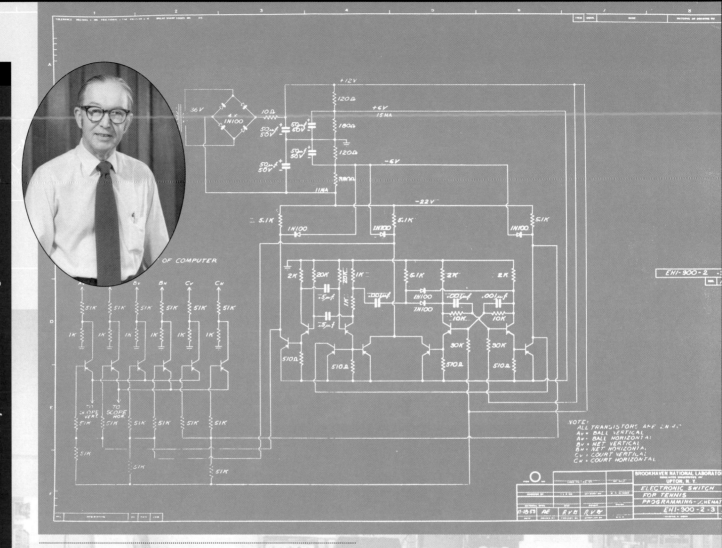

Willy Higginbotham and his schematic diagram for Tennis for Two.
At left, Higginbotham's own description of how Tennis for Two was played.

Spacewar!

In the summer of 1961, Steve "Slug" Russell* and some friends were trying to figure out how to best demonstrate the new PDP-1 computer that was being installed at MIT. In a time when most computers received input and delivered output in the form of punch cards or paper tape, the PDP-1 was remarkable in that it had a monitor display.

In a 1981 article in *Creative Computing Magazine*, J. M. Graetz, one of those involved in brainstorming the idea for Spacewar!, reported that they came up with the following three precepts:

- **It should demonstrate as many of the computer's resources as possible, and tax those resources to the limit;**
- **Within a consistent framework, it should be interesting, which means every run should be different;**
- **It should involve the onlooker in a pleasurable and active way—in short, it should be a game.**

Inspired by E. E. "Doc" Smith's *The Lensman* and *Skylark* novels, Spacewar was the first real computer game, as opposed to Higginbotham's Tennis for Two, which used hard-wired electronic circuitry, not a computer, to achieve its goals, and a model of great game design that's still fun to play today. The game was programmed into the PDP-1 in 1962, and for several years after that it was disseminated to college campuses across the country, ultimately spawning a number of rather significant ripples in the fabric of space/time or, more importantly, in the history of electronic games. Among the many whose first influence could be traced back to Spacewar are Nolan Bushnell, founder of Atari, and Joel Billings, founder of SSI.

In Spacewar, two B-movie–style rocket ships (called the "Wedge" and the "Needle" because one was shaped like a fat cigar and the other looked like a long slender tube) battled in computer-generated space. Players would flick toggle switches to make the ships change direction, and the ships would respond much like the zero-G Asteroids ships that would animate coin-op and Atari 2600 screens almost two decades later. Each ship could fire up to 31 torpedoes that would, in turn, appear as little dots traveling in the direction of the other ship. If the dot actually managed to intersect the shape of the other ship, it "exploded" and the ship disappeared. There were no particle effects and no stereo sound effects to mark the explosion. The other ship simply disappeared and was replaced by a mad scramble of dots to represent the debris of the destroyed ship.

Even in 1962, the programmers/designers were discovering the trade-offs between realism and playability. Peter Samson decided that the random-dot star map that Russell had originally programmed was insufficient. He used a celestial atlas to program the star map as the actual galaxy down to fifth magnitude stars, calling it (with typical hacker humor) "Expensive Planetarium." Another student added a gravity option. Another added a hyperspace escape option, complete with a nifty stress signature to show where the ship had left the system. The problem with hyperspace was

you never knew where you'd end up, and if you reappeared too close to the Sun and couldn't escape its gravity, well, you were toast. Later, "Slug" himself messed with the reliability of the torpedoes, but this was not well received by players, who liked their torpedoes to be accurate and reliable. Russell's refinements had leaped beyond his audience's ability to appreciate them.

Spacewar remains one of the truly great milestones in electronic game history. It directly influenced several of the great pioneers who came later. It was created before there was an industry, on a computer whose $120,000 price tag made it an unlikely commercial product. And yet, it remains a true gem of a game, as much fun to play today as it was then.

*"Slug" was Russell's nickname because, according to coworker Graetz, "he was never one to 'do something' when there was an alternative."

> *In the late 60s or early 70s, while hanging around at the Stanford University Student Union, I happened upon a machine that was the closest I had come to science fiction in real life. It was an electronic game, but not a pinball game. It consisted of nothing more than a TV-like screen and some buttons. It was, in fact, Spacewar, although by that time, the original toggle levers had been replaced by buttons. It also featured other improvements, including sun/no sun and negative/positive gravity (or none with no sun).*
>
> *My friend Steven and I played it pretty much undisturbed at the beginning of the summer break. By the end of that summer, though, there were crowds six deep around the machine, and a satellite monitor had been mounted high on the wall so people could watch the games in progress. I wish I had understood what Nolan Bushnell had known when he saw the same game at the University of Utah. It represented the beginning of a new era. (RDM)*

Screen from original Spacewar.

Steve "Slug" Russell and friends playing the original Spacewar game.

Reputed to be the original PDP-1 of Spacewar fame, now residing at the Computer History Museum at Moffet Field in Mountain View, California.

The original notes from the bus station where the first idea of video games was formally documented.

Below: Ralph Baer surrounded by his inventions.

Games on the TV?

Today it seems obvious that television sets were designed for playing games. Right? Well, in the early days of TV, it wasn't obvious—except to one engineer, Ralph Baer. Baer is a consummate inventor, and, convinced that games and TVs were made for each other, he became the "Father of Video Games."

After a stint in Army Intelligence in World War II, Baer obtained a degree in television engineering. His goal was to build television receivers. By 1951, he was working at Loral, then a small military contractor. He was given the job of building the "best TV set in the world." At that early date, Baer was already thinking about building TV sets with games built in.

"Somewhere along the line I suggested that we might include some novel features, like adding some form of TV game! That got the predictable negative reaction, and that was the end of that!"

It wasn't until 15 years later that Baer gave serious thought to the matter, but in 1966, he was still just about the only one doing so. Working at the time for another military contractor, Sanders Associates, Inc., he scribbled some notes in a bus station in New York, and on Sept. 1, 1966, he wrote a four-page paper outlining his ideas for a TV game system. Within five days, he had completed a schematic of his proposed system.

The first task was to make something appear on the screen. One of Baer's early decisions was to send the signal through the antenna input (the only one available) and to use channels 3 and 4, which are the channels still used today for video game consoles attached to the TV.

Baer got Bob Tremblay involved, and Tremblay built a vacuum tube device that could place two movable spots on the screen.

Fox and Hounds

"With that simple arrangement, we played a 'Chase Game' in which we pretended that one spot represented a fox and the other spot represented a 'hunter' or a 'hound.' The object of the game was to have the 'hound' chase the 'fox' until he 'caught' him by touching the 'fox' spot with the 'hound' spot. It was primitive, all right, but it *was* a video game, it *was* fun, and we were encouraged to forge ahead."

Shooter

Until this point, the entire effort was unofficial and had nothing at all to do with the work he was supposed to be doing. But Baer figured that he now had something to show, so he invited Herbert Campman, the company's corporate director of research and development, to see what he and Tremblay had created. The response was positive, and Baer received his first funding for the project—$2,000 plus $500 for materials.

Bill Harrison joined the team in January 1967. Baer's next innovation involved a toy gun, and Harrison designed some circuitry that allowed it to shoot the dots on the screen. "Now we could 'shoot' at that spot, and when we 'hit' it, the spot disappeared from the screen. Having the other player move the spot rapidly and randomly around the screen gave us a moving target. Gun games were born!"

The gun was a hit with Campman, too, and the team got more money and time to develop. New ideas and directions continued to flow, including some initial work with creating games to be played over cable TV. New people joined the project, including Bill Rusch, who had the idea to turn the video spot into a ball. "We batted around ideas of how we could implement games such as Ping-Pong, hockey, football, and other sports games. I am not sure that we recognized that we had crossed a watershed, but that's what it amounted to."

Brown Box

By November 11, 1967, the team had produced a working two-player Ping-Pong game. What followed was a system for programmable games, culminating in what Baer calls the "Brown Box."

What remained was to find a way to market the device. After showing it to all the major TV

The "Fox and Hounds" game hardware.

The Brown Box system that became the Odyssey.

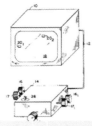

makers, a negotiation started with RCA. However, the RCA deal fell apart. But Bill Enders left RCA and joined Magnavox. At Magnavox, Enders championed Baer's game product, and ultimately the deal was struck.

The first home video game system, the Magnavox Odyssey, was launched in 1972. The Odyssey's legacy was far-reaching. Although it was a marginal commercial success, partially hampered by Magnavox's marketing strategies, it may have been the inspiration for Nolan Bushnell's introduction of Pong. (See the story on page 19.)

Ralph Baer didn't stop with the Odyssey. He helped develop Coleco's Telestar gaming system and invented Simon, Maniac, and a lot of other games and devices. He holds many patents and is still consulting.

Above: Ralph Baer's 1971 patent for "Television Gaming and Training Apparatus."

Above left: Ralph Baer with Odyssey Game, 1972.

15

Sometimes a Great Notion

The first part of Nolan Bushnell's story takes place in the mid-1960s. The day Nolan Bushnell first encountered Spacewar was the day that may have changed history. It was on the campus of the University of Utah. The discovery was especially fortuitous because Bushnell not only recognized a good game when he saw it, he knew what it could become.

Bushnell reveals, "In some ways I was smitten by Spacewar not just because it was fun to play, but I also saw commercial opportunity; I knew how much good games earned. But it was something I put at the back of my mind. It was running on an IBM 7900 or something like that. A big IBM machine. Certainly too expensive to be feasible economically.

"Now fast-forward to me coming to California in 1969 to work at Ampex," continues Bushnell. "I was an amateur-ranked Go player, and one of the guys I played Go with worked up at the AI lab at Stanford. He told me about the Spacewar game they had and I told him, 'I played that in college. I'd like to see how it works.' So he took me up there one evening and we played a lot of Spacewar. That rekindled my enthusiasm for the game and my belief in its commercial potential."

Bushnell's first project was Computer Space, a single-player version of Spacewar that he created in his spare time. For his workshop, he converted his daughter's room, and two-year-old Britta slept in the living room.

"My original plan was quite different from how it turned out. I originally planned to do it based on a Data General 1600—to have a minicomputer running multiple games. My technical addition, as I originally saw it, was going to be a very cheap monitor. Then what kept happening, the computer kept running out of cycle time—it was so blindingly slow. I thought the cost of the machine would outstrip its ability to earn. I almost gave it up. I cut down to four games, but that put the economics on the edge. I kept having to make the monitors smarter, taking over tasks. Then I had my real epiphany. 'Hell,' I thought, 'I'm not going to use the Data General. I'll do it all in hardware.' So I went from using a $4,000 computer to maybe $100 worth of components."

Ultimately, he completed the design of Computer Space, creating the whole thing in hardware. But he still had to find a way to market it. How that came about was another bit of serendipity.

"I had a dentist appointment and my dentist had another patient who worked at Nutting & Associates. I was chatting with the dentist through a mouthful of cotton about what I was working on. He said you should talk to this guy. And that's how I first heard about Nutting. They were a company who had done one product and were in trouble. They were not particularly successful at that time; they were looking for anything, so they jumped at it. Maybe a stronger company would not have taken the risk."

Computer Space released in 1971. It is widely considered an unsuccessful debut, but it did make money, and, more importantly, it gave Bushnell some idea of the demographics of video arcade games at a time when there was no such thing.

"Computer Space did very well on college campuses and in places where the education level was higher. However, there weren't any arcades as such back then. You had to put machines in bowling alleys and beer bars. That was the market. If you couldn't do well in Joe's Bar and Grill, you had no chance. Computer Space did horribly in the typical American beer bar."

THE 70s

Don't Look Back

The stage was set for the introduction of a new art form, and a new industry. The technological foundation was built. The earliest pioneers had seen farther than any others and had made their tentative steps along the path. The world was in flux, as new politics, new music, and new social consciousness began to spread throughout the United States and Europe. The 60s were over. A generation of young people dreamed new dreams and broke down the status quo. It was into that world that first Ralph Baer and then Nolan Bushnell made their humble offerings, and changed the world in ways no one could have foreseen. Once Pong became a household word, it was too late to turn back. The era of electronic games had begun...

Left, is Nolan Bushnell's manifesto of Atari's early corporate identity. It reminds us of the idealistic beginnings of this industry and of how much it has changed.

ATARI — GOALS

FAIRNESS

Fairness is the best single word which means play the game by the rules. We play hard, play to win, but we will play by the rules of local, state, federal and international law, as well as the standards of ethical business practice and fair labor relations.

An unethical corporation has no right to existence in any social framework. Besides, winning by cheating is, at best, a hollow victory.

PEOPLE

A corporation is simply people banding together in an organized fashion to produce products or accomplishments which would not be possible otherwise. When the goals of Atari and the goals of its people are in harmony, Atari is strong and its people are happy and satisfied. Therefore, Atari will:

a. Provide maximum remuneration and benefits to its people based on their contribution to its profits and goals.

b. Provide a work atmosphere in which a person can maintain his dignity and identity.

c. Maintain a social atmosphere where we can be friends and comrades apart from the organizational hierarchy.

d. Encourage and promote personal growth through education and training such as that we may all reach our individual potentialities.

e. Judge all people on the basis of their skills and contribution and not tolerate discrimination on the basis of race, color, creed, national origin, sex, appearance or personal life. At Atari, discrimination of the whites against blacks or blacks against whites; of the short hairs against the long hairs or the long hairs against the short hairs; the trained against the untrained; the experienced against the unexperienced, will not be tolerated.

f. Bring together people who enjoy what they do and are willing to strive to build a strong and innovative corporation in which we can all take pride and satisfaction and know that our part is well done. Our corporation will only be as strong as the sum of its parts.

PROFITS

Eventually, without profits, a corporation cannot exist. Therefore, all other goals except the first must be subservient to profits.

Profits should be large enough to fund our growth, share with our employees, and strengthen our corporate base.

Our profits should also be reflective of our contribution to those that our products serve. The best and most lasting business relationships are those in which all persons involved make profits in proportion to their income. By fairly pricing our products, we can keep ourselves, as well as our customers, financially healthy, and contribute to the overall growth of the industry.

PRODUCTS

We define our product as innovative leisure. We will build the best products possible, and serve our markets in such a way that through time the Atari name is synonymous with: quality, imagination, research, after-sale service, and social responsibility.

GROWTH

Our goal of growth will be aimed at expanding our current market through innovative products, as well as increasing market share through better solutions to our customers' problems. We will also grow by cautious entrance into allied fields, fields in which we can use our current successes to give us a competitive edge. Our growth will be dramatic, fueled by excellence in all areas, whether it be in research, finance, manufacturing, marketing or management.

CITIZENSHIP

We will remember that this society and its institutions have provided this climate for business activity. We believe that corporate citizenship is important to keep our institutions strong. We will be politically active for causes we feel are just. Our colleges and universities will enjoy our financial and personal support, and charitable causes will be supported.

Nolan K. Bushnell

17

1972:
The Magnavox Odyssey

I t was the first home video game system ever sold—anywhere! It was the first step toward what would ultimately become a multibillion dollar industry. It all started with Ralph Baer and his "brown box."

Ralph Baer took his "brown box" prototype to various TV manufacturers, convinced as always that video gaming was commercially viable. The first company to show interest was RCA, but after a long negotiation, the deal fell through. "Fortunately for us, one of the members of the RCA team—a guy by the name of Bill Enders—left RCA and became a vice president of marketing at Magnavox in their New York offices. And he had been very impressed with the demo."

Because of Bill Enders, Baer was invited to demonstrate the game to a group of Magnavox executives at the company's headquarters in Fort Wayne, Indiana. Baer tells us, "We demonstrated to a whole room full of guys who didn't seem to react very favorably. But the boss who was there, Vice President of Marketing Jerry Martin, said, 'We go with it.' And that was it; that was the beginning."

It took many months to turn the Brown Box setup into a mass-market machine, but in May 1972, the Odyssey Home Entertainment System was distributed to Magnavox dealers all over the country.

The original Odyssey was an extremely simple machine capable of generating two square spots to represent the two players

(the paddles), a ball, and a center line. There were no sound effects and no on-screen scoring. Using transparent colored overlays and six plug-in cartridges, the system could play 12 different games; however, many of the games required additional boards and other physical items such as dice or cards.

The Odyssey did not use integrated circuits, but rather consisted of 40 transistors and 40 diodes. The plug-in cartridges did not contain any electronics, but were used as jumpers to determine which of the electronics systems would be used for a set of games.

Other games and peripherals were available for the Odyssey, including a light gun that would react to any light source, which meant it could be aimed at a light bulb and react in the same way as when it hit a "target" on the game screen. However, since the system did not keep score, there was hardly any point in cheating.

Despite its relative simplicity by today's standards, the Odyssey might have done much better if it hadn't been for the perception, inadvertently and sometimes intentionally given by Magnavox salespeople, that the system would work only on Magnavox TVs. In its two-year lifetime, the Odyssey only sold around 100,000 units, though some sources report as many as 200,000. Only 20,000 light guns were sold.

The Odyssey was the culmination of Ralph Baer's experimentation that had begun way back in the 60s, and it clearly marks him as the first creator of the home video game and a visionary inventor.

Let the Games Begin

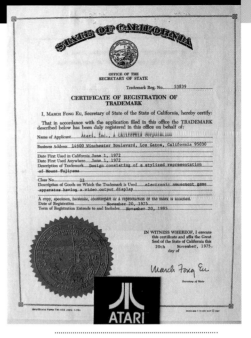

Registration of the Atari trademark in 1975 refers to the first use of Atari in June 1972. Note also that the design is described as "consisting of a stylized representation of Mount Fujiyama."

There are myths and legends, pioneers and prophets. There are geniuses and visionaries. In some ways, Nolan Bushnell has been all of them. While Ralph Baer may be known legitimately as the "Father of the Video Game," Nolan Bushnell can lay claim to the title "Father of the Industry."

Birth of Atari

Unable to come to an agreement with Nutting and Associates, the company that had funded his Computer Space project, Bushnell decided to form his own company with partner Ted Dabney. The company's original name was Syzygy, a term they picked from the dictionary that means "either of two opposite points in the orbit of a planet or satellite, especially the moon, where it is in opposition or conjunction with the sun." Simply put, it is an alignment of heavenly bodies. The name appealed to them as techies. However, a candle company had that name, and in June 1972, Bushnell picked the name Atari from his Go playing background. "Atari" is what you say when you have surrounded your opponent's stones and are about to take them. This also had special meaning for Bushnell and says something about his business philosophy.

After his lessons with Computer Space, Bushnell was sure he wanted to create a sports game this time. Something simple. He had obtained a contract to create a driving game for Bally, but he opted to begin even more simply. At this time, he was also managing a pinball route, to help fund the fledgling company.

He hired Al Alcorn, an engineer he'd worked with at

THE ROOTS OF PONG

Where there's innovation, there's often synchronicity. And so it was that, when Nutting heard about a home video game system being demonstrated at the traveling Magnavox Profit Caravan in May 1972, they sent Nolan Bushnell to check it out. Bushnell signed the guest book and saw the Odyssey.

Was this where the idea for Pong came from? Ralph Baer is convinced of it. Bushnell himself is not definitive.

"We already knew we were going to make a sports game. Simple is what we knew we had to do."

He did add, "Certainly I've never disputed that Ralph Baer created some of the first analog games. What we did was make them digital."

In any case, the decision to create a simple ball and paddle game may well have changed history. And, although Bushnell settled a lawsuit with Magnavox out of court and paid royalties for years after that, Pong was a monster hit, and the Age of Atari officially began late in 1972 when Pong was first introduced.

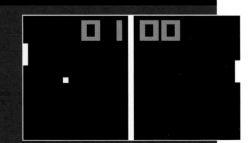

Ampex, to do the engineering for the next game. But before attempting the driving game, he told Alcorn to do a much simpler ball and paddle game. It was supposed to be a throwaway project, just to get Alcorn's feet wet. But Bushnell didn't say that. He told Alcorn that he had a contract for the game with General Electric—a complete fabrication.

Alcorn laughs about it today. "It's about the art of management. By definition, anything that is revolutionary or truly earth shattering is going to seem wrong at first. There are several ways to get people to do something. You can demand people to do it. Building enthusiasm works. At Apple it was called the 'Reality Distortion Field,' a term sometimes used to describe founder Steve Jobs' uncanny ability to convince people of just about anything. A white lie—not a big lie— Nolan was simply trying to get me to do the right thing for the wrong reasons. I could have resented it, but I think it was amusing, his way of doing it. I was stubborn and ornery enough that if he had told me the truth, I might not have worked so hard at it."

In fact, Alcorn completed the first hand-wired version of Pong in a week and a half. He then added some of the refinements that typified the great game, such as the "English" on the paddle and the ball's increase in speed as you played.

Originally, the paddles were just placeholders for a human figure holding the paddle, but the prototype proved to be fun to play. As Bushnell puts it, "Why gild the lily?"

The Andy Capps Pong prototype, front and back. Note the hand-wired circuit board and the Hitachi TV set.

Reality Distortion Fields

According to Alcorn, Bushnell actually had a contract with Bally/Midway to produce a pinball game and a video game (possibly a driving game) and was receiving regular payments from Bally. When Pong was completed, he realized

Early photo of Atari folks with their baby, Pong. Depicted from left to right are Ted Dabney, Nolan Bushnell, Fred Marenchek, and Al Alcorn.

THE CASE OF THE CRAMMED CASHBOX

When the first Pong prototype was done, they did a test installation in a bar called Andy Capps in Sunnyvale. Late at night they received a frantic call that the game was broken.

"We were worried about the games being reliable enough," says Al Alcorn. "They had to be robust enough to operate in a bar environment, which was relatively hostile. Silicon chips would burn out in those days, so we were concerned when we got the service call. We thought, 'Uh oh...' But the culprit was in fact the coin box, which was jammed up. That was very easy to fix. I can't say we really knew that this meant anything, but we did feel lots of relief. We really didn't know what we had at the time. We were just making it up as we went along."

that he was on to something and did his best to convince Bally that they didn't want the new game. First he told the Bally division that Midway wasn't interested. Then he told Midway that Bally didn't want it. In the end, he got them to pass on Pong. Having kept Pong for Atari, he decided to have Atari manufacture its own products. Alcorn remembers, "We originally intended to produce a game for the royalties, not make it ourselves. We had an argument about it at Andy Capps. Ted and I thought the whole idea of manufacturing was bullshit. Nolan had to convince us to be in the manufacturing business. In the end that turned out to be the best strategy."

Bushnell discovered that creating the cabinets came with its own headaches. "We wanted to go into higher profile places, which meant we had to tone down some of our ideas. I found that you couldn't please everyone, though.

"The real problem we had in those days was that we had no money. Venture capital was in its infancy at that time. In fact, we raised no VC until the company was highly successful. We always wanted to raise money. In those days we'd describe what we were doing and people would say, 'What? You want to put a computer inside a box and people put quarters in it. That sounds outlandish.'"

The end result, however, was staggering. As Al Alcorn

puts it, "Pong was a runaway smash hit in the coin-op amusement business. Prior to Pong, what was the big smash hit? There were pinballs, claws, driving games. Nothing like this. Pong was the biggest success anyone had seen."

A closer look at the original wiring of the first Pong prototype.

the newest 2 player
video skill game . . .

PONG

from ATARI CORPORATION
syzygy engineered
the team that pioneered video technology

The original Pong coll sheet. The back includes lines like, "a new product, a new concept, a new company" and "low-key cabinet suitable for sophisticated locations."

The 1972 commercial version of Pong.

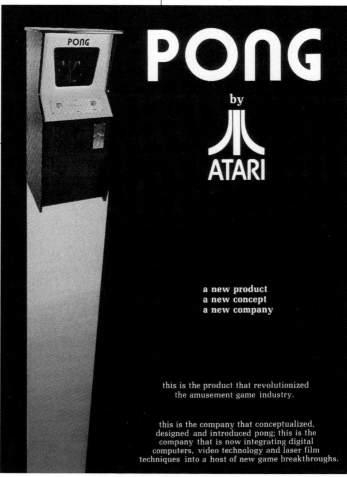

PONG

by

ATARI

a new product
a new concept
a new company

this is the product that revolutionized
the amusement game industry.

this is the company that conceptualized,
designed and introduced pong; this is the
company that is now integrating digital
computers, video technology and laser film
techniques into a host of new game breakthroughs.

"The Jackals"

Joe Keenan and Nolan Bushnell.

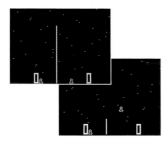

In Space Race, two side-by-side rocket ships would race toward the top of the screen while avoiding asteroids that flew horizontally across the screen. Midway's Asteroid was essentially the same game.

H owever they may have felt about being outmaneuvered by Bushnell, Midway quickly came out with their own Pong clone called Winner. But they weren't alone. Alcorn states, "Of all our first-run sales of Pong, I think a lot of them went to our future competitors."

In fact, by May 1973, Williams had introduced their version of Paddle Ball. By the end of the year, Chicago Coin had launched TV Hockey, Sega of Japan had introduced Hockey TV, Taito placed Pro Hockey in Japan, and even sports and amusement giant Brunswick dipped its toe in the water with Astro Hockey. Midway even built a follow-up machine to Winner called Leader, which allowed two or four players to play an elimination match of a Pong-style game, but the distinctive feature was the structure in the center of the screen (called the "center maze" in Midway's sales literature) that created interesting rebounds and ricochets.

Upon seeing the vast number of knockoffs of Pong, Bushnell and Alcorn realized that their own strength was in innovation. Alcorn says, "There were probably 10,000 Pong games made, Atari made maybe 3,000. Our defense was... 'OK. Let's make another video game. Something we can do that they can't do.' It wasn't easy. The company was building rapidly. It was much easier doing the first Pong with no distractions. Basically, though, the decision to do more games was defensive. Even so, it took some time to come out with our next game... Space Race."

Atari's second game was Space Race, which came out in July 1973. Midway released its own version of Space Race, called Asteroid (not to be confused with Atari's later mega-hit game, Asteroids). Nolan Bushnell referred to the people who produced copycat products as "the jackals" and was determined to beat them by innovation and originality.

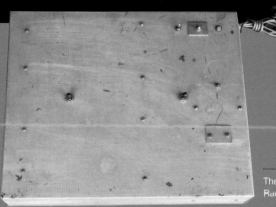

The original Space Race prototype box.

Kee Games

Sometimes getting around a barrier requires a little *extra* "innovation."

Atari quickly ran afoul of an established coin-op business practice wherein many regional distributors required exclusivity. "The problem was that our sales were limited by the nature of the distribution channel," says Alcorn. "One manufacturer could get only about one third of the market. Nolan's solution was to create another company that was perceived as a competitor. That company could grab another third of the market that we were losing to knockoffs."

Nolan convinced his next-door neighbor, Joe Keenan, to head the new company. When it started up, Kee Games "stole" two of Atari's top people, Gil Williams from manufacturing and Steve Bristow, Alcorn's top engineer. Publicly, the two companies were competitors, and there was considerable animosity between Bushnell and the upstart company, but secretly, they were one and the same. "Nolan and I even sat on the board of Kee Games," says Alcorn.

The two interrelated companies often used the same basic games in different cabinets, with minor modifications. For example, Spike by Kee is the same as Atari's Rebound (but with a special "spike" button), and Quadrapong by Atari is Elimination by Kee.

Combined, Atari/Kee released four titles in 1973 and an amazing 18 new titles (6 of which were variants on Pong) in 1974, including the next big hit game, Tank, which ironically came from Kee Games. Tank was the first arcade game to use ROM (Read-Only Memory) to remember the graphics, and it had an on-screen maze through which one or two players could maneuver. It was also so popular that dealers didn't care whether they had an exclusive on the machines or not. Meanwhile, Atari was running into management and cash-flow problems. Joe Keenan had turned out to be a highly effective leader for Kee Games, and so it was decided to merge the two companies and make Joe the president of both.

With the merger, Kee games went from this...

KEE GAMES

KEE GAMES
a wholly owned subsidiary of Atari, Inc.

...to this.

"We started a football game called Xs and Os, but then we thought a game with tanks would be better and made Tank instead." —Steve Bristow

new FROM KEE GAMES

SPIKE

THE "SPIKE" MAN COMETH... FROM KEE!

• FANTASTIC TWO-PLAYER GAME
• FOUR PADDLE GAME WITH HORIZONTAL & VERTICAL MOVEMENT
• SHORTER PLAYING TIME

KEE GAMES

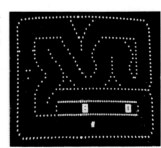

Somebody's Gotta Be First

Midway debuted TV Basketball in 1974, complete with
stubby, blocky players and two easily recognizable baskets.
They also developed a video baseball game called Ball Park
that cloned Ramtek's Baseball, released in October. In 1973,
Atari also launched the first maze chase game with Gotcha
and, in 1974, the first video driving game with Gran Trak 10.
The former didn't prove nearly as successful as Sega's later
(1976) Blockade, and the overhead perspective of the latter
didn't make it anywhere near the moneymaker of 1982's
Pole Position. However, these were the first games of their
kinds in genres that would later prove incredibly popular.

Even though Atari had started it
all with Pong, there were other
companies with bigger guns, and one
of them, Midway, licensed Taito's Gun
Fight, a clever little quarter gobbler
where two blocky, yellow cowboys
squared off with a cactus between
them. Coming to the U.S. in 1975, Gun
Fight was the first Japanese import,
a harbinger of things to come.

More from

Midway and Atari

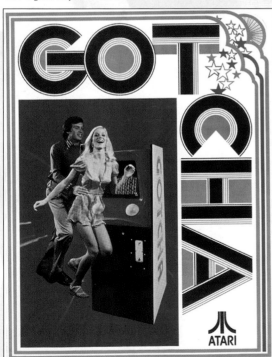

Midway's cabinets became ubiquitous.
Midway led in driving games in
1975 with Racer (a black-and-white
driving game), Wheels (overhead
perspective racing for one), and later,
Wheels II (overhead perspective
racing for one or two players). Atari's

best counterpunch was to release a big,
expensive console for one to eight players,
called Indy 800.

Midway also made arcade operators happy
in 1976. Seawolf, the classic submarine shooter with periscope and side-scrolling target
ships, became an arcade standard. Midnight
Racer, a 3D driving game with Hi/Low shifter,
was a major hit. The company even launched
Amazing Maze, a puzzle game reported to
have more than one million patterns. Sega
had a major hit, as well, with Blockade.
Blockade was a simple enough game where
you tried to avoid getting boxed in while you maneuvered
to hedge in your opponent and force him or her to crash.

But Atari hadn't given up on the coin-op business. Two
major games hit the cabinets for Atari in 1976. Night Driver
depicted a car hood in color so you could drive on a totally
black screen with white blocks representing the sides of the
road. The action was similar to 1982's Pole Position, but the
black screen allowed for a fast frame rate with the technology
of an earlier generation. Of course, Atari's biggest hit in 1976
was Breakout.

There is some discrepancy as to whose idea Breakout was.
Both Steve Jobs and Nolan Bushnell have claimed credit.
Whatever the truth may be, Bushnell did hire Jobs to create
the circuitry for Breakout. "Breakout was a funny situation,"
says Bushnell. "At that time, we had bonus programs, and
engineers could bid on the projects they wanted. When we

Gran Trak 10 used an overhead
perspective. The screen image
is from the original flyer.

were considering Breakout, ball and paddle games were considered to be dead, and nobody would work on it. So that's why I gave it to Jobs and Woz, because nobody in the company wanted anything to do with it."

Jobs took the job and got Steve Wozniak to create the circuitry. The deal was that they would receive a nice bonus for every chip they could remove from the basic 75-chip design. In a 72-hour stint, Woz was able to remove more than 50 chips from the

circuitry, and those who saw it considered it to be a true example of Wozniak's artistry. However, the final design was so tight, nobody could reproduce it. In the end, the circuits were redesigned with 100 chips.

Of course, Steve Jobs and Steve Wozniak went on to found Apple Computer (page 42), but they do have a place in the Atari legend.

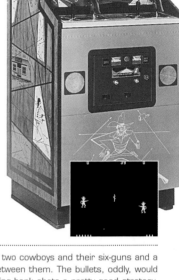

Midway's Amazing Maze had you racing through the twists and turns of a complex maze trying to beat the computer to the finish.

In October 1976, Atari released Night Driver, a racing game that gave an illusion of speed with very simple graphics.

Taito's Gun Fight featured two cowboys and their six-guns and a variety of obstacles between them. The bullets, oddly, would bounce off the edges, making bank shots a pretty good strategy.

GAME DESIGN 101

Nolan's Theorem: *All the best games are easy to learn and difficult to master. They should reward the first quarter and the hundredth.*

Mike Albaugh's corollary (as told by Joe Decuir): *The best games can be played with one hand, so you can have your beer or your girlfriend in the other.*

Albaugh's response: "Joe may be referring to the time I beat him at Tank while holding a beer. Not easy, given the two-joystick controls. On the other hand, we had both had several beers at the time. Some folks believe they play better 'a little loose.' I know that it's true for me, some of the time. On the other hand, I lost five bucks by believing Ed Rotberg could beat his 'clean and sober' best at Space Invaders in an 'altered state.' We deliberately sloped the control panels on games to prevent people setting drinks on them. We also put screened holes directly under the trackballs on Football, so if anybody poured a drink into it, it would just come out on his feet."

Al Alcorn with the original hand-wired home Pong prototype sent to Sears. Below: The return address label from Tom Quinn back to Alcorn. According to Alcorn, this box hadn't been opened since the 70s before these pictures were taken.

Homing In

The first wafer containing multiple Pong chips.

A lso in the mid-70s, Atari began another project that would ultimately have as big an impact in the home as Pong had brought upon the arcade scene. In 1974, Al Alcorn had Harold Lee, a chip expert, working on a way to create a custom chip that couldn't be copied. Lee wasn't sure that it was the best solution, given the rapid changes in technology, but he did say, "We can put all of Pong on a chip and hook it up to a TV set." Lee created the chip circuits, which Alcorn's wife would take each night to create wire-wrapped prototypes. Once the bugs were removed, Alcorn would return the corrected design. Ultimately, they had a chip design that they were pretty sure would work. They had created a feasible home system, but had no idea how they would market it.

Alcorn remembers, "We basically cold-called Sears & Roebuck in Chicago and stumbled across Tom Quinn, the buyer for sporting goods who was also the buyer for the Odyssey. He was at our doorstep within a few days. I think he perceived the potential better than we did."

But Quinn wanted exclusivity, and Bushnell wanted to explore his options, so they didn't immediately make a deal. "We took the home unit to Toy Fair in New York. Lots of buyers looked at it, but we sold exactly zero." Everywhere, it was the same. Nobody was interested, except for Sears.

Sears Tele-Games

The first version of home Pong was still a wire-wrapped prototype. This was sent to Sears in a custom wooden box. When it came time to demonstrate it, however, it didn't work at first due to interference from a broadcast tower on the top of the building. Alcorn did get it running, and ultimately Sears placed a Christmas order for 150,000 Pong machines, which were called the Sears Tele-Games system. "They paid the bills, did all the advertising," says Alcorn. "It was the best thing that ever happened to us." Still, in order to meet such a large order, Atari needed more money. Enter Don Valentine, the most influential venture capitalist of the time. Valentine was able to engineer a $10 million credit line, though part of his price was a seat on Atari's board, a position he took seriously.

Pong for the home sold for about $100, and was a phenomenal seller for Sears during the 1975 Christmas season. In focus group tests against the three-year-old Odyssey, Alcorn remembers, "What struck me was that, in the half hour the group was given to play each game, they spent most of their time putting the Odyssey together and making it work. With Pong, they hook it up and it's going 'beep, beep, beep' and people are having fun. Ironically, when they were asked what they

Pong-on-a-chip. The very first chip of the very first all-digital game.

would expect to pay, they rated the Odyssey higher because it had so many pieces. In retrospect, I think we underdesigned Pong. It was too simple."

Early Competition

After Atari's success in 1975, everyone wanted to get into the act by the holiday season of 1976. A staggering number of companies tried to introduce Tele-Games knockoffs in 1976, including Magnavox with their updated Odyssey 200 console, but none could match Atari's success, until a former leather company who also made aboveground swimming pools and a few toys entered the scene. Coleco introduced its Telstar system during that 1976 season with some last-minute help from Ralph Baer, who fixed a radio frequency radiation leak, and quickly, if briefly, rose to the top of the home TV game business. (See page 32 for more of the Coleco story.)

Controversy Erupts

Also in 1976, video games made the headlines and began a trend of criticism that has lasted until this day when Exidy released their controversial Death Race arcade game. Based more or less on the movie *Death Race 2000,* players would

Nolan Bushnell posing with the original Sears Tele-Games unit.

TELE-GAMES

ATARI

Above: Prototype of the original home Pong unit mounted on a wooden box. Right: The final unit.

Tele-Games photo courtesy of David Winter

27

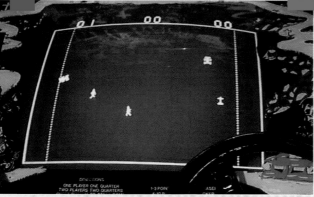

In 1986 Pete Kaufman, chairman of Exidy, created an even gorier game called Chiller that many arcades refused to carry.

compete at driving their cars over zombie pedestrians for points. The game started the violence controversy over video games and disturbed many in the game field. Atari, under Bushnell, had maintained a policy against killing recognizably human figures. Only 500 Death Race cabinets were ever made.

Cinematronics

In 1977, the next wave of innovation centered around vector graphics games. Cinematronics brought Larry Rosenthal's MIT master's thesis project to prominence. Cinematronics licensed and released the game. It was Space Wars, a new variant on Steve Russell's Spacewar! Using Rosenthal's "Vectorbeam" technology, on-screen images were created from detailed X,Y coordinates and produced crisper images than the blocky television-style graphics used in other games.

Space Wars had many of the variations that had earlier been added to Spacewar!, such as gravity/no gravity/ negative gravity, sun/no sun, and hyperspace (which would instantly send your ship to a random location that might or might not be safe). It also added incremental damage so you could slowly cripple your opponent. In the original game, one hit was all it took.

The first Vectorbeam game after Space Wars was Warrior in 1978. This was a one-on-one sword-fighting game with players controlling their hacking, bashing

warriors from an overhead perspective. The warrior figures, of course, were line-based figures displayed as animated outlines on the screen.

Tim Skelly, who was later to work on Armor Attack and Star Castle for the company, as well as Reactor for Gottlieb, not only worked on Warrior, but also helped design Rip Off in 1979. In Rip Off, players commanded futuristic tanks (little more than simple geometric shapes) on a playing field where triangles (representing fuel cells) filled the center of the screen and enemy tanks (in pairs and, at higher levels, in threes) would simultaneously try to remove the fuel cells and destroy the player's tanks. There was also a two-player mode where both players tried to fend off the enemy tanks in an early example of cooperative play.

In an interview, Skelly relates an amusing story that the starfield for Star Castle was actually the outline of a woman taken from a nudie magazine. Not many people recognized it for what it was, however.

The Next Generation at Home

By 1976, the collective creativity of arcade game designers had produced a wide variety of games, but only Pong and its cousins had yet come to the home. It was time for a change. Interestingly enough, the *first* steps toward a more versatile home game system did not come from Atari.

The Fairchild VES

The Fairchild Video Entertainment System (VES) launched in 1976 with a built-in Hockey/Tennis game and eventually supported 21 cartridges before Fairchild pulled the plug and sold the rights to Zircon. Zircon added five more cartridges before allowing the system to fade. The system retailed for $169.95, and the cartridges were $19.95 each. The first cartridge for the VES was called 4-in-1 and contained Tic-Tac-Toe, Shooting Gallery, Doodle, and Quadra-Doodle. This first cartridge was supplemented by Desert Fox, Video Blackjack, Spitfire, Space War, Master Mind, Labyrinth, and Backgammon/Acey Deucey during its first season. Ultimately renamed Channel F, the Fairchild system never sold well, and was soon to be overshadowed by Atari's next major advance, the Video Computer System, also known as the Atari VCS (later, the Atari 2600).

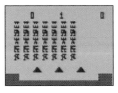
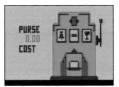
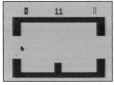

Fairchild's Channel F was one of the first multicartridge home consoles, but it achieved little success and was ultimately overshadowed by the VCS from Atari. Depicted below are several screen images from Channel F games.

Studio II

Also in 1976, RCA launched its Studio II under the magic price point for game machines of $150 and offered a variety of cartridges, also for $19.95 each (same as the Fairchild VES). The black-and-white graphics weren't very much better than those on the earlier Atari/Sears Tele-Games machines, but there were four different series of cartridges available to freshen the game experience: TV Arcade, TV Casino, TV Mystic, and TV Schoolhouse. Studio II didn't even make a ripple.

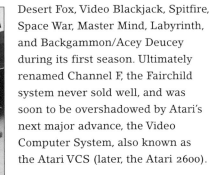

RCA's Studio II "Home TV Programmer" featured built-in keypad controls instead of paddles. It merits at least a footnote in the history of consoles for being one of the first cartridge-based units.

A Brief History of Early Handheld Games

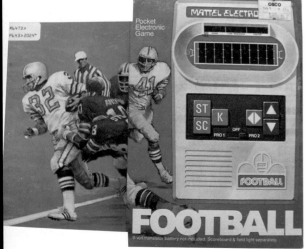

H andheld games first appeared in the 1970s. To a whole generation raised before Game Boy and other modern handheld game systems, a handheld game meant you got one—and only one—game. It was small and sat either in your hand or on a table in front of you, and it used a variety of different display types: anything from ordinary lights to a liquid crystal display (LCD) to a vacuum fluorescent display (VFD).

The earliest instance of a handheld game that we've been able to discover was a game by Waco made back in 1972 called Electronic Tic-Tac-Toe. This simple light-based tic-tac-toe game allowed players to slide plastic red or green tiles over the light to show they owned that square. After that Waco game, the first true electronic handheld games appeared around 1976 from Mattel.

Mattel

The first company to release a truly all-electronic handheld game (no mechanical moving parts, all solid-state electronics) was Mattel. The first of these games, such as Missile Attack, Auto Race, and Football, featured simple LED playfields with sound effects, and were immediate hits. Football, especially, sold in amazing quantities.

Michael Katz was director of marketing at Mattel at the time: "I first had the idea to make a game the size of a handheld calculator. I developed it with Richard Chang, who was the preliminary designer." Katz also says that the first game they released was Auto Race. "We wanted to test the market before we released Football, which we expected to do well." According to Katz, these simple games turned into a "$400 million category." Mattel went on to release about 15 games of similar design/play for several different sports. They then moved into even smaller LCD-based games and a couple of more complex, two-player games. Their biggest competitor was Coleco (see page 32), with their similar line of sports games (although Coleco moved into the head-to-head two-player games much faster than Mattel).

Entex

Entex started out with simple LED-based sports games, most of which featured head-to-head play. These were a little more playable than Coleco's head-to-head games, although they were also significantly larger. Entex followed the head-to-head games with their Arcade series, which featured some very popular arcade games (and rather good handheld versions of them). They also made two cartridge-based games, Select-a-Game and Adventure Vision, that are very collectible today, but didn't do too well when they were released.

Bandai

In the mid-70s, Bandai began making handheld games with some very weak sports themes, and they followed those with some arcade-themed games to compete with Entex. Bandai also released several promotional games for various companies, including Coca-Cola.

Bandai released more handheld games than any other company in the 70s and 80s, and they are still producing them today in Japan, including games for home console systems and Game Boy.

Milton Bradley

Milton Bradley is best known in the handheld arena for Microvision, the first cartridge-based handheld game system. Very primitive by today's standards, it had a 16x16-pixel LCD screen. It was very successful for a few years, but, ironically, only 11 games were released for it in the U.S. and a 12th one overseas. One problem was that MB refused to license games for the system—the only exception being Star Trek Phaser Strike (which was later changed to just Phaser Strike after MB decided not to renew the license). Space

Invaders was going to be released for this system, but when MB decided against licensing, the game was modified and released as Alien Raiders. MB also released

the far more successful and enduring game Simon in 1978.

Tomy

One of the earlier handheld game companies, Tomy's games in the early to mid-70s were mostly mechanical (and wind-up) in nature, with very simple electronics (motors/gears or lights).

In the 80s Tomy started making true electronic handheld games using VFD and LCD displays, following the success of Entex, Mattel, and others with their electronic games lines. They also developed a series of 3D, binocular-shaped games that were quite popular (including one with true stereo sound).

Other Companies of Note

Several other companies contributed to the development of handheld games:

Bambino: Sports games, competed with Mattel, Coleco
Nelsonic: Made Pac-Man, Frogger, Q*Bert watches
Nintendo: Game & Watch series, very popular with collectors
Parker Brothers: Merlin series, Q*Bert, Split Second, Bank Shot

Radio Shack (Tandy): Didn't develop their own games, but released a lot of handheld games licensed from companies like Bandai, Tiger, and Tomy

Tiger: Made several rare tabletop games. Among the rarest is their tabletop version of Star Castle. Tiger still makes many LCD handheld games.

NOTE: This section was written with the help of Rik Morgan. You can visit Rik's online Handheld Museum at http://users2.ev1.net/~rik1138/index.html

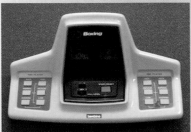

Coleco

Founded by Russian immigrant Maurice Greenberg, the Connecticut Leather Company began operation in 1932, in the midst of the Great Depression. Over the years, Greenberg and his son Leonard manufactured a great variety of items, gradually migrating into plastics and toys. They were enormously successful with many of their toys, especially their plastic wading pools. In 1962, they sold off the leather goods portion of the company, became Coleco Industries, Inc., and went public at $5 a share. In 1966, Greenberg's other son Arnold left his legal partnership to become Coleco's chief legal counsel and later its president.

Coleco was run by the Greenbergs—father and sons. It was the combination of Maurice's hard work and optimism, Leonard's manufacturing and engineering talent, and Arnold's financial and marketing skills that took Coleco to the pinnacle of success. In 1971, the company was listed on the New York Stock Exchange. Jim Gordon, who was director of creative services at Coleco, says, "Coleco was a New York Stock Exchange, Fortune 500 company that was run like a Jewish delicatessen. Whoever screamed last or loudest always got what they wanted. I loved every minute of it."

Coleco's entry into the electronic game field

came in 1976 when they introduced Telstar, a home Pong-type game. Arnold Greenberg relates that the company was heavily weighted toward spring and summer items. "Factory utilization was not as well balanced as it should be, which whetted our appetites for the game business."

Eric Bromley, who came from Midway and became Coleco's chief electronics designer, remembers the breakthrough that led to Telstar. "Originally, Coleco was looking for an analog device, saving nickels and pennies to get it under $100. With the GI (General Instruments) single-chip solution, you put this chip on a board, made an RF generator out of an LC (or later RC) oscillator, and added some gates to convert RGB signal to black and white. The chipset was

May 25, 1971, first day of trading on NYSE. From left: Melvin Gershman, Arnold Greenberg, NYSE official, Maurice Greenberg, Leonard Greenberg.

Among the products that were late to market in 1978 was the Telstar Arcade, which, had it been shipped on time, would have been one of the first cartridge-based game machines.

Telstar Arcade cartridges were distinctively triangular and contained a chip with entire games on each. According to Eric Bromley, they were not originally going to be silver in color. "The oscillators were generating too much heat and RF interference, so we used this aluminum coating as an RF shield."

Combat was a two-player tank game, another of Coleco's entries in the console market after the original Telstar.

maybe $8 to $10 at the time. Add some pieces of 'glue', as we called it, and your cost was around $12 to $20. At that point, Coleco could sell a game for $69.95. The formula—the magic price point—was cost times three."

Telstar was a huge success, and Coleco attempted to follow up by releasing eight new game systems in 1977. But a combination of events, including a 60-day dock strike, prevented them from meeting Christmas demand, and they were forced to liquidate below cost. According to Arnold Greenberg, "There was a kind of steady electronic trail. You would go from the basic Pong game into more sophisticated console-based dedicated video games. And by 1978, the world was changing and programmability was key and handheld was key."

The Fickle Finger of Fate

Forced to liquidate inventory after demand had subsided, Coleco suffered its worst losses in 30 years. In 1978 they were in financial trouble, but their recovery was equally rapid. Mattel had released the first of their handheld games, and Coleco immediately saw an opportunity.

It wasn't unusual for Arnold Greenberg to walk straight from the lab, having witnessed an engineering break-through, and schedule a product demo for the very next day, causing the product's designers to have to scramble to put something presentable together. Eric Bromley tells a story about how disaster turned into a bonanza: "One time, with almost no warning, we found ourselves demonstrating the prototype of our handheld football game, Electronic Quarterback, which was an upscale

version of Mattel's football game. Ours had passing, for one thing. The company's initial plan was to sell exclusively to Sears and move about 200,000 pieces. The salespeople had no faith in any product, and if they could sell anything, they were happy. Well, we sent over a shoebox with the electronics and a hand-built game unit that had 92 tiny hand-wired LEDs in it—some kid with tweezers and a soldering iron had spent maybe four weeks on it. But at the demo, one of the Sears guys accidentally tripped over the umbilical cord that extended between the prototype and the actual electronics in the shoebox; he sent the handheld prototype flying. I got it back in a bag, smashed into a hundred pieces—this $6,000 prototype. It was the best thing that could have happened to us. Sears didn't buy it, and we sold 3 million of them."

Coleco entered the handheld market in a big way. One of their winning strategies was to air competitive TV commercials featuring two actors dressed up as Mattel's and Coleco's football games. This competitive ad predated the famous Intellivision/Atari 2600 competitive ad by a few years and was the first of its kind in the toy industry.

Coleco's handheld line included a variety of toys, including their popular head-to-head line, which featured two-player competitive action.

Nolan [Bushnell] talked about using slip counters instead of analog delays. Analog devices would play differently on a hot day, for instance. The controls would behave differently. Nolan's concept was to use slip counters to digitize movement using vertical and horizontal counts. He got rid of all those timing devices. It was just brilliant. It was the most important thing that ever happened to video games, going out of analog to digital.

—ERIC BROMLEY

Mattel was first to market with their hand-held football game (which, as well as handheld baseball, has been re-released and is now available in toy stores). Coleco soon entered the handheld game business and produced a variety of products over the years.

Coleco's comparative TV commercial was the first of its kind in electronic game history.

In the 80s, Coleco and other handheld makers came out with mini arcade games based on popular arcade titles.

Designed by Nintendo, Space Blaster was in Coleco's 1978 catalog but, according to Eric Bromley, was never released.

35

Game Brain

tari's first response to the new cartridge-based systems was to develop a very simple multi-game console called the Game Brain. In actuality, Game Brain had almost nothing inside it. The cartridges were each self-contained versions of games Atari had previously released as stand-alone systems, such as Super Pong, Ultra Pong, Stunt Cycle, Video Pinball, and Video Music.

Game Brain was never released, in part due to the far superior system Atari was in the process of bringing to completion, and is considered a very rare collectible, as only a small number were created as prototypes.

Stella

Even before Fairchild came out with their Channel F system, Nolan Bushnell and his team had begun development on an advanced new system that incorporated interchangeable cartridges. Al Alcorn says, "At that time, game development was very expensive and required a custom chip every time. A microprocessor-based cartridge system was much better. The challenge was to design a system or base unit that was flexible enough to play a lot of kinds of games."

The original prototype of the VCS—code-named Stella after Joe Decuir's bicycle—the system that would ultimately become the first great home console system.

Ultimately, they turned to their Grass Valley facility—Atari's think tank. Steve Mayer found a chip that could handle the graphics and supply the speed and versatility to power the system they had in mind. It was the 6502 chip from MOS Technologies, designed by Chuck Peddle, founder of MOS. The 6502 was powerful for its time, outperforming and selling for less than competitive chips such as the Intel 8080 and the Motorola 6800 chip. Ironically, the chip that Atari eventually chose for their game system, the 6507, was a slightly limited version of the 6502 used in the first generation of personal computers.

Once the chip was secured, the team was assembled and included Jay Miner (see page 109), who was borrowed from Synertech (the company that designed custom chips for Atari); Ron Milner, who specialized on the sound module; Larry Wagner, a mathematician and game programmer; and Joe Decuir, a talented engineer.

The Atari VCS

The VCS entered the market with nine games: Combat (a variation on Tank, packed with the system), Air-Sea Battle, Basic Math, Blackjack, Indy 500, Star Ship, Street Racer, Surround, and Video Olympics. It also introduced several improvements over previous home console products. Its games were far more colorful, and its controls, which contained the usual knobs for controlling tennis-style games, also introduced something new to the home game systems, the joystick. Other innovations included game selector switches and difficulty settings.

The VCS did have some limitations, however. It was originally designed to handle simple games like Pong and Tank, as the screenshots on the next page clearly show. Nobody quite anticipated the incredible variety of games this system would eventually support. Its true versatility and potential did not really appear at first.

The VCS failed to live up to sales expectations its first Christmas season, much to the chagrin of Warner, who had invested around $100 million by that time (see page 40). There were various reasons for its lackluster performance, among them distribution problems and, possibly, competition from new handheld games, which were popular that season. Despite a slow start, the VCS was destined for greatness. Read on...

Stella, the bicycle... Still owned and operated by Joe Decuir.

In those days, it was very expensive to create a new game, so when we designed Stella, our intention was to save money. We were able to move significant functions out of hardware and into software. In doing so, the unintended consequence was to create a far more open system, to put the functionality in the hands of creative people who went way beyond what we, as the original designers, had expected. It comes down to a very important engineering principle. I remember, years later, hearing Bill Joy, who became chief technologist at Sun Microsystems, mention this principle—that not all the smart people in the industry work for you. We followed this principle by accident, and Stella's success was directly related to it.

—*JOE DECUIR*

Background: Hand-drawn architectural drawing of the VCS courtesy of Joe Decuir.

37

From Atari's first VCS catalog:

Strap yourself down, take a deep breath, and get ready. Ready for your new challenge-packed Video Game Program from Atari. You're destined for thrill after thrill, whether you're in the thick of a dogfight, screaming around a race track or dodging asteroids as you hurtle through space.

If this is your first Game Program, congratulations. But we've got others. All different, all in color (on color TVs), and all with more games and game variations per Game Program cartridge than anybody else. With new cartridges on the way all the time. So pick up the remote controllers, plug your new Game Program into Atari's Video Computer System™, and get ready for action. Atari action.

The Competitive Advantage of the VCS

"The VCS was much cheaper to build than any other system," according to Al Alcorn. "All the other systems were designed by semiconductor companies, and there was no incentive to reduce the use of silicon. The VCS had no frame buffer; all the other systems did. In those days memory was very expensive."

Alcorn continues: "The VCS was the most successful system because of the variety of games it could play, which was largely due to its elegant architecture. The competitors' architecture was too constraining and limited the range of games they could produce. The minimal architecture of Stella wound up being more flexible than even its designers imagined."

Explaining the Frame Buffer

Alcorn explained the innovation that made Atari such an unexpectedly long-lived and versatile system. "Actually it's quite simple. The obvious approach and the one used everywhere today is to have a large area of memory that represents each pixel on the display. That area is scanned out by special circuitry at high speed to drive a display. The computer can write to any part of the display and change the image. If the computer doesn't do anything, the display remains static. So if you had a display of 640 x 480 pixels of only 8 bits per pixel (256 colors), that would require 640 x 480 bytes or 307,200 bytes! Prohibitive in those days. So other game systems used larger pixels and 4 bits per pixel, but it was still the majority of the cost of the system. Stella relied on a very fast

microprocessor and a custom chip (Stella) that generated two lines of video on the fly. If the computer stopped (like if you pulled out the cartridge when it was running), the display turned to garbage. We had only 128 bytes of memory versus thousands of bytes in the competition. It was a bitch to program because the software had to do the job in a limited number of cycles or it missed the end of a scan line."

We actually put audio hardware in instead of trying to make the microprocessor do all the sounds. Being able to go beyond beeps and buzzes with a programmable sound module meant that you could use random noise for things like gunshots, regular sounds for motors and that kind of thing, and, well... beeps and buzzes, too.

—RON MILNER

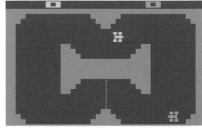

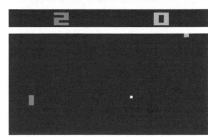

The first crop of games for the VCS were very simple and crude. Here are screens for Combat, Indy 500, Street Racer, and Video Olympics.

Stella originally accommodated 4K cartridges, but our first games were on 2K carts because those were the cheapest ROMs at the time. We saved about $1 in cost by using a 28-pin 6502 derivative (the 6507) and a 24-pin cartridge connector. If we had used a full 40-pin 6502 and a 30-pin connector, we could have easily supported the full 64K address space in the cartridge, and RAM, and even an expansion box. As it turned out, many companies performed a lot of tricks with the VCS to fake a read-write strobe in the cartridges, so they could extend the address space by bank selection. At the time, we never anticipated the system's longevity or the need for so much memory. We opted to keep the costs as low as possible.

—JOE DECUIR

Boxes from the first Atari VCS games.

WARREN ROBINETT AND THE EASTER EGG

It is standard procedure to place undocumented features and objects in games today. They are called Easter Eggs. But there had to be a first time, and it happened like this: Warren Robinett, a young programmer at Atari, would later go on to help found The Learning Company and to create the classic teaching game, Rocky's Boots, but he made his mark on game history first in 1979-1980.

"When I first went to Atari, I thought I'd died and gone to heaven. I was being paid to design games. But then, after about a year and a half, it started to dawn on me that Atari was making hundreds of millions of dollars and keeping us all anonymous. They didn't even give you a pizza if you designed a good game. There was no incentive at all. Nothing. That's when I had the idea of hiding my name in the game."

Warren created a very secret room in his VCS game Adventure that could only be accessed by selecting a single gray dot on a gray wall. If someone were clever enough to find the room, he found Warren's name written inside—completely against Atari policy. "I could have been fired if

anyone had discovered it, so I kept the secret for a year. It's damned hard to keep a secret for a year—especially a juicy secret like that—but I reasoned that if I couldn't keep the secret, then how could I expect my friends to do so. The game code would have been very easy for Atari to change if they had known about the secret room. But after 300,000 Adventure cartridges had been made and shipped around the world, it was too late.

"Being best known for inventing Easter Eggs in games is a bit irritating. I'd rather be known for inventing the action-adventure game. But, when it comes down to it, I'm happy anyone remembers my games from 20 years ago. At the time, I certainly wasn't looking 20 years ahead."

Although Robinett's Easter Egg was the first of its kind in a video game, hidden features were often incorporated into pinball games, according to former Midway and Coleco designer Eric Bromley. "At Midway, they had me create flaws so if a kid banged on the box a certain way they could get bonus score. Kids would look for these 'flaws,' but it would cost lots of quarters. We had a bunch of other tricks, too."

Big Changes at Atari

Meanwhile, back at Atari, ever the competitor, Bushnell realized that he would need to release the VCS in quantity and overwhelm his competition. In order to manufacture enough units, Bushnell began to look for another infusion of cash. The market was unfavorable for making a public offering, so the Atari board of directors decided it was time to sell the company. Bushnell approached Universal and Disney, but neither company was interested. However, Warner Communications was interested, and they sent Manny Gerard, a VP and Wall Street entertainment analyst, to go check out Atari. Despite Atari's unorthodoxy, Gerard

recommended that Warner buy the company. Put simply, the deal was consummated four months later for $28 million. It was the end of an era, though at first it seemed to be business as usual, but with more cash.

What happened next has been well documented in other books, including Steven Kent's *The First Quarter*. In short, the VCS did poorly its first Christmas, the video game business weakened significantly, and Bushnell's philosophy clashed mightily with that of the East Coast Warner conglomerate. By the end of 1978, Gerard had invoked legal clauses in the sale contract and removed Bushnell from Atari.

Warner installed Ray Kassar, a former vice president of Burlington, a textile company, as the new CEO, and despite the fact that the true "Golden Age" of Atari was just around the corner, many people believe that the clash between Kassar's buttoned-down, autocratic style and Atari's freewheeling, pot-smoking, "Work smarter, not harder" attitudes ultimately caused the company to come apart at the seams. To many Atari employees, Kassar came to be known, not so affectionately, as the "sock king" or the "towel czar" because of his background in the textile industry.

There were many tensions at Atari, which centered once again

Detail from the cover of one of Atari's newsletters.

Computers or Games?

With the amazing success of Apple Computer, it became clear that the age of home computers had arrived, and Atari intended to be a part of that revolution. The first Atari home computers, the Atari 400 and Atari 800, debuted in late 1979. However, Atari never really achieved anything like Apple's success, but the attention paid to the computer side did affect the game side of the company.

One person directly affected was Al Alcorn, who was working at the time with a select team on a special project called the Cosmos—a game system that used holographic technologies obtained by Atari when the developer of those technologies went bankrupt. In the end, Kassar refused to release Cosmos, prompting Alcorn to quit. With Bushnell already gone, the original team that had started the company was no longer there.

The Big Clash

Perhaps even more significant was the dissatisfaction of the chief designer/engineers at the company. Kassar had routinely refused to allow their names to be publicized with the games, and even changed some names when speaking about them to the press. Moreover, he refused to pay royalties, so, while some games were making the company many millions, the designers were given nothing to acknowledge their contributions. Take the case of Rob Fulop, whose Missile Command cart for the VCS sold 2.5 million copies.

around Kassar, his plans for the company, and his treatment of his creative team members.

His Christmas bonus was "the same as any secretary got—a certificate for a free Norbest turkey." "He was classical management," says Atari game designer Howard Scott Warshaw, of Kassar. "He was used to blue-collar and white-collar workers. You handled blue-collar workers, who were at the bottom of the org chart. You dealt with the white-collar workers. To him, software engineers, who were at the bottom of the org chart, were to be handled, but he didn't take into account that we were highly intelligent, creative people who didn't take well to being handled. He simply had no frame of reference for who we were."

Chris Crawford, pioneer game designer who worked for several years at Atari, also remembers Kassar's clash with the engineers. "He never could integrate smoothly with the engineers. There was always a war going on, which was stupid, wasteful, and destroyed morale." This situation ultimately led to the defection of some of Atari's brightest designers and the founding of competitive companies like Activision and Imagic.

Despite its problems, Atari was destined to make still more history during the Kassar years. The VCS did sell well the next Christmas, but it had still not reached its peak. Meanwhile, the unconventional designers at Atari were about to unleash some of the greatest games in video game history on the public. The Golden Age of Atari was just around the corner.

Meanwhile, Bushnell purchased back from Atari his pet project—the Videotime Theater franchise—for about $500,000, and proceeded to open the highly successful Chuck E. Cheese's chain of restaurants, where families could eat pizza and play games.

JUST ANOTHER
HIGH-STRUNG
PRIMA DONNA
from ATARI®

One of Ray Kassar's unfortunate comments was to call the Atari designers and engineers "high-strung prima donnas." Their response? This shirt. He also called his engineers "towel designers"— another famous bon mot.

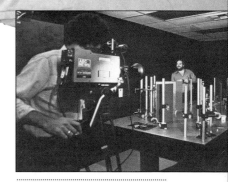

Al Alcorn in the holography lab, working on Cosmos.

Apple: A Modern Fairy Tale

Steve Wozniak, known popularly as simply "Woz," was already building electronic devices in the second grade. His obsession with building his own computer started almost as early. His first working computer was built in 1971 with his friend Bill Fernandez. They called it the "Cream Soda Computer" after the beverage of choice imbibed while designing it.

It was also Fernandez who introduced Woz to a skinny, quiet kid a few years younger but full of self-confidence. At the age of 12, Steve Jobs had gotten parts for a home project by calling Bill Hewlett, the founder of Hewlett-Packard, on the phone. He had actually worked at HP during the summer of his 13th year.

The combination of Woz and Jobs was incredibly fortuitous. Their diverse talents combined to create a true revolution. Both pranksters, they were notorious for their practical jokes, which often involved electronic devices created solely to freak people out. However, their first real enterprise was building "blue boxes" used to bypass long-distance charges on telephones. Inspired by an article in *Esquire* about the famous John Draper, aka "Captain Crunch," they built and sold "a ton" of them, according to Wozniak (who was known as Berkeley Blue to the phone phreakers).

Steve Jobs and Steve Wozniak working on the Apple II.

The Apple Computer

While working at HP in 1976, Wozniak designed and built a computer based on the MOS Technologies 6502 chip. The 6502 was a good chip, but most hobbyists of the time considered it harder to use as the "brains" of a computer than the Intel chips. However, its $20 price made it the chip of choice for Woz. It's unclear how this new computer got its name or why, but it's likely to have been Jobs' idea. After demonstrating the Apple I at the Homebrew Computer Club, where Woz freely passed out photocopies of his design to anyone interested, Jobs suggested starting a company. Woz, happy at HP, demurred; but Jobs' powers of persuasion were legendary, and ultimately they began Apple Computer on April Fool's Day, 1976.

Perhaps the rest would be a different history if it had not been for Jobs' confidence, ambition, and vision. After fulfilling an order for 50 Apple I computers for the Byte Shop, he went directly to Nolan Bushnell for advice on where to go next. Bushnell connected Jobs with legendary Silicon Valley

venture capitalist Don Valentine, who, in turn, connected
him with Mike Markkula, who had retired a millionaire from
Intel a year before and was enjoying his free time.

Markkula ultimately invested a considerable sum in Apple
and brought in Michael Scott from Intel to run the business.
Meanwhile, Wozniak was working on his "dream" computer,
the Apple II, which debuted at the first West Coast
Computer Faire in April 1977.

The addition of Regis McKenna as Apple's PR representa-
tive was the last significant piece in the puzzle. McKenna's
marketing savvy combined well with Woz's genius, Jobs'
charisma, and Markkula's business and marketing sense.
To make a long story short, the Apple II was a superior
machine, capable of displaying color graphics on a TV set or
monitor. The next year, Woz created the circuitry for Apple's
first floppy disk drive, which was a critical addition to the

Steve Jobs at
the Apple booth
at the West Coast
Computer Faire.

Steve Jobs in his
garage workshop.

The original
Apple II with
cassette
storage drive

43

machine, whose original cassette interface was slow, frustrating, and unreliable at best.

Then, one more critical element appeared—VisiCalc, the first spreadsheet program, which was the brainchild of Dan Bricklin of Software Arts and was sold by Personal Software. (For the complete story of the invention of VisiCalc, see Bricklin's excellent Web site at www.bricklin.com.) With the addition of the floppy drive and the revolutionary new spreadsheet program available only on the Apple II, Apple's sales exploded, and the company came to dominate the world of personal computers—for a time, at least.

Games and the Apple II

Games always figured into the Apple story. In fact, as early as second grade, Woz had created simple electronic games. Many of the engineers and programmers who helped create Apple had programmed games among their first efforts.

And, of course, Jobs and Wozniak had both been affiliated with Atari at various times, including their famous "4-day wonder" version of Breakout (see page 24 for more).

Woz's superefficient implementation of Pong got him a job offer from Atari, which he turned down, and his Breakout was a design wonder. "I hope that you run into the Atari folks who saw how few chips I used for Breakout," he told us. "But they couldn't understand my design. I probably couldn't either now."

Wozniak's first implementation of the BASIC computer language was called Game BASIC. "I made trade-offs in it just for games," he said.

Ever the prankster, Woz related one amusing story to me. "Apple did ship a 'Brick-Out' tape at one time. I think it still had my 'Easter Egg' in it, where you could put the game into an autoplay mode and the paddles would jiggle as though you couldn't control them, but they would never miss. I tricked some people, notably Captain Crunch, with this."

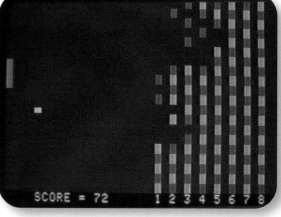

An early Apple II Breakout game.

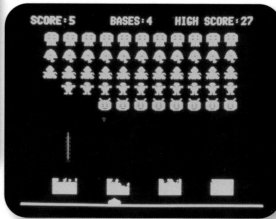

Apple's version of Space Invaders.

Apple put out several games, including a version of the popular Adventure and a Hangman spelling game.

The 1978 Invasion from Space...via Japan

S pace Invaders was like nothing else. It captured the imagination of a whole generation, and may have been singly responsible for the rebirth of the flagging video game industry.

Taito was one of the first Japanese companies to enter the video game business, and they had quite early forged a distribution alliance with Midway, Atari's chief competitor in the U. S. The first Japanese game to be imported to the U.S. was Gun Fight. But the game that changed everything appeared in 1978, once again distributed by Midway.

Space Invaders was in black and white only and used overlays to fake the colors at the top and bottom of the screen. It was the brainchild of Toshihiro Nishikado, a programmer at Taito, and there are many stories about its inception—most of them probably false. Whatever the truth, the implacable advance of the on-screen aliens and the hypnotic, *Jaws*-like sound effects created a whole new kind of challenge and tension. It was a game of concentration, courage, and hair-trigger reflexes.

Space Invaders was a game you couldn't win. In the end, the aliens would destroy your bases and your laser turret. It was only a matter of time. But Space Invaders did introduce something almost as good as winning—the high score—although the practice of saving players' initials was not yet implemented, so you couldn't prove that the high score was yours!

Space Invaders made history in other ways, as well. It caused a shortage of 100 yen coins in Japan, and it inspired a legal crisis in Mesquite, Texas (see sidebar, "The Space Invaders Crisis"). The Space Invaders phenom was not quite finished, however, and it played a significant role as the decade of the 80s began.

THE SPACE INVADERS CRISIS

After the release of Space Invaders, the citizens of Mesquite, Texas, became so furious at the misspent hours and dollars that they invoked a seldom-enforced city ordinance in order to drive Aladdin's Castle, a successful coin-op chain owned by Bally's (and later, Namco), from the local mall. The police chief cited a vague reference to Bally's alleged "connections to criminal elements," and the city created an artificial age limit of 17 years or older for patrons of the family-oriented arcade franchise. In lower courts, the city argued that they were trying to accomplish two purposes: (1) reduce truancy and (2) restrict minors from being exposed to people "who would promote gambling, sale of narcotics and other unlawful activities." The case was argued before the U.S. Supreme Court in November 1981 (years after the initial legal action) and decided in 1982 (City of Mesquite v. Aladdin's Castle, Inc., 455 U.S. 283). The U.S. Supreme Court, like the appeals court before it, ruled that the 17-year-old age requirement violated both the U.S. and Texas constitutions because it violated guarantees of equal protection under the law.

By the time of the final decision in the Aladdin's Castle case, a golden age of coin-op games had flooded the Bally's chain of storefronts, other arcades, restaurants, theater lobbies, and anywhere else arcade games could be placed.

Xs and Os

Neck and neck with Space Invaders—at least during the football season—was Atari Football, possibly the first sports simulation (as opposed to sports arcade) game, and certainly the first video football game to feature play selection. It featured four offensive plays and four defensive counter versions of the sweep, bomb, down & out, and keeper.

The game was based on another game called "Xs and Os" that had been conceived by Steve Bristow years earlier and abandoned in favor of Tank, and it retained its predecessor's use of letters to represent offensive (O) and defensive (X) players, giving it the look of an animated coach's playbook. The playfield also scrolled, displaying about 30 yards at a time, and stats appeared vertically along the sides of the playfield.

Atari Football was also possibly the first arcade game to feature the trackball. And it used the spherical control for all it was worth. A good game of Atari Football was a rigorous affair, with two-handed spinning of the controller, lots of body English, and plenty of blisters on the hands. The faster you spun the trackball, the faster your character (X or O) moved on the screen.

Atari Football scored big in the fall of 1978, keeping pace with the mega-hit Space Invaders—at least until the end of football season, when its sales dropped dramatically. The invading aliens hardly paused to notice.

In 1979, Atari came out with a two- or four-player version of the game that allowed for team play. In a four-player game, on offense one player was the quarterback while the other was the receiver. On defense both players were tackles. The four-player version was even more fun than the original.

- The world's first video attraction to simulate the actual play action of American football.
- Two players.
- New Trak Ball™ allows instant movement and control of key players in any direction.
- Offense can select 1 of 4 different run or pass plays.
- Defense can select 1 of 4 different plays.
- New add-a-coin feature adds continuous time-play.
- Versatile new cabinet is height-adjustable to 40" for standing play, 31" for cocktail table play.
- Built-in self-test system.

47

Bally Professional Arcade

ally's Midway arcade division had been a strong competitor to Atari throughout the 70s, and Bally decided to enter the home console race under their own corporate name.

We thought we were changing the world, and I thought this was a way that we could empower people to be creative and imaginative. I saw that this was a revolution. For a few months I held the record for the world's cheapest computer.

—JAMIE FENTON, BALLY PROFESSIONAL ARCADE DESIGNER

Bally began in 1932 as Lion Manufacturing Co., and in 1936 they moved to Chicago and adopted a new name—Bally Manufacturing Corporation. In 1969, Bally became the first publicly

traded gaming company on the New York Stock Exchange.

Their home system was first advertised in the JS&A mail-order catalog with a two-page ad for the Bally Library Computer in September 1977. The ad modestly claimed (in part): "The new Bally Library Computer provides more entertainment and services than man has ever dreamed possible from a consumer product."

Known more for slot machines and pinball games, Bally had not entered the home consumer market before, but they introduced the Bally Professional Arcade system in 1978 through computer dealers (and some TV dealers). It was a pretty good machine for its time. Based around the Zylog Z-80 chip, it had a number of interesting features. For instance, it came with two pistol-grip controllers with triggers and a rotating knob on the top. In addition to the controllers, it featured a keypad for data entry, and a version of BASIC for elementary programming.

Included on the system's ROM were Gun Fight (a color version of the Taito game originally distributed by Midway), Checkmate (a Blockade-style game), Calculator, and Scribbling (a sort of free-form doodle pad).

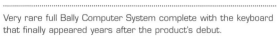

Very rare full Bally Computer System complete with the keyboard that finally appeared years after the product's debut.

Astrocade

The Bally system featured a high price tag—$100 more than the Atari VCS—and it didn't sell well. Early shipments were plagued by defects and had to be returned. Released in February 1978, it was off the market by 1979 or 1980. However, it was not dead and gone. It reappeared after Bally sold the rights to a new group of enthusiasts who formed a company called Astrovision. They marketed the new system first as the Bally Computer System, then later as the Astrocade, which also became the company's new name. Although the Bally system was never a top contender, it did have a moment of fame, appearing briefly in the movie, *National Lampoon's Summer Vacation*.

I remember that I bought it pretty much when it first came out. I eagerly awaited an announced keyboard that would have made the game system into a full computer, at least according to the local TV dealer where I purchased it. However, the keyboard never came out, and though I painstakingly entered some programs using the complex color-coded keypad overlay that came with the BASIC implementation, I abandoned my Bally system soon after Bally took it off the market. I had moved on to Intellivision by then, anyway. But I do remember playing many marathon sessions of Breakout on my Bally. (RDM)

1979: Atari Strikes Back

With the immense success of Space Invaders, Atari was losing ground in the coin-op arena. However, their response came in November 1979, and it was also quite out of this world.

Earlier that year, Atari had experimented with vector graphics games, releasing Howard Delman's Lunar Lander, which was a graphical version of an old mainframe rocket landing game. While destined to become a classic in its own right, Lunar Lander was quickly supplanted in the arcades by Ed Logg's first of several masterpieces, Asteroids. In fact, demand for Asteroids was so, well... astronomical... that several hundred Asteroids games were shipped in Lunar Lander cabinets just to fulfill the orders.

Ed Logg has provided us with some insight into the creative process that led to one of the all-time great arcade games. Not surprisingly, it started with Spacewar! (see page 12) "I had played Spacewar in 1971 or 1972 at the Stanford University Artificial Intelligence Lab and later at the University Forum (coffee shop). By the way, the Spacewar game in the Forum was two PDP machines linked together and was coin operated. So in a sense this was the first coin-operated video game that I am aware of. Of course, Pong was the first 'commercially' produced video game. Spacewar provided the controls and shape of the ships in Asteroids."

The original idea came from Atari's head of engineering, Lyle Rains. "He based his idea on another game at Atari, which had a large asteroid, which the

These original concept documents were taken directly from Ed Logg's original notebooks. They show how he created the vector formula for the Asteroids ship and also how he designed the font used in Asteroids.

player could not destroy. But players tried anyway. From that idea, I suggested that larger asteroids break up into smaller pieces to provide some strategy other than shooting everything." Logg also suggested adding a flying saucer, "otherwise the player could stall when there were just a few asteroids on screen. The big saucer was a random shooting saucer that introduced the player to the idea a saucer would come out when things appeared to be getting easy. The small saucer was more accurate because it aimed at the player with some amount of random error. As the score increased, his aim became more accurate. The first three saucers were always the large saucer. Thereafter the probability of a large saucer was reduced with each new saucer. The frequency of shots from the saucers was reduced with each new saucer too."

The usual way a designer knew he had a hit on his hands was when the other designers all wanted to play the game he was working on. Asteroids was no exception. "When the other engineers asked when I was leaving (so they could play), it became clear that I had an interesting game. Later in the project when I added the high score table, I would come in and see that many games had been played the previous night. However, I must say I would never have predicted that the sales of Asteroids would exceed anything the company had ever done before."

When we asked Ed for an interesting story about Asteroids, he said, "I have always been asked if I had thought of the lurking strategy where people get high scores by just shooting the small saucer. The answer is, I tried this strategy but I could not pull it off. I must also point out that at one time the small saucer would fire a shot just as he entered the screen. Often the saucer would not be visible and if you happened to be near, you would get hit before you had any idea where the saucer was. So I added a small delay before the saucer would take his first shot. This change was all that was needed to make the lurking strategy work."

Galaxian

Playing Space Invaders got to be a hypnotic exercise, and if you spent enough time shooting the moronic aliens, you could get pretty good at it. Then came Namco's Galaxian (also distributed by Midway), and it looked a lot like Space Invaders but in color. Galaxian was, in fact, the first true color arcade game. Galaxian's aliens were a whole lot smarter and more aggressive than those earlier invaders, and they hooked a lot of quarters from many a would-be protector of Earth. Oddly, we never really destroyed them all, as evidenced by the repeated appearance of the red, yellow, and blue flagship, which made cameo appearances in later games such as Pac-Man, Galaga, and Gorf.

Way Back When...

Turning back the clock, we want to focus on the parallel evolution of computer games, which, like video and arcade games, can trace their roots to mainframe computers. At the same time that Steve Russell was bringing Spacewar! to the PDP-1, Alan Kotok was finishing his B.S. project on the IBM 7090—a chess program that evaluated 1,100 positions per minute. By 1966, Richard D. Greenblatt's version, known as MacHack-6, became the first computerized chess program to enter an actual tournament. In the Massachusetts Amateur Chess Championship, the program scored one draw and lost four times (USCF rating of 1243). In 1967, the program became the first computerized chess program to beat a human player (USCF rating of 1510) by defeating Hubert Deyfus. In four amateur tournaments, the program went 3-12-3 (3 wins, 12 losses, and 3 draws).

Another early experiment was John Horton Conway's Life (1970), a cellular automata program that allowed you to set rules and watch what happened to your computer-based "lifeforms."

Also, though there may have been some earlier Star Trek programs on college mainframes before 1971, Don Daglow, currently CEO of Stormfront Studios, created one on the Pomona College mainframe during that year. Both Trek and Life went on to find renewed life in the personal computer world when Cygnus Software (later to become Interstel) released a slick version (for that era) of Trek called Star Fleet I, and Software Toolworks released Life

as part of a Golden Oldies package.

1971 was also the year that Peter S. Langston, one of the original Lucasfilm Games team, conceived of Empire while playing a board game with friends at Reed College. Inspired by the tabletop experience, he started coding the computer program in 1971. By the mid-70s, the game had proliferated to mainframes all over the country and was widely played on both college mainframes and on the Rand Corporation's (RAND) computer.

In 1972, an assembly language programmer named William Crowther was developing software for the routers that enabled ARPAnet (the Advanced Research Project Agency of the U.S. Department of Defense—later DARPAnet). This was the communications network commissioned in 1969 that was eventually to become the Internet. At that time, Crowther began work on a fantasy-based computer game based on his experiences as a spelunker. The game came to be known as Colossal Caves Adventure or, more simply, as Adventure.

Because of Crowther's involvement with the proto-Internet, this simple program ended up on the computers of colleges and defense contractors all around the world, influencing a whole generation of adventure game designers. Later expanded by Donald Woods at Stanford, Adventure's influence extended to the East Coast (Infocom's Zork in 1979), the West Coast (Roberta Williams' Mystery House in 1980), the industrial Northeast (John Laird's Haunt in 1979), and the tourist havens of the Southeast (Scott Adams'

> *I loved the excitement and camaraderie that animated those movements—something that's completely missing today. Getting rich dominates today. Back then, nobody anticipated that there would be money in it. We knew we were changing the world, but it was not big in money terms. It was big in revolutionary terms.*
>
> —CHRIS CRAWFORD,
> GAME DESIGN PIONEER

Radio Shack's TRS-80 was one of the first home computers.

PHOTO COURTESY OF RADIOSHACK CORPORATION

51

VAL FEELS ABOUT AMY

Gossip and Star Raider screens.

Adventureland in 1978). Internationally, it reached the UK in the form of Acheton, by Cambridge University's Jon Thackray, David Seal, and Jonathan Partington in 1978; Brand X (aka Philosopher's Quest), by Peter Killworth and Jonathan Mestel in 1979; and Roy Trubshaw's and Richard Bartle's Essex MUD in 1979. In Finland, Olli Paavola created Lord in 1981; Brad Templeton's and Kieran Carroll's Martian Adventure was completed in Canada in 1979; and Phillip Mitchell's and Stuart Richie's The Hobbit went on sale in Australia by 1983.

Crowther's game, intentionally simplified to appeal to his daughters, featured the original two-word parser (GET KNIFE) that inspired the Infocom crew to create ZIL (Zork Interpretive Language), which could understand complete sentences (see page 114). Another fan, Stuart Richie of Australia's Melbourne House, put his linguistic training to work in designing a parser for The Hobbit. Richie called his parser Inglish. Roberta Williams loved playing Adventure on a remote terminal, but wondered why no one had put pictures with the text (see page 134). Yet, everyone considered Adventure to be the seminal text adventure.

As the 70s progressed, more and more game programs appeared on college and corporate mainframes. In 1973, Gregory Yob was visiting the People's Computer Company. He tried out a few games and realized that many of them were simply 10 x 10 grids where you played "Hide and Go Seek" with the computer. Finding this unsatisfying, Yob created a maze based on a dodecahedron. The dodecahedron is essentially the modern 12-sided die used in tabletop games, and Yob used the lines representing the edges or facets of this geometric shape to represent the tunnels between the caves. Yob's game, Wumpus, required players to explore the dodecahedron and attempt to slay the Wumpus, a malodorous beast who hid in caves surrounded by pits and superbats, and had suckers on his feet to keep him from falling into those pit

traps. He would remain "asleep" until unwary or unwise adventurers would awaken him by firing an arrow and missing him. Once awakened, the Wumpus moved from cave to cave in a random pattern. If he ended up in the same room as the adventurer, he ate the adventurer. Hence, the odor associated with the Wumpus was designed to be an "olfactory" clue to the proximity of said monster. After all, the adventurer needed some hint that the monster was close before he or she ended up in the same room and the game was over.

The Home Computer Revolution

During the early 70s, as video games evolved and the industry around them grew rapidly, on a distinctly parallel track a revolution was in the making, and the revolutionaries were geeky hobbyists with an enthusiasm for electronics and programming languages. The computer was miniaturizing and, for the first time, becoming available to regular people.

The first computers were complex machines used only by a select few. "Prior to 1975, computers were associated with technicians in lab coats—the 'high priests' of the big machines—who would retire to air-conditioned environments with a problem to solve and emerge sometime later with a printout."[*]

Then came the kits like the Altair and IMSAI and the clubs like the Homebrew Computer Club. Hobbyists drove a business that nobody expected, and few of them ever considered money as a part of the equation.

The hobbyist market was about to give way to something much bigger, however. In April 1977, both the Apple II and the Commodore PET were unveiled at the West Coast Computer Faire. Tandy's nationwide Radio Shack franchise introduced the TRS-80 in September of that year. All three

---

Paul Freiberger and Michael Swaine, Fire in the Valley, *McGraw-Hill, 2000*

home computers began selling in quantities right out of the starting gate, and others, including Atari, quickly jumped in with personal computers. The era of the personal computer had arrived.

Commodore PET

Chris Crawford talks about his first reaction to the Commodore PET: "It was simply incredible how much they could put together and sell for only $600. In parts, separately, it would have been $1,000 or $1,500. My original reaction was suspicion." In part, Crawford's skepticism might have been well founded due to Commodore founder Jack Tramiel's reputation for heavy-handed business practices. "Business is war," he was quoted as saying. "I don't believe in compromising. I believe in winning."

Neither the PET (which stood for Personal Electronic Transactor) nor the TRS-80 could display color graphics, but they sold for less than the Apple II. There were definitely different camps at the time, each one swearing by its favorite system, but in the end, the Apple II, with its open architecture and color graphics, outlasted the others by many years, with its chief competition coming from the Commodore 64, a system that significantly emulated the Apple II.

Atari Computers

At Atari, first Nolan Bushnell, then Ray Kassar saw correctly that microcomputers represented a great opportunity, and the company shifted some of its focus toward making personal computers to compete directly with Apple. Unfortunately, this shift in focus may have resulted in taking away from Atari's strength and its bread-and-butter business—games.

Like the Apple and Commodore computers, Atari used the MOS 6502 chip to power its computers, with the addition of the custom graphics CTIA (Coleen Television Interface Adapter) chip. However, Atari's designers were hampered by FCC regulations limiting RF output. Apple had bypassed these regulations by not including an RF adapter with the system, which exempted them. (Apple RF adapters were sold as a third-party item.) Atari engineers rankled at the FCC restrictions, but had no choice but to design around them. Joe Decuir comments, "The disk drives were big and bulky, because they had to be managed by onboard microcomputer systems, and then they were slowed down by the 19,200 bps transfer rate. This was a crawl compared to the direct bus access that Apple had, but we were prevented from using the bus because of the FCC regulations."

The custom chips inside Atari's 400 and 800 computers were designed with games in mind. Again, according to Joe Decuir, "The Apple II was the obvious target to the engineering team, but we also conceived of the 800 as the next-generation gaming machine. In my opinion, it had no peer as a game console until the NES came out five years later in Japan." To cover both bets, Atari packaged the 800 with a real keyboard and some internal expansion capability, as the personal computer that could also play games, and the Atari 400 as the game machine that was also a computer. Later, Atari repackaged the chipset as a pure game machine, the 5200, which, unfortunately, wouldn't run 400/800 cartridges.

Automated Simulations

A utomated Simulations (later Epyx), one of the earliest computer game companies, emerged from a group of Dungeons & Dragons players, originally cohosted by Jim Connelley and Jeff Johnson. In 1977, Jon Freeman was invited into the group by Susan Lee-Merrow, who went on to work for Electronic Arts at its beginning and later became a major marketing executive for Brøderbund and Lucas Learning. Freeman had written several articles for *GAMES* magazine as well as a book, *The Player's Guide to Table Games*. He was working at the time on an updated version of the *Playboy Winner's Guide to Board Games*.

When Connelley purchased a Commodore PET to help with the bookkeeping side of his D&D campaign, he realized that if he could write and ship a game before the end of the tax year, he'd be able to write off the computer. So, he talked Freeman into adjusting the rules and creating data structures and scenarios (ship profiles, battle situations, maps, victory conditions, background stories, etc.) for a science fiction war game while Connelley did the programming. The game that launched Automated Simulations was called Starfleet Orion and took less than four months from conception (August 1978) to sales launch (December 1978). The company was named Automated Simulations sometime around Thanksgiving of the same year, primarily so that there would be a corporate entity for customers to pay.

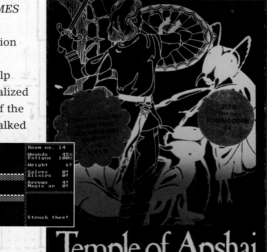

The game was successful, in spite of the fact that it required two players and had no computer opponent for solitaire play. "It was very simple, graphically," says Freeman. "Basically just dots on a screen. An explosion was an asterisk." Connelley and Freeman added a single-player mode in 1979 when they released Invasion Orion.

Temple of Apshai

EXPLORE A WORLD OF MONSTERS & MAGIC, HEROIC ADVENTURE! A FANTASY ROLE-PLAYING EXPERIENCE FOR YOU AND YOUR COMPUTER!

RESCUE AT R

YOU'VE GOT 60 M — IN REAL TIME— FREE TEN PRISO FROM A MAZE-L ALIEN MOONBAS

Background: One of several hand-drawn maps used to create Temple of Apshai.

The highlight of the company's early history was their Dunjonquest series of role-playing games, featuring three Temple of Apshai games and, later, Sword of Fargoal. To distinguish the role-playing titles from the strict science fiction games, they chose the sub–brand name Epyx, but it wasn't until 1982 that Epyx became the company's official name. (More on that later.)

They followed the Temple of Apshai with Rescue at Rigel, a science fiction game based on the same role-playing engine, and followed that with Crush, Crumble and Chomp!, in which the player got to be a movie-style monster on the rampage. This was years before Rampage revisited the same theme. Crush, Crumble and Chomp! came with a set of data cards describing each monster in detail.

Freeman remembers several other games created from 1979 through 1981, including Datestones of Ryn, Morloc's Tower, Hellfire Warrior (the first real sequel to Temple of Apshai), Star Warrior ("our first 'outdoor' quest"), Tuesday Morning Quarterback, Dragon's Eye, Upper Reaches of Apshai, Keys of Acheron (level design by Paul Reiche), and Sorcerer of Siva.

Under a third label, Mind Toys, Automated

Simulations created another pair of games—Jabbertalky and Richochet—in 1981.

Meanwhile, Jon Freeman's life changed significantly when he met Anne Westfall, who was in a neighboring booth at the West Coast Computer Faire in March 1980. Their meeting began what was to become a lifelong partnership. Westfall worked on some conversions of existing games, and the two worked together on Tuesday Morning Quarterback, which appeared first on the TRS 80 and later on the Apple II. They decided to strike out on their own in November 1981, and produced two games. One, called Pack Rat on the Atari 800, was never published. The other, Tax Dodge, was published by Steve Dompier's Island Graphics. Then one day they received a call from the head of a newly forming company. The "newly forming company" was Electronic Arts. The call was from Trip Hawkins. Their fortunes were about to change (see page 172). Meanwhile, Jim Connelley officially changed the name of the company to Epyx and continued to run it until 1983 (see page 150).

Crush, Crumble and Chomp!
The Movie Monster Game

WREAK HAVOC! SPREAD MAYHEM AND DESTRUCTION AS YOUR FAVORITE MONSTER!

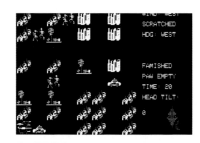

Crush, Crumble and Chomp! screen and data sheet.

Crush, Crumble and Chomp!
ARACHNIS

COMMAND		MEANING
R	Right	Turn right (90°)
L	Left	Turn left (90°)
H	Head	Turn head left/right 30° (aims Z & B)
N	Nothing	Do nothing (skip to end of turn)
M	Move	Move 1 square forward
J	Jump	Jump 2 squares forward (onto/ over buildings)
D	Descend (Dig)	Descend and move subsurface (up to 5 spaces)
N		North
E		East
S		South
W		West
U		Up to surface
G	Grab	Grab the human unit in the square in front of you
E	Eat	Eat the unit in your jaw (paw)
C	Crumble	Demolish the building/bridge in (the square in) front of you
W	Web	Weave an obstructing web in your square (bridge, road, or park only)
P	Paralyze	Cause nearby units to lose a turn
Z	Zap	Attack (with ray beam) flying units from the ground
B	Breathe Fire	Set fire to unit and/or building your head is facing
Q	Quit	Stop the game (temporarily or permanently)
#	Number (of points)	Check your current score

NOTES:
Arachnis has a weak Crumble (C) command, because its body lacks heft.

Copyright © 1981, Automated Simulations, Inc.
P.O. Box 4247, Mountain View, CA 94040

Going Where No One Had Gone Before...

As 1979 drew to a close, the game industry was poised to explode in all directions. Arcade games were just hitting their peak, and some of the greatest classics of all time were just around the corner. And the Atari VCS, with six million units already in homes around the U.S., was about to soar.

But the VCS would soon have company in the console market. Mattel, the powerful toy company, saw opportunity knocking, and they test-marketed their Intellivision game console in 1979. The first real home console war was brewing.

There were only a few companies marketing computer games at the time—Brøderbund, California Pacific, Automated Simulations, and SSI, for starters. Game designers like Dan Bunten, Richard Garriott, Doug Carlston, Bill Budge, Jon Freeman, Dave Lebling, and Marc Blank were already at work on projects that were to set the stage for the first real generation of computer games. Many other young designers were discovering the wonders of the new personal computers and writing their first programs. For instance, John Romero was already delving into the secrets of Apple Assembly language and graphics creation, writing programs in his head, and generally absorbing all he could.

Also at the end of the 70s, four Atari developers left and formed the first independent third-party game company to manufacture cartridges for the VCS, setting the stage for the future of the business. This company, Activision, was incorporated just as the first decade of video games came to an end, in late 1979.

The Last Straw

Activision came into being as a result of Atari's policies regarding authorship credit and royalties for VCS game designers. The problem came to a head with Ray Kassar in 1979, but problems with royalties and bonuses actually started at Atari earlier in its history. According to David Crane (one of the founders of Activision), during the VCS's first year there was a plan devised between engineering head Bob Brown and then president Joe Keenan that allocated 50 cents per console sold and a dime per cartridge to the engineering group, to be distributed as bonuses. However, that money never appeared, and management denied that the plan had ever existed. The engineers more or less laughed it off at the time.

Next, there was a written bonus plan, which was based on something called "Departmental Budgeted Operating Income," or DBOI. Some of the engineers referred to it as "Don't Bet On It." Somewhere in the tangle of legalese, this bonus also disappeared, though some of the top designers were taken behind closed doors, given 25 percent raises, and told not to tell anyone.

But the final straw dropped when marketing distributed a memo in 1979 that listed the percentage of sales of each VCS cartridge sold the previous year, and, referring to the top items on the list, it said something like, "These games are selling really well. Do more like this."

THE KASSAR TOUCH

Some of the engineers found out that Atari's cartridge sales for that same year had been about $100 million. It was a simple matter to do the math and determine how much each cartridge had made. Four designers— Al Miller, David Crane, Larry Kaplan, and Bob Whitehead—had accounted for 60 percent of the sales. "We went to see Ray Kassar with this information," relates Crane. "He told us we were no more important than the people on the assembly line who put the cartridges together." (It wasn't at that meeting, but at a later one, that Kassar claimed, "I understand creative people. After all, I worked with towel designers," a statement that was highly unappreciated by Atari's creative folk.) Ironically, it wasn't all about money. Most of the designers loved what they did. "I would say it was equal between designer credit and royalties," added Crane. "If Ray had given either of them to us, we would have been happy with it. But he gave us nothing."

THE 80s

At the beginning of the 80s, electronic gaming was entering its second decade as an industry; and it was ready to rock and roll. One blockbuster arcade game after another appeared on the scene. But now playing in people's homes was a rapidly growing list of titles—some original and some arcade conversions. Sales of the Atari VCS blossomed with the release of a licensed version of Space Invaders. Renamed Atari 2600, the venerable system suddenly leaped to the top of everybody's shopping list.

Mattel's Intellivision home console system launched in 1980, as well, and its superior graphics soon caught the public's eye. It was followed a couple of years later by ColecoVision.

Another revolution was happening, and it centered upon the home computer. For the first time, anyone with the patience and vision to do some programming and crude artwork could create and market a game. Creating games for arcade machines or home consoles required considerable equipment and technical knowledge, and actually putting them on the market required even more equipment plus specialized silicon chips only available from certain companies. Putting out a game for personal computers, by contrast, required only the computer itself and a disk drive with a blank floppy disk. (Even before disk drives, people put out games on cassette tapes, but those were tedious to work with and unreliable. In order for computer games to succeed, it's a reasonable assumption that the disk drive was a requirement.)

And so the stage was set for a roller-coaster decade of expansion, crashes, rebirths, technological advancement, and games galore!

!#?!

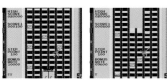

1980: The Arcades

1978 had Space Invaders, and 1979 had Asteroids and Galaxian. But 1980 had to be the king of arcade years to date, boasting a bumper crop in the range of 100 new games released in the U.S. and Japan.* 1980 is distinguished, not just for quantity, but by the sheer magnitude of its introductions. Even though not all the new releases were big hits, many set new standards and several are all-time hall of famers—in particular, Missile Command, Defender, and Pac-Man.

Space was a big theme in the arcades, as it had always been. In 1980 there were nearly 20 titles that began with the word *space* and another dozen or so that started with *moon* or *star*.* Several others had space themes, even if their titles didn't necessarily reflect it.

Here are just a few memorable titles from the more than 100 arcade releases of 1980.

Star Castle

Cinematronics had created several games after Space Wars, and in 1980 they came out with Star Castle, a game with stars, to be sure, but no recognizable castles. The stars, however, are a story in themselves. Looking for a different sort of star pattern, the designers used the outline of a centerfold from a girlie magazine.

Berzerk

Berzerk was, in some ways, the prototype of later games like Robotron: 2084, Gauntlet, Total Carnage, and Smash TV. When you began the game—to the disturbing sounds of "Intruder Alert! Intruder Alert!"—you found yourself in a room full of slow-moving robots that seemed to have it in for you. Although initially conceived in black and white, the first robots you encountered in the released color version—dumb yellow ones—were pushovers, since they couldn't shoot back. But later, you would have to handle the red robots, who did shoot back. Still, with some clever maneuvering, you could outshoot or outwit your enemies, all except for Evil Otto, a bouncing, fast-moving, and indestructible Happy Face, who would chase you inexorably to the death. The only hope was to make it to another room, and damn if your character didn't suddenly seem awfully slow even if his animation looked like it was running. Berzerk was one of the early games from Stern, a company that released a couple of dozen other games from 1980 through 1984, including the Konami game Pooyan, in which players took on the role of a mother pig. Berzerk is notable for being one of the first games to include synthesized voice. It boasted 31 synthesized words, including "Chicken, fight like a robot" and the attract mode comment, "Coin detected in pocket."

Crazy Climber

Crazy Climber was created by Nichibutsu and distributed by Taito. It was an odd little game with an equally odd hero. This guy just had to make it to the top of a 200-story building, despite having to dodge a lot of falling debris, nasty people who liked to close windows on his fingers, and an even nastier bird that pelted him with droppings.

Crazy Climber himself talked to you, which was relatively rare in games at the time. His repertoire of comments was limited, but the one we remember hearing the most was "Oh, noooo...," his last words as he

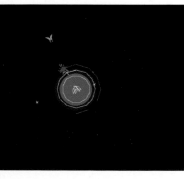

*Source: Killer List of Video Games (KLOV), www.klov.com

plummeted down to one of his three possible deaths.

Perhaps the most innovative aspect of Crazy Climber was the control system, which used dual joysticks to control the movement of his arms and legs in sequence—the only way to maneuver him. This control system reminded us of working a marionette, and was definitely a departure from any previous control methods.

Battlezone

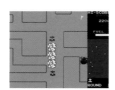

Atari had scored a hit with Tank in 1974, and Battlezone, which is credited mainly to Ed Rotberg, repeated the theme but with a decidedly different point of view. In fact, Battlezone may have been the first true first-person game—a distant ancestor to Doom and Quake. Although games like Night Driver and Tim Skelly's Tail Gunner had featured first-person viewpoints, neither allowed free movement, which Battlezone introduced to the arcades.

"The idea for the game came out of a brainstorming session," says Rotberg. "We knew we had the technology to do that sort of game with advancements in processors and in our vector generator."

Using vector graphics, the game put you in the role of a tank gunner rolling across a somewhat surreal landscape dotted with out-of-place geometry—cubes and cones and such—distant mountains, and enemy tanks. The enemy wasn't shy about firing their howitzers at you, and you had to stick and move, using the dual joystick controls, to stay alive. The radar sounds and on-screen instructions for locating enemy tanks ("Enemy to right") soon immersed you in this life-and-death duel. Failure was graphically represented by the sight of an incoming shell and the severe cracking of your windshield. For the first time, you felt the hit as if it were your own. And, no, you could not drive to that distant volcano.

Battlezone boasted another distinction. It may have been the first commercial game commissioned into the U.S. military. Well, not quite commissioned, but the U.S. Army did ask Atari to create a training version of the game based on the Bradley Infantry Fighting Vehicle (IFV). Ed Rotberg worked a grueling three-month schedule to complete the project. The military version of Battlezone contained a host of features not found in the commercial version, including a variety of ordnance, realistic trajectories, both friendly and unfriendly vehicles, two additional magnification levels, and a controller system with thumb, finger, and palm switches, none of which appeared in the commercial version.

Rotberg had his reservations. "I was personally concerned that Atari was getting involved with the military, and I was very much against it. The deal I made with them was that I would be completely exempt from doing any other military product."

Rally-X

Although it was not the biggest game of 1980, Rally-X was at one time expected to be just that. At the 1980 Amusement Machine Operators of America (AMOA) show, four major releases were being shown: Defender, Battlezone, Pac-Man, and Rally-X. Ironically, the one that was picked to be the big winner was Rally-X.

In fairness, Rally-X looked pretty good for its time. It was a top-down racing game with colorful graphics and cartoonlike action. It departed from other games of the time in that it featured saturated color on the screen instead of color figures over a black background. Given how new color was to arcade games, it must have seemed pretty amazing. However, its main claim to fame in the history of games was the introduction of the first bonus round.

Missile Command

Missile Command was another adrenaline pumper that put you in the basically hopeless position of defending your cities against incoming nuclear blasts. A morbid theme, to be sure, and a game you really couldn't win, unless you emulated the Olympic torch bearers and kept a defensive vigil at the controls in perpetuity.

It wasn't a question of winning, only of scoring and lasting as long as you could. Many an hour was spent fending off the bombs that appeared eerily in the sky above your bases. Round after round you spun the Trak-Ball and carefully rationed the antinuke missiles from your three bases, often aiming for the intersection of several incoming missiles for maximum efficiency. It was high tragedy when you

lost a city, worse if you lost a base that still had missiles.

Dave Theurer, the designer of Missile Command, describes the original concept: "Gene Lipkin told Steve Calfee that we should do a game where the country was being invaded by missiles. They showed me a picture of a radar screen and said take it from there. I hated radar screens because of the vanishing info, so I got rid of it. I had used the Trak-Ball in my previous Soccer game and decided it was the best controller for the task. In those days the trackballs were pretty big. We even had one that was the size of a bowling ball just for yucks."

Only about five of these rare prototypes were ever made. According to Dave Theurer, "The extra panel (see pictures at top of page) was originally designed to be part of the game play. We put it there to indicate the status of the various bases—how many missiles you had and the condition of your cities. We soon learned that when the players looked at the panel they lost track of what was happening on the screen. It was as if you had to drive your car and had to look on the floor of the backseat every five seconds. There were other reasons, such as the problem of light bulbs burning out, and we figured the arcade operators wouldn't want to go through the trouble of replacing them, meaning they would be meaningless anyway. Finally, eliminating the panel did save money, which was always a consideration."

Images of the Atari assembly line creating Missile Command units.

Answers to Missile Command Quiz Ground Zero and Armageddon

Defender

When it debuted at the 1980 AMOA show, Defender was universally considered to be too hard to be successful in the arcades. While the show attendees were betting on the ultrasimple Rally-X, Defender flew in under the radar to become one of the all-time great arcade classics.

They were right about one thing at AMOA. Defender was hard-core. Basically, the first time you played and tried to make sense of the two-way joystick and five buttons, you died in a matter of seconds. Defender wasn't for the meek.

To succeed at Defender, you needed a Zen-like concentration and ultimate coolness under pressure, the unique ability to see what was happening all around you while monitoring the radarlike topside scanner, and a complete oneness with the controls so you could react to any situation without getting killed. You not only had to shoot the alien Landers, Baiters, Bombers, Pods, and truly evil Swarmers,

but you also had to save the human abductees before they were turned into Mutants who would then add to your misery.

Once you achieved the zone, however, Defender could make you forget about everything else in life for as long as you could make that quarter last.

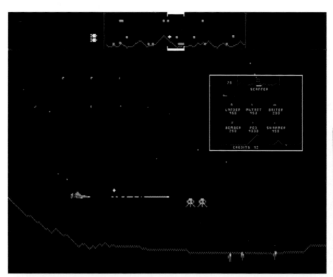

Stargate, aka Defender II, was even more insane than the original, and added yet another button control!

61

Pac-Man

In the brief history of video games before 1980, inspiration had come from many sources—predominantly sports and science fiction. But, once upon a time, magic struck when Toru Iwatani, a programmer for the Japanese amusement company Namco, stared at a pizza with one slice missing. It may have been the first and only time a game concept was inspired by an Italian entrée.

At any rate, Iwatani took his pizza and, with a bit of role reversal, turned it into a hungry character who just had to eat dots on a screen. This was the birth of Pac-Man. But Iwatani's vision was unique for many reasons. He purposely set out to create a nonviolent game, and a game that would appeal to female players. In both respects, he was more successful than anyone could have anticipated.

In fact, until this time there had never been a real *character* in an electronic game. Typically, the game environment was filled with nameless cars and spaceships and feature-less human stick figures. Though incredibly simple, Pac-Man was the first digital superstar of the video game era, the first character to capture the attention and imagination of the

world. And he wasn't alone. His cute but implacable enemies each had names, though they were changed from the original Japanese names. In fact, there was a switch on the Pac-Man cabinet that allowed different names for the ghosts, each of which also had a nickname. In all, there were 23 names for Pac-Man's enemies, 16 for the Japanese version and seven more for the American (see sidebar). Moreover, each ghost had a distinct personality.

Pac-Man was so popular that it spawned the first real licensing craze with toys, lunchboxes, Pac-Man cereal, popular songs, and even a Saturday morning cartoon show.

Pac-Man was the first electronic game superstar and the first game character to join the ranks of pop icons like Mickey Mouse and Bugs Bunny. This, more than any other fact, sets Pac-Man apart. The adorable, dot-craving, essentially nonviolent maze crawler set the stage for later characters such as Mario, Sonic the Hedgehog, and Lara Croft.

Originally titled Puck-Man, Namco and Midway wisely changed the name, fearing that vandals might alter the lettering with unfortunate and embarrassing results.

The original Puckman cabinet. (Courtesy of RePlay Magazine).

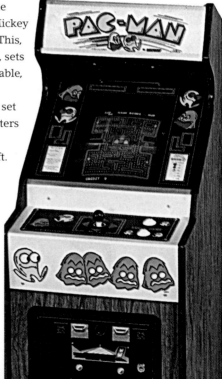

An unusual white Pac-Man cabinet.

THE 23 NAMES

Between the Japanese and the American versions of Pac-Man, the ghosts were each known by many names. There are 23 distinct name/nickname combinations, since "Pinky" appears in one of the Japanese versions as well as in the English version:

COLOR	JAPANESE ORIGINAL	JAPANESE ALTERNATE	ENGLISH
Red	Oikake ("Akabei")	Urchin ("Macky")	Shadow ("Blinky")
Pink	Machibuse ("Pinky")	Romp ("Micky")	Speedy ("Pinky")
Blue	Kimagure ("Aosuke")	Stylist ("Mucky")	Bashful ("Inky")
Orange	Otoboke ("Guzuta")	Crybaby ("Mocky")	Pokey ("Clyde")

Note: In Ms. Pac-Man, Clyde became Sue.

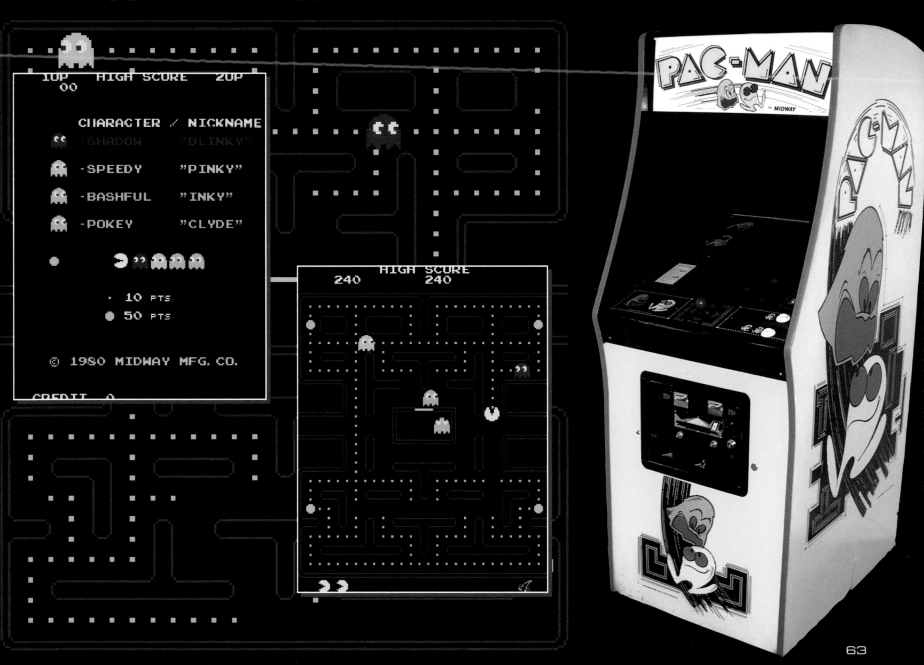

New Players: 1980

Despite its slow start, the Atari VCS had already sold around 6 million units by the end of 1979. In 1980, Warner struck a deal with Taito to release the hit game Space Invaders as a VCS cartridge. This was possibly the smartest move they ever made. Ray Kassar (see page 40) showed his marketing acumen by correctly predicting that people would go out and purchase the VCS just to get the Space Invaders game. And that's exactly what happened.

Releasing Space Invaders on the VCS caused Atari's sales to skyrocket and began the Golden Age of Atari.

Even as Atari was poised to enter its Golden Age, it was

also losing some of its best talent because of the friction between the designers and management. First it was Miller, Crane, Whitehead, and Kaplan joining Jim Levy to start Activision, which became the first third-party publisher in game history. Then it was Bill Grubb, starting Imagic—yet another competitor—and taking four important Atari folks with him (see page 74). Despite the fact that Atari was starting to enjoy the greatest game sales ever seen, and had become the fastest growing company in American history (until the dot-coms, anyway), the seeds of its doom were already being planted.

Activision

Activision started in 1979 with $750,000 in venture capital and loans, and unveiled their first games—Dragster, Boxing, Fishing Derby, and Checkers—at the Summer Consumer Electronics Show in 1980. By early 1981 they had added Skiing and Bridge. It was only the beginning. Activision was to achieve instant success, and like Atari, it created a culture of its own as well as its own legacy of memorable titles.

Four of Activision's five founders were, of course, its first

> *When we made the decision to leave Atari, we still didn't know where we were going. We saw that we had essentially three choices: one was to leave Atari and work as consultants. Atari was paying consultants three to four times what we made. Why not quit, consult back, and double our salaries? Or we could create a development house—one of the first third-party development houses. Our third choice was to form a company to market and distribute games, but this option contained a steep ramp in risk versus reward. There were a lot of issues to deal with.*
>
> —DAVID CRANE, ACTIVISION COFOUNDER AND CREATOR OF PITFALL AND MANY OTHER GAMES

Activision employees getting ready for their early Consumer Electronics Show.

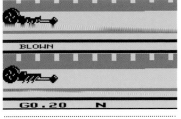

Screens from two of Activision's first games—Boxing and Dragster.

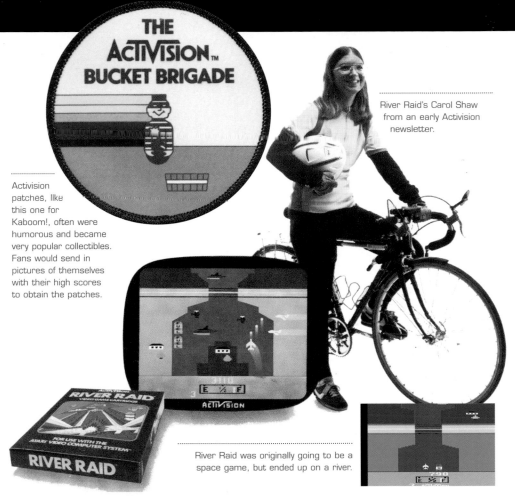

River Raid's Carol Shaw from an early Activision newsletter.

Activision patches, like this one for Kaboom!, often were humorous and became very popular collectibles. Fans would send in pictures of themselves with their high scores to obtain the patches.

designers, and they reaped the rewards of success in a way they never had at Atari. According to Jim Levy, "We were famous for our parties at the trade shows. It was a wild time, and we made the most of it."

Activision quickly grew and began to expand, making games for Intellivision and, ultimately, for home computers.

Early Hits

Activision's instant success was further fueled by a string of popular titles such as Larry Kaplan's Kaboom!, which was reminiscent of Atari's Avalanche, Steve Cartwright's stunt flyer Barnstorming, Bob Whitehead's Defender-like Chopper Command, and Carol Shaw's River Raid.

River Raid was originally going to be a space game, but ended up on a river.

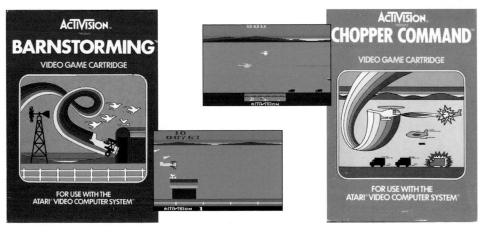

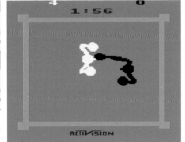

The early games from Activision were fun and addicting. Often, they were based on arcade games, as in the case of Kaboom! (far right) and Chopper Command (left). Steve Cartwright's Barnstorming (far left) was an original game.

The Best of the Best

Activision's designers were the best Atari 2600 programmers around, and they pushed the system to its limit, often pulling off technical, as well as design, coups. For instance, David Crane's Freeway, a Frogger-like game, was the first VCS game that animated 24 sprites simultaneously.

In 1982, Crane created the best-known VCS game of all time. Pitfall was a revelation, a tour de force for the VCS, and it helped usher in a whole new genre of games.

Pitfall was the first game to feature a running, jumping hero in a side-scrolling environment. Put another way, it was the first platform game, of which there have been about a zillion since. Think Lode Runner, Super Mario, all the way up to the 90s and Abe's Oddysee.

"Pitfall was our 18th game," says Crane, "and the single most amazing fact about it is that it took me 10 minutes to design."

Crane continues, "Doing a game is really a very complicated activity. There are thousands of ideas in your mind at one time, so the entire thing is self-consistent. Keeping track of all the details... and then the 20-hour days. After completing a game we had a downtime, which we used to misname as 'post-cartridge depression'. We would stare at the screen, play other guys' games, take time off. I was at that point, 'What am I going to do next?' I always wanted to do a game with a little

Designer Larry Miller, from an early Activision newsletter, and cofounder Al Miller's Dragster Club certificate.

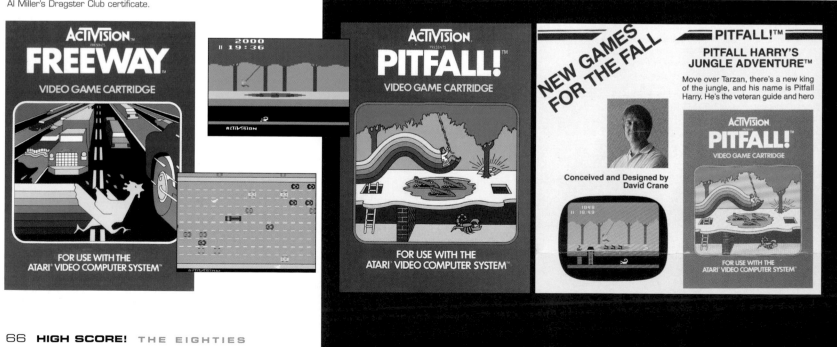

running man, so I took a blank piece of paper and drew a man. 'Where is he?' Put in path. Put in jungle. 'Why is he running?' Put in treasure and obstacles. That was the design. Execution took about 1,000 hours at the keyboard."

Crane drew from various influences. One of the cooler features in Pitfall was inspired by a Heckle and Jeckle cartoon in which they had to swing on vines over man-eating (or, in their case, crow-eating) alligators. In addition, the game's unique and clever above- and below-ground paths made brilliant use of limited space and increased the game play options. Pitfall Harry, the game's hero, had a greater repertoire of moves than any VCS hero to date, and he never even fired a gun or cracked a whip!

By 1982, when this picture was taken, Activision had grown considerably from its humble beginnings.

Activision's wholesome first catalog featured their four released titles plus the upcoming Skiing and Bridge.

Activision was famous for their parties in the early 80s.

67

Video Game Fans

Activision's promotion of their designers worked so well that fan letters began to pour in. Here are two happy customer service representatives surrounded by pictures of Activision fans.

Lots of fans sent in pictures of themselves, but none so fascinating as this one of a priest with an Activision patch sewn onto his robes.

SPACE SHUTTLE COMMANDER
ACTIVISION

COMMANDER ACTIVISION FEDERATION of STARBLASTERS

SPACE SHUTTLE PILOT
ACTIVISION

THE ACTIVISION TRAIL DRIVE

ACTIVISION ALL-STAR HOCKEY TEAM

SHORT-ORDER SQUAD
ACTIVISION

WING COMMANDER

ACTIVISION TENNIS

ACTIVISION SKY STARS

ACTIVISION FLYING ACES

FRIENDS OF DOLPHINS
ACTIVISION

With Activision's rise to success, Jim Levy was photographed for *Fortune* magazine early in 1982.

Newspaper ad announcing Activision's IPO in June 1983.

Circa 1983, this "family tree" shows all the early employees of Activision, including one Lawrence Probst, later to become chairman of Electronic Arts. The names of the five founders plus designer Steve Cartwright (Barnstorming) are at the roots of the tree.

Intellivision

In the late 70s Mattel was the biggest toy company in the world. They had scored big time with their first electronic foray—handheld games—and they were ready for more. In late 1979, they test-marketed their first video game system. In 1980, Intellivision (short for "Intelligent Television") hit the streets.

At first, Mattel was cautious. They hired contractors for low pay to produce the first games. When they did start making games in-house, they hired kids out of college. According to Intellivision game designer Keith Robinson, who now runs Intellivision Productions, Inc., "The company's marketing was oriented toward education and family products. Intellivision was seen as the heart of a computer system that would do family planning, stock analysis, teach you guitar… that sort of thing."

In 1981 Intellivision changed its focus and began the second unofficial age of Intellivision by releasing hard-hitting print and TV ads that directly compared their graphics to those of Atari's 2600. Intellivision clearly came out on top in those ads and quickly grabbed a 20 percent market share, outperforming the rest of Mattel.

Mattel's aggressive ads were seen as the first shot in a console war—the first of its kind—and the media was quick to respond. Although today we consider it commonplace to have competing video game systems on the market at all times, back then it was almost unheard of. Although Coleco had once run head-to-head ads against Mattel comparing handheld games (see page 30), this was the first such video game ad. For the first time in the brand-new video game business, consumers had a choice. Robinson puts it this way: "Before, the question was, 'Should I buy a video game system for my kid?' After, it became, 'Which video game system should I get my kid?'" Like Activision's challenge to Atari the previous year, this was a rite of passage for the young industry.

At around this time amid visions of a long and profitable future, Mattel opened Mattel Electronics, a whole new division of the company that had pioneered handheld games and brought us Barbie.

Mattel released the Intellivision console with other names in certain retail outlets. It was known as the "Tele-Games Super Video Arcade" in Sears stores, the "Tandyvision One" at Radio Shack, and (as in the photo), the "Sylvania Intellivision" in GTE phone stores.

The team of programmers and designers who made Intellivision's in-house games were called the Blue Sky Rangers. They were kept strictly under wraps; Mattel was afraid of their being stolen by the competition.

In addition to expanding the Blue Sky Rangers' ranks from 20 to more than 100 developers during the heyday of Intellivision, Mattel also attempted to expand the system into something approximating the computer that had been part of the original vision. The first add-on module for the system was IntelliVoice, a module that synthesized speech. Games like B-17 Bomber used the voice module effectively.

Mattel also promised a keyboard to complete its computer aspirations, but somehow the keyboard never quite made it to market. Finally, Mattel did release a keyboard, but it was a shadow of the promised peripheral. It was, in essence, too little, too late.

Intellivision's initial focus was to position Intellivision as the family computer system, but their winning strategy was to play hardball, although we may never again see a more unlikely spokesperson for video games than George Plimpton. Still, it was comforting to believe that the literati also played games. You can just imagine families all over the U.S. saying, "If it is good enough for George..."

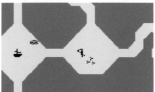

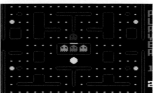

Screens of Major League Baseball, Advanced Dungeons and Dragons, Donkey Kong, and Atari Pac-Man.

Mattel eventually attempted to produce the long-awaited computer from scratch, but the resulting Aquarius system was even less impressive and even later than the ill-fated keyboard. Programmers considered it punishment to be assigned to create games for Aquarius, and designer Bob Del Principe's slogan for the system, which was released in 1983, was "Aquarius: System for the 70s."

Perhaps Aquarius would have succeeded in the 70s; but in 1983, it was just in time, along with Coleco's equally ill-fated Adam computer, to see the end of an era. For, even in the midst of unparalleled success, Mattel and Intellivision's ride at the top was to be short-lived.

As always, there were many contributing factors. For one, their own advertising, which stressed superior graphics, backfired on them when ColecoVision was released in 1982 with still better graphics. And second, the fateful year 1984

loomed ahead, and Intellivision's crash, along with the whole industry, was enough to cause Mattel to close down Mattel Electronics. However, Intellivision was not dead. The Senior VP of Marketing for Mattel Electronics, Terrence E. Valeski, bought the rights to the system and, using many of the Blue Sky Rangers, continued releasing new games through his INTV Corporation. Intellivision went on to become the only classic video game console from the early 1980s to compete against the Nintendo and Sega consoles in the late 80s. INTV Corp. finally stopped production of the Intellivision system in 1991, more than ten years after its introduction.

And still Intellivision lives on. Blue Sky Rangers Keith Robinson and Stephen Roney bought the rights from Valeski in 1997 and formed Intellivision Productions, which has brought the classic games to new platforms, including PC, Mac, PlayStation, and cell phones.

Minkoff's Measures team was named for a hiring test given to prospective programmers. Back row: Mike Minkoff, Steve Ettinger, Bill Fisher, Keith Robinson, Joe Ferreira, Ron Surratt. Front row: Julie Hoshizaki, Steve Tatsumi, Dale Lynn, Eric Del Sesto, Tom Lohff, Stephen Roney, Tony Ettaro. *Both photographs taken by Blue Sky Ranger Lee Barnes.*

Above: Don Daglow's Intellivision softball team, the Decles (a made-up word to describe the 10-bit programming for Intellivision). Back row: Gary Johnson, David Warhol, Robert Reeder, Eddie Dombrower, and Don Daglow. Kneeling: Tom Priestly. Front row: Judy Mason, Minh Chau Tran, Daniel Bass, Robert Newstadt, Mark Buchignani, and Mark Urbaniec (lying down).

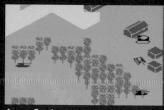
Armor Battle

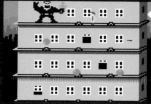
Astrosmash

Beauty and the Beast

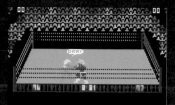
Body Slam Super Pro Wrestling

Boxing

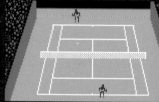
Championship Tennis

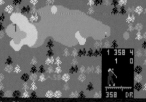
Chip Shot

Commando

Deep Pockets *(unreleased)*

Dracula

Empire Strikes Back

Frog Box

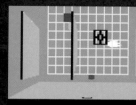
Grid Shock *(unreleased)*

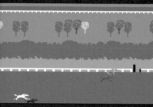
Horse Racing

Hover Force

Lock 'n' Chase

NFL Football

Microsurgeon

Motocross

Night Stalker

Space Armada

Happy Holidays *(unreleased)*

Sub Hunt

Swords & Serpents

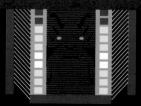
Maze-a-Tron

Imagic

After 16 years at Black & Decker and another two and a half at Atari, Bill Grubb resigned as Atari's vice president of marketing and sales in January 1981, intending to start a small marketing firm and get out of the world of big business. One of his clients was Activision, and seeing their success, he began to think there was room for another third-party company in the world of video games. It turned out that Denis Koble, who had been a designer at Atari for five years, was thinking the same thing. Soon there were nine people, including Rob Fulop, Bob Smith, and Mark Bradley from Atari, plus Bob Goldberger and Brian Dougherty from Mattel, whom Grubb had met while consulting.

Formed in 1982, Imagic was considered by some to be one of the best developers for the Atari 2600, relying less on arcade game remakes and more on original titles. They ultimately made games for Intellivision and ColecoVision, as well as for Commodore and Atari home computers.

In addition to their innovative game designs, such as

turnaround, but the rocket took off, and we rode the rocket. We went from zero to 350 people and sales of about $77 million in the first year."

The ride was a short one, however. Koble describes the atmosphere at the end, and some reasons for the discontinuation of the company: "We used to have a staff meeting every morning at 8:00 a.m. The industry was starting to fall apart, and every morning it was bad

I left Atari because they basically gave me no additional compensation except the free poultry for Missile Command. At that point in my life at 23, 10,000 bucks could have bought me a car. I got 2 percent and my name on my games at Imagic. It made my career.

—ROB FULOP, FORMER ATARI AND IMAGIC GAME DESIGNER

When I started at Atari, there were only 35 people. By the time I left, it was huge. At Imagic, I could get back down into the trenches... I remember a retreat at Pajaro Dunes and saying to Bob Smith, 'Bob, this is as good as it gets.' And it was true.

—DENNIS KOBLE, FORMER ATARI AND IMAGIC GAME DESIGNER

Rob Fulop's picture from Imagic's fanzine, NumbThumb.

linking two games (Atlantis and Cosmic Ark) as part of the same story, Imagic came out with some of the most colorful cover artwork of the time, some of which is reproduced here.

Imagic shot out of the gate, achieving instant success. Denis Koble remembers, "The company was founded with venture money, and the plan was to go public and make a big score. We were expecting a four- to five-year

news. Like the operations guy would say that we have more than 100,000 ROMs coming in next week, and we've already paid for them, but we didn't have orders for the games. The company was like a juggernaut, and you couldn't stop it on a dime. There were many financial commitments that couldn't be pulled back. Lots of people on staff. And meanwhile, the consumers had stopped buying."

Along with great games, Imagic created lots of great artwork for their box covers. Here's a small sample, along with some screenshots from Atlantis, Cosmic Ark, and Demon Attack.

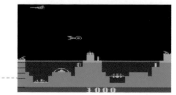

> *The Atari VCS wasn't very forgiving, and trying to learn the technology and invent a new game was like trying to build a house from toothpicks.*
>
> —ROB FULOP

> *I don't know. It's fun to be known and all the rest of it— the whole ego thing. But I guess I'd just as soon be rich and anonymous as rich and famous.*
>
> —DENIS KOBLE

> *Mark my words: There's going to be more money spent on video game advertising this winter than there will be on beer.*
>
> —BILL GRUBB, REFERRING TO IMAGIC'S PLANS TO ADVERTISE ON TV, EARLY IN 1983

1981 at the Arcades

One of the wonderful features of game playing is that when something is fun, it's *fun*. And what's fun can be made even more fun. This principle has been followed again and again in the history of electronic games, beginning with Pong and continuing to the present day.

One of the best examples of an idea that evolved into something better and better was the Space Invaders concept. Before Space Invaders, there had never been a game where you had a ship at the bottom of a screen and had to shoot down hordes of alien craft. But after Space Invaders, this became a game genre in itself, and games based on this premise kept getting better. Space Invaders led to Galaxian. After Galaxian came Galaga, and Galaga was like Galaxian on steroids.

Galaga

It's a good thing Galaga didn't come out first, or Earth would have been destroyed before we could pump up our wrists and fingers to fight them off.

Success in Galaga required the usual nerves of steel, but even more, a tireless button-pressing finger. Fortunately, if you could survive a while, you could gain a bonus ship. Yes, you had double the firepower, though you also had double the exposure to enemy fire and low-flying kamikaze alien ships. You also had to watch out for the tractor beam aliens who could steal one of your fighters if you were careless or unlucky enough to fall into their trap. With a well-placed shot, you could free it, but a careless or unlucky shot would kill your own man, causing you to increase your aggression level several times over. And Galaga had other surprises and unpleasant challenges. The game was full of tricks.

After a few waves of aliens, you were rewarded with a turkey shoot of a bonus round called the Challenging Stage. A bunch of ships flew out in predictable formation, but to get the whopping 10,000-point bonus, you had to hit 40 out of 40 of the suckers!

Gorf

Carrying the tradition of Space Invaders yet further, Gorf added its own inimitable presence. With an impressive vocabulary of phrases, Gorf hardly ever shut up, and it rarely had anything nice to say. One of Gorf's main innovations was the multimission arcade game. "I was a big fan of film history and D. W. Griffith," says designer Jamie Fenton. "I thought video games should have more than one theme."

In fact, Gorf consisted of five distinct missions, each a unique game. First there was the distinctly Space Invaders–like Astro Battles. Piece of cake. Next you had Laser Attack, in which you fought off more aliens, but had to watch out for the laser-firing support ships that could severely limit your mobility, and fry you instantaneously. Next came Galaxians. Yes, "We are Galaxians" again. From Galaxians you fought off a

bunch of ships squirting out of a space warp, and finally, as in Star Wars, you attempted to fire into the alien Flag Ship's reactor port to blow it up. The Flag Ship flew above you behind a shield and protected itself by dropping fireballs and chunks of its neutronium hull when you hit it.

Gorf was also the first to suggest a bit of role playing by means of its multistage story line and also by its use of military titles (six in all—ranging from Space Cadet to Space Avenger) to reward players' accomplishments.

Frogger

Probably everybody who ever played Frogger (and every writer who wrote about it) asked the question, "Why did froggy cross the road?" Why indeed? Our answer is, "It was fun." Not for the frog, of course, but for the rest of us. Frogger is one of those perennial classics that has been much imitated over the years.

The object was to get the frog across a bustling highway, then jump from log to log and turtle to treacherous turtle across a stretch of river, to one of the awaiting slots on the opposite bank, where there might be tasty flies as bonus treats. Sometimes you could offer a chivalrous ride to a Ms. Froggy, which also resulted in a bonus score. The pace of everything increased as you progressed through the game. Easy to begin, Frogger was surprisingly tricky to master, especially at higher levels—true to Nolan Bushnell's law of video game design—and its appeal was widespread and enduring, making it one of the true classics of arcade history.

Qix

In the early days of arcade game design, just about anything might turn out to be fun, and Taito's Qix was a pretty good example of how diverse games could be in the days before 3D graphics. This geometry lesson of a game required you to grab screen real estate by moving a small cursor across the blackness of Qix-infested space. The Qix was some malevolent (from your viewpoint, anyway) creature that would destroy your helpless cursor (called a *marker*) if it even touched the line you were drawing across the blackness. Other enemies, Sparx, chased you mindlessly, but relentlessly, and occasionally the line you were drawing would develop a fuse, which would burn down until you were toast.

If you could land the cursor safely on one of the screen's edges, however, or on the edge of already-captured space, you defined a new rectangular claim and reduced the Qix's domain while simultaneously gaining points, which were greater if you used the "slow" button. Each round had a goal—the amount of screen you had to capture to win.

For fans of the Etch-A-Sketch, there was some familiarity, as your cursor could only move in 90-degree angles and could only traverse space along the edges of its known universe, except when venturing out into the danger-filled blackness where the Qix moved randomly around. Qix players developed the extra benefit of being able to tell when 75 percent of a rectangle was filled in—a useful skill somewhere.

Ms. Pac-Man

Sequels often fall flat, but Ms. Pac-Man came on sassy and delivered the goods. With numerous subtle but effective improvements to the original game, Ms. Pac-Man was even better than the original. For the first time in video game history, women had a protagonist, and they

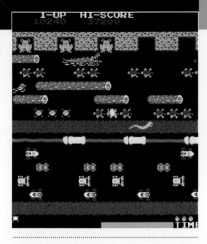

Frogger screen.

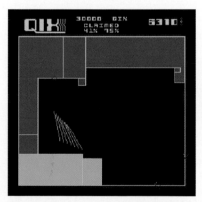

77

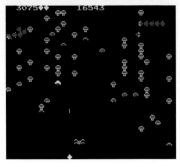

spent quarters in unprecedented numbers. If there was ever a love affair between women and video games, it had to be with Ms. Pac-Man.

Ms. Pac-Man came into being not in some Japanese pizza parlor, but around the MIT campus in Boston, and was the result of work done on enhancement boards for existing arcade machines.

The original intent was to create add-on boards that improved on game play for existing arcade games, thereby extending their viable life span in the arcade. However, following a lawsuit by Atari and subsequent out-of-court settlement, the designers approached Midway with an add-on board for Pac-Man. Midway, instead, suggested putting out a whole new game.

The original add-on had a Pac-Man–like character with legs, but that was not an acceptable option. Ultimately, however, the concept of a female Pac-Man came up. She was first Miss Pac-Man, then Mrs. Pac-Man, and ultimately she became the ultraliberated Ms. Pac-Man, the protagonist of the best-selling arcade game in U.S. history.

Ms. Pac-Man was an improvement over the original game, while still remaining true to its predecessor. The game was faster and included four mazes instead of one. Moreover, it did not allow for the kind of pattern memorization that many players had developed with Pac-Man. You had to play with skill, not patterns.

The four ghosts were back, but one was now named Sue (apparently after the sister of one of the designers), and the fruits got mobile, instead of waiting passively to be gobbled for bonus points.

Ultimately, men and women, girls and boys, all played Ms. Pac-Man, and the world had a new heroine.

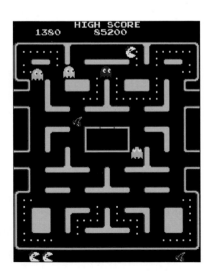

Centipede

I know Ed Logg didn't live in the house I once occupied in Hawaii where foot-long centipedes occasionally dropped from the ceiling to scare the bejeezus out of us, but ironically, he was designing one of my favorite arcade games at about the same time I was dodging the genuine article. Thus, I have a very personal relationship with Centipede.

Centipede was a brilliant game in every respect. The smoothness of motion using the Trak-Ball, and the rapid-fire attack, could whittle away a mushroom faster than you could say "millipede." The title character itself seemed to have many lives, and, once hit, the centipede's segments would strike out on their own, taking new paths through the forest of mushrooms. Dodging the ever-annoying spider while attempting to get the maximum points by blasting it at point-blank range added to the intensity, and of course there were cameo appearances by some of our other favorite insects: poisonous scorpions and fast-falling fleas that left a trail of new fungus behind and announced their presence with a descending slide whistle sound.

Ed Logg on Centipede

We initially had the centipede running in a field of mushrooms that could not be destroyed. The spider was created from the start just like the small saucer in Asteroids. It was designed to keep the player moving. At our first review, Dan van Elderen asked why we could not shoot the mushrooms. From that suggestion the game really changed. The centipede segments would leave mushrooms when killed, the spider would remove them, and the flea created columns of mushrooms, which I thought would be the ideal strategy to trap the mushrooms. The earwig would cause the centipede to drop to the bottom to create a sense of panic.

Many years after Centipede was released, I happened to be walking by Industrial Design and noticed that the players were only playing the second player on a cocktail version of Centipede. A cocktail cabinet has the second player facing the first so the software must reverse the field of play. I asked them why they were doing this, and they said the second player gets better scores. I checked my game code and indeed there was a bug. Instead of the spider reducing his range as the player's score increases, the second player's spider was *increasing* his range, making it easier for the player.

Two Centipede posters. The one on the left is the one Atari released. The original poster (from Ed Logg's personal collection) featured a somewhat blurry naked green woman coming out of a colorful mushroom patch. Judged too risqué, it was abandoned, and this may be the only one remaining.

Centipede board game from Milton Bradley.

> [On Millipede]There were several ideas we wanted to add to Centipede to make the game more interesting. For example, having multiple spiders made the game really frantic. I also wanted to add some variations, like waves of mosquitoes and other bugs that come after certain levels. After one level, the field of mushrooms changed based on the game of Life* (a mushroom would grow if there were two or three neighboring mushrooms). This was created to break up any pattern the players may have created that I had not foreseen.
>
> —ED LOGG

*See page 51 [Ed Conway's game of Life]

79

Tempest

The first game featuring Atari's color vector graphics, Tempest was a bright and colorful game that could baffle the unwary. Instead of the linear movement of Space Invaders games, you got to spin your odd crablike ship around one of 96 geometric shapes. Clockwise or counterclockwise, you spun, shooting at the advancing menace of flip-flopping red thingies and avoiding, at all costs, *avoiding* the spikes.

Tempest was an unreal game that required you to rethink your approach and stretch new video game muscles. It was all too easy to find yourself overwhelmed and not know, literally, which way to turn. And the game was tons of fun to play. You may not have had a clue what it was about or why you were bent on destroying these odd bits of alien geometry, but you just knew it had to be in a good cause.

TEMPEST

© MCMLXXX ATARI
BONUS EVERY 10000
CREDITS 2   FREE PLAY

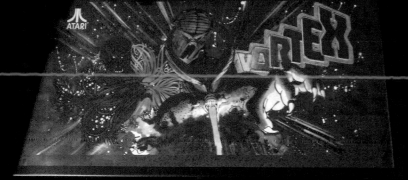

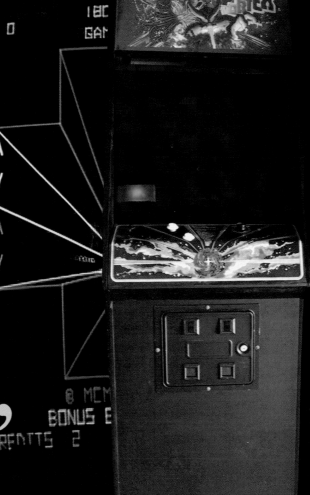

" We had a book of ideas that we kept, and one idea I had wanted to do was a first-person Space Invaders. I loved Space Invaders, and I thought it would be great in first person. Atari had a new color vector display under development, and they said I could use it. But when I completed my first version of the game, it was OK, but nothing special. At the first design review, Gene Lipkin said it sucked, and that was my feeling, too, but I still thought with some changes I could make it work. I mentioned a nightmare I had with monsters coming out of a hole in the ground and said, 'I can take this first-person Space Invaders and make it into a tube, and the monsters will come out like a hole in the ground,' and they said, 'Try it.' So I made a bunch of different shapes and made the necessary changes, and at that point people started coming into the lab and playing it a lot and making it hard for me to get my work done, which was the traditional way we knew we were onto something. When we field-tested it, it did really well. A large part of the game's popularity was that the controller was fun, and you could sit there and spin when you were waiting for something to happen. It had a nice feel to it. "

—DAVE THEURER, TEMPEST DESIGNER

Like Missile Command, Tempest went through some name changes. Its first moniker was Aliens, which was the name of a famous Ridley Scott movie. Next came Vortex, which might have made some sense in the context, but, as designer Dave Theurer states, "I kept having a bad feeling. It reminded me of a feminine hygiene product." Put to a committee vote, the name that stuck was also Dave's favorite alternate—Tempest.

Donkey Kong

The story of Donkey Kong has been told often. And for good reason. It was in Donkey Kong that we first met one of video game history's most enduring characters, even if he was only a carpenter known as Jumpman at the time. It was Shigeru Miyamoto's first video game (for an interview with this legendary designer, see page 238). It was the beginning of an era and a portent of the future.

Nintendo had not done well in the U.S., though their Radarscope game had only slightly trailed Pac-Man in popularity in Japan. But, of 3,000 Radarscopes shipped to the U.S., 2,000 remained unsold. When Miyamoto was given his first game assignment, the plan was to use the remaining 2,000 cabinets for the new game. A far-too conservative plan, as it turned out.

Miyamoto created a story line about a gorilla who runs away from his master, a carpenter, and steals the carpenter's girlfriend. The carpenter must chase the gorilla through a series of industrial settings to rescue the girl. The name Donkey Kong was Miyamoto's best dictionary-aided attempt at creating an English title meaning "stubborn gorilla."

Other than a lawsuit by Universal Pictures over the similarity of Donkey Kong to King Kong (which Nintendo won), the game climbed the charts a lot faster than that carpenter was able to climb those girders. It was a tremendous hit. It also introduced what we like to call the "save the princess" theme that would later be repeated in Miyamoto's Mario and Zelda games, as well as other games such as Prince of Persia.

Donkey Kong's protagonist—no, not the ape, but the man—was originally called Jumpman. But later, he was renamed after Nintendo's U.S. head Minoru Arakawa's landlord. He became Mario, and later changed professions to become a plumber. But that was all to come.

The game itself was clever and required patience, good timing, and whatever it takes for a puny human to go up against a giant ape. The cartoonlike musical background was similar to the music of later Nintendo games.

1982 at the Arcades

Arguably, 1980 and 1981 were the most significant years in arcade game history. However, creativity and technology continued to advance, and 1982 brought us several additional all-time favs.

Food Themes

Two games brought food to the forefront of the arcades: Atari's Food Fight and Midway's Burger Time. Food Fight was an all-out brawl, with watermelons, pies, and other delectables flying as you tried to pick off some decidedly unfriendly chefs. Burger Time was far more construc-tive in its vocational training. The ultimate goal here was to walk across various hamburger parts to cause them to fall onto platters, ultimately construct-ing tasty burgers. Would-be short-order chefs would be advised not to tromp on the burger parts during assembly, but the technique worked for our hero, Peter

Pepper, whose only defense against his various enemies— Misters Hot Dog, Pickle, and Egg—was to hustle his portly butt up and down ladders or to spray pepper in their faces to freeze them temporarily.

Dig Dug

The game's title starts out like some grammar lesson on the verb "to dig," but the game itself is a classic. Dig Dug himself was a little guy who liked to tunnel underground and do some vermin eradication by means of his handy-dandy pump weapon. The pump would literally blow Dig Dug's enemies up like balloons until they popped. Of course, for extra cleverness points, you could lure a few pursuing Pookas and Fygars under a rock, which you conveniently caused to fall at just the right time. The real trick was that your enemies had a way of moving around without tunnels, which often meant curtains for the unwary Dig Dug.

In a way, in contrast to the early arcade maze games, Dig Dug was like a make-your-own maze game. Its clever play style, cute graphics, and nifty challenges elevated it to an all-time favorite. Many games imitated it, and even Maxis' SimAnt, which came out years later, brought back Dig Duggian memories.

Created by Namco, Dig Dug was the first coin-op import licensed by Atari.

Mr. Do!

At about the same time as Dig Dug, Universal released the first of several Mr. Do! games. Mr. Do! was a clown who carried around a magic ball and ate cherries. Not that it has to make sense or anything, but Mr. Do! was similar to Dig Dug, and pretty much as fun to play. However, it lacked that certain something to take it to Dig Dug's heights... er, depths?

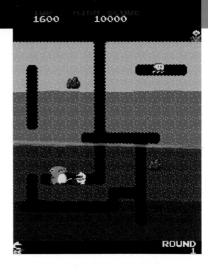

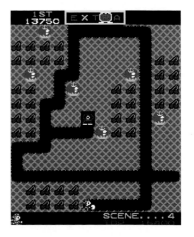

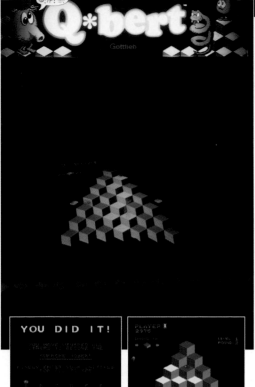

Q*Bert

Although Dig Dug and Mr. Do! were definite runners-up for 1982's "cute award," that year's unquestioned winner had to be that ultra-endearing alien hopmeister, Q*Bert. This nonviolent critter just had a need to hop around, changing the colors of the platform tiles on a playfield that gave the illusion of being 3D—no doubt part of its appeal. And instead of hopping in a straight line, Q*Bert took the angles and hopped diagonally, just to keep the spatially challenged on their toes.

Q*Bert was plenty of fun to play, with its strange cast of characters, including Coily the snake (dumb as a limp rope)*, Slick and Sam, who liked to undo Q's hard work, and Ugg and Wrong-way, whose trick was to turn our hero's world upside down. Q*Bert talked a little during the game, but his words were really gibberish pieced together by messing around with the speech synthesis.

Originally, Q*Bert was meant to shoot from his rather ample proboscis, and the first proposed title of the game was "Snots and Boogers," which, for obvious reasons, was scrapped. The second title, "@!#?@!," was actually printed on some test cabinets that went out, but ultimately the good folks at Gottlieb realized that a pronounceable name was something of a plus. In a brainstorming session, they came up with the idea of combining cube and Hubert, making Cubert, then Q-Bert, and, finally, Q*Bert—the winner!

For a more detailed version of the Q*Bert story, check out these two Web sites: http://users.aol.com/JPMLee/qbert.htm http://www.coinop.org/features/qbstory.html

*Warren Davis, designer of Q*Bert, offers this in Coily's defense. "I have to take issue with your description of Coily as 'dumb as a limp rope.' He actually had a learning disability, and should be treated a little more sensitively."*

Get the ultimate high score and become the Supreme Noser!

Before it was Q*Bert, it was @!#?@!

Pole Position

When you hear the name Pole Position, think of every racing game that has come since because Pole Position defined the genre. It was the first driving game to capture the feeling of the track, and the skill involved required all your attention. Shifting gears, anticipating the next turn, dodging aggressive drivers, and making that first qualifying lap were all a part of the experience. Pole Position was the first great driving game, and the first that truly satisfied our need for speed at the arcades.

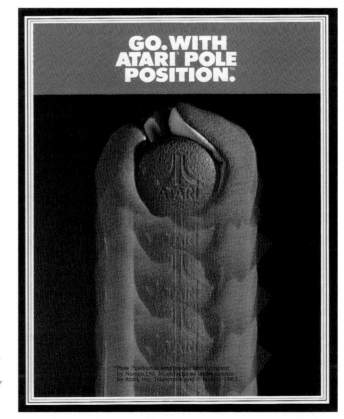

Joust

Joust always struck us as one of the weirdest games we'd ever seen. Gravity definitely played a major role in the game. You were mounted on an ostrich, with a lance in hand, and would fall to the nearest platform (or into the molten lava below) if you stopped flapping, which entailed constantly hitting the "flap" button. This odd means of transportation, combined with the fascinating physics built into the game, made it completely absorbing. The game's stilted use of Ye Olde English (as in "Thy Game Is Over")

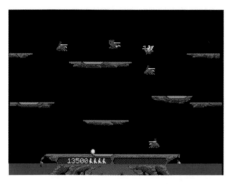

clashed with common sense about as much as the flying ostriches.

Oddly, unlike real jousting, altitude was very helpful, which in some ways made it similar to dogfighting in very unwieldy, underpowered aircraft. You couldn't vanquish your foes from below, but only from above, so you would sometimes flap-flap-flap into a superior position, then drop on your unsuspecting victim.

Joust boasted its share of enemies, including several types of buzzard-mounted jousters, the dreaded pterodactyl, and the mysterious hand that would reach out from the lava and grab your bird. But by far the best opponent was generally standing (or sitting) right next to you. In two-player mode, you could choose to play cooperatively, which had its merits, but there was no challenge so satisfying as going up against your friend, and that was part of the great appeal of Joust. A cooperative game could suddenly turn into a full-on duel to the death between friends.

Tron

It might have been a box-office flop, but Disney's Tron was just this side of orgasmic for geeky gamers like us. It was our secret fantasy brought to the big screen. And so discovering Midway's Tron in the arcades was the closest thing to being in the movie that any of us could ever hope for. We'll admit that lust for total immersion into the Tron experience has since been replaced by *Holodeck* fantasies from Star Trek, but in those days, Tron was it.

The cabinet had that je ne sais quoi, that glow of neon that was just cool, and the joystick was completely satisfying in your hand. The game itself was plenty hard, which meant lots of quarters spent in order to experience all of its scenes, the best of which was based on the famous light cycle sequence in the movie. Cool scene, cool game play.

Tron was the first game based on a movie license, and promised a wonderful synergy between Hollywood and games. However, later attempts to link movies and games soon disillusioned us and proved that Tron was the exception, rather than the rule.

Donkey Kong Jr.

Clearly, Shigeru Miyamoto wasn't monkeying around when he decided to do a sequel to Donkey Kong. In Donkey Kong Jr., he flip-flopped roles on us, and we were perfectly happy about it. Instead of playing the irate carpenter, this time you

got to play the ultracute scion of the original ape, as he attempted to rescue papa from that very same carpenter, now named Mario. Mario would one day soon change professions and become our favorite hero, but not now. In this game, he was the heavy, and it was Junior who had to save the day.

Donkey Kong Jr. wasn't just the first official appearance of Mario, it was also a great game, much improved from the original. It is another indication of Miyamoto's budding genius that the sequel to his first hit game showed so much improvement. Its four levels were loaded with challenges, rewards, and imaginative touches galore. Junior's personality shines throughout, and Miyamoto's comic touches and melodramatic music set the stage beautifully.

Robotron 2084

After Defender, Eugene Jarvis did the even more intense Stargate, then took a little time off. When he came back to Williams, what he gave us was Robotron 2084, which I like to think of as Berzerk gone berserk. Jarvis obviously didn't subscribe to Isaac Asimov's three laws of robotics; the mechanical monstrosities of Robotron were out to destroy all humanity. Your mission was to save the last human family—Mommy, Daddy, and little Mikey—who seemed to have a tendency to wander aimlessly among hordes of robotic assassins of various shapes and sizes. The most insulting enemies were the Brain Robotrons, who could turn Mommy, Daddy, or Mikey into zombielike killing machines called Progs. Some of Robotron's metal menagerie, like the Hulks, were blocky and indestructible, but most would succumb to a well-placed shot.

The real charm of Robotron, in addition to its high adrenaline production, was its use of two 8-direction joysticks, one for running

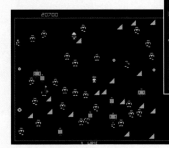

(which you did a lot) and one for shooting. That meant you could shoot in just about any direction while you were on the move, which did give you an increased tactical advantage if you could keep a cool head. But there were just way too many dangers to relax for a moment, except perhaps briefly after you had cleared one of the incessant waves. In Robotron, you knew that death was just around the corner, and every minute you survived was a victory. If you had met Eugene Jarvis back then, you would have shaken his hand and then bummed a quarter off him so you could play again.

Zaxxon

If people occasionally had trouble with the pseudo-3D perspective of Q*Bert, they really freaked out when they first encountered Zaxxon. This little gem of a game initially caused bafflement among the ranks of players for whom the two-dimensional game had become second nature.

Somehow most of us made the necessary perceptual leap and, keeping half an eye on the altimeter conveniently

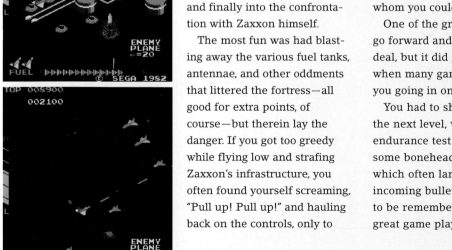

positioned on the left side of the screen, courageously maneuvered and blasted our way over and under the obstacles of the fortress, past the oncoming delta-winged spacecraft in the space level, and finally into the confrontation with Zaxxon himself.

The most fun was had blasting away the various fuel tanks, antennae, and other oddments that littered the fortress—all good for extra points, of course—but therein lay the danger. If you got too greedy while flying low and strafing Zaxxon's infrastructure, you often found yourself screaming, "Pull up! Pull up!" and hauling back on the controls, only to

watch your nifty little craft plunge nosefirst into a brick wall or electric barrier.

Ultimately, we came to call Zaxxon's POV an "isometric perspective," and it has been used effectively for years in other games, such as Diablo. But once upon a time, it was brand spanking new.

Time Pilot

While neither the history nor the avionics of Time Pilot would stand the test of close scrutiny, the game itself was a blast. The back story had something to do with traveling in time through five stages from 1910 (the very genesis of manned flight) through the year 2001, which at the time was the far, far future. The bottom line was that you got to shoot a lot of stuff all over the place while doing loop-de-loops with your aircraft in two-dimensional space and laying down a carpet of rather large, slow bullets. Granted, the enemies you faced in each successive time period got tougher, but the premise remained the same: shoot everything. Well, except for the occasional parachutist, whom you could collect for a nifty bonus score.

One of the great feelings in Time Pilot was the ability to go forward and backward. Sure, that sounds like no big deal, but it did give you a great sense of freedom in a time when many games were essentially "rail" games that kept you going in one direction all the time.

You had to shoot down a lot of enemies to advance to the next level, which was fun, but it sometimes became an endurance test to see how long you could avoid making some bonehead move and zigging instead of zagging, which often landed you smack on another plane or an incoming bullet or missile. In any case, Time Pilot deserves to be remembered, not for its science, but certainly for its great game play.

Moon Patrol

Cruisin' on an afternoon in your moon buggy would have been relaxing, if it hadn't been for all those nasty flying saucers, giant potholes, boulders, and other menacing obstacles that kept appearing. Good thing your particular vehicle came equipped with dual-firing guns (up and forward) as well as a handy jump control. Although Moon Patrol might not qualify as one of the all-time great games, it did distinguish itself by being the first game to feature parallax scrolling, in which the background moved at a different rate than the foreground. This gave the game a slightly more realistic distance effect. Moon Patrol was the only imported game licensed by Williams (from Irem in Japan). Moon Patrol was also one of the early games to allow you to continue playing by inserting a quarter before a timer ran out.

1983 at the Arcades

The hits kept on coming all through 1982, and 1983 began the same way. Several pivotal games were released in 1983, not the least of which were Dragon's Lair, the first laser disk game, and Mario Bros., which first introduced the world to Mario and Luigi. Although the arcade business was about to take a tumble, companies such as Atari, Midway, Cinematronics, and Nintendo continued to produce great games.

Dragon's Lair

Dirk the Daring was kept pretty busy finding his way to the great dragon Singe, who had, for reasons only dragons know, kidnapped the fair Daphne. Even at 50 cents a pop, Cinematronics' Dragon's Lair—the first laser disk game to be released (if not the first to be developed)—caused an instant sensation. With art and animation from Don Bluth Films, who also did the *Secret of NIMH*, the game was stunning, funny, and more graphically rich than anything previously seen in the arcades. It was like

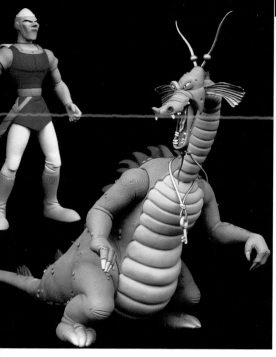

stepping into a Saturday morning cartoon.

Dragon's Lair's weakness, however, was game play. The game consisted of a series of branching decision points. Learning which decision was right or wrong could cost quite a few quarters and require you to see your hero, Dirk, turn into a crumbling skeleton before your eyes countless times, but ultimately the persistent player was treated to a reunion scene with the sexy Daphne, and a road map of the game imprinted in his or her head. It is interesting to note that Gottlieb's Mach 3, which came out within two weeks of Dragon's Lair, did better business. But Dragon's Lair is remembered as a landmark product, synonymous with the introduction of the laser disk game.

Mario Bros.

You met him first as the aggrieved victim of a giant malevolent ape in Donkey Kong. He was a carpenter then. Next, with a new name (Mario) and still a carpenter, he morphed into a nasty man who had captured the giant ape, forcing poor Junior to risk life and limb to rescue his daddy in Donkey Kong Jr. Finally, he must have gone through some self-help seminars and vocational training, because now he was just about the most endearing character since Mickey Mouse, and he was a plumber, to boot.

Joined in two-player action by his sidekick Luigi, Mario had a knack for clearing the sewer of unwanted turtles called Shellcreepers, aggro Sidesteppers, irritating Fighterflies, and the treacherous Slipice that could make Mario and Luigi stick frozen to the ground.

Game play was pretty simple. Get under a creature and jump to flip it over, then kick it off the screen. You got points for kicking it, and you could also collect a bonus coin when it rolled out. The crablike Sidesteppers required two bumps from below and got pretty worked up after the first one, picking up speed and looking kinda angry.

The game was at its best as a two-player game. You could play cooperatively, but more often than not, one person would flip something over and the other player would go grab the points. Not fair, you say? But that was Mario Bros. And you could get revenge with a well-timed bump on your buddy, sending him into an oncoming enemy. So there!

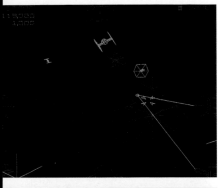

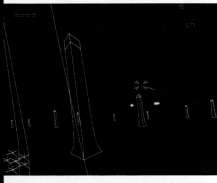

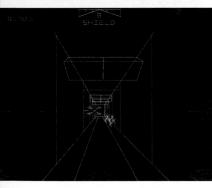

Star Wars

The Force was with Atari when Ed Rotberg began his last game, Warp Speed, before leaving the company. Don't remember Warp Speed? Maybe that's because it never came out. But under a new team and with a nifty license from George Lucas, it did become a most awesome and adrenaline-pumping game of Star Wars. According to Rotberg, "The guys who completed it did a great job. About the only piece that I contributed was the controller." At any rate, it makes a good trivia question.

Star Wars was a marvel of design. The cabinet art and control layout were superb, and the game play was intense. Of course, you played Luke Skywalker at the controls of an X-wing fighter, and you frequently heard voices—the voice of Darth Vader, "I'm on the leader," or Obi Wan Kenobi, "Use the Force, Luke!" Meanwhile, R2-D2 would be talking to you in the background, but you probably didn't understand what the little droid was saying. Or did you?

True to the movie plot, you had to engage in some nasty dogfighting with a horde of TIE fighters in the first stage, then blast away at the gun towers on the surface of the Death Star. Finally, if you made it this far, you got to fly the dramatic trench run, avoiding all dangers and remembering the Force until you tossed your torpedoes into the miniscule exhaust vent that was the Death Star's Achilles' heel. If you were good enough, you'd be inducted into Princess Leia's Rebel Guard—the high scorers' honors.

Of course, the other two movies from the original trilogy also came to the arcades, but it was the original Star Wars that most of us will remember best. And Star Wars in the arcades was a harbinger of great games to come. Later products for the home computer, such as X-Wing and TIE Fighter, involved us even more deeply in the movie plot, but nothing could compare to the experience of playing at the arcade, especially in the cockpit version of the game. Inside the dark confines of the cockpit, you came to believe, as long as your quarters lasted anyway, that you really did live a long time ago, in a galaxy far away.

Atari's Dan Osborne shows George Lucas how to use the Force in his cockpit version of Star Wars.

Spy Hunter

Pole Position was the first driving game we really hauled ass in, but we were limited to a racetrack and a couple of gears. By 1983, we were ready for something a little more deadly. Enter Bally/Midway's Spy Hunter, which introduced to the arcades a car fit for 007, enemies to shoot and destroy, and cool Peter Gunn music. There was even a weapons van that you drove into at high speed, reminiscent of the popular TV show *Knight Rider*.

You had a nifty assortment of weapons, ranging from smoke screens to missiles, with which to cream whatever got in your way. Or, you could play bumper cars and simply knock those nasty bad guys off the road, where they'd crash and burn satisfyingly. Of course, they often tried to return the favor.

Spy Hunter let you play through on a timer with unlimited cars. You could crash as many times as you liked, and your trusty replacement truck would dish out another car. Of course, crashing wasn't recommended, but it happened

as your car often skittered out of control in the heat of the battle. In the later stages, you traded in your Bond car for an equally fast and deadly speedboat on a river (switching from asphalt to water), but the idea remained the same.

Spy Hunter 2 came out with a two-person view and a new isometric perspective, neither of which was a hit with arcade fans.

I, Robot

I, Robot was not one of the greatest arcade games of all time, but it did have the distinction of having a cool name, and of being the first game to use full 3D polygon graphics. It was the first of many, to be sure. It was a strange game, but fun to play. And its sense of humor was evident right from the beginning, when our heroic robot is told he can't jump. That's right. The rule from on high is, "No jumping!" And so begins the saga of the robot who must jump. And, when you weren't jumping, you could just make cool pictures in "Doodle City" for a few minutes.

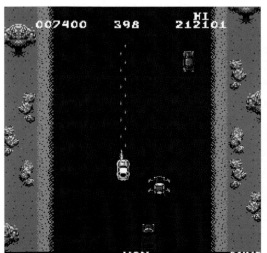

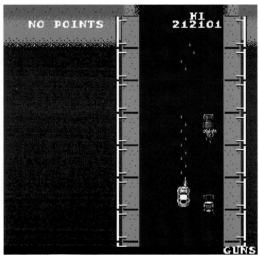

1984 at the Arcades

By 1984, the arcade business had hit bottom, and the number of top games dwindled considerably. However, two fighting games (Karate Champ and Punch-Out!!) and one classic marble game did appear that year.

Punch-Out!!

Nintendo's Punch-Out!! simply reeked of personality, and it was a lot of fun, as well. Taking on the likes of Glass Joe, Bald Bull, or Mr. Sandman with your wire-framed, goofy-faced challenger, you couldn't help but smile, until you tasted the canvas anyway. The game included a play-by-play announcer, which, although it sounded as if it had a fishbowl over its head, nevertheless made you feel like you were at Madison Square Garden.

When the K.O. bar lit up, it was time to deliver the final blow, the coup de grace, the big whomper. Time to deck the dude!

Punch-Out!! was a great boxing game, and the first of its kind. You had to mix it up, and each successive challenger required better technique. You had to mix up your punches, use defense, and finish the guy off when the K.O. lit up.

In true Nintendo style, the characters were very cartoon-like, and some of them could even stick and move pretty well.

Marble Madness

Whereas "Roll Out the Barrels" would have been a good theme song for Donkey Kong, TV's *Rawhide* theme ("Rolling, rolling, rolling...") would have fit Atari's Marble Madness at least as well. But, while the spherical protagonist of this game was a geometric shape without superpowers, it rolled through a truly surreal 3D world. Even in arcade games, where, let's face it, reality is not the benchmark, Marble Madness set new standards for imagination and was much imitated in subsequent years.

Mark Cerny was a champion arcade gamer and, while working on a physics degree at UC Berkeley in the 70s, managed to be the first documented player to roll over the scoreboard on Defender. He subsequently got a job as a teenage wonder programmer at Atari, where he was asked, "Why do you want to spend the best years of your life before you burn out at Atari?" His answer? "I didn't think I'd burn out." Ironically, Cerny's resume was sent to Atari's human resources department, and, thinking that it was a job application, they sent him a rejection letter. "It said, 'We'll keep you on file,'" remembers Cerny. "Lucky I didn't go through normal channels to get my job."

When he started at Atari, he worked on Qwak! and Major Havoc. In 1983, he began working on the concept design for Marble Madness. "Originally, I thought of using the touch screen but soon decided it was a dead end." He decided instead to use Atari's trusty Trak-Ball for the controls. "I don't think this has ever been printed," he said, "but originally the Trak-Ball was going to be motorized. It would move along with the marble. So, if you were going downhill, for instance, the Trak-Ball would be spinning, and to slow down the ball, you'd stop or slow down the spin. But it was too hard to implement."

Cerny went on to work on many games and was part of the teams that did Crash Bandicoot and Spyro the Dragon. After serving as president of Universal Interactive in the mid-90s, he left and ultimately created his own company, Cerny Games. He's still making games, and assures us that he hasn't burned out yet.

Vectrex

It was the first vector graphics console system for the home. Vectrex was first shown by General Consumer Electronics (GCE) at the Summer CES in Chicago in 1982 and hit the market in time for Christmas with a price tag of $199. It included an Asteroids-like game called Mine Sweeper. Milton Bradley purchased GCE in 1983, but, despite critical praise, sales were disappointing, and by 1984 Vectrex was discontinued.

The Vectrex box, with its nine-inch screen, looked like a black version of Apple's Macintosh, which appeared some years later. Despite the fact that it was the perfect system on which to play home versions of games like Asteroids, Battlezone, and Tempest, to name a few, Vectrex's timing was bad. It came out at a time when the video game industry was on the verge of collapse. Only 30 games were produced for the system.

Vectrex was also monochromatic, which might have been perceived as a limitation. To display color in games, Vectrex used colored plastic overlays, harkening back to the first Odyssey system. (A color version with a clever layered color phosphor system was developed, but never marketed. One prototype still exists.)

Whatever the reasons, not that many Vectrex machines were sold, and yet it remains one of the most fascinating and innovative products that never got to live up to its potential.

Jay had made a speech-sampling device. One day he had us all shout, 'Back to work!' in unison. He put it in the box and whenever he thought someone was shirking, he'd pull it out and play 'Back to work!' from it. That was how I got the inspiration to put voice in Spike.

—TOM SLOPER, GAME SYSTEM DESIGNER

JAY SMITH ON VECTREX

One day John Ross picked up a one-inch CRT that had been used in some military instrumentation. It was maybe six inches long, and I think it had just a numerical display. But that started us thinking about making a handheld game from a TV tube. This led to a small game that was optioned to Kenner Toys. It was called a Mini-Arcade and used a five-inch CRT. We proposed using a vector scan instead of raster, and our first prototypes used oscilloscopes. But Kenner was pretty much a pure toy company, so they ended up turning it back to us.

Ed Krakauer, who had been at Mattel and later started General Consumer Electronics, saw our prototype around September 1981. He got very excited, but said it needed a larger screen and had to be done by the next CES in June. We put on an incredible crash effort to do it.

We gave it a nine-inch screen and turned it vertical so it would look different from a TV. It was designed using the Motorola 6809 processor, and the entire ROM was 8K— 4K for the built-in game, Mine Sweeper, and 4K for the operating system.

Jay Smith was the former head of Western Technology and is known by fans as the Father of the Vectrex.

ColecoVision

C oleco was always a player throughout the 70s, but they hit their zenith—and their nadir—in the 80s. It started with a fateful trip to the bathroom.

The high point of the arc came with the release of the graphically superior ColecoVision console system. ColecoVision was a far superior game system at the time, and Coleco marketed it aggressively. From its debut in August 1982 until its demise in 1984, hundreds of thousands of consoles and close to 10 million cartridges were sold for this system. In all, 170 games were made for ColecoVision, but the one that made all the difference was Shigeru Miyamoto's classic game, Donkey Kong.

How Coleco scooped the home market with Donkey Kong is a story in itself. It started with Eric Bromley, Coleco's head of game design and development, who was visiting Japanese companies looking for content for the upcoming system. "While at Nintendo, I had to use the bathroom, which was on a different floor; and I walked past a machine that intrigued me. I asked if they would show it to me. It was Donkey Kong, and I knew immediately that we had to have it. They said they wanted, I think, one or two dollars per cart, which was a great deal (AU: A great deal (arrangement), not a great deal of money) back then; but they also wanted about $200,000 wired to them within 24 hours. I waited until it was about 7:00 a.m. in the States, then called Arnold Greenberg, Coleco's president. I said, 'Arnold, are you sitting down? I got the greatest game I've ever seen. The deal is reasonable. They only want a buck or two per unit. However, they want two hundred thousand in advance.' I took the phone off my ear and waited for the screaming to die down. Finally he asked, 'What's it called?' And I said, 'It's called Donkey

ColecoVision expansion modules included a fancy joystick, a driving module (which included a plug-in pedal), a rollerball, and the Atari 2600 converter.

Kong.' He asked, 'Why do they call it that?' I told him, 'Because they think it's funny.' First thing he wanted to do was change the name. Anyway, he said yes, and I went out to a restaurant with Yamauchi-san and his daughter and we wrote the contract on a cloth napkin. I kept the napkin."

But that wasn't the end of the story. Later, Nintendo actually made a better deal with Atari; and in a hotel room during a Consumer Electronics Show, Bromley was told to get it back at all costs. He got Minoru Arakawa, founder and president of Nintendo of America, out of bed and spent two hours "arguing, begging, pleading, and cajoling." In the end, Arakawa agreed to return the deal to Coleco, saying, according to Bromley, that he'd "never seen any American stay up all night pleading for something like this, and if you put that much into the product we can't lose."

Besides having superior graphics, ColecoVision also boasted the ability to play all Atari 2600 cartridges using a special adapter called "Expansion Module #1," the first cross-platform adapter. Of course, this spurred a lawsuit by Atari, but Coleco prevailed. With the adapter, ColecoVision could legitimately claim to run more software titles than any other system. Coleco followed their Atari adapter with a standalone Atari 2600 clone called the Gemini, again the first time a manufacturer had cloned a competitor's game system.

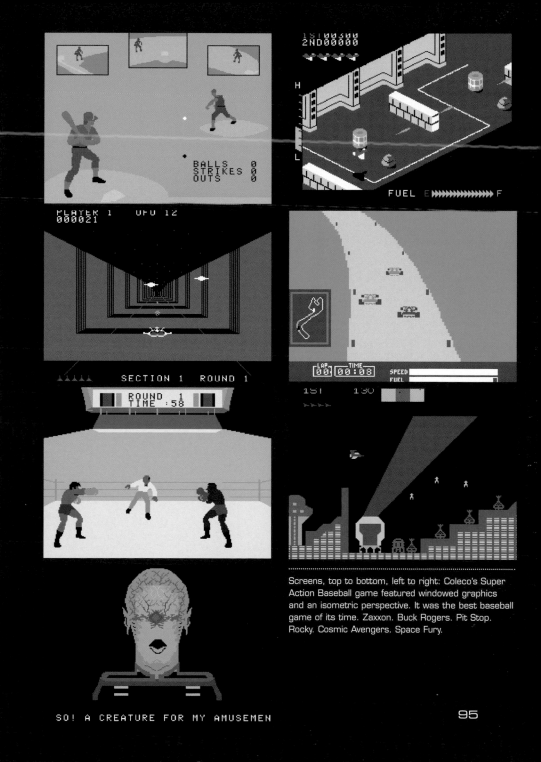

Screens, top to bottom, left to right: Coleco's Super Action Baseball game featured windowed graphics and an isometric perspective. It was the best baseball game of its time. Zaxxon. Buck Rogers. Pit Stop. Rocky. Cosmic Avengers. Space Fury.

95

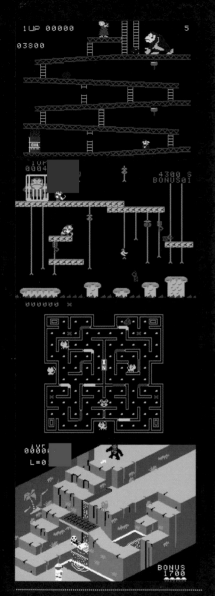

More ColecoVision games: Donkey Kong, Donkey Kong Jr., Mouse Trap, and Congo Bongo. Of course, it was Donkey Kong that launched all the hubbub!

I went to Japan with Leonard Greenberg and we visited Yamauchi, the president of Nintendo. At the time, we were doing some joint product development with them. They were interested in buying ColecoVision from us for 10 percent above our cost, but Leonard wanted to sell it to them for 10 percent below our regular selling price. The negotiations broke down and Yamauchi said, 'We'll develop our own game system, then.' I heard Leonard laughing, thinking these guys wouldn't come up with anything that could compete.

—BERT REINER, COLECO'S HEAD OF ENGINEERING AND PRODUCTION

Coleco's other best-seller was the Cabbage Patch doll. They even had a Cabbage Patch game.

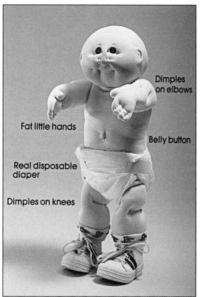

Dimples on elbows

Fat little hands

Belly button

Real disposable diaper

Dimples on knees

Adam

Perhaps no system demonstrated the adage "Timing is everything" better than Adam.

Adam was an incredible idea—an inexpensive computer system, complete with monitor and printer, for little more than the price of a video game system. The Adam plan, according to designer Eric Bromley, was to create the ultimate user-friendly computer system. It was a bold and exciting idea. Unfortunately, Adam had many reliability problems, and a great many of the machines had to be returned. It also, unfortunately, hit the market just as the video game phenomenon went boom and died.

"Adam was capable of having no instruction manual...we just needed a place for the warranty and how to plug it in," says Bromley. "If there were three possible ways to do something, they would all work. You could do things in any order. The theory about Adam computer was that the operating system and the three major applications were the same. You plug in one chip and up came the word processor. Plug in another chip and it would be a spreadsheet/database, or a graphics program. The operating system was underneath, so we just bank-selected the part of the operating system we wanted. There was no loading, just the application with a simple menu system for operating it."

The big marketing coup of Adam was the release of an exclusive version of Donkey Kong Jr., and consequently there was a lot of excitement around the Coleco booth at that Winter CES in Las Vegas. People were lined up four deep around the displays to see dramatic presentations of Adam.

However, Adam's ability to play Donkey Kong and Donkey Kong Jr. caused a bit of havoc. Nintendo had licensed the video game rights to Coleco, but had licensed the computer rights to Atari. Given that Adam was able to play ColecoVision cartridges, but was at the same time a computer, a great brouhaha erupted. Nintendo's Arakawa sums it up with classic understatement. "It was a big mess. How do you define the line between computer and video games? We had a difficult time trying to satisfy both of them."

In the end, Coleco won the right to sell both versions of Donkey Kong. They were also parties in a lawsuit brought by Universal Studios, owners of King Kong, which alleged that Donkey Kong was a copyright infringement of Universal's movie star ape.

Nintendo and Coleco won the legal battle, but even the great Kong couldn't save Adam.

The video game crash and the disaster of Adam nearly killed Coleco. The company was saved by its Cabbage Patch dolls, which were hitting their peak at the time. However, only a few years later, Coleco finally succumbed and went out of business. Adam was their last foray into the world of electronic devices.

Also available for Adam were several computer and arcade titles, such as Dragon's Lair (pictured).

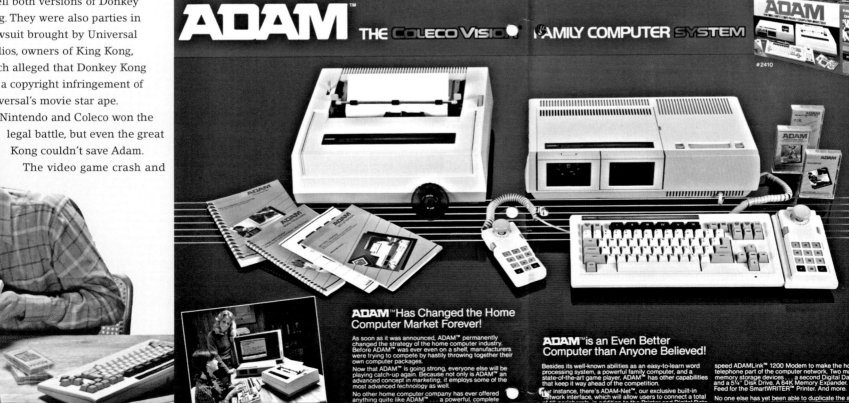

Before he left Atari, Nolan Bushnell held a huge party at his mansion in Woodside, CA, which had previously belonged to the Folgers (Folgers Coffee).

Meanwhile, Back at Atari

In the early 1980s, Atari was sitting on top of the world. VCS sales took off, and, at its peak, around 26 million systems had made it into people's homes—an unprecedented number. Likewise, cartridge sales were in the millions for top titles. The arcade division was pumping out hits in a booming market. Money was pouring in. It was Atari's "Golden Age."

Atari Stories

The Atari 2600 required its own breed of programmers. It was difficult to program for, and it took a particular kind of person to pull the best performance out of the games. Many Atari 2600 game developers were highly independent and eccentric, and there are a lot of stories about the free-wheeling atmosphere at Atari in those days. Nolan Bushnell called it a "passionate, almost religious quest. And the more religious fervor, the better and more interesting the games turned out to be."

"Once Upon a Time at Atari"
Howard Scott Warshaw not only designed games during the so-called Golden Age of Atari, but he has also created a one-of-a-kind video documentary series entitled,

"Once Upon a Time at Atari." The video series features interviews with several of the principal engineers at Atari during the early 80s.

Among my favorite stories is one that involves George Kiss, then director of software (whose morning question upon arriving at work was, "Is there anyone in jail?"), and Larry Kaplan, who had helped found Activision and then returned to Atari as a vice president. Kaplan offered Kiss a specific salary bonus. "Or," he said, "you can have your score in Defender." According to the story, Kiss wracked up a great Defender score.

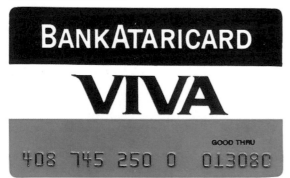
In the golden days of Atari money flowed so freely that they jokingly made their own credit card.

BANKATARICARD

VIVA

GOOD THRU

408 745 250 0 01308C

Ray Kassar with then Mayor Diane Feinstein at a cable car fundraiser in San Francisco. Kassar took the opportunity to show off Atari's Model 800 computer.

Crown Prince Henri of Luxembourg poses with the Millipede game he took back home with him after touring Atari in 1983.

After the formation of Activision, the concept of designer royalties was back on the table, though it was still not the standard arrangement. One colorful character, Todd Frye, whose exploits included something his colleagues called "walking the walls," and who believed that "lack of direction promoted initiative," went to Ray Kassar with a proposal: or maybe it was the proverbial "gun to the head." At any rate, he demanded a royalty for the game he was working on or he would quit and join Activision. The game was Pac-Man, and if Frye had stopped work on it at that time, they would have missed the Christmas season and lost a fortune. Kassar had no choice but to say yes. Frye received a dime for each 2600 Pac-Man cartridge sold. Atari sold 10 million. Frye pocketed a million bucks.

In "Once Upon a Time at Atari," Frye states, "In some ways it was irresponsible of Atari. I mean, it was a life-threatening thing to put that much money in the hands of such mono-maniac, egomaniac, neurotic freaks who were under so much stress to produce. The only reason you did well at Atari is for some reason you wanted to be stressed."

Probably the biggest irony is that Frye's Pac-Man port was a very poor imitation of the arcade version and, despite its stellar sales, tarnished Atari's reputation at a time when the competition was heating up.

E.T. Phone Home

Back in the days when Howard Scott Warshaw was creating games for the Atari VCS, he was given the opportunity to create one very big game. The catch was that he had to create it in only six weeks. Although some people might have refused so parsimonious a deadline, Warshaw saw it as a challenge. The game was E.T.

Atari had paid something like $20 million to Steven Spielberg for the rights to the game, and they expected it to be huge. However, despite the fact that Warshaw was actually able to get a game up and running in five weeks, the game had a snowball's chance in hell of meeting consumer expectations—not in 5 weeks or even 25 weeks. However you look at it, E.T. was a very well-publicized failure, not something Atari needed that 1982 Christmas season. Following the problems with Atari's 2600 version of Pac-Man, E.T.'s failure has been held responsible for further eroding consumer confidence in Atari products, and in video games in general. Although at the time few people at Atari were antici-pating it, they stood on the brink of a massive meltdown.

George Oppenheimer was the creative force most responsible for Atari's ads and brochures.

Publicity shot showing Don Osborne (national sales manager), Lyle Rains (chief of engineering), and Mary Fujihara (vp of marketing).

99

During the early 1980s, Atari was divided into two camps—
the arcade division and the VCS developers.

With the release of Space Invaders on the VCS, sales rose astronomically.
Suddenly Atari was selling millions of cartridges.

Out of hundreds of VCS games, we've put 30 on these pages.
Can you match the boxes with the appropriate screen images on the next page?

Answers on page 103

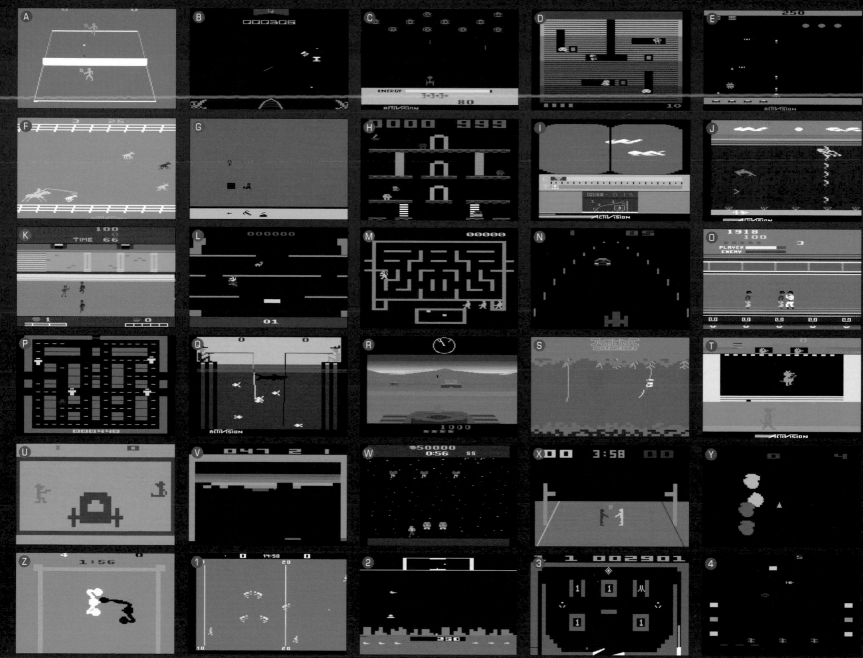

RECEIVER

Concepts and Ideas

Designers at Atari were always looking for new ideas for games, and often drew up storyboards and game descriptions to illustrate those concepts. On these two pages are several games that were drawn up but never released—a rare glimpse into the conceptual work of Atari's designers.

THE GREAT POGO RACE

LUMBERJACK

HAUNTED MANSION

ECEIVE

CYBERBALL

PACK RAT

The Boom and the Bust

The home console business was changing. After only a few boom years, the astronomical growth of the industry finally caught up with it. The video game crashed, and crashed hard, in 1983-1984. There are many causes for the meltdown of the video game industry. After Activision successfully defended against Atari's lawsuits, the way was open to third-party publishers. Jim Levy, Activision's president, recalls, "Imagic started in 1981, and I remember that by the Consumer Electronics Show in the spring of '82 there were as many as 50 software companies."

The Crash

If you look at the history of video game technology going back to Pong, there's a rough cycle of 6 to 8 years between the introduction of a new technology and the time that it peaks. What happens in a technology-driven market when it peaks depends on what happens at the beginning of the next cycle. Pong games gave way to the VCS and the cartridge-based home systems. In later years, at the end of the Nintendo Entertainment System's cycle—the cycle of 8-bit consoles—there were once again massive losses. Other cycles were not as disastrous, as long as a new platform was ready to carry the sales at the time of transition, such as when the Super NES reached its peak and the Nintendo 64 and Sony PlayStation were introduced. Each cycle of 6 to 8 years, a new technology is introduced to a new generation of gamers, primarily those players between 9 and 16 years old.

Back in the early 80s, third-party software companies began to sell game software, each looking for a share of the market. By spring of 1982 there were at least 50 companies creating games for the Atari 2600, and each was looking for maybe 5 percent of the total market. According to Jim Levy, "Our projections at Activision, which we believe were pretty accurate, estimated that the total 1982 cartridge market would be about 60 million units. Activision had between 12 percent and 15 percent of the market. We planned to sell maybe 7 or 8 million cartridges and manufactured accordingly."

But Atari was caught up in their success and didn't take into account the new competitors when forecasting how many cartridges they would sell. They planned to sell 60 million cartridges, which would have been 100 percent of the market! And each of the new software makers planned to sell 1-2 million cartridges themselves. If you do the math, there were simply too many games coming out—as much as 200 percent of market demand—and many of these were rush jobs of dubious quality and appeal. This situation would create a huge problem by the end of the year.

By the end of 1982 there were huge backlogs of software sitting in warehouses. A whole bunch of what Levy calls "the Johnny-come-lately's" were getting no sell-through and were running out of cash. They were not getting paid because their product was not selling through at retail, but they still had to pay their suppliers. Many of these newer companies began dumping products at cut-rate prices.

Even though some products, like Activision's Pitfall and River Raid, continued to sell extremely well, there was widespread concern during 1983. Early in that year, Mattel announced that they were getting out of the electronic games business, closing the doors of Mattel Electronics.

Activision sold off some of their older inventory at reduced prices. By the second quarter of 1983, Atari began to dump products, both financially and literally. It is now well known that Atari took millions of cartridges out into the desert in New Mexico and buried them, although it was not common knowledge at the time. Panic began to set in. Once again, according to Jim Levy, "By the middle of 1983, it was run for the exits and hope you could get there before the building collapsed.

"I kept wondering when Atari was going to dump all that inventory—they had huge inventories—and the answer they gave me was that they wouldn't dump... that it had value. But they did start dumping at really low prices, and once they started to dump, it was over. Atari collapsed, and took the whole industry with it."

Aftermath

By 1984, the business of video games was in shambles. Jim Levy continues: "We had 400 people at our peak in mid-1983 and 95 at the bottom 18 months later. We went from $50 million in revenue per quarter to maybe $6-7 million. And we were lucky. We were coming into PC software, although it was a small market then, and we had strong international sales. We also had plenty of cash. If we had been exclusively Atari 2600 in the U.S., we would have gone out of business."

Even though the crash has generally been associated only with the video game market, it had significant effects on the computer game market. Trip Hawkins, whose Electronic Arts was new and still small at the time, also remembers it well: "It was terrible for everyone. Almost all of the retailers that had been carrying games were either driven out of business or dropped the category as Atari went down. So, it took two years to rebuild a new retail network. Also, consumers saw so much bad press about Atari that they got the idea that video games were 'out' and cut back on game purchases. It was a tremendously difficult platform transition and wiped out many companies.

"Computer game companies like EA were struggling in a very small, difficult market, and it was not until Commodore sold a lot of C-64 disc drives and Tandy sold a lot of PC compatibles that the market got strong enough to keep EA and others going. After that, the NES took off."

It took years for the industry to recover. The young computer game industry continued to grow as more and more computers found their way into people's homes. But the single biggest reason for the recovery of the video game market has to be laid at the plunger of our favorite plumber—Mario—and the coming of the Nintendo Entertainment System to America.

Despite their ultimate success, even Nintendo felt the effects of the crash. According to Howard Lincoln, former chairman of Nintendo of America, "It was a really incredible collapse, and the impact of it lasted for years. Even after the NES was successful we kept hearing about the Atari collapse—all the way into the 1990s. For years, during the dog days of summer when sales typically drop, we'd have retailers saying it must be the start of another collapse."

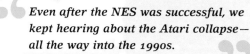

Even after the NES was successful, we kept hearing about the Atari collapse— all the way into the 1990s.

—HOWARD LINCOLN

FACTORS IN THE VIDEO GAME CRASH OF 1983-1984

ANALYSIS BY JIM LEVY AND RUSEL DEMARIA

Transition Cycles: **The years 1983-1984 would have been natural transition years for the business, according to the cycles we've observed since. And there wasn't anything sitting there to take up the slack. The home computer couldn't do it, and Nintendo's next-generation system wasn't out yet. ColecoVision was not quite enough of an advance, and, in any case, Coleco wasn't a company that could drive the transition.**

Atari's Hubris: **Atari believed that no matter what anyone else did, they could sell 60 million cartridges in 1982. And** much of their 1982 creative output was very weak. One executive was heard to boast, "I can put horseshit in a cartridge and sell a million of them." In fact, Atari produced more Pac-Man cartridges than there were systems. When asked why, one Atari manager said that they thought people would want to have a second copy at their ski house. Yes, someone said that.

Oversupply: **You had 50 software companies when there should have been 5, every one producing a couple of million carts—60 million by Atari. Activision produced probably 6-7 million and sold 80-85 percent. What you ended up with was over 200 percent of demand being** produced, and half of it was still in warehouses or on shelves at the end of the year. In 1983-1984, everything went into the toilet. Games were selling for $5. "The only thing that saved Activision was that we had plenty of cash," says Levy, "and even so, it took three years before we were able to break even again."

Perceived Competition from Home Computers: **Some people in the business wondered if home computers would supplant home video systems. Arnold Greenberg, former president of Coleco, says, "We joined the parade of those who got caught up with the coming of the home computers; even as we devel-** oped it the drumbeats could be heard." Fear of competition by home computers was definitely in some people's minds.

Lack of Faith: **I remember being on the show floor at CES during 1983 and 1984 and hearing many of the retailers, and even some of the press, referring to video games as a fad and comparing it to the Hula Hoop, one of the famous fads of the 1950s that more or less defined the transitory nature of fad-based businesses. In those people's minds, video games were a short-lived phenomenon, something that would die and never be seen again. No wonder they were ready to bail and get out. (RDM)**

After the Crash,
Arcades Live On

Paperboy screen.

Original Paperboy design sketches showing different (mostly unfortunate) outcomes.

The video and arcade game industry took some time to rebound, but Atari did release two all-time classics— Paperboy in 1984 and Gauntlet in 1985.

Paperboy

Paperboy was conceived by Dave Ralston, who also designed the hit arcade game 720. According to Paperboy programmer John Salwitz, "Dave was working on one of Gravitar designer Rich Adams' games. We called it Akkaahhr (which stood for 'also known as Rich Adams'). Dave had been talking about a game involving a paperboy on a bicycle for some time. It had won the 'best game' at a brainstorming session, though most of the best brainstorming games never got built. But Dave had been a paperboy as a kid, so that was part of his inspiration. At the brainstorming session, he showed a transparency of a

street much like the final game images, then flipped it over to show riding on the other side."

One of the few other games that directly influenced Paperboy was Sega's Zaxxon, with its three-quarter isometric view. Otherwise, Paperboy was something original and different. In fact, it was even more different at the beginning. Salwitz remembers, "Originally, it was downright wacky. It always had the riding dynamics and the paper-throwing, but for a while it was kind of bizarre. We had pianos running down the streets,

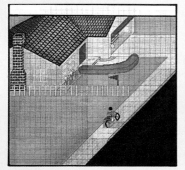

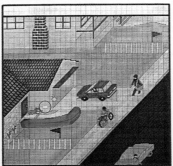

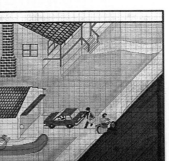

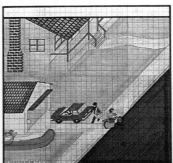

huge nails, and ducks in business suits."

After some "horrific focus groups," the project was nearly killed. But Don Traeger, who came in as a new marketing lead on the project, helped save it by bringing it back to something more accessible. Again, Salwitz remembers, "Instead of pianos, there were cars. Some things that are incredibly obvious now were not so obvious then. That refocusing and refiltering was as much an invention as anything. What we learned was that any time you diverge from what is accessible or mainstream, unless you are incredibly lucky or gifted—or both—you cut out a big portion of your market."

Gauntlet

As we did with Asteroids and Centipede, we asked designer Ed Logg to share some of his insights into his classic game, Gauntlet. He relates some of the inspirations that led to the game's concepts as well as some of the challenges inherent in creating a four-player game with hordes of enemies on technologically primitive equipment.

"My son was heavy into Dungeons & Dragons, which was very popular at the time. The original proposal for Gauntlet was made with characters and pieces straight out of D&D. Other inspirations included a game called Dandy, which gave me the idea of having multiple players play at the same time, as well as the concept of items, which would increase the player's health.

"Gauntlet had some interesting challenges because the game could not have been done the way I wanted on the hardware that existed. So the engineer, Pat McCarthy, added features on top of existing hardware. In addition, I planned to have as many as 1,000 characters running around at any one time. So with the slow processors we were using I had to come up with a technique to solve the collision problem.

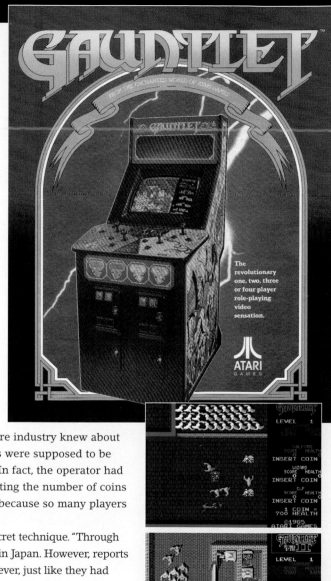

Once we had the hardware and software algorithm, the rest of the game came together very well. Of course, with a game like this we needed many levels to challenge the players. So while I was on vacation many other programmers and engineers came up with many of the level designs you see in the game today.

"Balancing the game also presented challenges, especially when more than two players were involved simultaneously. We went through several variations before settling on the final algorithm. However, I recently looked over the initial proposal, and I must say the game turned out more or less just as it was initially envisioned.

"The first time we field-tested this game at a small arcade, the entire industry knew about it within a few days. Since field tests were supposed to be secret, this was extremely unusual. In fact, the operator had installed a sign above the game limiting the number of coins a player could play at any one time because so many players had come in to play it."

Logg also relates a story about a secret technique. "Through Namco, we sold many Gauntlet units in Japan. However, reports came in that players were playing forever, just like they had done with Asteroids and Centipede. I could not believe this until I received a videotape showing their technique. Indeed it was possible with two of the four characters. I will leave it as an exercise to the readers to figure out which two."

Hmmm…

Playing with Keyboards— the Computer Cometh

"VIC Commandos" (left to right): Kim Tomczyk (standing), product manager Mike Tomczyk, Bill Hindorff, and Andy Finkel. Hindorff and Finkel created many games for the VIC 20 and C-64. The photo was taken by team member, Neil Harris.

Between TV series, William Shatner served briefly as the spokesperson for Commodore's VIC 20.

Home computers were becoming ever more common in people's homes and at the workplace. Products like VisiCalc on the Apple II and, later, Lotus 1-2-3 on the IBM PC helped legitimize personal computers and increase sales. And that meant more customers for computer games. During the period 1979-1980, a staggering number of companies began creating computer games. The list of companies basically tells the story of the 80s—Origin, Sirius, SSI, Muse, The Learning Company, Sir-Tech, Edu-Ware, plus Brøderbund and Epyx, which had begun slightly before 1979.

Commodore

Commodore was founded by Auschwitz survivor Jack Tramiel in 1954, originally to repair typewriters. But Tramiel was willing to gamble on new technologies, and over the years he developed adding machines, office furniture, and, in the early 70s, transistorized calculators.

The sale of transistor calculators was highly competitive, and Commodore came close to going out of business. Tramiel saved the company by borrowing $3 million from Irving Gould, a Canadian financier. He also purchased MOS Technologies to control the cost and supply of the chips he needed. Tramiel shifted the gears of his company and began making home computers. He believed in "Computers for the masses, not the classes." In 1977, Commodore released their first home computer, the Commodore PET, which was designed by Chuck Peddle.

VIC 20

In the early 1980s Commodore hit on the ultimate product line— truly low-cost, user-friendly machines. Introduced at the Consumer Electronics Show in 1980, the VIC 20 was originally called the MicroPET, but the name was changed before it was released in 1981.

With only 5K of system RAM, the VIC 20 was a highly underpowered color machine that was little more than a keyboard with a hookup to a TV. Its miniscule RAM apparently goes back to Jack Tramiel's edict that the designers use 1K chips in the design because Commodore had a surplus. Despite, or perhaps because of, its simplicity, the VIC 20 sold phenomenally well.

Commodore 64

In 1982 the Commodore 64 was introduced, and it was a much-improved version of the VIC 20, with 64K RAM and a custom sound chip. The C-64 went head to head against the Apple II as everyone's favorite game-playing machine, and most computer game makers began to support both systems almost routinely. Commodore sold 22 million C-64s in 1983, and over its lifespan, the C-64 sold more systems than any other single computer in history.

Amiga team photo.

Amiga Stories

Once upon a time, two Florida doctors with a few million dollars to spare thought about opening a department store franchise, but somehow ended up funding a computer company. They hired Jay Miner from Atari and Dave Morse from Tonka Toys, and the team set about secretly creating the next killer game machine. The company's public name was Hi-Toro ("high bull"), according to codesigner RJ Mical.

Dave Morse

As a cover, the company began marketing peripheral game products like the Joyboard. They even hired the skier Suzy Chaffee (known for a series of Chapstick commercials) to demo the board. But secretly they were working on the ultimate game machine. According to Mical, "It was always a game system from the beginning. It only changed by definition because someone wrote on a piece of paper that it was a personal computer. When I met with the hardware guys and saw the diagram on the white-board that was clearly labeled 'computer,' it had ports for disk drives and keyboards and the like, but I said, 'Game system?' and they chuckled and said, 'Game system!'"

According to codesigner David Needle, David Morse deserves tremendous credit. "Without a doubt, there would be no Amiga if it were not for his strong and solid support and leadership at the corporate, product, engineering, and personal levels."

By the time the system had been developed, the company was deep in the hole. They offered the machine to many companies, but the only one that made an offer was Atari. However, Jack Tramiel was aware of their financial situation, and offered them a very low per share price, which kept going down the longer they dickered. The company was saved by a phone call from Commodore, Tramiel's former company, which ended up buying Hi-Toro for $4.25 per share—more than four times Tramiel's best offer.

The name of the company was changed to Amiga, "because it was friendly and welcoming, and it came before Apple and Atari in the alphabet," says Mical, whose title was Director of Intuition. (The name of the interface was "Intuition.")

The Amiga ended up being overshadowed in the market-place by the IBM PC and its clones and by the Apple Macintosh. But to its designers, it was a holy mission. "We all had a really deep passion for what we were doing," says Mical. "What we were doing was for the greater good of man. We believed that computers would become omnipresent. We wanted to create a computer that was as powerful as the big guy's computer, but at a low cost so everybody could afford it."

Not many game publishers specialized in games for the Amiga. One notable exception, however, was Cinemaware (see page 216), a company whose games often demonstrated the early superiority of the Amiga.

This was the first Amiga prototype ever shown publicly—at the 1984 Consumer Electronics Show. According to co-designer, RJ Mical, "The three stacks, two standing and one lying on its side, are the original prototypes of the three Amiga workhorse chips, with all the logic of the chip implemented using high-speed CMOS. Each one connects via a monster cable into a motherboard which was nicknamed Lorraine after the wife of the boss, Dave Morse.

"People at CES didn't believe the Amiga could be that powerful, so during the show they kept looking under the skirt of the table to 'see where the real computer was.' Surprise! It was the Amiga, man!"

Cinemaware (see page 216)

THE DOG'S TALE

Dave Needle tells a rather tall tale, but one that is in keeping with the slightly mystical bent of the Amiga team. "Jay's dog Mitchie sat at his feet for most of his time at Amiga, watching Jay's every move. There are many Mitchie stories, including how Al Alcorn got the dog a security badge at Atari. Often, Jay would be at some difficult part of the design, and he would draw a potential solution. The dog would look at it and shake her head 'no.' Jay would erase a part and draw another circuit. Mitchie would then nod her head up and down in approval, usually with some quiet mumble (I don't speak dog, but Jay may have). My desk was next to Jay's, and I witnessed this event many times. Yes, Jay was the father of the Amiga, but Mitchie was responsible for many parts of the design."

Jay Miner and codesigner, Mitchie the dog.

Bob Whitehead's Hardball featured smooth action and some interesting innovations like determining pitch location.

Accolade

In late 1984, two of the Atari refugees who had cofounded Activision decided that they had experienced enough of the cartridge world. They didn't like the fact that Activision seemed so rooted in the console world, even after the 1983 crash. So, Alan Miller and Bob Whitehead once again formed their own company to create games on home computers and once again, as with Activision, decided not to serve as corporate executives. And, once again, the company was given a name that began with an "A." This time, however, Miller deliberately scrutinized the dictionary to find a satisfactory name that would come before Activision in the phone book.

Miller and Whitehead settled on the name Accolade because the idea of applause suited their artistic sensibilities. "Interestingly," says Miller, "Acclaim was also on our short list of names and was later chosen by two other ex-Activision employees, Greg Fischbach and Jimmy Scoroposki, for their game company." Both Miller and Whitehead expressed their great appreciation of Jim Levy as the head of Activision, but they wanted to go their own way. "We always thought the world of his talent," says Whitehead. "But he was, in a way, trapped in the video game business. We wanted to go in a different direction."

Tom Frisina

Looking for someone to run the company and leave them free to be creative, they first turned to some Activision veterans, Tom Lopez and Allen Epstein. But Lopez decided to move on to Microsoft, and Epstein became a venture capitalist. Ironically, Epstein was later to step in as president and CEO at a crucial point in Accolade's history, but the inaugural president was Tom Frisina, a veteran of both home electronics and one of Nolan Bushnell's Catalyst companies. (Catalyst Technologies was a company Bushnell formed in

1981 to serve as an incubator for new technology companies.)

Tom Frisina had left the home stereo industry to manage Androbot, Bushnell's robotics company, which attempted to build home personal robots. Frisina and Bushnell didn't see eye to eye, however, and so he was glad to take the reins at Accolade when the job was offered.

Meanwhile, Miller and Whitehead targeted the Commodore 64 as their primary platform and started work on their pet projects. "The profit margins were completely different," says Whitehead. "You could produce a computer game on a floppy disk for probably a tenth of what it cost to produce a cartridge. Of course, you still had to create quality software to succeed."

From the Old West to Outer Space

Miller adds, "Our initial creative goal at Accolade was to expand the scope of what video games had been up to that time and appeal to a much wider audience. Bob and I had been doing games for eight years at that point and had in fact been developing them since the very

Alan Miller's Law of the West seemed like something right out of television's classic *Gunsmoke* when it first appeared.

beginning of programmable games. We were interested in emulating other, more popular forms of entertainment such as movies and television. In Law of the West, I chose to develop a game similar to the movie *High Noon* and tried to explore on-screen interpersonal communication. Bob chose to emulate televised baseball and was brilliantly successful with Hard Ball. Mike Lorenzen (who also came from Atari and Activision) emulated the television show *Star Trek* with Psi-5 Trading Company. We were also targeting an older audience than we had at Activision because we wanted to appeal to a larger audience. I would be remiss if I did not

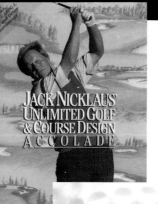

Jack Nicklaus' Golf featured some of Nicklaus' famous golf courses using the Mean 18 game engine.

mention that Mimi Doggett created all of the art for these three games, and Ed Bogas composed the music."

Whitehead remembers the start-up mentality at the beginning. "What you need in a successful game is a balance between freshness and familiarity," says Whitehead. "In Hard Ball, we achieved both. The over-the-shoulder view behind the pitcher was familiar to TV audiences. And we added some innovations for the time, such as being able to control the pitch using the joystick, being a coach, and having names for our player lineups." Amusingly, the player names were taken from Accolade's staff, their families, and employees of their agency.

Artech and Distinctive

One of Accolade's philosophies was to bring in outside talent to supplement their in-house designers. "At Accolade we tried to have about half of the original titles done by employee developers and half done by external development groups," says Miller. "It was our policy to have all ports done by external groups because the internal group's efforts were focused on original creations."

Two Canadian development teams, Artech and Distinctive Software, made considerable contributions to Accolade's product line. Artech produced Dambusters, Ace of Aces, and Fight Night. Distinctive, after a couple of years doing ports for Accolade, ultimately developed the very popular Test Drive series and later went on to become a top designer

for Electronic Arts' sports games.

Accolade had a number of other significant products. Rex Bradford's original golf game, Mean 18, became the Jack Nicklaus Golf series. "It was a perfect fit," says Whitehead. "Jack Nicklaus prides himself on his course designs, and Mean 18 had a course designer. It was brelatively easy to get the license." And there was also Test Drive, the first in a highly successful series that helped set the standards for future driving games.

New Directions

Eventually Frisina left and went on to form 360 Pacific, but Accolade continued to produce a variety of interesting titles. By the end of the 80s, they had created a graphic adventure engine with a reverse parser to compete with Lucasfilm's Secret of Monkey Island series and, more specifically, Sierra's Leisure Suit Larry series. Infocom veteran Mike Berlyn unveiled a wild adventure called Altered Destiny, and Activision veteran Steve Cartwright went head-to-head with Leisure Suit Larry as his Les Manley went in a Search for the King and got Lost in L.A. Another great series of games from Accolade was Star Control, by Paul Reiche and Fred Ford, which mixed space exploration with space battles and weird aliens.

Although Ace of Aces had the same name as the booklet game from Nova Graphics, it featured a lot more action and had missions like the later flight simulators.

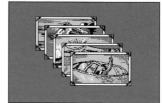

In the days before high-resolution, 3D, and animated cut scenes, the stage was set with still photos.

Star Control

After Paul Reiche III finished working with Jon Freeman and Anne Westfall on Archon and Archon II (see page 172), he teamed up for a while with old friends Evan and Nicky Robinson in a company called R3 (pronounced "R-cubed"), though he also had his own company called Supreme Brain Software. R3 pitched a game called Teratasaurus (which means "mutant dinosaur"). The game eventually became EA's Mail Order Monsters. R3 also did World Tour Golf, but then Reiche went off to work as art and technical director for an ad agency called SoftAd.

"One day I found myself in Detroit wearing a suit and about to go visit Ford and General Motors, and I realized that the pods had gotten me." Reiche returned to what he loved—designing games. For his next project he wanted something that, in his words, "combined thoughtful aspects of game play with twitchy ones, scratching the same itch as Archon." Inspired by the original Spacewar (see page 12), he decided to add some simple strategy to the space combat aspect of the game.

Working with his new partner, Fred Ford, he started with two ships and then began creating characters, eventually figuring that they'd be able to create 12 alien races and still have the game done in time. In the process, he created one of the all-time villainous races in the history of computer games—the Ur-Quan. "I'd seen an article in National Geographic about predatory caterpillars in Hawaii. There was a picture of it hanging and grabbing a moth from above.

I was fascinated by the concept of a creature that clung to the ceiling and hung down over you." However, Reiche, who thinks about a lot of things other than computer games, knew he wanted a villain with more than just mindless destruction as a motive. "Why would they travel all that way, spend all that time and energy, just to blow you away?

They'd have to have some economic or religious reason, or something." So, he created a race of slavers.

Another inspiration for the strategy portion of the game was Orson Scott Card's fabulous novel, *Ender's Game.* "I imagined what it was like fighting the Buggers remotely."

Star Control was primarily a simple exploration and combat game. But its sequel, Star Control 2, is still called by many avid fans quite possibly the best computer game ever written. "We wanted to do more than just whip out more ships and rule variants, so we thought, 'Let's try a science fiction adventure role-playing game. In the first Star Control, there was no timeline, so we had to rationalize the circumstances that caused these aliens to come all the way across the galaxy to enslave people. What was the ecological niche that caused the Ur-Quan to be solitary and violent? At the time, I was also curious about troubled childhoods and how they affect people's lives, so I thought, maybe the behavior of races could be defined by their past experience as well. Maybe they were slaves in the past. But who enslaved them, and why?"

That the graphics in Star Control 2 are rich and full of character is no accident. Reiche hired a number of excellent artists, including George Barr (who had done art for Archon II), Erol Otus, and Iain McCraig, to help create the characters and ships. With spot animations, they brought the 2D paintings to life. Reiche comments that later games, which used 3D-rendered characters, "didn't have the same charm as the hand-painted ones."

Fans of Lucasfilm Games' Monkey Island, Reiche and Ford created a complicated conversation system. Says Reiche, "The way Monkey Island handled conversations worked really well for humor. You had multiple choices in what you could say, and the contrast between your choices allowed you to lie or be crazy. In one sense, multiple choices blows the drama, but the contrasts are great for humor, and it also

lets the player control how long they want to spend in the conversation tree.

"Originally, we thought to model the space science really accurately, and I did a lot of study of stars and planets, but we found that level of detail became boring, and anyway we mostly ended up generating ice balls or Venus-like worlds. We decided that some level of abstraction was necessary to keep people from losing themselves and getting lost in the details."

Star Control 2 is a beautifully crafted game, with a great mix of action, exploration, humor, and a rich cast of alien characters and races such as the Chenjesu and Mmrnhrmm (who fused to become the Chmmr), the Zoq-Fot-Pik, the Syreen, the ever-cowardly Spathi, and many others.

Although there was a Star Control 3, it was not done by the original team, and was not considered nearly up to the standard of its predecessor. Today, there is a Star Control Web Ring, with lots of intense and detailed information— more than you could ever need, no doubt, about the Star Control games and their wacky universe.

I know it probably sounds weird, but when I design a game like this, I make drawings of the characters and stare at them. I hold little conversations with them. I ask them, What do you guys do? And they tell me.

—PAUL REICHE III

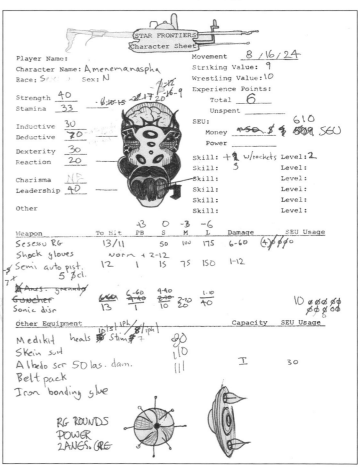

One of Paul Reiche's original stat sheets, used in developing Star Control.

113

Infocom

Infocom founders:
Marc Blank,
Joel Berez,
Albert Vezza,
JCR Licklider (Lick),
Christopher Reeve.

I f you ever noticed that the name Infocom doesn't sound like a game company, your observation was more astute than you might have guessed. Although you probably read earlier in the book how M.I.T.'s Dave Lebling and Marc Blank were inspired by Adventure and began work on a game known as both Dungeon (its official name, but one Dungeons and Dragons owner TSR objected to with a threatened lawsuit) and Zork (a reference used by the creators for any unfinished project), Infocom originally intended to exploit the popularity of Zork and move the profits into the much more lucrative world of business software.

Al Vezza, one of the powerbrokers at the M.I.T. computer lab, proudly demonstrated Dungeon at many conferences and realized that the game had commercial potential. On June 22, 1979, Vezza joined with Blank, Lebling, Joel Berez, and a few other staff and students to capitalize Infocom. Their goal was to parlay game publishing into a software empire like the then-powerful Lotus Development Corporation. Indeed, the "Lotus obsession" was a major cause of Infocom's downfall.

Speaking Zorkian

Although the mainframe version of Zork (also known as Zork: The Great Underground Empire) had been fully functional since 1977, the TRS-80 and Apple II versions weren't released until late 1980. Unlike other adventure games of

the time, Zork and its sequels, Zork II and Zork III, featured a language called ZIL (Zork Interpretive Language). Marc Blank created ZIL using a language developed at M.I.T.'s Dynamic Modeling Group called MDL ("Muddle"), which in turn was based on LISP (which stands for "list processing"). ZIL, which was designed specifically for creating games, went beyond checking VERB and OBJECT against the game's database. Instead, ZIL interacted with the player to sort out clarifications and assumptions. If a player typed **open the door** in a room with more than one door, ZIL would return a question, "Which door do you mean?" As a result, ZIL was by far the strongest parser in gaming until reverse parsers, using word lists, came along to assist gamers further.

Cover from a very early
TRS-80 version of Zork.

Razzle-Dazzle

Infocom's marketing department insisted that the finest graphics processor was the human mind and that they were serving computer gamers best by allowing players to imagine the action.

Leather Goddesses of
Phobos even featured a
scratch 'n' sniff card.

Moreover, their text-based games did not require graphic conversions, so they could easily be ported to every machine imaginable, from mainframe through CPM-driven units to Apple, Atari, Commodore, IBM, Texas Instruments, and a half-dozen foreign operating systems.

To compensate for the lack of razzle-dazzle on screen, Infocom soon developed a tradition for creative packaging. 1982's Starcross was a science fiction game packaged in its own flying saucer. It also contained one of the most interesting "bugs" in Infocom history. Author Dave Lebling defined the "beam" in the game as though it were a "person." As a result, it could be talked to and directed rather than merely used or manipulated.

1982's Deadline (Marc Blank), a classic murder mystery, came packaged with documentation designed to imitate a lab report, coroner's report, statements taken by police, and other forms of evidence. 1983's Suspended (Mike Berlyn) used the plastic mask of a cryogenic sleeper to make the product jump off the shelf, and featured a map of the cryogenic complex and six vinyl markers to represent the robots. 1983's Planetfall (Steve Meretzky) featured color postcards from interplanetary tourist traps, a Stellar Patrol ID card, a recruitment brochure for the SP, and a personal diary. 1984's Cutthroats (Mike Berlyn) came with a book that had a map of four shipwrecks, as well as a price list/tide table because the player was supposed to explore a shipwreck to find a treasure. Another

Infocom trademark of documentation was the magazine parody called True Tales of Adventure, found in Cutthroats.

Mind Food

Yet, the real Infocom miracle was in the quality of the games themselves. The stories within the games were so fascinating and the environments created by the "Infocommies" were so rich that other products were designed as well. Novels were published under the Infocom mark. Science fiction author George Alec Effinger novelized the original Zork, and fantasy author Robin Bailey did the same for Enchanter (Blank and Lebling's 1984 tale of an encounter with a wizard named Krill). Also, since Infocom games were noted for having tough puzzles, a force rose up to meet the need for clues. M.I.T. graduate Mike Dornbrook built Z.U.G., the Zork Users Group. He developed a line of books called *Invisi-Clues* that enabled you to get help with one puzzle without having to glance at solutions to other puzzles. Later, Dornbrook became an official part of the Infocom marketing brain trust, but not until the profits from Z.U.G. had built a beautiful home for him in which he still resides.

Nor was Infocom, like so many game companies, trapped in a situation where its authors had to keep making the games harder and harder (and more esoteric) in order to satisfy the core audience. The designers tried several ways to shake up the mix. Zork III appeared in 1982 and reversed the course of the previous two games. Instead of gaining points for solving the hard puzzles, Zork III gave points to players for doing easy, obvious things like climbing down a cliff to get a treasure chest. Yet, you didn't get any points for solving hard puzzles like opening the treasure chest. There were only seven points to be earned in the entire game. The idea was to get players away from

Deadline's "Interlogic" concept included independently acting characters with their own action and choice paths in a timed game, a first for adventure games.

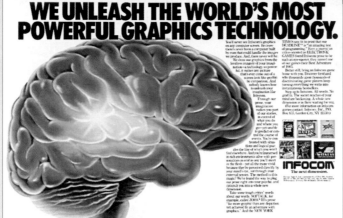
Infocom's games may not have had graphics, but their ads were both graphical and funny.

their obsession with points and back to the story.

Sometimes, the attempt to expand the audience was moderately successful, such as when Stu Galley wrote Seastalker in 1984 to be Infocom's first junior adventure. Sometimes, the attempts backfired. In 1984, for instance, Steve Meretzky designed a sequel to Enchanter, using the title Sorcerer. To reach a wider audience, Sorcerer was advertised on the back cover of *Boy's Life* magazine. Controversy arose when one postal worker unilaterally (and illegally) decided that he would not deliver the magazines because they were advertising a satanic product. Could this event have subtly inspired Brian Moriarty's postman protagonist who tries to save his village in his 1985's Wishbringer?

Sometimes the attempt to widen the audience was phenomenally successful. 1984's Hitchhiker's Guide to the Galaxy paired Infocom's master of mirth, Steve Meretzky, with his novelist equivalent, the brilliant Douglas Adams. The game was proportionately as successful as its namesake, and a new audience discovered Marvin the manic-depressive robot and company, while the old audience struggled with the babelfish puzzle and pondered peril-sensitive sunglasses.

When Brian Moriarty proposed his Infocom masterpiece, Trinity—a complex, ethically and emotionally challenging game built around the Manhattan Project—he was encouraged

Douglas Adams and Steve Meretzky (pictured above) adapted Adams' classic *Hitchhiker's Guide to the Galaxy* to the computer.

to go in a different direction. As a result, he published 1985's Wishbringer, an introductory-level game that sold remarkably well and was conceived around the idea of putting a glow-in-the-dark rock in the box as a marketing gimmick like the old maps, books, and postcards. At the same time, Dave Lebling was finishing the Enchanter series with Spellbreaker, an expert-level game that did not perform up to expectations.

Infocom had one other 1985 project that did not perform up to expectations. Entitled Cornerstone, it was a product without a plot. It was a database application firmly positioned between the programming-heavy dBase series by Ashton-Tate and the limited, but easy, VisiFile. It was more versatile than the latter, but didn't require the expertise of the former. Vezza, Berez, Blank, and Cornerstone author Brian "Spike" Berkowitz thought Cornerstone would be the foundation of the company's future. Indeed, Blank bet Berkowitz a dinner in Paris that Infocom stock would not sell for less than $20 per share by 1987. Instead, Infocom had become so weak by the end of 1985 that they became a takeover candidate.

Brian Moriarty with a DEC System 20. Note the Apple sticker on the right edge of the photo.

The New Infocom

In February 1986 Activision purchased Infocom for around $6 million—considerably less than the $20 per share envisioned by Blank, which would have yielded more than $60 million. At first, all parties tried to play well together. Activision CEO James Levy dressed up as a bride for a mock wedding ceremony at Infocom headquarters, and the company's official newsletter, *The Status Line* (formerly the *New Zork Times*), reported that "We'll still be the Infocom you know and love." The acquisition seemed cordial even when the company's humorous underground newsletter, *InfoDope*, made fun of Levy. Articles joked about Levy trying to get Infocom to widen their range of titles and create simulations. (*InfoDope* suggested titles like Tugboat Simulator and Empire State Elevator Operator.)

Infocom published more titles in 1986 under Activision than they had been able to market in 1985, and still more in 1987. Indeed, Activision hired the famed acting troupe Second City to perform at their party where they unveiled 1987 hits at that summer's Consumer Electronics Show. It seemed a well-made match.

Yet, the acquisition was no longer cordial when Levy stepped down and Bruce Davis took the reigns at Activision. Two years after the purchase Bruce Davis decided that, in retrospect, Activision had overpaid for Infocom, and initiated a lawsuit against the Infocom shareholders in an attempt to get some of the money back. The Infocom shareholders were shocked and incensed by this, and fought a prolonged litigation as a matter of principle. Davis, who was a lawyer, invoked a clause in the sale contract, "making vague claims, and, over time, increasing the amount he was requesting," according to Mike Dornbrook. Years later, even after Activision entered bankruptcy, the suit was settled for about two percent of the legal expenses that had been incurred, just to make it go away.

Davis also forced Infocom to publish Infocomics in 1988, an intriguing idea from Tom Snyder Productions that tried to capitalize on the crossover between comic readers and computer game players with $12 products that would come out on a serial basis. Unfortunately, the experiment overlooked how much comic readers enjoy art and decided to bypass established writers, artists, and intellectual properties in order to exploit the Infocom intellectual properties. Infocomics bombed, and as morale began to deteriorate, underground humorists began to publish such things as a memo to join the "Bruce Youth" movement and "turn in" their fellow employees whenever they heard a discouraging word against their corporate "fuehrer."

In addition to the Infocomics failure, Davis pushed and pushed for more graphics in Infocom releases. Activision's commitment to Apple caused them to publish Quarterstaff, a Macintosh-only game featuring lots of interface innovations, but sales were so low that it was never ported to another machine. Marc Blank wrote Journey, an illustrated adventure that allowed point-and-click navigation throughout. Dave Lebling attempted to create a Shogun that would do for James Clavell's novel what Meretzky had done for Douglas Adams' masterpiece. Bob Bates attempted the same with the Arthurian legend in his game Arthur. Yet, the marketplace perceived the graphics as either too little, too late, or as too incidental to the games, while Activision observed how quickly the graphics drove up the development budgets and reduced profit margins.

All of the corporate controversy and Hollywood-style accounting overshadowed the marvelous quality found in Meretzky's Zork Zero, 1988's graphical prequel to the series that had started it all, and BattleTech: The Crescent Hawk's Inception, Westwood Associates' role-playing game based on FASA's BattleTech universe. Those games were successful until corporate overhead butchered their financials. As a result, Activision sent Joe Ybarra to Massachusetts to reduce the overhead by an impossible amount or else pull the plug. By then, the "Great Underground Empire" was slated to be six feet underground. Other titles were marketed as Infocom titles, but the creative unit no longer existed.

Improv group Second City performed for Activision at the 1987 CES show.

Screens from some of Infocom's later graphic adventures (top to bottom): Arthur, Circuit's Edge, BattleTech: The Crescent Hawk's Inception.

Richard Garriott & Origin Systems

"Three important events happened in 1974," says Richard Garriott. "First, my sister-in-law gave me a copy of *Lord of the Rings*. Second, I discovered Dungeons & Dragons. And third, I became acquainted with my first computer. In combination, these three events began a love affair with the computer that has continued to this day." Garriott's passion for computer games soon surfaced. He even convinced his high school to let him use their one and only teletype machine to link to a remote computer so he could start writing his games, and to establish a special course "with no teacher, no other students, and no curriculum," whereby he could experiment. During high school, he wrote 28 small games, which he entitled D&D1 through D&D28. The game that ultimately became Akalabeth was D&D28B, and was never intended for release. However, while working a summer job as a salesman at the local Computerland, he was encouraged to sell it. "I made a substantial investment of personal assets in Ziploc bags and Xerox copies, and hung a few copies on the walls of the store. One of them found its way to California Pacific, and they offered to publish the game. They sold 30,000 units, and my royalty was $5 per unit. Something that had taken four to six weeks to create had earned me $150,000. 'Not bad,' I thought, and I started work on Ultima, which essentially used Akalabeth as a subroutine."

Richard Garriott with the original paper tape code of Akalabeth. Inset, as well as to the left, a reel of Akalabeth tape.

As a teenager, Garriott and friends (Jeff Hillhouse and Chuck "Chuckles" Bueche) built a ride they called the "Nauseator." "It was a ride that spun on two axes. When you were in it, you didn't feel dizzy, but 15-20 minutes later, everyone who rode it felt sick. So we called it the 'Nauseator'." Interestingly, Jeff Hillhouse was Origin's first employee and still works there today.

Many Faces of Akalabeth

Garriott's first game was Akalabeth. On this page are several covers and pack-in sheets for the original game. Below, in a picture taken in 2001, Garriott is playing Akalabeth on an old Apple II.

Welcome, foolish mortal into the world **AKALABETH!** Herein thou shalt find grand adventure! Created by Lord British

© – 1980, California Pacific Computer Co.

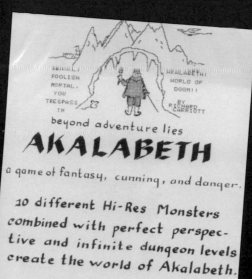

FOOLISH MORTAL, YOU TRESPASS IN

AKALABETH WORLD OF DOOM!!

BY RICHARD GARRIOTT

beyond adventure lies

AKALABETH

a game of fantasy, cunning, and danger.

10 different Hi-Res Monsters combined with perfect perspective and infinite dungeon levels create the world of Akalabeth.

for Apple II w/48K and Applesoft R.O.M.

AKALABETH WORLD OF DOOM

Beyond Adventure Lies...

AKALABETH WORLD OF DOOM

designed by LORD BRITISH

48K 13 of 16 Sectors

JUST 34.95 on diskette

A TOP OF THE ORCHARD SOFTWARE PRODUCT
from California Pacific Computer Company

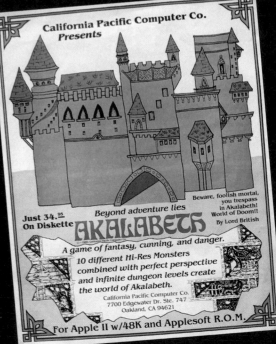

California Pacific Computer Co. Presents

Just 34.95 On Diskette

Beyond adventure lies

Beware, foolish mortal, you trespass in Akalabeth World of Doom!! By Lord British

AKALABETH

A game of fantasy, cunning, and danger.

10 different Hi-Res Monsters combined with perfect perspective and infinite dungeon levels create the world of Akalabeth.

California Pacific Computer Co. 7700 Edgewater Dr. Ste. 747 Oakland, CA 94621

For Apple II w/48K and Applesoft R.O.M.

The Ultima Series

The first Ultima was originally titled "Ultimatum" but soon became Ultima I. I still remember how much fun it was to play—my first RPG (RDM).

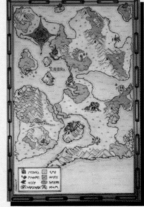

Each of the Ultima games included a cloth map, and sometimes other interesting items like coins and metal ankhs. Here are the cloth maps for two of the first Ultimas.

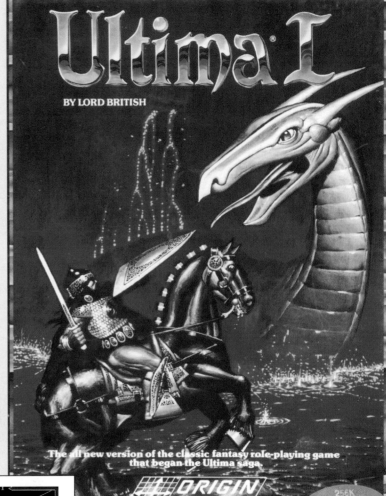

The all new version of the classic fantasy role-playing game that began the Ultima saga.

The original Ultima I came out in a Ziploc bag. This cover was the first re-release version.

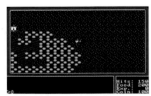
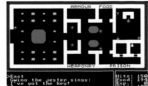

Screenshots from Ultima I (left) and Ultima II (right).

Garriott's alter ego was Lord British, a character he played both in real life and in the Ultima series. His original game credits read "Lord British" as well.

Below: Raising the sign on Origin's first big office building in Austin, Texas.

Below right: Garriott's role-playing roots continued in the new building with medieval duels on the front lawn.

Garriott put himself and his friends in the Ultima games. In addition to being Lord British, he was Shamino, one of the recurring characters.

One of many wonderful paintings created by Denis Loubet for Origin's games. This is a photograph of the original art for Ultima VI.

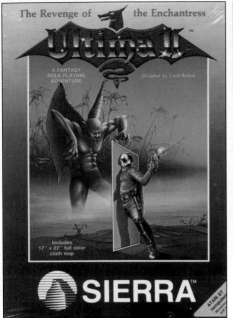

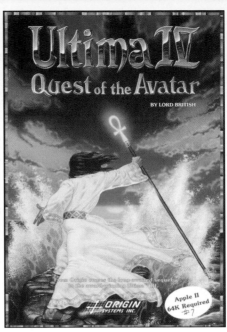

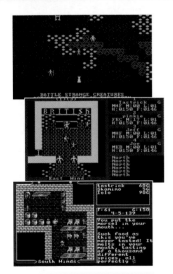

Screenshots from Ultima II, III, and IV.

When California Pacific went out of business, Garriott found that many companies wanted to publish Ultima II, but only Sierra would package it the way he wanted, with a colorful box and cloth map. Ultima II was also the first assembly language program he had ever written. Up to this point, all his games had been written in BASIC.

Ultima III was Garriott's second assembly language program. It was during the programming of this game that Garriott made the decision to rewrite each new Ultima completely from the ground up, a practice he continued for each of the Ultima releases.

In Ultima IV, Garriott took a big risk. He included ethical puzzles and a concept of accountability in the game. "I was very worried that it would flop," he says, "but when it came out, it became the first Ultima to make it to number one on the charts. Ultima IV is special, also, because, if you think of the first three as 'Richard learns to program,' Ultima IV was

where I learned to tell a story."

Ultimas V and VI continued the story begun in Ultima IV, with some considerable story development and plot twists. It marked the first time Garriott had considered story

FALSE IMPRESSIONS

In Ultimas V and VI, Garriott created a fearsome race of creatures called the Gargoyles. Throughout these games, you fought and killed them when you could, feeling good that you were ridding the land of a terrible enemy. But, by the end of Ultima VI, you discovered that the Gargoyles were really very civilized, and that you had been systematically, if unknowingly, destroying their world. To me, this is one of the most brilliant moments in computer game history, where I was given the opportunity to come face-to-face with my own ability to create prejudice, and how ignorance can create false impressions. (RDM)

consistency. "The first Ultimas were really inconsistent, and had a lot of disconnected elements. Starting with IV, I began to create a consistent world and storyline."

Ultima VII was a major rewrite of the code and game style. The graphics were far more three-dimensional, and there were a lot of other activities available to the player, even baking bread. Garriott's comment: "I consider Ultima VII to be the most finished of the Ultimas. I liked the concept of the black gate that could allow the guardian to step in. I love the pattern of the game and the pattern of play. One of the best stories. My own critique is that it was probably too large." Looking at Ultima Online, which was first conceived around the time of Ultima VII, you can see the basic elements of the online game to come.

Screenshots from Ultima V, VI and VII.

Ultima VII was also the second time I got to be a character in a game. If you went to the small town of Cove, you could meet the bard named DeMaria! (RDM)

A Time of Transition

Following their sale to Electronic Arts, Origin continued work on the Ultima series with Ultima VIII. However, as Richard Garriott remembers it, there was considerable pressure to get it out, and it was released "before its time." Garriott recalls, "The high concept of the game was good, with a new balance of action-oriented puzzles and storyline, but it was the most unfinished of our projects."

Ultima IX was the final Ultima in the series. Because of the early indications of success of Ultima Online, its development was a difficult process, ultimately leading to Garriott leaving Origin. However, the game was completed and marked the end of the story begun back in the early 80s.

In its early days, Origin was briefly located in New Hampshire. When they moved back to Texas, some of the employees remained behind and formed a new company, originally called Blue Sky Software (not to be confused with the Blue Sky Rangers of Intellivision days). Led by Paul Neurath and Doug Church, they created state-of-the-art games, ultimately changing their name to Looking Glass. In 1992 they created a first-person 3-D dungeon crawl that was set in the Ultima world and became Ultima Underworld. This ground-breaking product helped set the stage for the era of first-person games that was to come.

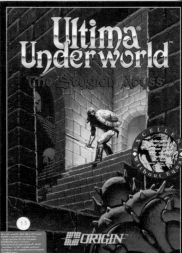

Brøderbund

Starting in the late 70s, Doug Carlston's first games were the episodes of the Galactic Saga written in BASIC for the TRS-80.

Gary, Kathy and Doug Carlston, founders of Brøderbund.

S hakespeare asked us, "What's in a name?" Perhaps it was Doug Carlston who proved that a rose really *would* smell as sweet by any other name.

Even before Roberta Williams (see page 134) published Mystery House, The Wizard and the Princess, and Mission: Asteroid, Doug Carlston, who was a bored attorney at the time, had designed a space-opera style game on his TRS-80 computer. Carlston had taught at an integrated school in South Africa, and was once ousted from the country during the apartheid era for his sympathies. He used many African names for locations and people in the series of games he invented, called Galactic Saga. The name he chose for his company came, oddly, from an unsavory group of merchants

called the Broederbond, an Afrikaans word meaning "association of brothers."

Most people didn't know the origin of the company's name, and it was commonly believed that the name was Swedish, an impression reinforced by the use of the null sign instead of an "o" in Brøderbund. Whatever people believed about the name, Brøderbund was one of the first successful computer game companies. Carlston and his siblings, Gary and Kathy, started their business in Eugene, Oregon, but eventually moved to the San Francisco area. They brought us such memorable games as Lode Runner, Prince of Persia, Carmen Sandiego, and, most popular of all—Myst (see page 257).

Brøderbund released tons of products during the 80s, many of them classics destined to become models for the next generation of game designers.

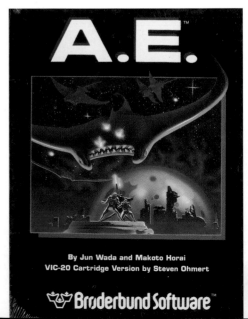

By Jun Wada and Makoto Horai
VIC-20 Cartridge Version by Steven Ohmert

In 1982, Brøderbund began selling games from the Japanese company Star Craft, with early games designed by Tony Suzuki and Jun Wada, who were among the first Japanese game designers to achieve celebrity in the U.S.

1982

Choplifter! was a huge best-seller, the first game to beat the then best-selling VisiCalc spreadsheet software on the Softalk sales charts of the time. It was also possibly the first game to be "ported" from computer game to coin-op, and it was certainly one of the first games that involved rescuing hostages (after Defender). It came about a year after the Iran hostage crisis. The game's designer, Dan Gorlin, remembers, "I was in a computer store and watched as three mothers came in to get that game 'where you rescue the hostages.'" He continues: "A lot of professionals in the game business now tell me that Choplifter was a big influence on them. It kinda freaks me out; like inventing dynamite or something."

1983

Lode Runner was similar to many other arcade games of the times, but it contained a dizzying number of levels with a lot of clever puzzles. Even better, Lode Runner had its own "editor" program, making it perhaps the first game

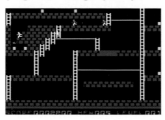

that allowed you to create your own levels—a true classic.

1984

The Ancient Art of War was a ground-breaking war game that featured troop formations and strategy, as well as various bits of advice from Lao Tzu. You picked your general and then operated on a grand strategic map. Once a battle was set up and you had decided how to

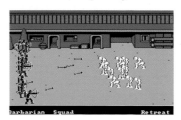

deploy your troops, you could watch the action in an animated battle.

125

Let us introduce you to the next dimension of arcade adventure and excitement . . .

Brøderbund games stretch your vision and imagination to the limit. Computer gamesters everywhere are discovering our incomparable Atari, Apple, VIC-20, and IBM PC programs, and they're not going back to anything less. So next time you're looking for new worlds to conquer, look to Brøderbund.

Brand New from Broderbund!

A.E.™
by Jun Wada and Makoto Horai

The A.E. are coming! Beware! Squadrons of menacing sting rays are streaking down from the sky to attack you. Wave upon wave elude the firepower of your remotely-fired, trigger-action missiles. You're doomed to be pestered forever unless you drive these waves of A.E. ("rays") out of the solar system, deep into the outer waste-lands of space. APPLE II/II+, 13 or 16 sector (48K Disk). Joystick or paddle controlled. Also available for ATARI 400/800 (48K Disk). Joystick controlled.

SERPENTINE™
by David Snider

Giant serpents set forth to slay their slithery cousins. To add to the fun, the snakes lay eggs and fight ferociously to protect their young! A fast arcade style game with many levels of play. APPLE II/II+, 13 or 16 sector (48K Disk). Keyboard or joystick controlled. Also available for ATARI 400/800, joystick controlled (8K Cartridge/16K Cassette/24K Disk).

THE ARCADE MACHINE™
by Chris Jochumson and Doug Carlston

Create your own arcade games! It's easy! N[o] programming knowledge needed. Comes wit[h] a selection of full color monsters (or you desig[n] your own), dramatic explosions and sound e[f]fects, automatic high scoring features, and more. Requires APPLE II+ or an APPLE II wit[h] Applesoft in ROM or RAM and a 16 sector con[troller (48K Disk).

Pleasures and

CHOPLIFTER!™
by Dan Gorlin

With realistic throttle action you maneuver a daredevil rescue chopper. You fight off enemy jet fighters and air mines above, and tank fire and air-to-ground missiles below, to rescue hostages held behind the lines and bring them out alive! APPLE II/II+, 13 or 16 sector (48K Disk). Requires joystick with two buttons. Also available for ATARI 400/800, joystick controlled (16K Cartridge/48K Disk).

APPLE PANIC™
by Ben Serki (ATARI and IBM versions by Olaf Lubeck)

The apples will get you if you don't watch out[!] Forced to flee from pursuing apples in a multi[-] level mansion, you set traps for your pursuer[s] along the way. A fast arcade style game wit[h] great graphics and animation. APPLE II/II+, 1[3] or 16 sector (48K Disk). Keyboard controlled[.] Also available for the ATARI 400/800, joystic[k] controlled (16K Cassette/24K Disk), and for th[e] IBM PC with graphics adapter card. Keyboar[d] controlled (64K Disk).

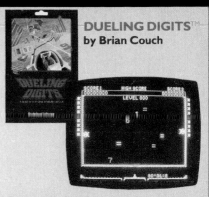

Famous Beginnings at Brøderbund

1984

Raid on Bungeling Bay might not have been considered one of the great classics from Brøderbund, except for one thing. It was the first published game by a young designer named **Will Wright**, who, only a few years later, would create the ground-breaking game **SimCity**.

1985

Jordan Mechner (see page 292) filmed his brother running and jumping, then rotoscoped the images into his first game, **Karateka**. Using kicks and punches, you had to run through a bunch of screens of baddies to rescue the princess. The ending was great. If you ran right up to the princess, she kicked you in the head and it was "Game Over." You had to start all over again. If you politely walked up to her, though, you won! Karateka was the initial model upon which Mechner later made the classic game Prince of Persia (1989), also from Brøderbund.

1987

MacroMind's **Maze Wars+** was distributed by Brøderbund and came out long before the company released Director (not to mention Dreamweaver or Flash) and changed their name to **Macromedia**.

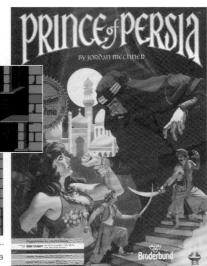

Prince of Persia

Quintessential Edutainment

Even though a few companies, such as The Learning Company, had previously combined entertainment and learning on computers, Brøderbund became known for such games and really popularized the so-called "edutainment" genre.

1983

One of the ultimate typing games, MasterType helped many budding typists have fun while learning, a theme that would continue throughout Brøderbund's history.

1985

The game that truly defined the term *edutainment*, the Carmen Sandiego series remains one of the most popular educational games ever. Besides Where in the World..., there were versions of the game for the U.S.A., America's Past, Space, Europe, Time, and a special edition for Japan.

1992

The Living Books series, which featured animated and interactive children's books, was another wonderful addition to Brøderbund's legacy of edutainment titles.

Brøderbund Games of the Early 1980s

On this and the next few pages we've reproduced many of the game box covers done by Brøderbund in the 80s. These images were provided courtesy of company founder Doug Carlston, who graciously let us rummage through 31 huge boxes of games!

Games of 1981

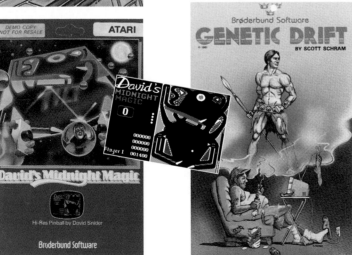

> *I vividly remember the Arcade Machine. I made a lot of little arcade games, and even placed second one month and fourth another in the contest Brøderbund held, which meant my games were on the back of the next month's release. (RDM)*

Brøderbund Games of the mid-1980s

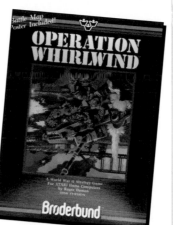

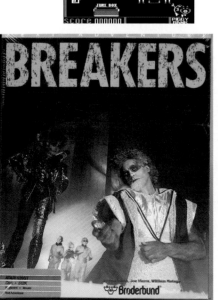

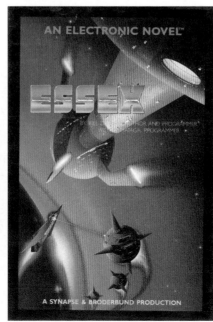

Brøderbund Games
of the Late 1980s

1988
From Choplifter!'s
Dan Gorlin.

1989
Lucasfilm was just
becoming a game
publisher, but they
hadn't yet started on
their own series of
Star Wars titles.

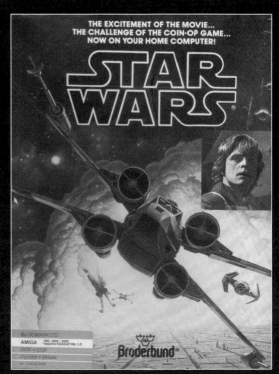

APPLE IIC Plus/IIas (ONLY)
128K • 3.5" Disk
Keyboard
FANTASY ROLE PLAYING
By Ian Boswell and Martin Buis

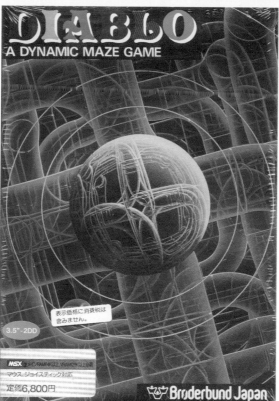

3.5"-2DD

定価6,800円

Brøderbund Japan

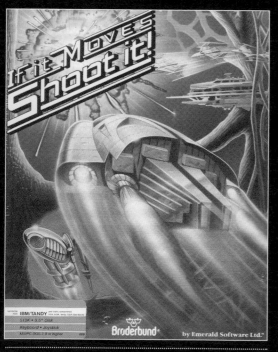

IBM/TANDY
512K • 3.5" Disk
Keyboard • Joystick
MS/PC-DOS 3.8 or higher
by Emerald Software Ltd.

One of my favorite game titles. (RDM)

We've included Diablo, which was only available in Japan, because of its very familiar title. No relation to Blizzard's megahit game of the 90s.

In addition to the games depicted on these pages, Brøderbund also created the Living Books series, Print Shop, the Bank Street series, and many more products of all kinds, ranging from games to education to home productivity. They also distributed games for many other companies including Origin, New World, Maxis, Synapse, and Cyan. They introduced such popular games as Prince of Persia, SimCity, Manhole, Cosmic Osmo, and Myst.

Doug Carlston with Mike Cantor, one of the founders of MacroMind, which later became Macromedia.

17 PAUL DRIVE
Brøderbund Software

Ken and Roberta Williams

Sierra: Computer Game Pioneers

> *Colossal Cave changed my life. I owe a lot to Will Crowther.*
>
> —ROBERTA WILLIAMS

YOU ARE IN THE FRONT YARD OF A LARGE ABANDONED VICTORIAN HOUSE. STONE STEPS LEAD UP TO A WIDE PORCH.
ENTER COMMAND?

ierra is one of the longest-lasting computer game companies still in existence today and has for many years been one of the biggest. In their first 20 years of operation, they published more than 150 products—most of them games—but they also published compilers, word processors, and many other home productivity and educational products. Sierra employed hundreds of talented designers, artists, programmers, and other creative people and helped pioneer many of the most significant developments in the history of computer games. They were first with a graphic adventure game, first with a color-filled graphic adventure, first to use sound cards and video cards, first to put out a CD-ROM game (Mixed-Up Mother Goose in 1988), and first to create a significant online enterprise (The Sierra Network in the early 90s). They also produced several of the longest-running series in gaming history, beginning with King's Quest.

More Adventure

In 1979, Ken Williams started a small company called On-Line Systems. He was working for various clients, doing mostly financial, communications, and database work. When the Apple II computer came out, Williams saw the need for a Fortran compiler and began work on one.

Meanwhile, his wife Roberta was at home with a new baby and time on her hands. Ken had been bringing his TRS-80 computer home and had a link to the mainframe at one of the companies he was working with. Roberta discovered a game on that mainframe. It was called Colossal Cave—the original Adventure game. Working with a Teletype connection, which printed out descriptions of the game's scenes, Roberta quickly became engrossed in this new form of entertainment.

After completing Colossal Cave, Roberta began looking for more games like it. Other than some games from Scott Adams's Adventure International, she found little. Suddenly inspired, she thought perhaps she could create a game of her own. "That's where I sat down at my famous kitchen table with tons of paper and started mapping and putting down ideas," says Roberta.

ON-LINE systems

Presents

MYSTERY HOUSE

HI-RES ADVENTURE #1
THE BEST IN HI-RES ADVENTURE
by
Ken & Roberta Williams

$24.95
Disk 48K
Apple II or II Plus
Machine Language
DOS 3.2 or 3.3

MYSTERY HOUSE

by
Ken & Roberta Williams

What is an adventure game? According to the dictionary, an adventure is a hazardous or daring enterprise, an exciting experience; to risk, hazard, to venture on. One who goes on an adventure is a venturer. A seeker of fortune in daring enterprises, a speculator. In essence, an adventure game is a fantasy world where you are transported, via your own computer. You are the key character of the fantasy as you travel through a land the likes of which you will find in books that take you, through your imagination, to the world it is creating.

Through the use of over a hundred Hi-Res pictures you play and see your adventure. You communicate with HI-RES ADVENTURE in plain English (it understands over 300 words). All rooms of this spooky old house appear in full Hi-Res Graphics complete with objects you can get, carry, throw, drop or?

In this particular HI-RES ADVENTURE game, you are transported to the front yard of a large, old victorian house. When you enter the house, you are pulled into the mystery, murder and intrigue and cannot leave until you solve the puzzles. Your friends are being murdered one by one. You must find out why, and who the killer is. Be careful, because the killer may find you! As you explore the house there are puzzles to be solved and hazards to overcome. The secret passage-way may lead you to the answer.

ON-LINE systems

36575 MUDGE RANCH ROAD
COARSEGOLD, CA 93614
209-683-6858

"I wanted something with a good story, but it also had to be a game. Stories tend to be linear—beginning, middle, climax—and I needed to expand into 'What if they want to do this? Or that?' My main inspirations were Agatha Christie's *Ten Little Indians* and the board game Clue. I used the idea of Clue to pull me out of linear thinking."

In about a month, the game was entirely designed, but of course the next step was programming. Despite a background in computer science, Roberta was not an accomplished programmer. She needed Ken for the technical side, but he wasn't showing any interest. "Ken noticed what I was doing, but I think he thought, 'Isn't that cute?'" So, one day Roberta hired a babysitter and invited Ken out to a romantic dinner. "Well, he should have been suspicious, and maybe he was. Maybe he wasn't as dumb as I thought. Anyway, we went to a steak place in Simi Valley and had a nice dinner and some wine. We talked about his Fortran compiler and the Apple computer. Then I said I wanted to tell him what I was doing, and I saw his eyes glaze over. Finally, he looked at his watch and said, 'I'll give you five minutes.' I still remember the moment when he started actually listening. I could see it in his eyes. I'll never forget it. It changed our lives."

The next day, Ken called his partner in the Fortran project and said he was dropping it. He was going to work with his wife on a game.

Mystery House

During their dinner conversation, Ken and Roberta had decided that the game should have pictures, and from that point the development happened very quickly. By May 1980, On-Line Systems released Mystery House: Hi-Res Adventure #1, packed in Ziploc bags and often hand-delivered to computer stores. And they were still working at the kitchen table. They ultimately sold 80,000 copies at $25.95 each.

"Mystery House was the first computer game with real graphics in it," says Roberta. "About two months later, Richard Garriott came out with Akalabeth, which I would say had even nicer graphics, but Mystery House was the first. Before that it was all Pong-like lines and Xs and Os."

On-Line Systems gradually expanded, releasing at least three more games in 1980—Skeetshoot, the little-known Hi-Res Football, and The Wizard and the Princess/ Adventure in Serenia—and seven more products in 1981. "When we started Sierra, we had no idea how big the computer industry was going to become," remembers Roberta. "We thought computers and software would always be a small industry, of interest only to hackers and hobbyists like ourselves. Well, we were wrong. Our little software business quickly outgrew the space available on our kitchen table, and the operations had to be moved to the den and spare bedroom."

Three covers for The Wizard and the Princess, the second game in what became the Hi-Res Adventure series, one showing IBM's version, which was called Adventure in Serenia.

> *The Wizard and the Princess was a breakthrough game. Ken created the game to draw the lines on screen and then wrote a routine to fill in the colors. There's no way he could have fit all those graphics on a disk, but by using draw commands and the fill routine, he could put a ton of full-color graphics in the game. A lot of people afterward used similar techniques. Of course, if he had used page flipping, he could have made the graphics fill invisibly to the player, and we would have been wondering how he got all those images on the disk!*
>
> —JOHN ROMERO,
> COFOUNDER IDSOFTWARE

Porting the Arcades

Sierra didn't only make adventure games. They also made quite a few early action games, many of which were ports of arcade games. In 1981, On-Line Systems released Missile Defense (Missile Command), Crossfire (Exidy's Targ), Jawbreaker (Pac-Man), and Frogger—the only one they licensed, and the weakest of the lot.

Hi-Res Football, a little-known Xs and Os sports game that On-Line Systems did in 1980, is one of their earliest games and one that is rarely included in lists of the company's products. They also did a Hi-Res Soccer game. The original cover was from a painting by Roberta's mother, but she had so overendowed the cheerleaders in the picture that some retailers wouldn't carry the product. The cover was quickly redone.

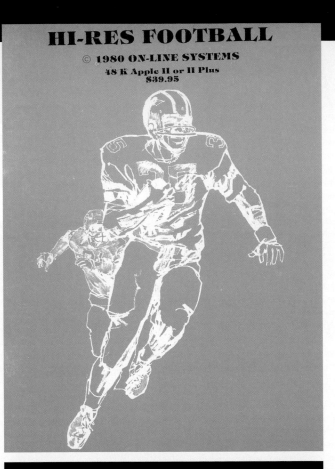

NO MORE CARTS FOR SIERRA

It is not well known, but Sierra also did, briefly, create some games for the Atari 2600, including Texas Chainsaw Massacre and Winnie the Pooh. However, caught in the video game crash of the mid-80s, they ended up with a lot of excess inventory, which plunged them into financial troubles. This experience stayed with Ken Williams. In 1984, he went to Japan and brought back Nintendo's FamiCom system. Al Lowe recalls, "I vividly remember playing Mario, and we all thought it was so much fun." But when it came to producing titles for the NES when it came to the States, Ken said no. "Definitely, getting burned with excess inventory was a major reason why we never went into carts."

MISSION: ASTEROID
HI-RES ADVENTURE #0

$19.95
Disk
48K REQ

MISSION: ASTEROID is an introduction to the HI-RES ADVENTURE family of games. This adventure is slightly easier and a little shorter than our other HI-RES ADVENTURE games. MISSION: ASTEROID is designed to acquaint beginning Adventure players to the wonderful world of Hi-Res Adventure.

In this adventure you find that an Asteroid is about to hit the Earth and destroy it. It is your mission, as an Astronaut, to rocket to the Asteroid and blow it up before it reaches Earth. You must fight through the Red Tape at Mission Control, then enter the Rocket Ship and learn how to fly it. I hope you have a flight plan or you will never find your way through space to the Asteroid. Be careful with the explosives, as they can be very dangerous if not handled correctly. This game should provide weeks of Adventure.

OVER A HUNDRED HI-RES PICTURES. (Looks great on b/w and color televisions).

FULL 21-COLOR!! HI-RES GRAPHICS. (Each room is a work of art).

YOUR GAME MAY BE SAVED FOR LATER CONTINUANCE.

RUNS ON BOTH 48K APPLE-II AND APPLE-II PLUS.

THIS EXCITING GRAPHIC GAME WILL CHALLENGE YOUR IMAGINATION AND TEST YOUR CREATIVITY EVERY STEP OF THE WAY!

APPLE II/APPLE II PLUS SOFTWARE.

ON-LINE SYSTEMS

Mission: Asteroid was actually created after The Wizard and the Princess, but was easier and smaller, so it was later renamed as Hi-Res Adventure #0.

SierraVision was the brand Sierra used for many of its early games.

1982's Time Zone was one of the most ambitious adventure games ever made. Shipping on an astounding six double-sided floppy disks, it consisted of 1,500 screens and 39 interlocking scenarios. In many ways, it was a tour de force, but it was also more adventure than most players could handle, and the original asking price of $99 was too steep for most people's wallets.

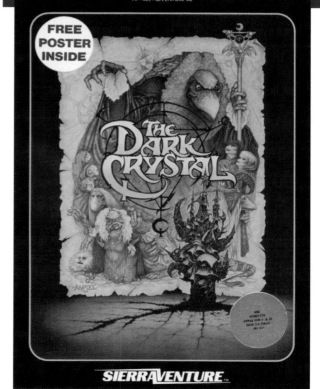

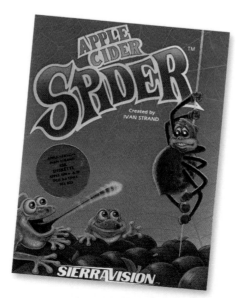

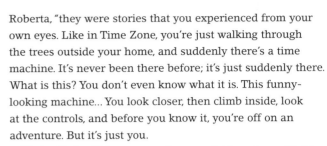

King's Quest®

Sierra had developed a relationship with IBM early on when the computer giant published Adventure in Serenia. So when IBM was developing the PCjr (code-named Peanut), which was supposed to be a low-cost consumer machine, they approached Sierra to see if they wanted to create a game for the new machine.

"They gave us prototypes and explained the capabilities of the machine. It could do a lot more than the Apple II at the time, with 128K of memory and more colors. They said, 'We want something like The Wizard and the Princess, but we want it to push the machine's capabilities,'" remembers Roberta. "I had always wanted to do animation in my games, and have more colors. Up to then the adventure games had been first-person perspective. I had the idea to do something different, so I said, 'I want to create a world with a little guy running around and you control him.' But if you had a little guy running around, you had to give a sense of dimensionality in the picture. He has to go behind things like trees and rocks and stuff."

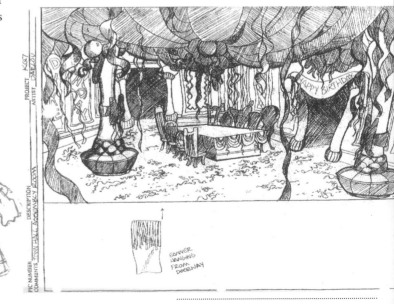

The concept of the third-person adventure game completely changed the way adventure games were created, and Sierra had to create a whole new game engine to produce King's Quest and the games that followed.

The change wasn't only technical, however. "In the old games," remembers

Roberta, "they were stories that you experienced from your own eyes. Like in Time Zone, you're just walking through the trees outside your home, and suddenly there's a time machine. It's never been there before; it's just suddenly there. What is this? You don't even know what it is. This funny-looking machine... You look closer, then climb inside, look at the controls, and before you know it, you're off on an adventure. But it's just you.

"But with the little guy running round, it's not you, it's him or it's her. Suddenly that character has to be defined, and I actually think the story becomes more defined. Before, it was a little more loosey-goosey. There weren't a lot of really well-defined characters, and I think the worlds were a little more loosely organized, partly due to my own inexperience as a writer. But once you start thinking in third person instead of first or second, you have to think, Who is this person and how is he going to interact with other characters? When it was you, it was your personality. Now it was someone else with his or her own personality."

About the time Roberta was beginning King's Quest, she was also completing The Black Cauldron.

ROSELLA AS A TROLL

Original drawings for King's Quest 7.

Ken and Roberta Williams

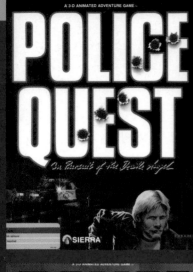

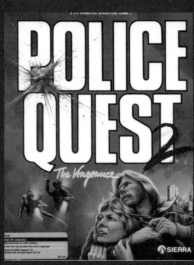

More Quests

With the success of King's Quest, Sierra launched several more Quest games, drawing upon a variety of designers, each of whom had a unique and individual approach to the newly formed third-person adventure game genre. Like King's Quest, each of the new games initiated a series of games, as they were all very successful. The first was Police Quest, designed by ex-cop Jim Walls. This was a serious crime adventure using the King's Quest engine.

Where King's Quest was a lighthearted fantasy adventure and Police Quest was an attempt at serious police drama, the next series had tongue firmly in cheek. When Scott Murphy and Mark Crowe (Two Guys from Andromeda) came up with an idea for an adventure game set in space, Ken Williams gave them the go-ahead. Williams had a great respect for the creative process and would let his creative people run with their ideas. "I wanted my designers to be the king of their product, and nobody was going to mess with their creativity. And if it didn't sell, they didn't get invited back."

Space Quest™, which came out in 1987, starring a rather dim-witted janitor named Roger Wilco, sold very well, and Murphy and Crowe were definitely invited back to produce several sequels. Roger Wilco's adventures were loaded with odd puzzles, humorous situations, and quirky dialogue. Along with Leisure Suit Larry and Lucas's Maniac Mansion (which also released in 1987—see page 200), Space Quest helped usher in a new era of humor-based adventure games.

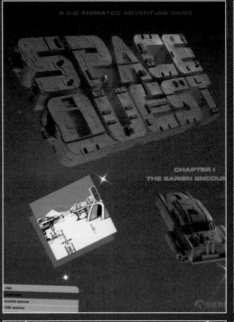

Leisure Suit Larry

At the same time Roger Wilco was being prepared to pratfall into the game market, veteran game designer Al Lowe was preparing to introduce another, at least equally lame character, basing the new game on Sierra's sole text-only game, Chuck Benson's Softporn Adventure. "I took the design for Softporn, kept the locations and puzzles pretty much, and then started on the text. Chuck was a great programmer, but wrote dialogue like an engineer," says Lowe. "So we took Softporn, which has no central character... and created a dorky character. By this time, of course, we were doing all this new 3D technology, and so I commented that the original game was so old it should be wearing a leisure suit. I guess that's how Larry's outfit came into being. It was coincidental that Scott was doing something similar with Roger Wilco. However, Larry was even dorkier than Roger—he was simple and dim-witted. He operated further down on Mazlov's hierarchy of needs."

Larry was a huge success, and there were two sequels, at which point Lowe considered the story to be done. "I wrapped it up and tied a big bow on it," he says. "I was tired of it. By the way I ended it I thought I had made it pretty final. I had Larry fall out of his world and land in Sierra. It was

my homage to *Blazing Saddles*. So Larry meets Ken Williams and gets a job. He starts typing and he's programming the first scene for the first Leisure Suit Larry."

However, the series had become so popular that people were asking for more. As a joke, Lowe did another game, but called it Leisure Suit Larry V, and in it he referred to events from the fourth game that never existed.

After finishing the Larry series, Lowe did a game called Freddy Pharkas: Frontier Pharmacist, a spoof on westerns inspired by the Zucker Brothers games like Airplane. The original version was very successful, so they did a second version with speech instead of printed text.

Gabriel Knight™

Originally hired as one among a group of in-house writers, Jane Jensen helped Jim Walls with Police Quest 3 and then wrote and designed with Roberta Williams on King's Quest VI. Following that, she was offered the opportunity to create her own series. "I guess at the time I wrote the proposal," says Jensen, "I was influenced by some of the adult graphic novels like *Sandman* and *Hell Raiser*. Also, I had already done some work on a mystery series concept that dealt with paranormal mysteries and featured a parapsychologist. All that got boiled down to Gabriel Knight."

The first Gabriel Knight game, Sins of Our Fathers, featured an excellent voice-over cast, including Tim Curry, Michael Dorn, and Mark Hamil. Its dark, adult themes met with considerable critical success. Says Jensen, "It was very gothic and a little bit more violent and a little bit more sensual."

The sequel, The Beast Within, which was done with real actors in full-motion video, also received critical acclaim. But keeping the same depth of detail while shooting real actors was a challenge. "We shot a 600-page script," says Jensen. "It was very difficult, but we accomplished a lot, given our time and budget."

With the third in the series, Blood of the Sacred, Blood of the Damned, they moved from real actors to 3D characters. Jensen comments, "It's really difficult to get 3D actors to look good and to emote."

The Gabriel Knight series has an unusually large female fan base, according to Jensen. "It has a sort of mystery/romance feel to it. Especially with GK2, it had a very Anne Rice homoerotic quality."

Phantasmagoria®

With the growing popularity of the CD-ROM, Roberta Williams became inspired to try something new. "I always

liked horror or thrillers and suspenseful stories and movies. I thought it would be fun to see if it could be done in a computer game, but I was convinced that you couldn't really scare people like you could in movies. 'Hey, don't open that door!' I figured we needed to use real actors. I wanted it to be really scary. Most of the games that tried to be scary didn't seem scary to me."

Using blue screens and setting up each camera shot exactly to the 3D models of the house and rooms they had created, they began to shoot the actors to blend into the scenery. However, like 7th Guest, they ran into difficulties with a sort of halo effect around the actors, and had to spend a lot of time on postproduction, cleaning up the images by hand. "I got a nasty reputation around Sierra for being so picky," says Roberta. "I kept sending the pictures back because I could still see the blue at the edges."

Screens from Phantasmagoria.
Above: The blue screen set. Above right: Scenes from the game.

Original Phantasmagoria storyboards.

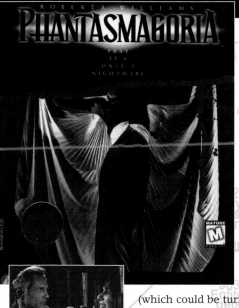

The game shipped on a whopping seven CDs, garnering some attention for sheer size, and it generated a good deal of controversy. It contained a lovemaking scene, a rape scene, drug abuse, and several violent death scenes (which could be turned on or off). It was definitely for adults, and Sierra suggested an age limit of 15. "Originally it had nudity in it, too," says Ken Williams, "but in the end we chickened out and removed it."

Despite some uneven press, the game sold well. Its puzzles were kept intentionally easy to allow new gamers to enjoy it, and it was very strongly marketed. Given its content, Phantasmagoria managed to stir up considerable controversy and was not only banned by various retailers but also by the Australian government.

End of an Era

Sierra had grown to be a huge company, and ultimately acquired smaller companies such as Dynamix. In 1996, Ken and Roberta Williams sold the company to Cendant Corporation, a multifaceted company with many interests and subsidiaries. The couple then retired after 18 years of running the company. It was the end of an era. Sierra continued to make games, many of them exceptional, but the company's personality changed. It was no longer a mega–"mom and pop" concern.

Among the many fine games to come from Sierra in the 90s was a first-person shooter—not one of the genres for which Sierra had been previously known.

Half-Life®

After Doom, the first-person shooter became the de facto standard for game publishers. One after another, games imitated id's masterpiece. Some, like Interplay's Descent, gave new dimension to the game by adding a mind-twisting flying element. Others, like Apogee's Duke Nukem, added humor and attitude. And id's own Quake was an amazing 3D world and another technological breakthrough. But few in the genre, if any, really told a story.

Valve and Sierra changed that. Half-Life, while still in the mold of a first-person shooter, added drama, story, and character interaction to a great action game. Perhaps because of that (or even in spite of it), Half-Life was received both in the market and critically as one of the best games of 1998, spawning a number of sequels. Following in the tradition first established by id with its Doom WAD editor, which allowed anyone to create levels for Doom, Valve also included an editor with Half-Life, which meant that lots of additional scenarios ("mods") were created and shared by users on the Internet. Some of these Half-Life mods were good enough to be included in the excellent 2000 release, Half-Life: Counter Strike.

Sierra put out a staggering number of games in over two decades of production, and we've included a few of them here. Also of note is the Quest for Glory™ series. Under the Dynamix label, Sierra put out even more great games, such as The Incredible Machine™ and Starsiege: Tribes™.

Dynamix

EA photo from Arctic Fox, with Kevin Ryan, Jeff Tunnell, Damon Slye, and Richard Hicks.

During high school, Damon Slye began programming versions of existing games like Mastermind and Star Trek on an 8K Commodore PET. Against his parents' better judgment, he went out and bought an Apple II. "They thought I should save the money for college. They had no idea what I was doing in my room all that time." What he was doing was programming his first original game—Stellar 7. At the time, Jeff Tunnell was running a computer store, and Slye began working for him. "Damon was working on a font-making program, and I was doing some games in the back room," recalls Tunnell. "One day I needed a routine written, and Damon did it for me in assembly language. I realized then that I was never going to be that good a

programmer, and I began thinking about being a producer and designer and doing the business aspects."

They formed Dynamix in 1984 and soon published Slye's first game, Stellar 7, through SEC and Chris Cole's Sword of Kadash, through Penguin, a company that sold games and graphics tools for Apple II and C64. Sales of Stellar 7 were somewhat disappointing, despite the fact that a lot of people seemed to have the game. Slye says, "I think we sold around 8,000 units. Hit games were selling on the order of 80,000 units back then. I was mystified, especially since everyone I met had played it and loved it. Apparently it had been heavily pirated." The game had many fans, however, including author Tom Clancy, who once called Slye to tell him how he had played it every day when it came out.

Fateful Decisions

With the disappointing sales of their first games, the young company was just scraping by, but they received some encouragement when Joe Ybarra from Electronic Arts called out of the blue to suggest making a deal with them. Nothing happened for several months, remembers Slye, "So we gave him one last call. We let him know it was now or never—we needed a contract or we'd have to close up. He sounded surprised. 'Why didn't you say so earlier?' So he finally invited us to come to EA to pitch a game idea. We all piled in a van and made the long drive to San Mateo." They pitched a game to EA. "After the pitch, all the EA guys around the table one by one gave us the green light," says Slye. "It seemed

Early Stellar 7 covers, which were designed by Damon Slye.

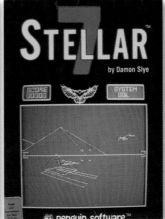

like a done deal. After they all left the room, Joe nixed the idea! It was quite a letdown." But Ybarra had another idea—a tank game for the still-unreleased Amiga. "Joe told us the Amiga was on the order of 10 to 20 times more powerful than a Commodore 64. And EA was supporting it heavily. So of course we jumped at the chance to develop on it."

While they were developing the tank game, they worked on prototype systems that, according to Slye, "looked like something out of a mad scientist's experiment... It was a steel black box with wires coming out everywhere, and the keyboard had a wooden case." Slye continues, "After many all nighters, and lots of pizza, the result of our efforts was Arctic Fox. The game was really an evolution of Stellar 7. Instead of having seven little basic arcade levels, Arctic Fox was one epic quest with many simulation and strategy elements. Instead of monochrome wire-frame graphics, it had 32 colors and solid-fill. Arctic Fox was a cool game, and it was the first original title that EA shipped on the Amiga.

"Unfortunately, the Amiga didn't sell as well as we'd all hoped. I remember an email Trip Hawkins sent out to all the Amiga developers that was titled 'If You Know 6502 Assembly Language, Start Coding!' It was quite a shock after Trip had been singing its praises for so long. But Trip was a smart guy, and his quick about-face was the right decision."

While Tunnell worked on Skyfox II for EA, Slye went to work on his next original game, Abrams Battle Tank. He had this to say: "Both Spectrum Holobyte and MicroProse had very realistic tank simulations in the works. In our game, the player was put in command of a lone tank and would take off across the countryside, taking on everything that came his way, including not only other tanks and infantry, but helicopters as

well! Ours was not very realistic. Tank warfare does not really lend itself to a solo experience: it's about platoons of tanks mixed in with infantry and air support, but our approach was a reflection of our prior games."

While Slye was working on Abrams Battle Tank, Tunnell became interested in adventure themes and movielike techniques with a game called Project Firestart. The company's founders began to concentrate, then, on these different aspects of game design—

I like to find a subject that offers interesting choices to the player. You don't try to simulate the facts, but to create the same kinds of tensions that would occur in the real world. The important thing is the psychology. I was beginning to develop this understanding in A-10 Tank Killer, and continued it through my other products.

—DAMON SLYE

WHY THE TANK KILLER?

"A-10 Tank Killer was a big advance, especially for me in understanding how to make a really good simulation," says Slye. "I'd always wanted to do a flight sim for the PC, but I wanted something different from the standard jet sim, which had been done many times. We had learned that basic marketing teaches that when you develop a new product, you can either build something a little better than the competition, or make something different; and that it's almost always smarter to make something different. Find an untapped niche. When I was searching for a cool combat airplane to simulate, I came across the A-10. It was the antithesis of the F-16 and the other modern jets: Instead of a sleek, beautiful, swept-wing, supersonic, high-tech dogfighting machine, the A-10 was a green, ugly, straight-winged, slow airplane designed to fight down low, alongside the grunts on the battlefield. What it lacked in grace and beauty, it made up for in personality and firepower. This was an untapped niche.

"In addition, it seemed to me that since the A-10 was designed to work closely in conjunction with friendly forces on the ground, and against enemy ground units, all of these additional elements would create more compelling game play, and more choices for the player, as well as the possibility of introducing some storytelling (through radio messages and requests from friendly ground forces). A-10 Tank Killer was the first game Dynamix published as a label, and it was also the first simulation that supported the new 256-color VGA graphics. It sold very well. Later when the Gulf War came along, the A-10 was featured in many CNN pieces, and the sales of the game really took off."

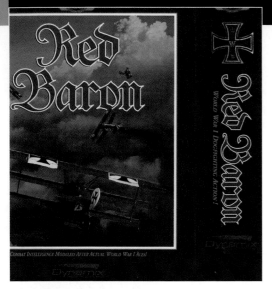

Some of Damon Slye's research photographs of a real Fokker, from the making of Red Baron.

Slye on simulations and Tunnell on adventure and movielike games. The company actually released an astounding eight products in 1989, including multiple ports for Activision (among them the original Mechwarrior game and Ghostbusters II) and their first two as an affiliate publisher for Activision—A-10 Tank Killer and David Wolf Secret Agent.

"Hey, We Should Just Buy You Guys."

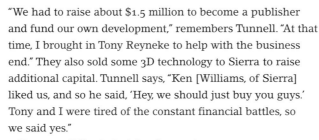

"We had to raise about $1.5 million to become a publisher and fund our own development," remembers Tunnell. "At that time, I brought in Tony Reyneke to help with the business end." They also sold some 3D technology to Sierra to raise additional capital. Tunnell says, "Ken [Williams, of Sierra] liked us, and so he said, 'Hey, we should just buy you guys.' Tony and I were tired of the constant financial battles, so we said yes."

"It was a difficult decision for us since we were so emotionally invested in Dynamix," says Slye, "but it was the right decision. Ken, who understood entrepreneurial motivation, did a great job with the transition. He allowed us to maintain our identity and most of our autonomy, provided sufficient incentives to us, and gave us the support we needed to grow into a successful label for Sierra."

The company grew rapidly then, expanding from around 30 people to more than 100. In 1991, they released four titles, including The Adventures of Willy Beamish, Heart of China (in which renowned martial arts instructor Sifu David Leung played a principal role), Nova 9, and Red Baron.

Red Baron was a great game. Set in the biplanes of World War I, it captured the feeling of the relatively slow-moving dogfighting of the era and was a delight to flight simulator fans. Slye comments that "jousting in biplanes at slow speeds, up-close and personal with the opponent, creates a pretty exciting, compelling experience. It remains one of my personal favorites of the games I've worked on."

Around this time, Tunnell, like Bilbo with the Ring, "was feeling stretched and thin." He broke away to form his own development company, Jeff Tunnell Productions (JTP), but continued to produce for Dynamix. "We did a remake of Lode Runner, before retro became big, 3D Ultra Pinball, and Trophy Bass. I remember when I suggested Trophy Bass, everybody laughed at us, and Ken Williams looked me in the eye and said, 'This had better work.'" It did work. In fact, Trophy Bass was one of Dynamix's most successful games along with 3D Ultra Pinball. "Few people realize that the simulation games for which we are so well known actually were not our biggest money-makers. When I returned as the head of Dynamix in 1995, I developed the idea of making the simpler games like 3D Ultra to pay for the others."

After Red Baron, Slye began work on Aces of the Pacific, which covered the air war in World War II in the Pacific theater. "We (or I) were a little too ambitious and optimistic on our goals for this product. Consequently, it was the most grueling development experience the rest of my

team members and I ever went through. There was a lot of overtime, and far too many all-nighters. We made the classic mistake of adding people to the project when it was behind schedule, in the hopes of speeding things up. This added to the chaos and probably made it even later than it would have been. Eventually we did finish it (though it had lots of bugs and we had to do a patch), and fortunately it was a big hit. I think we built the right game, but I think my mistake was not realizing how long it would take to build. Had we

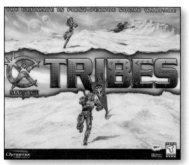

known, we could have planned a more orderly development."

Slye's last product at Dynamix was Aces Over Europe, which featured WWII air combat in Europe. "We added more combat AI, support for better graphic resolution, new planes, campaigns, and maps. Having learned from our mistakes, we released a clean product with very few bugs, and we managed to work only a modest amount of overtime."

In the same year that Aces Over Europe was released, Dynamix released a little game that made a big impression. "The idea came from a comment that Damon made, maybe ten years earlier," recalls Tunnell. "It was at a time when products like Music Construction Set were popular. Damon said, 'It would work if we could put together little machines.' I thought, 'Man, that's cool,' and ran off and did a little design. I held onto that design for ten years, but when I started JTP, I thought it was time to do it."

Incredible Fun

Working with Kevin Ryan, Tunnell created the ultimate Rube Goldberg computer game, in which the player had

to solve puzzles or create free-form gadgets by putting together an odd assortment of items, such as cannons, light bulbs, bowling balls, cats, pulleys, scissors, and various gears and widgets.

"Incredible Machine was put together by me, one programmer, and one artist on a total budget of about $35,000," says Tunnell. "We did a second product as an add-on and put it in a cool package. We sold about 250,000 units for a total budget of around $75,000 at that point." The Incredible Machine quickly became one of Dynamix's most memorable products.

Dynamix continued to produce quite a few games, but one of the most notable series evolved from the fact that Dynamix had done the first Mechwarrior game. When Mechwarrior-style games began to be very popular, Dynamix decided to create one of their own and came out with MetalTech: Earthsiege in 1994. After several more products in the Earthsiege world, Dynamix took the back story of Earthsiege and created a much bigger universe for Starsiege in 1998. However, Starsiege was costly to produce and fell short of the company's expectations.

Nevertheless, also in 1998, Dynamix came out with Starsiege Tribes, a first-person shooter designed to be played online by teams of 16 players. Tribes was the first such online cooperative team game. It also featured the ability to play both indoors and outside on a large landscape, with the players flying around using personal jet packs. Thousands of Tribes teams were developed, and the product was a significant success for Dynamix.

In 2001, Sierra officially closed down the Dynamix offices in Eugene, Oregon, sadly closing a chapter in this history.

I think one of the secrets to a great simulation is the idea that what you want to model—what's really important—is not the specific facts and data associated with the vehicles, but rather the experience and choices that exist in the mind of the player. It's all about psychology. So, the designer's focus should not be on the vehicles, but on the experience created within the player's brain. Due to shortcomings in computing power it's not possible to model reality; therefore, sometimes you have to change the 'facts' to get closer to the truth. I began to understand this in A-10 Tank Killer, and utilized this principle more fully in Red Baron, Aces of the Pacific, and Aces over Europe.

—DAMON SLYE

Sirius Software

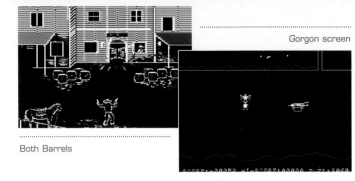

Gorgon screen

Both Barrels

ike so many early computer game companies, Sirius was formed in the late 70s when one brilliant creator teamed up with a visionary marketer. It began when Jerry Jewell, a sales manager at a Sacramento, California Computerland, met Nasir Gebelli. Gebelli had made a little slideshow on the Apple 2, which the pair turned into the first graphics editing product for the Apple—EZ Draw. Gebelli then began producing games, first Duck Hunt and Both Barrels, then the Galaxian-like Space Eggs, which he programmed in 30 hours straight. Next he produced Gorgon, a game so much like Defender that Sirius later settled with Williams Electronics to avoid a copyright suit.

Gebelli was a brilliant programmer, described by id Software cofounder John Romero as "a god." Most of the Apple 2 programmers of the day imitated Gebelli, to the point of using some of his code. He was a magician with the Apple 2 computer.

Jerry Jewell relates a story about being approached by Steve Wozniak, the creator of the Apple 2: "Wozniak came up to me at the third West Coast Computer Faire, and he wanted to thank me and Nasir. He said, 'I had an airplane accident not long ago and had amnesia. While I was convalescing, they brought me my Apple and your games. I think your games helped me recover my memory.' For years after that, he would invite us to parties and get us VIP tickets to things like the US Festival."

The early days of Sirius were like those of so many pioneering companies, with work going on in apartments and at night or on weekends. But the sales of Space Eggs and Gorgon really skyrocketed, and then Apple Computer placed a $1.5 million order for their products for redistribution. "We had a $3.5 million first year," says Jewell. "Not bad. Of course, the inventory that Apple bought sat in warehouses and was never distributed."

Iron-on tattoo that came with Space Eggs (hold up to mirror).

By Mark Turmell • A Product of Sirius Software, Inc.

I Fried The "Space" Eggs

Copyright 1981 * By Sirius Software

Space eggs

"It Will Crack You Up"

By Nasir • A Product of Sirius Software, Inc.

Jewell remembers the atmosphere of the early days of computer games being much different from today's more competitive industry. "Everybody knew each other. I mean Sierra, Brøderbund. Like if we were going to come out with a racecar game, we'd tell them, and they wouldn't do a racecar game right then. We didn't share programmers or anything, but we did cooperate in that way to avoid diluting the market."

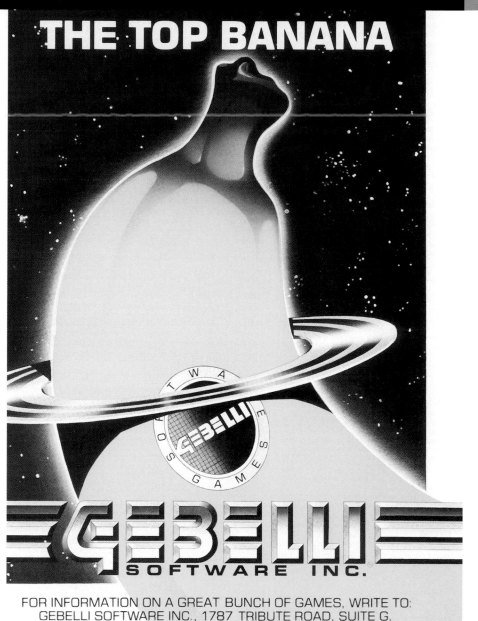

THE TOP BANANA

FOR INFORMATION ON A GREAT BUNCH OF GAMES, WRITE TO:
GEBELLI SOFTWARE INC., 1787 TRIBUTE ROAD, SUITE G,
SACRAMENTO, CALIFORNIA 95815 (916) 925-1432

Nasir Gebelli later went on to form his own
software company and placed ads like this.

149

Epyx

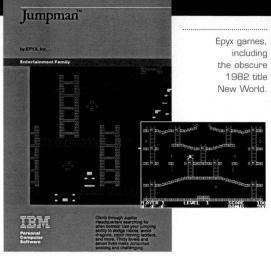

Epyx games, including the obscure 1982 title New World.

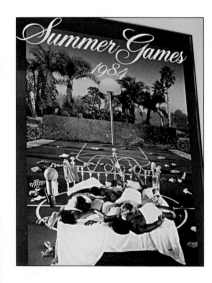

E pyx evolved from Automated Simulations (see page 54), and went through several incarnations during the 1980s and into the early 1990s. After Jon Freeman and Anne Westfall left, Jim Connelley continued the company. He released Randy Glover's 1983 hit, Jumpman, which, ironically, was based on the main character from Donkey Kong. By that time, Donkey Kong's Jumpman had become Mario, and apparently Nintendo wasn't concerned about the similarity of Jumpman to their game, nor of the sequel Jumpman Jr.'s similarity to Donkey Kong Jr.

Meanwhile, tensions erupted at Epyx, and Connelley and a bunch of programmers left. Michael Katz then took over as head of the company. Katz instituted immediate changes.

"Epyx was known for strategy games, and the board members wanted to see the company be more mainstream, which meant action. We created a new category, action/strategy, and changed our company logo to show the Thinker with a joystick. The first product in that category was Pitstop, a pure auto race game in which you had to decide based on gas usage and tire wear when to go into the pits. If you waited too long, you'd either run out of gas or tires would blow. You also controlled the pit crew. Pitstop became the demonstration model and lead product of the new positioning of Epyx."

Katz mentions that Epyx was the first software company to make activity products from toy licenses, such as Mattel's Barbie and Hot Wheels and Hasbro's GI Joe. Epyx was also the first company to categorize their game types and to put a recognizable logo on their products so that consumers could tell what kind of game they were buying. For instance, a mortarboard represented an educational product, while a joystick represented an action game.

Also in 1983, Epyx merged with Starpath (formerly Arcadia), headed by Bob Brown, who had been one of the chief architects of the Atari VCS. Again, according to Katz, "They had shelved a multievent sports product. We saw it, and with the 1984 Olympics coming to Los Angeles, we told them to finish it and make it an Olympic product. That was Summer Games."

Summer Games was an excellent title that featured several Olympic events and allowed up to eight players to compete. In some cases, two players could compete at the same time. Each event had its own control system and generally involved some frantic keyboarding or joystick manipulations.

Summer Games was the beginning of a highly successful franchise for Epyx, for which the company is most often remembered. They produced a sequel to Summer Games as well as Winter Games, World Games, and the very popular California Games, in which you competed in skateboarding, footbag, surfing, roller skating, a Frisbee-like game, and BMX racing. California Games II, which came out in 1990, added hang gliding, jet skiing, skateboarding, bodyboarding, and snowboarding to the series. Perhaps the weirdest game, though not officially part of the "Games" series, was Purple Saturn Day, which involved a sort of intergalactic Olympics with pseudofuturistic events like time/space piloting.

Epyx produced quite a few other games, including Impossible Mission, an excellent action platform game, their Street Sports line of games, Sub Battle Simulator, and

Dragonriders of Pern (based on the Anne McCaffrey novels). Epyx was also the original publisher for the first games from George Lucas's game group (see page 198). On this and the following page, we've included cover art from a variety of Epyx titles over the years. Note the Infogrames armadillo logo on the Israeli version of Project Neptune.

The World's Greatest Football Game was done by Gilman Louie's Nexa Software, later to merge with Spectrum Holobyte (see page 192).

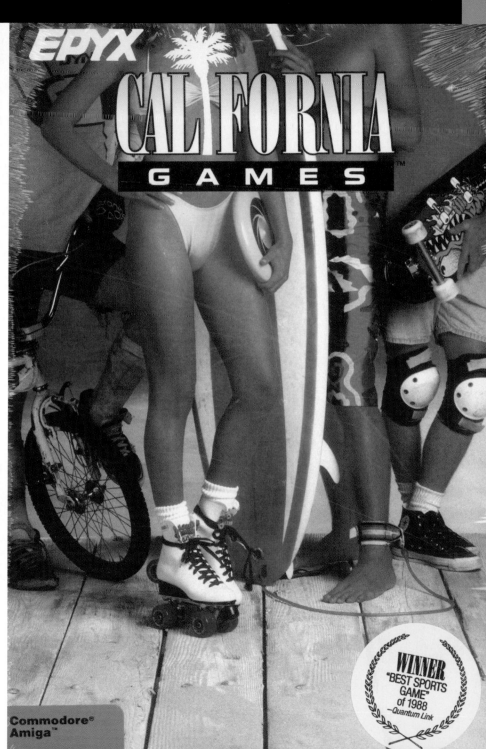

Commodore®
Amiga™

The Computer Game Developers Conference

Original board of directors: (back): Nicky Robinson, John Powers, Dave Walker, Brenda Laurel; (front): Tim Brengle, Stephen Friedman, Chris Crawford.

Chris Crawford had been a game evangelist at Atari. It wasn't surprising when he gathered some of his developer friends at his home in March 1986 for the first Computer Game Developers Conference (although it was dubbed a "symposium" originally). "We sat around in a circle," remembers Crawford, "and everybody just talked about game design issues. I had a clipboard with questions to ask, just in case, but I never needed it. We talked about game design in the morning and business issues in the afternoon."

After the first small gathering, Crawford realized how valuable the experience had been. "We learned an enormous amount from each other." So he planned a second conference for September of the same year. This one was more organized, and it took place in a hotel in Milpitas. This time 120 people showed up. "I won't say that everybody came," says Crawford, "but a sizable proportion of the design community showed up. Everybody was wandering around thinking, 'Golly gee, look at all those people facing the same problems as me. I used to be all alone, and now I'm not.'"

Crawford deliberately chose small spaces to ensure that the conference would feel crowded, which would force people to mingle. This mingling was to become a significant aspect of all the later Computer Game Developers Conferences.

Originally, CGDC gave out awards to publishers. At the time, says Crawford, the publishers were concerned that these conferences were going to become a game designers' union. "They had every right to be concerned—when the developers put their heads together they realized that many were getting screwed." However, the real purpose of the conferences was to mingle and share information.

In the early days, there would be a banquet to accompany the awards ceremony, and most of the developers came in costumes. A guest speaker would deliver some message to the gathered crowd of developers. "The most memorable speaker was novelist Bruce Sterling, who told us we, as game designers, were writing in sand," recalls Crawford. "He gave quite a rousing speech."

The Game Developers Conference expanded. In a politically charged atmosphere, Crawford left the leadership role, and the conference was ultimately sold to publishing company Miller Freeman. The conference now hosts thousands of attendees; however, many who attended it in the early years look back nostalgically to a time when it was just "us," the core developers. Many industries have major shows where manufacturers and publishers display their work. The game industry has always attended shows such as the West Coast Computer Faire, the Consumer Electronics Show, and more recently the games-only E3 Expo, but the Game Developers Conference was unique. It was about the creation of games, for the creators of games. It established a community of developers and fostered mutual respect and lifelong friendships.

The first Computer Game Developers Symposium. In the front row: Gilman Louie, unidentified person, Jeff Johannigman, Ivan Manley, unidentified person, unidentified person, Chris Crawford. In the back rows: Stephen Friedman, Sean Barger, unidentified person, Kellyn Beck, Cliff Johnson, unidentified person, unidentified person, Brian Moriarty, Carole Manley, Tim Brengel, Gordon Walton, unidentified person, Thurston Searfoss, Mike Jones.

A game designer costume. Right: *Softalk* magazine editor Margot Comstock and coauthor Rusel DeMaria at the banquet.

The Wizardry of Sir-Tech

GALACTIC ATTACK

A real-time space war simulation written in USCD PASCAL for your APPLE II or III

Sir-tech SOFTWARE, INC.
6 MAIN STREET OGDENSBURG, N.Y. 13669
(315) 393-6633

RUNS ON ANY APPLE
(DOS 3.3 or PASCAL, 48K and 1 disk required)

Wizardry

A Game of Fantasy & Adventure

by
Andrew Greenberg & Robert Woodhead

©1981 SIR-TECH SOFTWARE, INC.
& ANDREW GREENBERG

REQUIRES
48K, 1 disk, Dos 3.3
APPLE COMPUTER

ote: The story of the Wizardry series is very difficult to tell because there is considerable disagreement among the principal players in the story. Here, then, are the highly condensed basics.

Mortal Enemies

Other than Electronic Arts, most of the early computer game companies were started and run by the game developers themselves. Another exception was Sir-Tech Software, which began more like modern companies, with the combination of creative and business people. In some ways, it all started at Cornell University when Robert Woodhead had a nasty surprise. "I was thrown out of college for a year for low grades. I guess I had been spending too much time programming and playing games on the PLATO network."

Andrew Greenberg was the system administrator for that same PLATO system Woodhead had been spending too much time on. "Part of my job was to kick people off of the games, and Robert had made it his mission in life to play games on PLATO. So we were automatically each other's enemies."

During his imposed year off, Woodhead wrote Galactic Attack, a single-player version of one of the PLATO games, and began work on a dungeon-style game he was going to call "Paladin." A few weeks after beginning Paladin, he heard about another student who had written a dungeon game. It was Andrew Greenberg, who remembers, "He was stunned

to hear that I'd written a game because I was, by definition, a professional spoilsport."

Woodhead remembers, "Andrew had two things going for him. He had already written a game in BASIC, and he had a really good name for it—Wizardry." The two met and agreed to collaborate, dividing responsibilities during a weekend meeting. However, their partnership was anything but smooth. Greenberg recounts their working style: "We were like night and day. We spent all our time quibbling and criticizing each other. Our friends said if you locked us in a room together, there'd be a lot of screaming and yelling, and later, when you opened the door, there'd be blood dripping from the walls, and in the center of the room there would be a diskette." Today, the two are great friends, but their mutual respect only became clear later, when they each read positive statements about the other in the media.

During that same period, Woodhead had been programming

Wizardry inspired and entertained a whole generation of game players, including Robin Williams, Harry Anderson, and the Crown Prince of Bahrain, who actually called Sir-Tech on the phone.

some database and accounting programs for Fred Sirotek, an entrepreneur who owned several businesses. After showing some products at a computer show, Woodhead and Norm Sirotek, Fred's youngest son, decided to form Sirotech Software in 1981. Their first product was Infotree, a database created by Woodhead. The company was ultimately renamed Sir-Tech, according to Robert Sirotek, "because Norm and I kept getting phone calls in the middle of the night and early morning from end users."

Wizardry

Months later, at the first Boston Applefest in 1981, Woodhead brought with him possibly the first public beta version of a computer game. The beta version was called Dungeons of Despair, and it consisted of a few specially designed levels of Wizardry. He sold them at full price, promising the completed game later and asking for feedback. "We had a clue that we were onto something when we counted the money that night in the hotel room, and there were several thousand dollars on the bed.

"The Dungeons of Despair scenario was us exercising everything we could do to make sure the game was solid," says Woodhead. "We wanted people who bought

it to test it for us. Proving Grounds of the Mad Overlord was later play-tested for two to three months by fanatical players running 24 hours a day. They found very subtle bugs and really did tweak and tune the difficulty of the game considerably."

One of Wizardry's ultimate strengths was the extent to which it was tested and played before it was finally released. Both Woodhead and Greenberg admit that they owe a great

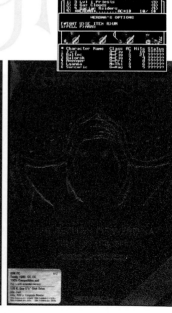

KNIGHT OF DIAMONDS
THE SECOND SCENARIO

deal to the many testers who spent hours on the game. They also drew inspiration from Dungeons & Dragons and from the PLATO games. "We added a concept of story and plotline to what we'd seen on PLATO, where it was 'hack-hack-kill-kill-occasionally something interesting happens-run away...'" adds Woodhead.

Proving Grounds of the Mad Overlord, the first Wizardry game, was a great success. More importantly, through a combination of mesmerizing game play and effective marketing, it became one of the most influential products in the early history of computer games. Rob and Norm Sirotek, who ran the company, concentrated on marketing the games and building the infrastructure of the business, while the design duo of Woodhead and Greenberg came right back with a sequel, Knight of Diamonds—essentially a scenario disk for the same game with new dungeons and some tougher puzzles. (Clever players with advanced characters figured out how to teleport to the bottom and work their way back, thereby avoiding some of the challenges.)

Sometime around the creation of the third Wizardry, Legacy of Llylgamyn, Greenberg moved to Boston to begin work on Star Saga, an amazing text-based science fiction adventure. Woodhead then created The Return of Werdna (Wizardry IV), the toughest of the initial Wizardry epics, with Roe Adams. The concept was great—this time you play the evil Werdna, out for revenge—but in the end, Wizardry IV proved possibly too difficult. In addition, it was completed late, coming out in December 1987. The Wizardry series was losing ground.

The Next Phase

Enter David Bradley, whose first published game was Parthian Kings from Avalon Hill. Afterward, he began working on a role-playing game, but Avalon Hill didn't want to compete

with Sir-Tech and suggested he offer his game to them.

Bradley went to Sir-Tech and struck a deal to create Wizardry V: Heart of the Maelstrom. But at that time, Wizardry IV wasn't yet complete, and Sir-Tech opted to wait and deliver the games in order. According to Bradley, it was two years before Wizardry V finally came out in November 1988, although it was completed much earlier. Wizardry V also included an introduction by Andrew Greenberg and his wife, Sheila.

Robert Sirotek gives great credit to Bradley's work on Heart of the Maelstrom. "Wizardry IV was by far our worst commercial failure; Wizardry V saved the Wizardry product line. We very likely would not have continued with the Wizardry products if it were not for the success of Wizardry V."

Along with Woodhead, Bradley credits Richard Garriott's Ultima series with being one of his main inspirations. "I considered that Heart of the Maelstrom was a greatly expanded role-playing game. Ultima was the other series putting content back into the

Deep Space was one of Sir-Tech's few non-Wizardry titles, most notable because it was created by Paul Neurath and Edward Lerner, who later went on to form Looking Glass Studios and produce many great games, including Ultima Underworld.

games, and, as Garriott went with a third-person view of the characters, I elected to stay with the traditional Wizardry first-person viewpoint."

Bradley knows Wizardry as few others could, given that he rewrote the whole system from the ground up in Wizardry VI: The Bane of the Cosmic Forge. He expresses great respect for the work of Woodhead and Greenberg, and worked hard to preserve what he calls, "the spirit that makes Wizardry Wizardry." Among the changes Bradley implemented was the use of full-color graphics for the first time in the Wizardry series, which up until that point had stayed with the original line-drawn mazes.

Wizardry VII: Crusaders of the Dark Savant was a complex game that pitted the player against several computer-controlled enemies, all seeking the same 13 map pieces that could lead to a valuable artifact. In the game, players were transported from the world of the previous game into this new scenario, which included some surprises such as aliens and space travel. Bradley comments, "I regard this game as my true masterpiece. It was very nonpredictable and nonlinear. Everybody who played it had a different experience."

In 2001, Sir-Tech finally released Wizardry VIII, possibly the final installment of this great series.

These cards are from a Japanese card game based on the Legacy of Llylgamyn, called Tiltowait. Wizardry fans will remember that Tiltowait was one of the most powerful spells in the game. Ironically, their fighter character is called Mifune, and back when I played the game obsessively, my Samurai was also called Mifune. Sheer coincidence, no doubt. [RDM]

Wizardry was huge internationally. Here are a French version of Wizardry, a Japanese board game, and a detail from a Japanese anime laser disk. Below are Sir-Tech's founders in Japan with executives from Banpresto Co. Ltd., a division of Bandai, while they were opening up connections with the Japanese console makers. Wizardry was among the first computer games translated to the Nintendo Entertainment System.

Another one of Sir-Tech's early products was a great maze game called Star Maze. You flew a sort of Asteroids-style ship through a complex series of mazes, shooting and avoiding surreal enemies like the crawling caterpillar, and often bouncing off the walls. It was great fun.

Opportunity Knocks:
The Story of SSI

Joel Billings in 1980.

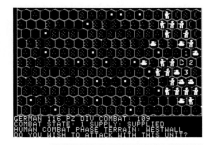

The 116th Panzer Division (next to the #3 attacker) is ready to join in the attack on the unfortunate U.S. 106th Infantry Division in 1981's Tigers in the Snow, a hex-based version of the Battle of the Bulge.

In the summer of 1979 Joel Billings was on vacation, preparing to go to business school in the fall. A champion paper and board game war gamer, Billings considered creating war games on the computer, thinking there might be potential sales in the emerging microcomputer market. Having just studied marketing surveys in school, Billings decided to start by putting out a questionnaire in a couple of local hobby/game shops. Being in Silicon Valley at the time, he found that about 20 percent of the war gamers who filled out his survey had access to computers. On the questionnaire he had written, "If you're a programmer and interested in programming war games, call me."

Two important events occurred then. First, he received a call from John Lyons, an experienced programmer and a war gamer. Lyons commented, "Now I know what opportunity looks like when it knocks."

The second important event was meeting Trip Hawkins, then at Apple, who convinced Billings that the Apple II was the way to go. "I credit Trip with evangelizing the Apple II to me, whereas I only knew about the TRS-80, which would have been the wrong computer."

Billings met with investors, which is how he first heard about Trip Hawkins, but ultimately, he started Strategic Simulations, Inc., using family money instead of outside investment. SSI's first game was Computer Bismarck. Billings says, "We started with an easy situation. John called it a Fox and Hounds game. We realized that artificial intelligence would be a real challenge, but in this one all you had to worry about was, 'I'm the Bismarck and all I want to do is run away.' Our early AI was more like an expert system. Using our expert war game experience, we asked ourselves what should it do in each situation and had it pick path 1 or path 2, and so forth." Despite its simplicity, the artificial opponent for the solitaire game—Otto von Computer, as the programmers called him—was so respected that he stayed around for 1981's Torpedo Fire.

After several simulated days, the British admiral (human player) has yet to catch sight of the legendary Bismarck as its artificial admiral (Otto von Computer) attempts to break out into the North Atlantic.

Business in High Gear

By 1982, SSI had published 17 games, with 8 of them using the familiar hex grids of war games. Most importantly, the fledgling SSI had already recruited several designers and programmers for a raft of new games. Charlie Merrow (later to design Fighter Command) would design Computer Air Combat (the game that inspired Russell Sipe to start *Computer Gaming World* magazine) and Computer Baseball. Dan Bunten was recruited to design Computer

Quarterback and Cartels & Cutthroats; Roger Keating (later of Strategic Simulations Group (SSG) fame with Reach for the Stars and Warlords) would program Southern Command with its version of the Arab-Israeli War of 1973; Gary Grigsby (later of Kampfgruppe, War in Russia, Pacific War, and Battle of Britain fame) would design several games; and the trio of David Landry, Chuck Kroegel, and Dave Walker were recruited to program Tigers in the Snow and Battle of Shiloh.

In addition to these games, SSI published two hybrid board game/computer game efforts: Napoleon's Campaigns 1813 & 1815 and Road to Gettysburg. Both games came with board game maps, but all movement and combat was resolved on the computer. The games were not entirely popular because they portrayed "fog of war" and "limited intelligence" all too well. It was difficult to tell what was going on, even with the map. Later, a version of Napoleon's Campaigns allowed you to resolve battles with 15mm miniatures and to type in the results so that the computer could referee strategic movement and set up smaller battles for you.

Although Gary Grigsby would unveil the first two "monster games" on the computer during 1982 (Guadalcanal Campaign) and 1983 (Bomb Alley), and AI genius Roger Keating was putting the finishing touches on RDF 1985 (his hypothetical war between the Americans and Soviets in the Persian Gulf), SSI wasn't betting all of its marbles on historical combat. Contemporary with Grigsby's games were Paul Murray's Warp Factor (ship-to-ship combat in outer space) and Tom Reamy's Galactic Gladiators (man-to-man tactical combat with a scenario editor).

Also in 1983, SSI unveiled a boxing strategy game called Ringside Seat. The boxing game played well and featured statistics on all the famous athletes in the days before player associations and major sports federations demanded a royalty for such use. There was only one problem. The freelance designer who sold the game to SSI used the statistics from an Avalon Hill board game called Title Bout to create his database. Indeed, entire game mechanics were stolen from the board game. Naturally, Avalon Hill took legal action against SSI—also including Computer Bismarck in the case. It was ultimately settled out of court. Ironically, Avalon Hill had published a computer version of Title Bout, but it was only available on one computer platform, and it didn't sell very well. However, James V. Trunzo, the designer of Avalon Hill's Title Bout, later used his database and mechanics to create other computer boxing games, most recently APBA Pro Boxing.

SSI put out three other titles in 1983 that offered nonmilitary challenges. Epidemic required players to stop a space spore–spawned epidemic, Geopolitique 1990 required diplomatic as well as military acuity, and Fortress was an abstract war game (somewhere between Othello and Go) that "learned" how you played and built strategies against you.

In 1984, the company broke into the fantasy adventure field with Questron. Once again they became embroiled in a legal situation when it turned out

John Lyons

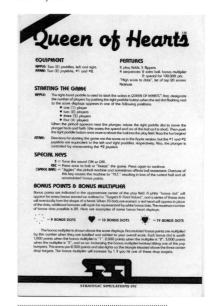

SSI did mostly war games in the beginning, but they put out a few other titles. Here's an obscure game called Queen of Hearts from the early days of SSI.

With Napoleon's Campaigns 1813 & 1815 and Road to Gettysburg, the maps were so large that you needed reference points on the screen and a printed map on the side in order to keep up with the action.

Maze Rats: An entire gang of robots (G,A,R,M,S) has ganged up on the Armour team (Q,L) after traversing the maze from right to left.

Ali Is the Greatest: Using the Stick & Move strategy, Ali was able to hold off Sonny Liston for a unanimous decision in three rounds.

Any resemblance between Questron's graphics and those of the Ultima series was purely intentional.

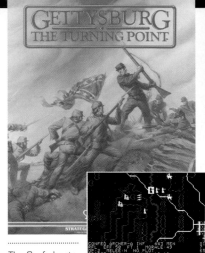

that the designers of Questron had basically redone Ultima. "We were showing Questron at a trade show in January, two weeks before it was to come out," says Billings, "and some Origin guys came out and said it was a rip-off of Ultima." Some tough negotiations later, SSI worked out an agreement. "At that stage, there was no way we were not going to release it," Billings recalls. Questron was not only popular with SSI's customer base, but was successful enough to attract the attention of the new powerhouse on the block, Electronic Arts. EA hired the brothers who designed Questron to build Legacy of the Ancients for their 1987 season. This time, SSI was the company taking legal action, and the brothers were required to fulfill their Questron contract and design Questron II for SSI. Of course, real gamers knew that Questron II was pretty much Questron III. The same brothers went on to create Legend of Blacksilver for Epyx, which could be considered Questron IV.

As always, SSI continued to intersperse war games of the highest possible quality into the mix. The military games included Gary Grigsby's War in Russia and a couple of new takes on the genre—a tactical battle game called Field of Fire and a flight simulator of sorts called 50 Mission Crush. Yet, the publisher was unafraid to experiment with games like Rails West (railroad building in the western frontier of the United States) and Colonial Conquest (multiplayer strategy in the expansionist era).

For war gamers, however, the high-water marks for SSI war games came in the mid-80s. Kampfgruppe, the award-winning game of armored combat on WWII's eastern front, was hailed by every reviewer and made Grigsby into a cult hero among military buffs. It was also the era of Gettysburg: The Turning Point by Chuck Kroegel and David Landrey. The game marked the beginning of an American Civil War series where, unlike previous games with their fixed historical orders of battle, you could be surprised in the same way that

a real general could be surprised. The Civil War series for SSI was a staple for the company until everything was overwhelmed by the Advanced Dungeons & Dragons phenomenon.

Yet many people forget that SSI's venture into the world of AD&D actually followed a successful line of fantasy releases like Wizard's Crown, Gemstone Warrior, and Phantasie. In fact, the original idea for the AD&D series was

The Confederate commander avoids conventional wisdom and charges Union cavalry on the first turn of Gettysburg: The Turning Point.

to use the Wizard's Crown engine and force-feed the licensed game's role-playing mechanics into it. Fortunately, that didn't happen, and the "gold box" engine evolved out of this initiative. (See the next section for more information on SSI's D&D games.)

War gamers felt slightly miffed when SSI became so successful with its role-playing license, but the truth was that during the height of AD&D success, SSI was publishing more military titles per year than before. Plus, some of Gary Grigsby's most intricate designs appeared in this era. Games like the Panzer Strike series, Second Front (War in Russia on a grand scale), and eventually, Pacific War offered challenges never experienced before. The granddaddy of all strategic-level war games, Pacific War was so intricate that experienced war gamers used a two-page checklist to make sure they took advantage of every move.

Dungeons & Dragons

In 1987, TSR Incorporated informed interested bidders that it was ready to license Dungeons & Dragons to a computer game company. D&D had inspired many games already, such as Dungeon Master, Wizardry, and Ultima, but none of them were licensed, and TSR got nothing from them. They had looked into making computer games themselves and discovered that it was not practical for them.

At least ten companies contended for the potentially rich license. One of them was SSI, and Joel Billings remembers: "If you think of it, they were really doing war games. So we thought, who would be better for it than us? Most of our guys were both war gamers and RPG players; so we took this very seriously and outlined a whole series of different products, not just one. In the final decision, we were up against EA and Origin, but they were just proposing one title, sort of like the movie license model. I think our broader vision won us the contract."

The deal was consummated at the Consumer Electronics Show (CES), and SSI started work on several titles: Pool of Radiance, an adventure that took place in TSR's Forgotten Realms campaign setting and the first of the "gold box" series; Heroes of the Lance, an action game that was developed in Europe by U.S. Gold and did best on the Nintendo Entertainment System; and Dungeon Master's Assistant, for use with D&D campaigns.

Similar in appearance to Interplay's The Bard's Tale, Pool of Radiance offered much more detail and number crunching. More importantly, it offered authentic D&D statistics, character classes, alignment, mechanics, and nomenclature. Among other innovations, the game placed the characters in a mock 3D terrain and used three different levels of sprite graphics to suggest the differences between short-, medium- and long-range encounters.

The next gold box game was Curse of the Azure Bonds, where SSI ran into a play balance dilemma. By allowing players to bring experienced characters from Pool of Radiance, they had to make the game playable for beginners and for people with built-up characters. Their solution was to have most of a player's weapons and equipment stolen at the beginning of the game. They took a lot of criticism for this decision and had to come up with new solutions for play balancing in the future.

The D&D license was a huge boost for SSI. War games had always had a limited audience. Fantasy had more players, and D&D was as big as you could get in the fantasy genre. At that time, SSI entered into a complex deal with Electronic Arts, which had the best distribution in the business, giving up 20 percent of the company for a $2 million cash infusion. However, by the time SSI paid substantial royalties to TSR and the distribution share to Electronic Arts, their overall profitability suffered. Billings had this to say: "The deal with EA was both good and bad for SSI. It ended up being one of the key factors in SSI's ultimate demise. But if I had it to do over again, I'd probably do the same thing. I'm not much for second-guessing."

SSI did continue to produce war games, but it was clear that the fantasy genre was their best source of revenue, and much of their resources were devoted to those games going into the 1990s.

By 1990, SSI realized it was time to look for a new approach, and that's when they teamed up with Westwood (see page 184) to create the landmark game, Eye of the Beholder.

Publicity photo of Trip Hawkins and Joel Billings announcing the partnership between EA and SSI.

161

Panzer General, Steel Panthers, and Other Generals

One of the most successful and innovative war games of the 1990s was inspired largely by Daisan-Ryku, a Japanese war game for the Sega Genesis that was never released in the States. This game managed to captivate the interest of many of the designers at SSI. The game it inspired was Panzer General, a campaign game, which placed the player in the role of a German general fighting a series of battles played across beautiful landscapes. Panzer General's success spawned a number of other products, and the graphics continued to improve with almost every new version. Although Allied General, the first sequel, was a disappointment (having been created by an outside developer), later products included Fantasy General, which introduced fantasy elements to the series (such as mage or warrior campaigns); Panzer General II, with options to play German, U.S., British, or Russian sides; and People's General, which was set in the post–Cold War era. Finally, they released Rites of War, a well-designed Warhammer variant based on the Panzer General II engine, and Panzer General 3D. These last two suffered from coming out after the company had been purchased by a series of

In the initial Panzer General, you could only play the role of a German commander. Later releases allowed you to take any side of both the historical and fantasy conflicts portrayed.

new owners, and never got much marketing. However, by the time the company released the People's General, a postmodern Communist campaign using the same basic engine, the units looked so real that they upstaged the landscapes on the battlefields, causing them to look phony by comparison.

All the General series games featured smooth-as-silk mouse interfaces, the games flowed well, and the sound effects and voice acting were terrific. The games were not without controversy, however. The details of explosions and bodies flying caused some stir, and there was criticism of the game's perspective being exclusively from the Nazi side.

The truth is that SSI's Joel Billings knew all too well the alliterative marketing axiom that nothing makes money in war gaming except for "Nukes, Nazis, and NATO (and sometimes, Napoleon)." In addition, Billings knew that in games that revolved around tanks and planes, the Germans had the best equipment through much of the war. So, it is no surprise that the first entry in what came to be known as the General series was based on German air and armor.

Steel Panthers

In 1995, about 18 months in marketing time after Panzer General's phenomenal success, another series did extremely

The units in People's General looked so crisp that they made the battlefields and buildings look unreal.

Panzer General II not only offered multiplayer play and better graphics than its ancestor, but also offered campaigns from four different sides: U.S., British, German, and Soviet.

well for SSI. Again, the subject matter was tied to World War II. SSI's longtime genius, Gary Grigsby, returned to the scene of many of his finest moments. The designer of Kampfgruppe, Overrun, Panzer Strike, Typhoon of Steel, and a host of other tactical combat games (Guadalcanal Campaign, Bomb Alley, War in Russia, Second Front, and the great classic, Pacific War) created what many believe to be the ultimate armor simulation.

The original Steel Panthers offered tactical combat with meticulously modeled tanks and terrain that looked almost three-dimensional. Scenarios could be played in a couple of hours, and a scenario editor allowed players to build their own combat scenarios. The complexity of play was represented by the program's translucent calculations for armor penetration, movement effects upon aim, and terrain effects. The simplicity was enhanced by having each unit's movement range highlighted on the map, as well as a host of additional options for moving entire tank divisions at once (in formation!).

Where Panzer General had great explosions and special effects to reflect the results of battles, Steel Panthers allowed you to lay down smoke to avoid battles or use indirect fire to attack the enemy. Instead of merely seeing the final results of combat, war gamers were treated to watching shells bounce harmlessly off approaching Tiger tanks and infantry ambushes pop up in the detailed woods terrain. Steel Panthers also offered a robust Morale model that often had outnumbered and outgunned units retreating whether you ordered them to do so or not.

More Panthers and Still More Scenarios

User-generated scenarios started to proliferate and to be swapped over the still-new World Wide Web. Then came Steel Panthers II in 1997. Whereas Grigsby's modern armor sequel to Kampfgruppe, Mech Brigade, had been superior in

design but inferior in sales, the modern armor sequel to Steel Panthers was a major success. Perhaps the successful implementation of armor in Desert Storm affected sales. Perhaps it was the ability to use a familiar system in launching guided missiles, building tactics around reactive armor, and the ability to play campaigns where you could upgrade units after the battle and purchase support units before the battle. Players who thought Desert Storm was too one-sided could play earlier Arab-Israeli conflicts or simulate Korean and Vietnamese conflict actions. Better yet, they could continue to build their own scenarios…and they did.

In 1998, Steel Panthers III released. It used the same basic engine as the prior two efforts, but it was significantly more complex. Steel Panthers III offered 40 scenarios and six campaigns. The scale was enlarged to 200 yards per hexagon compared to the 50-yard hexes of the previous games. Most importantly, players could no longer simply charge in a modern parody of the Light Brigade. A new command control point system meant that players had to make reasonable decisions that reflected solid combined arms doctrine. Although Steel Panthers III covered everything from WWII to the modern day, it was more like a complete modern warfare game than its predecessors. Combined arms were much more important, and aficionados are continuing to build their own scenarios and distribute them on the Web to this day.

DAISAN-RYKU

I remember seeing a parade of people coming in and out of Chuck Kroegel's office when I was visiting in late 1993. They were playing Daisan-Ryku, a Sega Genesis game from Japan. I remember their comments about the fluid way that you could order units about with the Sega controller, as well as the emotional stake you would gain by shepherding units from one battle to the next. The next time I visited SSI, the Daisan-Ryku addicts had managed to incubate that something special into something even more special—Panzer General.

—JLW

Trip Hawkins & Electronic Arts

It seems that some people are destined to do great things. Trip Hawkins is one of them. Most people know that Trip Hawkins started Electronic Arts and helped create a revolution in the business of computer games. Few, however, know his roots.

"I got my professional feet wet by starting a little business to market a tabletop football game I'd devised in 1972," says Hawkins. "In the days before computers, I played not just board games, but the kind of board games that simulated interesting things, like NFL football. Accu-Stat was an excellent game and used dice and charts to allow realistic uses of strategy and player characteristics and stats. It was the precursor to John Madden Football.

"Of course, I was 19 years old and had no idea what I was doing," continues Hawkins, "so the business failed. But it was perhaps the most important experience of my work life because I discovered my love for creating games could combine with a passion for entrepreneurship, and that failure could be used to just add fuel to the furnace. For years, my best friends would say that the only reason I started EA was so that someday I could make another football game.

"In 1980, I had only been out of school for two years, and yet I knew that I was already part of something very special and powerful and that I would have a very interesting career. At Apple I learned a lot about thinking big from Mike Markkula and Steve Jobs, and I learned how you could be a small company in a huge industry and still think and be the leader. This was reflected in the 1980 National Computer Conference trade show, where tiny Apple was a darling of the show and showed a lot of class by taking all the show attendees to Disneyland for free."

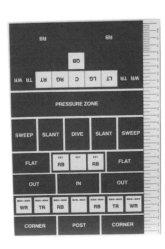

Trip with another Apple employee, John Couch, in 1981, examining a memory subsystem circuit board for the Apple Lisa. "Since I helped Apple get a great story," says Hawkins, "Steve Jobs was pleased and had the photo framed and gave it to me as a gift."

Electronic Arts: The Plan

The original plan for Electronic Arts involved three principles that turned out to be prescient. "After failing with Accu-Stat, I was determined to start another business and to do so successfully," Trip Hawkins remembers. "So I was more deliberate and patient about timing and wisdom. I knew what I wanted to do and collected ideas and thoughts over a period of years. But I also felt that a really 'big idea' was required to make a business work. The big idea for EA was the concept of the software artist—treating the creative talent like artists. But there were two other ideas at the founding, represented in this plan, that proved in the long run to be equally critical. One was organized, efficient, cross-platform development using our own proprietary tools and technology. The other was direct distribution to retail stores. This original plan document is a bit amazing in how well it predicts the future, although our financial model for EA was ludicrously optimistic, as is the case for many startups. What made EA a winning company was the combination of strategic vision with the raw ability to adapt from mistakes and adjust and stick with it."

....
October 8, 1982: The original business plan for Electronic Arts, then called Soft-Art.

In famous venture capitalist Don Valentine's office in 1982, presenting the EA business plan. Dave Evans was one of the new company's first producers. Trip came up with the idea of a game producer by combining aspects of film, recording, and business software development project management into the job. The role of "producer" has remained a standard part of game development ever since.

SUMMARY

THE OPPORTUNITY

The retail value of home computer software will grow from $100 million in 1982 to $2.9 billion in 1987. During this time the home computer will emerge as a significant new communications medium for play, discovery, fantasy, and experience for 22 million upper income, well-educated families worldwide. SoftArt hopes to become one of the leading software suppliers to this market.

THE BUSINESS

A system for producing and marketing a broad line of advanced consumer computer software developed by independent designers.

THE STRATEGY

Starting in 1983 with 18 products, primarily "better games", SoftArt will develop a broad software product line for the home. It will be critical to develop three assets: Talent, The Marketing Delivery System, and Technical Leadership.

TALENT will be developed via a group of "Producers" who will synthesize the functions of movie producers, record industry A & R people, and technical product managers. Their goal will be to get the best possible home computer software products out of independent designers working under contract.

THE MARKETING DELIVERY SYSTEM will include direct sales to retailers, bold and visionary print advertising, and innovative and distinctive product packaging and point of sale merchandising. The goal is to achieve broad distribution with a broad, branded product line that sells itself.

TECHNICAL LEADERSHIP will include the development of advanced software tools, anticipating hardware technology advances, and providing assistance and creative stimulation to designers. The goal is to efficiently produce better products that get the most out of the consumer's computer.

KEY FIRST YEAR EVENTS:		
10-82	First designers sign
11-82	Company debuts at AppleFest
12-82	Major financing complete
1-83	Show first products at CES
4-83	First products ship
9-83	Company turns profitable

FINANCIAL GOALS:	'83 Sales	'84 Sales	'87 Sales	Long-Term PAT
	$4.2M	$20M	$192M	12%

FUNDING REQUIREMENTS: $2,000,000 additional investment
($206,000 already invested)

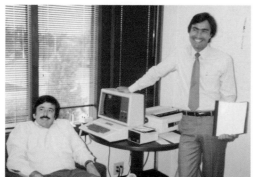

Presenting the business plan with Rich Melmon, the first employee Trip hired, as sales and marketing executive. Trip is leaning on his "trusty" Apple II, which was also used by Bruce Zweig to program initial versions of his best-selling MasterType game.

Leave the Room,
Lose Your Vote

Trip's first proposed name for the new company was Amazin' Software, which was universally disliked by the first 11 employees, including Bing Gordon. "We were going to go with Soft-Art, but it was taken, so we had a meeting at Pajaro Dunes to determine a name," Gordon recalls. "Trip said we had to have a name before the night was over, and anyone who went to sleep lost their vote. That was typical of

Trip. Trip could always wear people out. He could go and go. If you leave the room, you lose your vote. The other part is, if you're in the room, you get a vote. Anyway, I liked Electronic Artists because it reminded me of Mary Pickford and the original United Artists 'anti-studios' in Hollywood. However, Steve Hayes pointed out that we weren't the artists... that we worked with them. We didn't develop our own in-house project until five years later with Skate or Die. Tim Mott suggested Electronic Arts. It was after midnight by then, and that's the name we adopted."

Trip Hawkins (right) and Bing Gordon holding the football (below) at one of EA's Pajaro Dunes retreats, probably circa 1984.

David Maynard with one of the early EA game development cross-platform artist stations, circa 1984.

"EA's first real office, where we had a lease and our own furniture, was in San Mateo on Campus Drive with a nice view," according to Trip Hawkins. "Here, in one of the two conference rooms with windows, Steve Hayes and I are obviously enjoying the view while contemplating something important. This would have been in 1983. Steve and David Maynard were the first two technical staff hired by EA, both joining in 1982 prior to our first venture funding."

EA's first retailer proudly displaying his Electronic Arts releases.

Early Days at EA

May 1983 at the first EA warehouse in South San Francisco. "All 21 employees at that time went to the warehouse to pack and ship the first orders in company history," says Trip Hawkins. "I was taking a break and probably looking around for something else to do. I would later personally hand off the first order to a customer who drove over to pick it up."

I founded EA in 1982 and we shipped our first games in May of 1983. By September, we were already way behind on our plan and feeling like we might go bust. These key objectives were posted around the company walls and given to everyone during that stressful launch period, and much discussion took place about them on an ongoing basis. These objectives became a rallying cry for survival and a kiln for the EA culture.

—TRIP HAWKINS,
FOUNDER,
ELECTRONIC ARTS

KEY OBJECTIVES
TO BE MET BY 10/1/83

1. 800 GALLERIES PROPERLY INSTALLED

2. 8 COMMODORE PRODUCTS "IN THE BAG"

3. 1,000 COMMODORE OUTLETS SIGNED UP

4. ALL SET FOR COMMODORE AND IBM OPERATIONS

5. "BETA" SOFTWARE FOR 2 HOME MANAGEMENT TITLES

6. EVERYONE READY FOR SEASONAL VOLUME

7. SUCCESSFULLY HOLD OVERHEAD SPENDING AND HEADCOUNT

8. EVERYONE'S SANITY INTACT!

90% done

impossible! we're all insane already!

Among the early employees depicted packing software are Nancy Fong (left), still VP of Creative Services, and Susan Lee-Merrow (top left), who went on to become a longtime executive at Brøderbund and Lucas Learning.

167

We See Farther

This handmade mockup of EA's "We See Farther" poster was used at the West Coast Computer Faire in 1982. It became part of what was then known as "The Manifesto."

"This poster, made in 1982, captured in one image the concepts and vision of Electronic Arts," Trip Hawkins tells us. "'We See Farther' became our rallying cry and a touchstone in hard times that made us keep going. It was conceived of by Andy Berlin and Rich Silverstein, who EA worked with as freelancers and who made EA their first client when they formed their own agency. GBS became a major force in advertising and did the famous 'SEGA!' campaign years later."

(A Manifesto)

We See Farther.

Who We Are.
We are an association of electronic artists united by a common goal:

We seek to fulfill the enormous promise of personal computers.

Already the personal computer has proved itself beyond question as a facilitator of unimaginative tasks. The beginning of its applications for entertainment and personal development are to be seen all around us.

What is not to be seen is the extra dimension of quality and imagination that will make the difference between a mere device and an extension of human potential.

We, as a company and as individuals, mean to bring that dimension of quality and imagination to personal computer software. And by doing this, we mean to make the personal computer all it can be.

As a turbocharger for the imagination. And as the mind's first true creation in its own image.

Where We Are Going.
As we approach the end of the decade we will witness dramatic changes in the way people see themselves and the world around them.

The software arts will be a principal agent of this change.

Because software is interactive in nature, it has the power to bring minds closer together than any other expressive medium ever has.

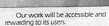

Our work will be accessible and rewarding to its users.

The work we publish will be work that appeals to the imagination as opposed to instincts for gratuitous destruction. They will be programs that encourage exploration, discovery, curiosity and creativity. They will entertain and educate at the same time, and help to eliminate the artificial and misleading distinctions between "games" and "educational" programming.

Above all, we will work with an overriding concern for quality, integrity, and the unimpeded progress of imagination.

Not only will we adhere to these values in our own work, but we will also support the efforts of others working towards the same ends.

And while our initial efforts may be seen merely as "better games" and "more imaginative education programs," they will finally be more than this.

The company we are and the products we will disseminate will create their own values and meanings, free from

the restraints and compromises of existing categories and previous forms.

In this way we have the opportunity to contribute work of new and additional value to people all over the world. Work that learns from the past rather than borrowing from it. And therefore, work of greater benefit for the future.

How We Work.
Most businesses today are founded on the idea of making the greatest possible profit in the least possible time.

We are not.

We are founded on the idea of accomplishing great things. And in the belief that it is possible to have a certain amount of fun in this process.

To do this, we will create a special environment for talented independent software artists. A supportive environment in which big ideas are encouraged and given room to grow. A caring environment in which basic human values like mutual respect and honesty are combined with a dedication to quality and professionalism.

We see creating such a company as its own reward.

We see profit as the material adjunct that will follow our accomplishments.

It is, we realize, a non-traditional way of starting a business. But as this is a non-traditional business itself, we believe our approach to be the right one.

And while we are few in number today and apart from the mainstream of the mass software marketplace, we believe we have both time and vision on our side.

We invite you to join us.

ElectronicArts

CAN A COMPUTER MAKE YOU CRY?

"Can a Computer Make You Cry?" was the first EA poster/ad generally distributed. It appeared in several magazines in 1982, including Scientific American. For the first time, the actual developers of games were featured. Included in the picture are Mike Abbot and Mark Alexander (far left front and back rows), who created Hard Hat Mack, EA's first platform hit; Dan Bunten (back row, second from left), who created M.U.L.E. for EA; Jon Freeman and Anne Westfall (third and fourth from left, back row), creators of Archon and co-creators of Murder on the Zinderneuf; Bill Budge (far right, back row), creator of Pinball Construction Set; John Field (second from left in front), who created Axis Assassin and The Last Gladiator; David Maynard (front right), who created WORMS.

WE SEE FARTHER

ELECTRONIC ARTS

An early EA group shot, including a very young Paul Reiche III, who helped design both Archon and Murder on the Zinderneuf.

Year by year, the company continued to grow, as evidenced by this later photo. Among the recognizable faces in the crowd is Chris Crawford, who worked with EA at one point in his long career.

The next important promotional poster was the famous "We See Farther" poster and ad. Using the same photo as the "Cry" ad, this poster further illustrated EA's philosophy of featuring the artists while publicly stating the company's manifesto.

Pinball
Construction
Set

A video construction set™ from BudgeCo

Rare BudgeCo poster for
Pinball Construction Set.

Bill Budge

Games with built-in scenario design software have become a staple in today's game market. Thanks to an independent programmer, EA became one of the first companies to market a game that let you "roll your own" games.

Bill Budge began programming in high school. He worked at Apple Computer for a short time, where he first met Trip Hawkins, programming for the Apple II and somewhat for the Lisa project. At Apple, he created Raster Blaster, a pinball simulation with realistic physics and a do-it-yourself game product that featured raster graphics (though it did require some programming), which was sold by California Pacific. In 1981, he started BudgeCo to market Raster Blaster.

While at Apple, he spent time around the early Macintosh developers, and it was the Mac's graphical interface that inspired a couple of his products. One was a Mac-like toolbox and product called Mousepaint for the Apple II, and the other was the Pinball Construction Set, which he first released through BudgeCo. Pinball Construction Set was one of the first game products that set the player's own creativity loose, and after Trip Hawkins approached Budge with a good offer, it became one of the flagship products for Electronic Arts' debut.

> *For me, the ultimate video game has always been playing with computers to create the ultimate video game.*
>
> —BILL BUDGE

Bill Budge at work in the 80s.

Screenshot of the Apple II version of Pinball Construction Set.

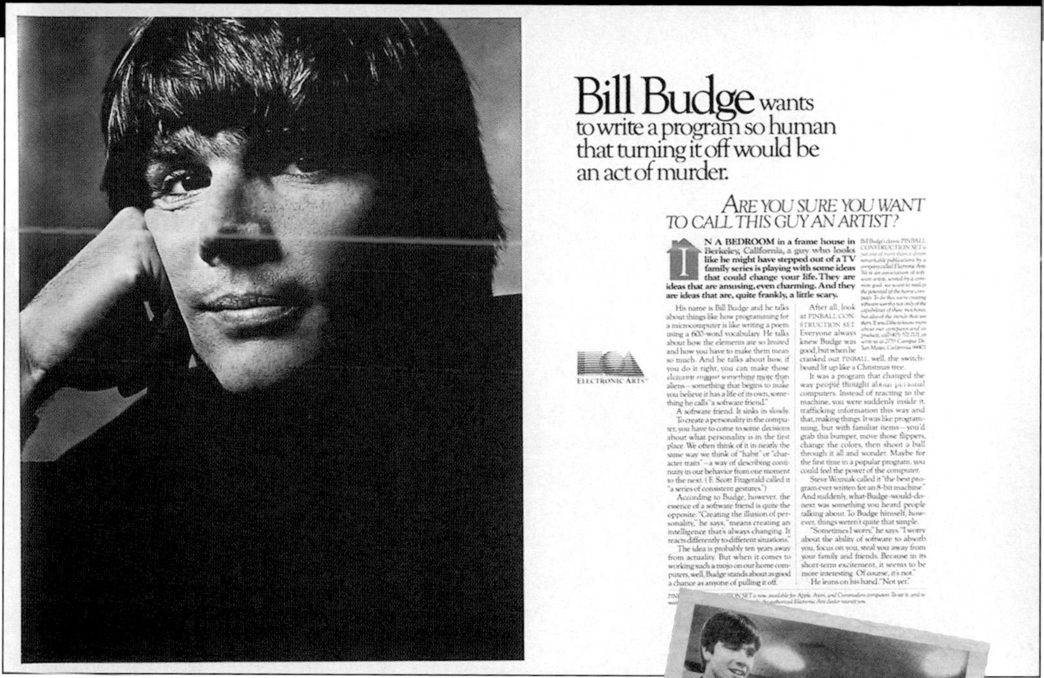

Bill Budge wants to write a program so human that turning it off would be an act of murder.

ARE YOU SURE YOU WANT TO CALL THIS GUY AN ARTIST?

IN A BEDROOM in a frame house in Berkeley, California, a guy who looks like he might have stepped out of a TV family series is playing with some ideas that could change your life. They are ideas that are amusing, even charming. And they are ideas that are, quite frankly, a little scary.

His name is Bill Budge and he talks about things like how programming for a microcomputer is like writing a poem using a 600-word vocabulary. He talks about how the elements are so limited and how you have to make them mean so much. And he talks about how, if you do it right, you can make those elements suggest something more than aliens—something that begins to make you believe it has a life of its own, something he calls "a software friend."

A software friend. It sinks in slowly.

To create a personality in the computer, you have to come to some decisions about what personality is in the first place. We often think of it in nearly the same way we think of "habit" or "character traits"—a way of describing continuity in our behavior from one moment to the next. (F. Scott Fitzgerald called it "a series of consistent gestures.")

According to Budge, however, the essence of a software friend is quite the opposite. "Creating the illusion of personality," he says, "means creating an intelligence that's always changing. It reacts differently to different situations."

The idea is probably ten years away from actuality. But when it comes to working such a mojo on our home computers, well, Budge stands about as good a chance as anyone of pulling it off.

After all, look at PINBALL CONSTRUCTION SET. Everyone always knew Budge was good, but when he cranked out PINBALL, well, the switchboard lit up like a Christmas tree.

It was a program that changed the way people thought about personal computers. Instead of reacting to the machine, you were suddenly inside it, trafficking information this way and that, making things. It was like programming, but with familiar items—you'd grab this bumper, move those flippers, change the colors, then shoot a ball through it all and wonder. Maybe for the first time in a popular program, you could feel the power of the computer.

Steve Wozniak called it "the best program ever written for an 8-bit machine." And suddenly, what-Budge-would-do-next was something you heard people talking about. To Budge himself, however, things weren't quite that simple.

"Sometimes I worry," he says. "I worry about the ability of software to absorb you, focus on you, steal you away from your family and friends. Because in its short-term excitement, it seems to be more interesting. Of course, it's not."

He leans on his hand. "Not yet."

ELECTRONIC ARTS

Budge's notoriety grew quickly, and EA even made a "poster child" of him.

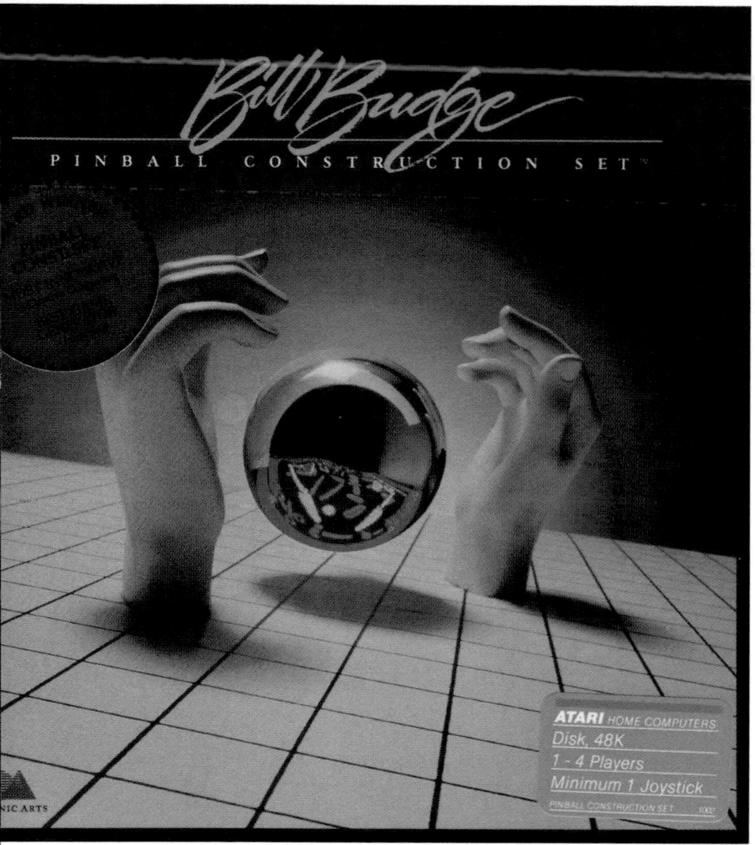

> ***"Electronic Arts sent me on an 'Artists Tour' to promote their games, like a book author or a rock star. I showed up at one department store in Boston wearing blue jeans, a T-shirt, and sneakers. The manager was expecting me to work behind the counter selling games, so I had to buy a whole new outfit in the men's department. That was when I realized that game programmers weren't rock stars."***
>
> —BILL BUDGE, GAME DEVELOPER

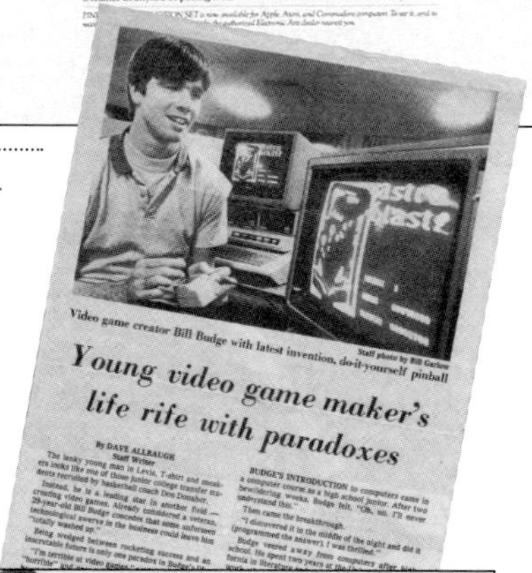

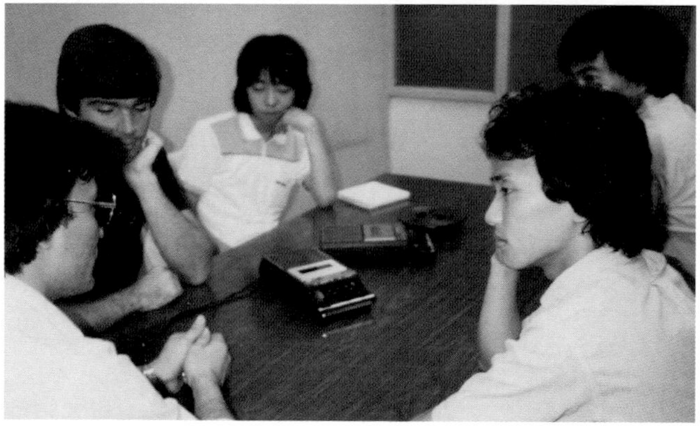

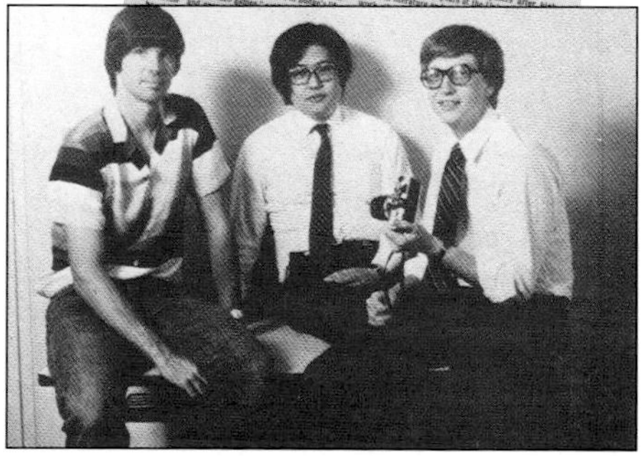

In an ambassadorial trip to Japan in 1981, Budge and Brøderbund's Gary Carlston met with Japanese programmers, including Tony Suzuki (Alien Rain and Galaxian) and Jun Wada (AE). Budge also ran into a very young Bill Gates.

Jon Freeman & Anne Westfall

Jon Freeman and Anne Westfall were among the original software "artists" who helped launch Electronic Arts. However, they were already veterans of the young industry, having created several games for Automated Simulations and on their own.

"One day we got a call from Trip Hawkins—the day that EA was incorporated," Freeman recalls. "It truly came out of the blue. He contacted us based on a classified ad that we'd placed, basically as a favor to a magazine, in its new classified section. It was a pretty big surprise because our copy of the magazine was missing the classified page. We didn't know it was there. When Trip called and said he'd seen that ad, we were pretty skeptical. We thought it was some sort of weird scam.

"We agreed to meet Trip, however, and were impressed that he was the first person we had ever encountered who offered an advance against royalties," Freeman continued. "Although the cash involved was incredibly meager by current standards, it

was far more than anyone else had ever offered. At that point, advances were not commonplace. His notion that the developers make games and the company handle the publishing sounded very good. We had left Automated because we wanted to concentrate on developing games, not running companies and dealing with politics. Of course we had no idea if EA was going to succeed, or what it would become.

"Ultimately, our talks settled on our two strongest ideas—Archon and Murder on the Zinderneuf, and we said, 'Pick one,' and Trip said, 'Why don't we do both?' It was exciting and somewhat scary at the same time.

"I had met Paul Reiche at a trade show, and, with two games to do in six months, we asked him to join us along with our friend, Robert Leyland. Robert did the programming on Zinderneuf, and Anne programmed Archon. Paul and I worked on design for both products."

ARCHON
BY ANNE WESTFALL AND JON FREEMAN & PAUL REICHE III

THE LIGHT AND THE DARK

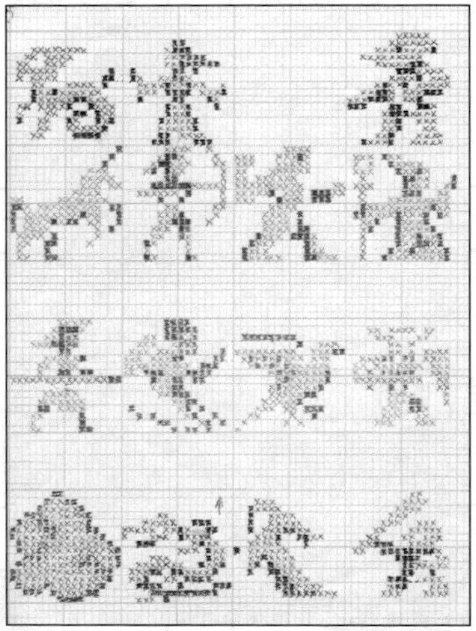

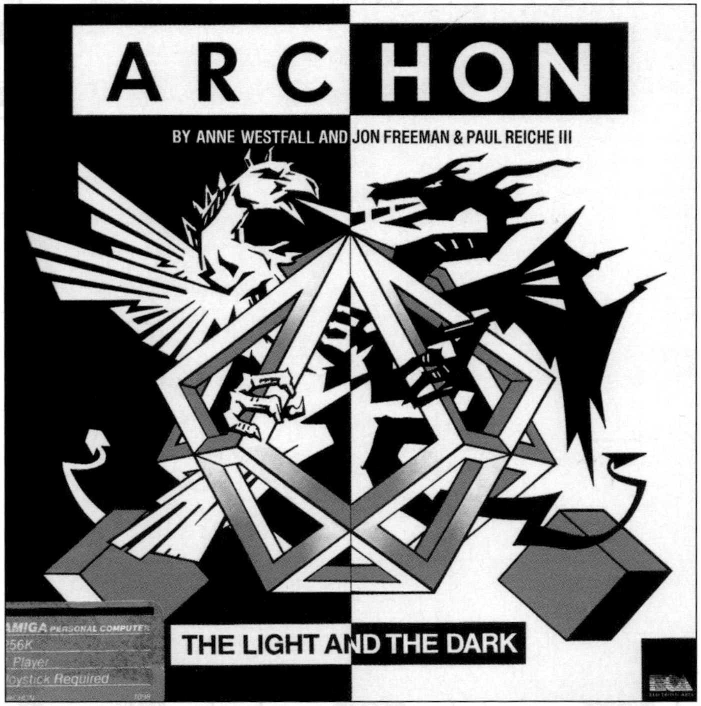

Archon was simply an amazing game; in my opinion the quintessential computer board game. It had great rules and strategies, like chess, with the addition of arcade-style battles that made it a true computer game. The shifting balance of light and dark was brilliant. One of my all-time favorites.

(RDM)

Archon featured both board play on an ever-changing board and real-time battles in a separate arcade battlefield.

George Barr is a noted science fiction and fantasy artist who worked on several game projects with both Jon Freeman and Paul Reiche. Here is an original drawing depicting the two possible winning screens in Archon Ultra.

MURDER ON THE ZINDERNEUF.

BY ROBERT LEYLAND AND PAUL REICHE III & JON FREEMAN

Murder on the Zinderneuf was a murder mystery set on a dirigible. You were given a choice of detectives you could play; each of them had various styles of questioning suspects.

The detective (you) on the Zinderneuf had to question suspects and locate clues to solve the murder mystery.

MURDER ON THE ZINDERNEUF

ORIGINAL PROGRAM BY ROBERT LEYLAND
DESIGN BY PAUL REICHE / JON FREEMAN

ELECTRONIC ARTS

FREE FALL

(C) 1983, 1984 FREE FALL ASSOCIATES & ELECTRONIC ARTS

Dani Bunten Berry

She started life as Dan Bunten and was one of the young visionaries at the genesis of computer gaming. The first and most ardent proponent of social and online gaming, Dani Bunten Berry died in 1998 leaving a legacy of games, articles, personal courage, great friends, and an esteemed position in the history of electronic games. When he made the transition from SSI to EA, Bunten created game history—with a game that was just "too weird" to sell.

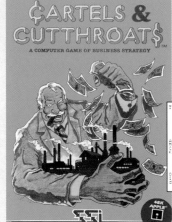

1981: Cartels & Cutthroats was Bunten's second Apple II title for SSI. This economic simulation game was designed for up to six simultaneous players. Trip Hawkins tried to obtain the rights to it from SSI, and when they refused, Bunten offered to produce another game for the newly forming Electronic Arts.

Screens from Cartels & Cutthroats on the Apple II.

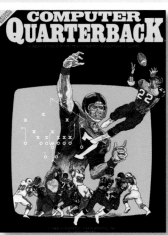

1978: Wheeler Dealers, a multiplayer stock market simulation game for the Apple II, came in a cardboard box, not a Ziploc bag, and sold for an astounding $35. It included special buttons used to play the game. A truly innovative product of which only 50 were sold.

1979: Bunten created Computer Quarterback for SSI. Originally a two-person game only, a single-player mode was added at the last minute at SSI's insistence.

1982: Cytron Masters was Bunten's last game for SSI. It featured strategy and real-time action and pushed the Apple II hardware to its limit.

M. U. L. E.™

A game in which up to four players attempt to settle a distant planet with the so-called help of a mule-like machine they all learn to hate.

DAN BUNTEN
BILL BUNTEN
JIM RUSHING
ALAN WATSON

ELECTRONIC ARTS

M.U.L.E.™
by *Ozark Softscape*
"A must-have."
— *Electronic Fun*
"May well become the Monopoly of computer games."
— *Personal Software*
"Graphics, sound and humor are superlative."
— *Creative Computing*
"Recommendation? Buy it."
— *Softline*
BEST MULTI-PLAYER GAME OF THE YEAR
—*Electronic Games*

C64, At

1983. Based loosely on ideas from Robert Heinlein's *Time Enough for Love*, M.U.L.E. was, and is, one of the classic games of all time. This was the first game credited to Bunten's company, Ozark Softscape. Brian Moriarty, a longtime friend and colleague of Bunten's, described it as an "unprecedented example of computer-moderated parlor gaming. By combining the resource management of Cartels & Cutthroats, the auctioneering of Wheeler Dealers, and the futuristic setting of Cytron Masters, M.U.L.E. sustained an exquisite play balance of teamwork and rivalry, bitter cooperation, and delicious treachery." Though it initially sold only 30,000 copies, it has inspired many game developers as well as ongoing Web sites devoted to it.

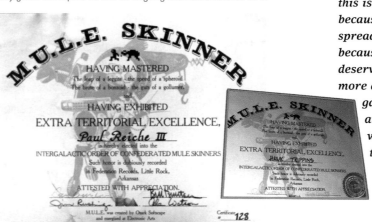

Many people (including one "Hawk Trippins") prized their M.U.L.E. Skinner certificates and still have them today.

Login was a major Japanese game magazine, and they named our game, M.U.L.E., the best game of 1983. Of all the myriad awards I have received over the years, this is one of my favorites because our notoriety had spread to Japan and also because M.U.L.E. richly deserved it. M.U.L.E. won more awards than any game in EA history and yet did not sell well because it was too weird.

—*TRIP HAWKINS*

The SEVEN CITIES of GOLD

OZARK SOFTSCAPE PRESENTS
A GRAPHIC ADVENTURE INTO THE...
HEART OF AFRICA

ROBOT RASCALS

IBM XT, PC, AT,
TANDY 1000, Compaq
256K 2-4 players
IBM Color Graphics Adapter req'd
ROBOT RASCALS $305

by Ozark Softscape   ELECTRONIC ARTS™

1984: The Seven Cities of Gold was Bunten's first real commercial hit, selling 150,000 copies and winning several awards. Following his own traditions, he created a game that featured real-time action, strategy, and exploration with a historical context and even some educational value. The one irony was that it was his first single-player-only title.

1985: The next game Ozark wanted to produce was based on an Avalon Hill board game, but the execs at EA applied some leverage and convinced them to produce a sequel to The Seven Cities of Gold. Heart of Africa was not, however, nearly as successful as its predecessor. Ironically, some years later, Sid Meier did tackle that Avalon Hill game. It was called Civilization.

1986: Heart of Africa was the last game Ozark produced for a single player. With Robot Rascals they went in the opposite direction and required the participation of four players. Featuring a deck of real playing cards, this game was a turn-based action and strategy game. Billed as a "family game," it was mostly ignored by the buying public.

/ "Hi, we're from Europe. Where's the gold?" /
A SECOND CHANCE to GET
the NEW WORLD RIGHT.

SEVEN CITIES of GOLD
from ELECTRONIC ARTS™

Dan Bunten and Trip Hawkins

JOEL BILLINGS ON THE EARLY DAYS

In hindsight, Dan Bunten was critical to SSI's development. He was the first nonemployee to submit to and publish a game with SSI, and his game was the first non-war game published by SSI. Up until then I assumed we would create all our games in-house. In early 1980, just after Computer Bismarck was published, Dan contacted me and submitted his beta version of Computer Quarterback. We published it in September 1980, and it was the office favorite for at least a year. We organized a league that included employees at SSI and others working at other companies involved in the production and printing of the game. It was clearly the most fun two-player game we made in the early years, and arguably in the history of SSI.

Dan was very low-key, funny, and easy and enjoyable to work with. After publishing three games with SSI, Dan let me know that he and Trip Hawkins had spoken about the possibility of his doing his next game with EA. (This was when EA was just forming.) He was very interested in having his games make it big by going with EA, but at the same time expressed worry that EA might not survive. No one knew whether the market could support the money EA was going to put behind its products.

Trip offered to give SSI stock in EA to buy out our option on Dan's future work. In what turned out to be a financial mistake, I didn't jump at the chance to get EA stock. Trip ended up offering Dan a contract we

couldn't match, and Dan decided to take a chance with EA. M.U.L.E. was the result. Despite the awkwardness of Dan's move from SSI to EA, you couldn't help but root for this tall (at least that's how I remember him), smiling guy who wanted to make games people could enjoy together. In that way he was unique among all the computer game designers I've met.

I probably hadn't seen Dan for ten years when I bumped into him at an E3 in L.A. in 1995 or 1996. Although his sex had changed, she was the same tall, happy, smiling person I had known ten years before. I will always remember her fondly as a great game designer and uniquely warm personality in the computer gaming business.

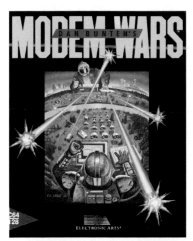

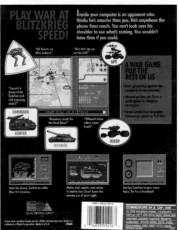

1988: Constantly innovating and pushing the envelope, Bunten's last game for EA was Modem Wars, the first game from a major publisher to feature modem-to-modem play. Many of the synchronization and latency challenges faced later by online game developers were first solved in this game.

1990: Command H.Q. was released by Microprose and, like Modem Wars, featured modem-based war gaming.

Dan Bunten was one of the best at game design. He knew how to organize a game system and draw players into it. He also had a very playful sense of humor that he would work into his designs along with a great intuition about what would be fun. In addition, his sensitivity and kindness made it very rewarding to work with him.

One of my favorite memories of him was that whenever I saw him he would give me a free chiropractic adjustment. His father had been a chiropractor. So he'd have me fold my arms and then he'd stand behind me and lift me off my feet by my elbows, and my back would go, 'pop.' Man, I could use one of those adjustments right now!

—TRIP HAWKINS

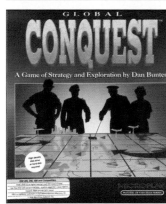

1992: Global Conquest featured four-player online war gaming and, according to Brian Moriarty, its absorbing mix of real-time action and resource development was the design prototype for an entire generation of combat simulations, including Dune II, Warcraft, and Command and Conquer.

I remember a scene at a Computer Game Developer's Conference in the late 80s or early 90s. I was seated in the lobby of the hotel on couches with Dan Bunten, Will Wright, Richard Garriott, and Sid Meier. I had the morbid thought that if someone tossed a grenade into this gathering, computer game development would be instantly destroyed. Fortunately, no such thing happened, and I was in game fan heaven. (RDM)

Dan Bunten with Brian Moriarty, Chris Crawford, Steve Peterson, Eric Goldberg, and Robert Gehorsham at an early Computer Game Developer's conference.

EA Sports

BY ERIC HAMMOND, LARRY BIRD & JULIUS ERVING

I t is little known, because he didn't publicize it much at the time, but the earliest games in what has become the immensely popular EA Sports line were principally designed by Trip Hawkins, EA's founder. He personally recruited celebrity figures such as Larry Bird, Dr. J, Earl Weaver, and John Madden, and he worked directly with them to formulate some of the greatest and most influential sports games of computer gaming history. Hawkins spent extensive amounts of time with his experts. For instance, he tells us, "the first design session I had with Madden took place over a 3-day period on a train winding its way across the USA."

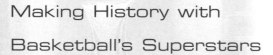

Making History with

Basketball's Superstars

1983's One on One was the first true licensed sports computer game, and, as such, it marks the beginning of an era. Moreover, it was a great game to play. Despite its very crude graphics, the game was painstakingly crafted to simulate one-on-one basketball play between two of the living legends of the game, Julius Erving and Larry Bird. Erving met with Trip Hawkins and Eric Hammond of Electronic Arts and shared his insights into the game with them, helping bring more realism to the player's experience.

The following quotes from Julius Erving came from a design session with Hawkins and Hammond.

> *Things will break for you if you have patience. That's very high on the list.*
>
> —*JULIUS ERVING*

Publicity photo of Michael Jordan looking at the Commodore 64 version of Jordan vs. Bird: One on One.

PHOTO COURTESY OF COMPUTER GAMING WORLD.

The capability to make a shot is, I think, directly attributed to having the right to miss it. If I can go to the foul line, and I have the right to miss the shot, I will make it more often than if I didn't have the right to miss it. If you have made five or six baskets in a row, you have the right to miss it anywhere on the court. So you are going to go out there and you are going to take that shot.

—*JULIUS ERVING*

ONE·ON·ONE WITH GODZILLA

Asked who would win the most in ten games between him and Larry Bird, Erving replied, "I could play ten games against Godzilla and I'd feel that I'd win most of them."

Jordan vs. Bird: One on One

It was natural to follow a great one-on-one game with an even greater one. With Michael Jordan's rise to prominence in the NBA, Electronic Arts made the logical choice for a sequel to their first One-on-One product and paired Jordan and Bird in this 1988 release. This game, like its predecessor, was great fun to play, whether you liked to stand back and pop 3-pointers with Bird or drive to the hoop and perform 360 jams with Jordan. The players' images improved noticeably, as well, and were based on actual images of players in action.

ISBN 1-55543-244-1

EA IRC
01816

COMMODORE 64 & 128*
64K; *in C64 emulation mode
1541 or 1571 disk drive re
Joystick required
1-4 players
JORDAN VS BIRD

Earl Weaver Baseball

Baseball has often been described as something of a ballet, where athletes stretch, pirouette, and jump with amazing and graceful agility. So, it should be no wonder that one of the finest computer baseball game ever made had its inception in ballet. A young programmer named Eddie Dombrower was fascinated by ballet and created the world's first computerized dance notation program. With

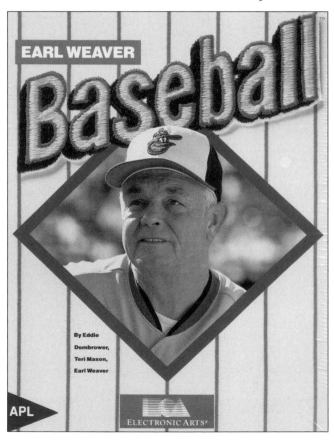

EARL WEAVER
Baseball

By Eddie
Dombrower,
Teri Mason,
Earl Weaver

APL

ELECTRONIC ARTS®

Earl Weaver Baseball, Dombrower was able to combine the programming of intricate body movements with his love of baseball. He had already created World Series Baseball for Mattel's short-lived Intellivision console system. Now, he was ready to program the game where the ball reacted according to a physics model and the on-screen athletes moved like they should.

The grand slam came when Earl Weaver, the Hall of Fame manager for the Baltimore Orioles, agreed to consult on the game. With Weaver's help, Dombrower was able to get it all right: movement, physics, and strategy. The lineups followed Weaver's philosophy, the default positioning of

fielders was based on Weaver's handling of similar game situations, and there was even an interactive database where players could "Ask Earl" what he would do in a given game situation (based on Weaver's book, *Earl Weaver on Strategy*).

The physics model for Earl Weaver Baseball was state of the art, and although later games would improve on the physics model, EWB was the first of its kind. In fact, Don Daglow, the producer of EWB, would eventually direct his own Stormfront Studios to produce Tony La Russa Baseball II with temperature and humidity factors, height of grass, and slant of the basepaths for every major stadium. Yet, Earl

Weaver Baseball was the first game to truly cross-reference the statistical matrix of random numbers and existing statistics with formulas that considered wind, outfield wall distance and height, fielder's speed, runner's speed, and ball velocity. Unlike the pure statistics-based sports games and the pure reflex-based arcade games that were published prior to EWB, players suddenly had to consider the configuration of the stadium and the simulated weather when they were planning lineups and strategy.

John Madden Football

EA's first football game was called Touchdown Football and came out in the early 80s. However, the game that was to burst on the scene, set the new standard, and become the best-selling series in EA's history was ignited by the irrepressible John Madden. It isn't well known that Trip Hawkins worked directly with Madden to develop the game. What more can we say? A true classic, and a great series. The first to bring playbooks and realistic detail to electronic football games.

Original John Madden play diagram, framed and hanging on Trip's wall.

JOHN MADDEN FOOTBALL™

IBM

ELECTRONIC ARTS®   Robin Antonick and John Madden

More Electronic Arts Games

After its dramatic debut in 1983, Electronic Arts quickly became one of the most important computer game companies in the world. With only six products in May 1983, they exploded a year later with 42 products.

EA Games of the 80s

Chuck Yeager's Advanced Flight Trainer

Two things made the 1987 product Chuck Yeager's Advanced Flight Trainer notable. The first was that it was really what it said it was— a flight trainer. For those of us who were one jet shy of liftoff, AFT was aerial boot camp but much more fun. The second thing that distinguished the product was Chuck Yeager himself, although the product was well under way before EA struck a deal with General Yeager. The wry humor of Yeager's comments when you nose-dived into the turf—"That's no way to treat a plane," for one— somehow made all the difference. As they had done with many of their sports titles, EA arranged for their designer, Edward "Ned" Lerner, to meet with General Yeager to glean some of his particular wisdom. "It was something of a culture clash," remembers Lerner. "The design team were all of 25, and he was over 60 at the time. I remember him touching the joystick somewhat disdainfully and saying, 'I do the real thing.' But he was a good sport about it."

Budokan: The Martial Spirit

Budokan was a wonderful martial arts game that came out in 1989. Michael Kosaka, an artist working at Electronic Arts, designed the game to be a "serious" martial arts game. Kosaka was studying the Japanese martial art Aikido at the time and wanted to do something that captured the spirit of real martial arts training. "I remember that the concept was sold accompanied by one of my really crude hand drawings of two guys in Kendo uniforms hitting each other in a dojo. No full-color storyboards and dialogue scripts, no elaborate preproduction with models and overhead slides. It was seat-of-the-pants, get-outta-the-way development back then."

Using martial arts books for reference, Kosaka and several other artists worked with EA's proprietary animation tools to draw each frame of the animation by hand. The result was well worth it, because Budokan had exceptionally smooth animation for its time. Attempts to videotape EA employees falling on wrestling mats "ended up being more for staff comic relief than actual animation reference," adds Kosaka.

The name Budokan was taken from a yearly martial arts festival in Japan, but Kosaka later found out that it is actually just the name of a big auditorium. "It would be like calling a game 'San Francisco Cow Palace.' But to us, it sounded cool and exotic, and we also remembered the rock album *Cheap Trick: Live at the Budokan*."

CHUCK YEAGER'S Advanced Flight Trainer
COMMODORE 64 & 128*
C64 emulation mode
1541 or 1571 disk drive
joystick recommended
ELECTRONIC ARTS®
By NED LERNER

Starflight

Starflight was EA's first role-playing game on the IBM PC, although it started out on the Atari 800 and then the Commodore 64. The decision to make the game on the IBM PC was, at the time, a radical thought. According to designer Greg Johnson, "People were saying that the PC was not a machine anyone wanted to play games on." In 1986, after three years of effort, the game was released. "When we were building Starflight we were just about as naive as they come," says Johnson. "Electronic Arts was still very new and had only about 30 employees. For all of us on the team it was our first game; most of us were straight out of college. We really didn't have a clue about how to build a game like that."

What Johnson calls "a game like that" was an ambitious and complex effort, especially for its time. Starflight allowed the exploration of a vast galaxy that was never the same twice because each planet was generated as fractal graphics on the fly. In some ways, it was like Star Control, which came out years later.* There were ships, random planets to explore, aliens to encounter, and the opportunity to build up wealth by mining and colonizing the planets. It was also a lot of fun to play.

Starflight was the first PC game to go platinum (sell more than 250,000 units). Johnson remembers, "The game was almost canceled any number of times. I think most of our success was due to the amazing focus of our lead programmer Tim Lee. Several of us had a hard time surviving through those three years, and there were countless disappointments. It was all driven by the idealistic dream of walking into a store and seeing your game on the shelf, all the time only half believing that was really possible. In retrospect it was one of those life-defining experiences you're grateful for but would never want to have to live through again."

Greg Johnson went on to help design Starflight 2 and made some contributions to Star Control (see page 112). After working with so many aliens, it's not too surprising that he eventually created two of the wackiest aliens ever—ToeJam and Earl (see page 249).

Sentinel Worlds I: Future Magic

Karl Buiter had published a detailed space exploration game on the Apple II called EOS, or Earth Orbit Station. It required tons of disk switching and had an interface that seemed complicated enough to require NASA training. The good news was that he learned enough from the experience to put together a tremendous effort called Sentinel Worlds I: Future Magic.

Like Starflight before it, Sentinel Worlds I: Future Magic required you to build and train a crew before you could launch. Unlike Starflight, you weren't likely to lose the chance to get the ultimate win from botching one encounter. Gamers who preferred puzzles and resource management gravitated toward Starflight.

Indianapolis 500: The Simulation

Indianapolis 500: The Simulation, from Papyrus, was just what it claimed. It modeled racecar performance, featured working rearview mirrors, variable race lengths, and a lot of additional detail. Prior to 1989, racing games were about as realistic as the Autopia at Disneyland. Design teams might get the top speeds right and the exterior design right, but little attention was paid to physics, the effects of damage, wind effects, oversteering, gear ratios, and fuel limits, among 1,001 other details. In fact, you drove on such a rail in earlier games that you didn't even see your car spin out, much less turn around the wrong way. Indy 500 was the first racing game that allowed you to spin the car completely around and travel the wrong way on the track. Hardly good racing, but it made for exciting game play. Indy 500 established the baseline for what other racing games would become.

---

*Johnson and partner Mark Voorsanger regularly shared ideas with Paul Reiche and his group. "Paul Reiche was really the mastermind behind the communications system in Starflight," says Johnson. "And I made some contributions to Star Control. We often helped each other out."

Westwood

Louis Castle

Brett Sperry

1985 saw the humble beginnings of a company that would ultimately change the face of computer gaming. Their first project, a C64 port of the Temple of Apshai series, netted them all of $16,000, just enough to cover expenses.

Louis Castle, who cofounded Westwood with Brett Sperry, gave us some background on Westwood's history; for instance, how they very nearly created the first real-time action RPG: "We literally rewrote the entire product, graphics and programming... We made it a real-time, top-down dungeon crawl—like a very primitive version of Diablo or Gauntlet. But that's not what Epyx was expecting, and they said, 'No you can't do that. It needs to be turn-based.'"

Even though the Apshai port was released as a turn-based game, the lure of real-time action remained. The young company continued to port games and worked on several titles for Epyx, including World Games and Super Cycle, ultimately getting the chance to create games of their own design.

Westwood's first original game was Mars Saga for Electronic Arts. "We lacked the experience to finish a totally original product. Mars Saga turned out OK, but it could have been great. It had great fundamentals but lacked a strong story element and presentation. It needed more characters and events to pin it together."

Their first big product was Eye of the Beholder, which was published by SSI. "We wanted to do a D&D game, but SSI was pretty tight with the license, so we did a couple of other games for them—Questron and Hillfar, which was sort of a D&D puzzle game." Inspired by FTL's Dungeon Master, which came out in 1989, Eye of the Beholder was a real-time dungeon crawl set in the D&D system and was a big hit in 1990.

Westwood was sold to Virgin in 1992, which gave them an infusion of cash. Virgin then released Westwood's first true adventure game, Fables & Fiends: The Legend of Kyrandia Book One.

At the time, Westwood was working on another real-time game based around medieval knights and sorcery. Concerned about the game's potential appeal, they began to consider changing it to something more contemporary—"think tanks and money as a resource, oil wells and other stuff like that," Castle recalls. "We were fascinated by Rescue Raiders (Choplifter with units) and Military Madness. And Brett was a huge Dune fan. When Virgin said they had the Dune license, it all fell into place. Brett realized that spice was the perfect common resource for both sides to fight over."

The original name for the game was Dune, but Virgin had a Dune

DUNE·II

The Building of A Dynasty

Westwood
STUDIOS

Distributed exclusively by GAMES

adventure game project under way. Known as Dune II, the resulting game became the model for the real-time strategy (RTS) genre. "We knew it had to be a multilayered game with building and protecting buildings and units, not a game of wanton destruction." In many ways, Dune II was the culmination of the work that had begun with that original Apshai port. Real-time games soon exploded, with Blizzard's Warcraft and Westwood's Command & Conquer series playing leading roles. Ironically, it all started with a swords and sorcery game that took a few unexpected turns and became a science fiction classic.

Westwood has gone through many identities. They were originally known for porting existing products, but have been variously known for sports, RPGs, adventures, and real-time strategy games. This is only a small look at their origins and early landmark products. As a part of Electronic Arts now, they have continued to make great games throughout the 90s and beyond.

In late 1990, SSI teamed with Westwood again for their first true 3D product in their AD&D line. They had a fresh face in DragonStrike, but not a commercial success. DragonStrike was a 3D flight simulator in which players would fly astride fighting dragons in a mission-based campaign setting. DragonStrike was designed for both the PC and the Amiga, though much of the low-level copper and blitter code had to be rewritten in order to get a decent frame rate on the Amiga. To show how much technology has changed, the entire 3D code library for DS fit in 10 kilobytes of memory, and the routines could generate around 1.5 megabytes of map data. The data had to be compressed and generated with each frame because the program had to reuse the memory and didn't have enough buffer to keep even the visual part of the map in the buffer.

FABLES&FIENDS
THE LEGEND OF
Kyrandia
BOOK ONE

KING'S QUEST® games
and Sierra On-Line, Inc.

I bet I can catch
a teardrop!

"Companies that skyrocket up are on a path to explode. Lots of young companies make one hit, and if you let that get to your head, it can really destroy you. You can be a victim of success as easily as a victim of failure."

—LOUIS CASTLE

185

MicroProse

Sid Meier at an early game show.
Right: Bill Stealey with his plane,
Miss Microprose, and two passengers,
Russell Sipe and coauthor Johnny Wilson.

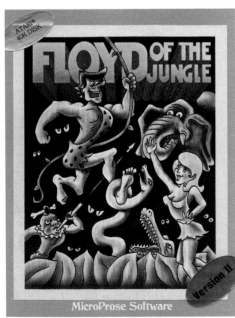

nother of the most influential computer game companies of the 80s, MicroProse began after a challenge playing a coin-op arcade game. The scene was an arcade at the old MGM Grand Hotel (now Bally's) in Las Vegas. Both J. W. "Wild Bill" Stealey and Sid Meier were working for a Baltimore-based defense contractor, and were attending a meeting for the company at that hotel. They met over an Atari coin-op game called Red Baron (not the Dynamix/ Sierra game for the PC), where "Wild Bill" was challenging all comers.

Red Baron used wire-framed graphics to depict World War I aircraft. Most of the units had a console cabinet with a seat that allowed you to sit in a cockpit and shoot down enemy planes with your unlimited supply of ammunition. Sid Meier watched Stealey racking up victories and finally decided to take the challenge. When Meier blitzed past all of the experienced pilot's high scores, Stealey couldn't believe it. He asked Meier about his flight experience and was chagrined to discover that he was merely a computer systems analyst and had beaten the high scores by analyzing the simple moves used by the artificial pilots in the game and predicting those moves in advance.

Since Stealey had already done some bragging, Meier countered with a bold assertion of his own. Meier claimed that he could design a better game in one week on his home computer than the Red Baron

game that was raking in quarters in front of them. Stealey didn't want to be outdone, so he assured Meier, "If you can write the games, I'll sell 'em."

It took longer than a week. In a tradition that goes back to the earliest days of programming, Meier's schedule slipped and it took a whole two months to finish the game. As promised, Stealey took Hellcat Ace on the road and immediately sold 50 copies on his first sales call. As a result, it seemed like money in the bank to form a company. According to Stealey, "MicroProse started on a bet between us. We decided to sell just enough software to pay off our cars. Then, in the first year, with me carrying all of MicroProse in a satchel, we did $200,000 on the back of Hellcat Ace."

The original idea was to call the new company "Smugger's Software," based on the acronym S.M.U.G., which stood for Sid Meier's User Group. Fortunately, they opted for a more assonant double pun. MicroProse was supposed to stand for the microprofessionals who designed and programmed the games. It also represented the idea that their code was prose in the sense of being an art form, like literature. Even so, the small company started out as a homespun operation, with products distributed in plastic bags and manuals produced on a dot-matrix printer.

The company's first products were Hellcat Ace, Chopper Rescue, and Floyd of the Jungle. Stealey says, "Floyd of the Jungle was my favorite. It was the first game to allow you to hook up four joysticks on the Atari 800. And Chopper Rescue let you play with two players, one pilot and one gunner."

Sid Meier relates that he had many influences through the years. Games like Space Invaders, and even Pong, convinced him that the electronic medium could generate intensity. He also mentions the work of Dani Bunten Berry (née Dan Bunten) (see page 174)—especially The Seven Cities of Gold. "I was blown away by how epic it was. It probably led to Sid Meier's Civilization. Up until that time, I was writing airplane, submarine... smaller games in scope. I saw how you could spread out across the map and didn't have to be constrained by the size of the screen. I did Pirates! right after seeing Seven Cities. Later, Dani told me that in Pirates! we had done all the stuff she had wanted to do with Seven Cities, which turned her loose to concentrate on multiplayer games. She was evangelical about multiplayer."

Sid Meier is legitimately considered one of the greatest game designers in history, and he had a rather unique approach to game design. Instead of plotting everything out in detailed design documents and flowcharts, he would spend late nights coding working prototypes of the game long before the product reached the alpha stage, where game coding usually begins. Meier would bring in new builds almost daily for his coworkers to play, test, and critique. Later, as he added researchers, musicians, artists, and codesigners to his teams, they would shake down the semidaily builds and make suggestions, which, in turn, Meier would turn into improved code. At times, Meier would have perfectly working code and would rip it all out with his typical refrain, "We had it in there, but it wasn't fun, so we took it out." There are very few designers who can code as rapidly as Sid Meier or who have his instinct for fun.

Commentary from Sid Meier

Sid Meier has graciously provided us with commentary on

each of his games over the years, starting with Hellcat Ace. He tells a story not only of his own accomplishments, but of many aspects of the evolution of game design during the 80s and into the 90s.

Hellcat Ace

My first attempt at a combat flight simulator, based on a trick I had worked out that rotated the horizon quickly and moved it up and down. We could only push so many pixels back then, so I used this trick to make it look like you were flying. Today, we laugh at it.

Chopper Rescue

This was a side-scrolling arcade game like Choplifter, but Choplifter had a better swooping effect. It was a game where I was discovering player missile graphics on the Atari—a million things flying around shooting at you, hostages waving on the ground—a full-bore arcade game... dropping bombs and shooting everything... It was not realistic in any sense.

Solo Flight

This was the first game that really broke out nationally. It came when I was learning to show a 3D world. It came out around the same time as SubLogic's (later Microsoft) Flight Simulator, but ours was easier to fly and not quite as detailed. I think we were the first to show a shadow on the ground so you could gauge your altitude. It helped set the tone for us— the combination of realism and fun. My personal aphorism is, "When fun and realism clash, fun wins."

NATO Commander

It was not even fun to play. It was just bad.

F-15 Strike Eagle

F-15 started with our experiments in wire-frame rotations.

MicroProse Software

> *All our early games were written in something we called 'Sidtran.' It was Forth-like, very interactive, and let us change a few lines and start playing again. Sidtran gave us a lot of flexibility. We used it at least through Pirates.*

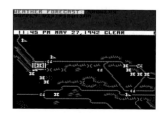

Decision in the Desert was a real-time combat game before they were popular.

Sid Meier's F-15 Strike Eagle raised the ante on flight simulation by adding realistic features and a huge manual.

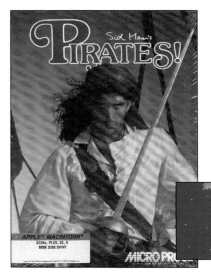

When that became an airplane, it said "dogfight." We found ways to show that on screen with fairly complex ideas for the time—radar, bombsites… ideas direct from the real Air Force. Bill put a lot of his knowledge into it. I think we were the first to have chaff and flares. Also, a bit of a MicroProse trademark, we included a 100-page manual, so you felt like you got some insight about how things were done in the real world. It was something that seemed realistic and was fun to play.

Conflict in Vietnam/Crusade in Europe/Decision in the Desert

These were aberrations—hex-based war games that were part of my growing up, but didn't make the best translations to computers. But these games turned us loose to find a new language for computer games that was not tied to board games. Overall, the fun of the industry is figuring out how to use a new medium, finding a new model.

Silent Service

One of my better games. There was a game called Gato (see page 193) somewhat before us, and I remember playing it and saying, "Hey, this could be a good game." But in my mind it had copped out in some ways and didn't have the mixture of fun and realism that I thought would be fun. So, we basically stole the idea and made a cool World War II submarine game set in the Pacific. The innovation I remember was the map you could zoom into, and keep zooming down even to individual islands. We used a sort of fractal idea that included the whole Pacific. It was a gigantic playground to

Pirates! is one of the finest games ever made, and probably the best example of mixing strategy, role-playing, and action in one game. Anyone who hasn't played Pirates! should try it! (RDM)

play with submarines. This was the first time I had done a significant amount of research on a topic.

For a long time it was just subs with torpedoes, but Stealey said we needed something more exciting. "Can't you get on the surface and shoot it out with guns?" He said it so many times that we finally said OK and put in a deck gun. From that moment on, he was a game designer, and he would just have to say "deck gun" to mean that we needed excitement and cheap thrills. It was a running joke. (In fact, "Wild Bill" relates that he was demonstrating Silent Service to a potentially big client who was skeptical of a submarine game. "There were three ships and I got one of them, and then the other two were chasing me. I got blown to the surface, got one with a torpedo, and shot the last with the deck gun, and they all cheered and ordered 25,000 units. Thank god for the deck gun.")

Pirates!

Pirates! was a reaction to the RPGs, where it was kill this monster, get five exp, kill that monster. I didn't enjoy them. And adventure games, which I called "pick up the stick games." You know. You're in a room with a glass, a stick, a brush. You pick up the stick. They promised excitement, storytelling, and plot that I didn't think they delivered. I said to myself, "I'm going to try to write an adventure role-playing game that is the way I want it, with the focus on excitement, romance, story… and takes you from one high point to the next and doesn't bog you down in killing the same monster again and again. Pirates was a neat topic, and I took a movie fun/excitement approach to it as opposed to a realistic approach. We had no shame putting a lot of "arrghh mateys" in there. It seemed like a nice combination of sword fighting, exploring the big map, meeting with a governor and wooing his daughter, land battles… well, we won't talk about the land battles. But one mistake we didn't make was to make the action parts too involving, like we did later in Covert Action. You don't want the player to get too involved in the action and lose the thread of the story.

Red Storm Rising

We all read the book and thought it was cool, but what I recall about that was meeting Tom Clancy. Before we could do the game we had to have an audience with Tom Clancy. Bill had what I call his "virtual flight suit" on and was totally in Air Force mode. He wanted to convince Tom that we were legit and knew what we were doing. And we did have a good meeting with Clancy. And we were lucky. They gave us plenty of leeway. I worked a lot with Larry Bond (who later did Harpoon), and he was a very heavy-duty simulation kind of guy. We tried to be pretty hard-core with that game. It was a pretty good game, but not one of my favorites—maybe more complex than fun. In the end, I found that I didn't like doing licensed games.

Gunship

That was a fun game and became a test bed for everything I knew about flight games. The one unique thing was learning how a helicopter worked, how different it was from an airplane. It was also the first game where I didn't write all the code. We started to have teams of programmers once we got into 3D. We had a very smart guy, Andy Hollis, who did the 3D programming on Gunship.

Note: Hollis went on to garner fame as the lead designer on Electronic Arts' Jane's series of simulations.

F-19 Stealth Fighter

F-19 was probably our biggest out-the-door success. It was also the first game we wrote for the IBM PC. We had a cool mapping system that I sort of borrowed from Pirates!—a big map, where if you swooped down toward the ground, there

I remember interviewing Tom Clancy during the Winter CES in Las Vegas prior to Red Storm's launch. Tom had just received word during the morning that the Naval Institute Press was claiming that they owned the rights to Clancy's favorite protagonist, Jack Ryan. At one point, Clancy became so agitated at a question I asked that he threw his cigarette forcibly at the ashtray, missed it, and caused ash to fly across the table at me. My colleagues and I laughed at Clancy because of his naivete about software. He said that Red Storm Rising would be the best submarine simulation ever because it was all ones and zeros and, once you had it right, you didn't need to do it again. Even after numerous versions have been done with better graphics, I hate to admit it, but I agree with him. It's still the most entertaining and playable submarine simulation ever. (JLW)

were buildings and roads and the idea of a big world. Of course, we did it by cheating. And also there was the idea of an airplane that half the time would try to avoid fighting. It added a suspense element that was a little bit new. We were riding a wave of militarism and modern hi-tech; the Cold War was still on. There were rumors about the Stealth bomber in the news. It was the right product at the right time. And we had the technology, too... the different views like the missile cam, the bomb cam. We claim to have invented a lot of those camera views, as well as the full-time camera in the corner of the cockpit that showed you the plane you were locked onto. This solved the problem of having planes in the distance be dots on the screen, and you couldn't tell what they were doing. With all the views, we almost felt like movie directors. F-19 was the last flight simulator that I wrote. I felt that it was everything I knew about how to write a flight simulator, and I never felt the need to write another one after that. That didn't mean that Bill didn't keep asking me to write them, though.

Covert Action

We have a problem we call the "covert action problem," which is when action sequences take over the game. It was an international spy game with clues to unravel in different cities, and as you played, the game would break into various action sequences—break into building, car chase,

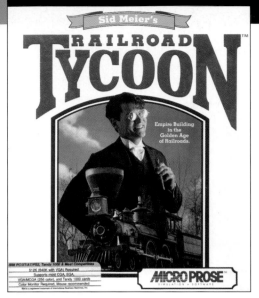

decode message—and each game was cool on its own, but almost too cool in that it took you too far away from the plot. It pointed out clearly how lucky we had been with Pirates! to have balanced the plot and action segments so well. This was a case where the whole was less than the sum of its parts.

Railroad Tycoon

This was the first game that started the whole "Sid's God game" thing, but it started off simply as a model railroading game about laying down track and watching trains with switches and signals. I showed it to Bruce Shelly, and he was into railroads and history and had done a board game called 1830 about trains, so I developed the rest of the game to make Bruce happy. I put in all sorts of stuff that I knew he would like, and he really contributed a lot to the game. We tried to make it fun and touch on all the cool parts like building track, seeing the economics, the tycoons of the day, covering the sweep of history.

Civilization

My first intention with Civilization was to make a real-time game that would emulate SimCity on a global scale, but it didn't work. I put it aside and wrote Covert Action. When I came back to it, a light went on in my head, and I realized that it would be a turn-based game. From that point on, Civilization was one of the smoothest developments of all the games I've made. It's amazing how few things we had to undo in the game. Even the tech tree. I just threw together a bunch of technologies, expecting to have to go to the history books afterward, but that ended up, with one or two exceptions, to be the tree we used in the game.

Civilization had many influences. SimCity in its turning the world away from destruction toward construction, the idea

F-19 had an amazing bug in it. In the simulation, you could run completely out of fuel and still glide in to finish your mission. Besides that, ironically, the game had already shipped and was 'out the door' before 'Wild Bill' Stealey discovered that the plane wasn't to be called the F-19 at all. Stealey was attending a briefing at the Pentagon when he realized that MicroProse had put their branding into the wrong aircraft designation. (JLW)

that it's just as much fun to build something as to destroy it. Empire, which had that "uncover the map" quality. Railroad Tycoon with the idea of economics and building and all it had.

One defining quality of Civilization is the concept of simple systems interacting to create complexity. On their own, the finances, military, and so forth are all easy to understand, but combined, they create a complex experience. And also there's the concept that you are the king. You get to make all the decisions that influence the course of history. Civilization is reputed to have this "one more turn" quality. You're always planning ten moves ahead, and you just gotta play one more turn. You've ordered a lot of chariots, you're researching gunpowder—you're always in the middle of things and projecting ahead. There's seldom a good stopping point. There were lots of cool touches. In a solid game system, you can do so much cool stuff. You could take one of your populace and turn them into something like a tax collector or an entertainer. Our entertainers looked like Elvis. One of our little jokes.

CPU Bach

How do you top Civilization? I admit I ducked the issue and let other people do Civ II. So I went off and did CPU Bach, which was as far away as you could get from what I had done before—on purpose. If I tried to top myself every time, I'd go crazy. I started it on the PC, but somehow Trip Hawkins convinced me that there would be a 3DO machine in every living room, right next to the stereo. And it did have a lot going for it, even if it didn't turn out exactly that way. At any rate, CPU Bach was a fun product, and I'm proud to have an aberration like that in my life.

Magic: The Gathering

The most complex, bizarre, strange development process I've ever been through. The irony is that halfway through the project, we had a great game, but during the second half we made it worse and worse. We had to make a lot of changes to fit the licensor's requirements and had to take a lot of the cool stuff out.

Gettysburg

Gettysburg was a game I'd been wanting to write for at least 20 years. When I was eight years old, I was sent off to Switzerland where my father's family lives, and the bribe to get me to go peacefully was an American Heritage book on the Civil War. It was the most amazing book with full-page battle maps, paintings that looked like the battle was actually happening. I always wanted to capture that in a computer game, but it took advancements in technology to allow a thousand figures to march across the screen, shooting and marching and all. It's a niche product, but I think it's the best Civil War game out there, and I'm happy with how it turned out.

Civilization III

Where Civ II added more units, more technology, more stuff, Civ III takes the approach of widening the game, like having culture, diplomacy, trade resources, things that were overshadowed perhaps by the military aspects of the original game. It's true to the spirit of the original with new game play elements that interact in the same way. Much of what we put into Civ III came from our players. We've gotten a lot of feedback, and many people have asked for ways to win besides capturing the world. And we've added some interface elements from real-time strategy games, putting as much on the main screen as possible.

More from MicroProse

In addition to Sid Meier's brilliant designs, MicroProse was the home of a host of other talented designers. Arnold

Hendrick, formerly of board game publisher SPI, and Lawrence Schick, formerly of Coleco's electronic game division, collaborated on a Japanese version of Pirates! Mixing tactical battles, role-playing elements, and action sequences, Sword of the Samurai is a great game that never received the acclaim of its predecessor. While Schick went on to craft Task Force 1942, a detailed World War II naval simulation, Hendrick parlayed his military history background into the original M1 Tank Platoon. Then, Hendrick created the most detailed role-playing game imaginable. Darklands was one part detailed historical setting (Germany during the 15th century) and another part open-ended fantasy. Unfortunately, Darklands arrived over budget, past due, and with hundreds of thousands of lines of discrete code instead of the promised software engine that could craft 15th-century Italy and 15th-century Britain as its heirs apparent. It also arrived with so many bugs that it ran through seven patches before it was playable on the average machine.

MicroProse also scored with a group out of Texas. Steve Barcia's SimTex group gave the company a mega-hit in Master of Orion and duplicated the feat with Master of Magic. In 1994 MicroProse also collaborated with Mythos Gaming to produce X-Com, which set new standards in turn-based strategy gaming. X-Com was followed by several sequels.

MicroProse was ultimately acquired by Spectrum Holobyte and later, by Hasbro. At the time of this writing, the MicroProse trademark is owned by Infogrames, though the company, as such, no longer exists. Sid Meier founded Firaxis games, and continues to produce great games such as the Alpha Centauri series.

Spectrum Holobyte: Converging Paths

A round 1979–80, Gilman Louie was developing TRS-80 games for a company called Voyager, the first being a Star Trek type of product. He later began working with the Apple II and Atari 800 systems and formed a development company called Nexa, working for Activision, Epyx, and others.

"My big break came when I was at our six-by-six booth at the West Coast Computer Faire in 1983 and a young executive from Microsoft/ASCII approached me saying he didn't know there were any Japanese-American game companies. I'm not Japanese, but I didn't say anything. At the time, I was

WW II GATO-Class Submarine Simulation
Spectrum HoloByte Inc.

The original Falcon, done as a cartridge for the Japanese MSX system.

Louie worked with writer Rob Swiggart to produce Portal, arguably the first computer novel.

The Real Dogfight Simulator.

$29.95

$ 1 Rebate
See offer inside

For 16K Model I
Level II TRS-80

1980: "Battle Trek for the TRS-80, the first game I designed and sold."—Gilman Louie.

MSX   ROM PACK

スターシップシミュレータ

株式会社アスキー

1984: Starship, another MSX cart, "my third Star Trek game," says Louie.

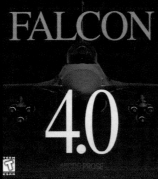

that we'd sell maybe 10,000 of them, but we sold 100,000, and Sega licensed it for their Master System in 1984." The game debuted in the U.S. in 1985.

Joining Forces

Meanwhile, in 1983 Phil Adam and Jeff Sauter started a company called Spectrum Holobyte ("spectrum" meaning color, "holo" meaning 3D, as in hologram, "byte" being a digital representation). They produced a World War II submarine simulation called Gato. "We had trouble getting it on the shelves," says Adam, "so I sent out 3,000 games at no charge to various stores, then called all 3,000 the following week. The first time we got a purchase order for 48 pieces, we popped open the champagne." By the fall of 1984, Gato became the number one game on many charts. Adam adds, "Not many people know that Gato was originally designed for the PCjr. Not many companies were founded around the PCjr and survived."

Spectrum followed by creating Orbiter, a space shuttle simulation. It came out two weeks before the *Challenger* disaster.

About that time, Paul Saffo, of the Institute of the Future, showed Louie's Falcon game to technology writer and pundit Stuart Alsop. Alsop knew about Gato and brought the two companies together, suspecting a good match. Meanwhile, despite the fact that Adam and Sauter were already in negotiations with Activision to sell their company, Gilman Louie managed to convince them to work out a business plan to form a publishing company and do Falcon for the Macintosh and the Amiga. Somehow Activision got a copy of the business plan and, according to Louie, "offered me a $250,000 development deal to make it go away. I knew we had something then, and I ran out of that meeting to talk to Phil while Jeff was in another meeting with Activision. But Phil was getting ready to go to England to meet with Mirror-

Above: 1988 CES booth. Phil Adam is on the right. Also, 1989's booth. Below: Gilman Louie getting the chance to check out an F-16.

consulting and doing various jobs out of my mom's house with all my fraternity brothers from San Francisco State."

Shortly thereafter, he received a surprise visit from eight Japanese businessmen who had called from the San Francisco airport. While his mother was serving tea and asking embarrassing questions, somehow he was offered funding to do a flight simulator for the MSX—a Z80-based computer in Japan. He could choose the F-15 or the F-16. He'd be working with 16K of RAM and a 16K cartridge.

"I was embarrassed and could only imagine what these guys, whose cards had ASCII on one side and Microsoft on the other, were thinking. Then Mr. Hamada said , 'We started in a house half this size.' I said yes to everything." The product Louie created was called Fighting Falcon F-16.

"It was complex and allowed head-to-head fighting on two computers using the joystick port and some nifty communication software we wrote. I figured it was pretty nitchy, and

Gilman Louie was featured in a national magazine ad for the Amiga with a screenshot from Vette!

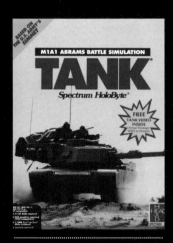

Spectrum's Tank is based on the U.S. military's networked simulation/training simulation, SIMNET.

soft, so I went with him. We showed our business plan to the British and ended up doing a deal with Robert Maxwell and forming Sphere, Inc., as the holding company, with Spectrum Holobyte as the publisher."

The deal gave Maxwell 80 percent of the company. Louie and Adam each took 10 percent. Sauter took Spectrum's hardware division, which was not part of the Maxwell deal. Four years later, Adam left to join Interplay, but not before participating in several big developments in the company's history.

Ironically, one of the first projects the new company had set its sights on was to create a game based on Tom Clancy's *Red Storm Rising*, but the deal with Maxwell got held up, according to Adam "because Gilman had a computer system he wanted to be a company asset and Maxwell's people didn't want to pay for it." The Red Storm Rising contract went to MicroProse instead (see page 189).

When it was released, Falcon was a huge success, critically and commercially, ultimately coming out on the IBM PC in 1987. Known for its realism and technical accuracy, Falcon went on to be the quintessential modern jet simulator—the standard by which other modern combat simulations were to be judged for years afterward. In each subsequent version, it became more and more detailed and realistic, despite hitting some turbulence along the way.

Tetris

While Falcon was flying high, another game more or less airdropped into their laps. It came to them by way of Hungary and they paid $11,000 for the rights to it. It was the antithesis of a detailed simulation like Falcon. It contained a mere seven blocky shapes, no Gouraud shading, no complex rules of engagement, and no huge manual. The game was called Tetris. The Tetris story, which is a tale in its own right, is covered separately on page 196.

Bankruptcies and Near Misses

Falcon was so realistic that Spectrum Holobyte was approached to create a low-cost military trainer through General Dynamics. They were given access to many design specifications and other information, but then it turned out that they couldn't do it, after all, since they weren't military contractors and didn't work in ADA (the standard military programming language named after "Ada" Lovelace (see page 6)). "So we took all the design specs and the information we learned working with General Dynamics and the pilots, and we made Falcon 3," says Louie.

As Falcon 3 was approaching its launch date, Robert Maxwell died in a mysterious boating incident, and it later turned out that the Maxwell empire was bankrupt. Moreover, the bankruptcy people were convinced that millions of dollars of missing pension funds were somehow hidden at Spectrum Holobyte. As part of the liquidation of the Maxwell businesses, the bankruptcy officers were going to sell Spectrum if Louie couldn't raise enough money to buy it back. "I told Bill Stealey at MicroProse about my situation, and he immediately loaned me $300,000, saying, 'We can figure out what to do about it later.' He literally wired me the money the next day."

The money from Stealey bailed out the company temporarily, but it wasn't a long-term solution, so Louie went to venture capitalist Vinod Khosla, who was working with Trip

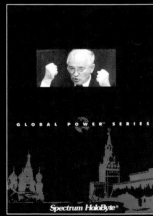

1991: Crisis in the Kremlin, a bold product that places you in the role of Mikhail Gorbachev, which ironically predicted the coup attempt on his leadership of the Soviet Union.

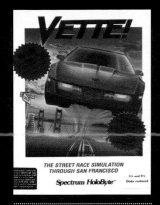

THE STREET RACE SIMULATION
THROUGH SAN FRANCISCO

Spectrum HoloByte

Hawkins at the time on the funding of 3DO. With Khosla's investment, the company was not only able to continue, but also secured investment from Paramount and, along with it, the license to do Star Trek games.

While all this was taking place, however, Spectrum was forced to release an already-delayed Falcon 3 before it was really ready, and the product initially was badly bug-ridden. It was months before a series of patches finally produced a stable version. The product sold well despite its problems, and when it was finally patched together, it flourished.

With new investment, the company took on new life. Tetris, Falcon, and the Star Trek license obtained from Paramount launched them quickly from a $7 million company to a $26 million company. It was at the height of this success that Bill Stealey came back to Louie with a problem of his own. His board was going to take the company from him if he didn't raise something like $12 million in ten days. With Khosla, from Kleiner Perkins, and Spectrum Holobyte's CEO Pat Fealy, Louie launched a campaign to purchase MicroProse and allow Stealey to keep his shares. Ultimately, they were successful, and MicroProse and Spectrum Holobyte essentially merged.

Louie remembers that the merger worked out well for the first year, but then it became clear that the two companies had very different cultures and expectations. The company's stock went up, but then started to fall as the two cultures clashed. After trying to sell unsuccessfully several times, they sold the combined company to Hasbro and ultimately were purchased by Infogrames. Gilman Louie left after that and started working for the CIA.

Having fun with chess, this insert was included in National Lampoon's 1993 spoof of the Chess Master series, Chess Maniac 5 Billion and 1.

195

Tetris

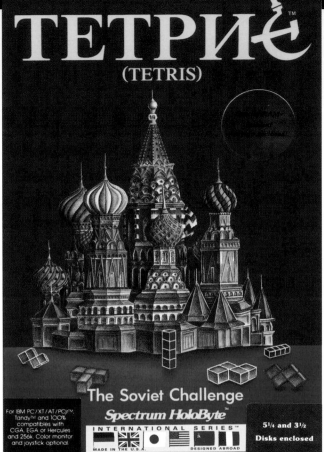

Alexey Pajitnov

Pajitnov with Henk Rogers and
colleague Vladimir Pokhilko.

The original Japanese Game Boy
version of Tetris.

I n 1979, Alexey Pajitnov graduated from the Moscow Institute of Aviation with a degree in applied mathematics. From the university, he went to work at the Ministry of Science, the main research institute in the Soviet Union. His job involved artificial intelligence, speech recognition, and what he calls "really serious, well-established, boring work." He adds, "I liked it, though, and spent 60 hours a week programming this stuff."

But Pajitnov had other interests. "Basically for all my life I was interested in kinds of mathematical puzzles or diversions, or some deep intelligent jokes," he says in a Russian accent. "When I got access to computers, that passion immediately found a place, and once I had a more or less reasonable operating system, I started putting together games and puzzles."

Pajitnov's first inspiration for Tetris was a game called Pentominos. "It was available at toy stores in Russia. It contained shapes that would fit into a box. You would take out all the shapes, and then you spent a good hour putting them back." Pajitnov became quite good at Pentominos, and even read a book written about it.

"One day, I decided to put together a game based on this puzzle, and I decided to put it on the computer. When I wrote the procedure to rotate the shapes, it worked very quickly when you pressed a key, and it was so amazing to see it moving on the screen that I wanted to see a game in real time. That's how the idea of Tetris was born."

There were other steps to take, however. First, since the original five-square shapes of Pentominos created too great a variety for Pajitnov's intentions, he reduced it to four squares per shape, making a total combination of seven possible shapes.

From this point, naming the game was easy. "Pentominos was named from the Greek for the number 5. I figured I would take the Greek word for the number 4, *tetra*, and that became Tetris. But I soon realized that if you just placed the shapes into the box, the game would soon be over. I needed

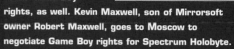

Handheld Japanese Tetris game, called "Tetris Jr."

a way to get rid of the shapes so the game could continue. And I noticed that when an entire line was full, it was kind of dead—you can't do anything with it—so I decided to take it away and leave space for more pieces."

The scoring system was another aspect that made the game unique. "You get a score in advance with each piece as it appears, and you spend part of the advance score while you think about where to put the piece. There are no bonus points for combinations, no points for clearing lines. There's simply a certain potential of points for each piece. And, of course, as the game progresses, the amount of the advance increases, but the pieces fall faster and you have to think faster."

The pieces appear randomly, and Pajitnov points out that "it was truly random. There was no bias to one shape over another." But Pajitnov did consider other refinements, such as a garbage area and making the square shapes invisible, "since you didn't have to rotate them, anyway." But in the end, he kept it simple. "I realized that I had better not touch anything because I could spoil it by adding complications."

The original game was developed in 1984 on an Elecronica 60 computer with a monochrome monitor. When it was ported to the IBM PC in 1985, with a whole 16 colors, the pieces were each given an individual color. "I do remember that the T piece was yellow," adds Pajitnov.

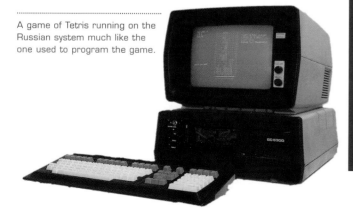

A game of Tetris running on the Russian system much like the one used to program the game.

A RIGHT TWISTY TALE

The story of how Tetris found its way to the world is very complex and involved a lot of legal folderol. Here is a very brief summary of events as remembered by Henk Rogers (currently coowner of The Tetris Company, which handles all worldwide Tetris-related products) and Phil Adam, who was at Spectrum Holobyte when Tetris was introduced.

● 1984: Alexey Pajitnov invents Tetris.
● Tetris somehow finds its way onto computers in Iron Curtain companies.
● Robert Stein, who has a company of developers working in Hungary, discovers it and licenses rights to Mirrorsoft in England. He subsequently goes to Russia and acquires some of the game rights he has already licensed to Mirrorsoft, but not all of them.
● Mirrorsoft licenses computer rights to Spectrum Holobyte, which then licenses console rights to Atari spin-off Tengen.
● Spectrum Holobyte packages the game for personal computers in the U.S., stressing the Russian angle, even hiring Ronald Reagan and Mikhail Gorbachev look-alikes.
● In 1987, Henk Rogers, a computer game publisher in Japan, discovers Tetris at the Spectrum Holobyte booth at CES. From them, he licenses personal computer rights for Japan.
● Rogers seeks console rights, first from Spectrum Holobyte, then Tengen, and publishes Tetris on Nintendo's FamiCom system in Japan. Robert Stein agrees to represent Rogers in seeking Tetris rights for handheld games such as Game Boy.
● Months pass, and Stein does not deliver handheld rights. Rogers learns that someone has approached Nintendo to do a Game Boy Tetris. Rogers asks Nintendo president Minoru Arakawa to give him a little time and heads off to Moscow himself.

● Meanwhile, Spectrum Holobyte has approached Nintendo about Game Boy rights, as well. Kevin Maxwell, son of Mirrorsoft owner Robert Maxwell, goes to Moscow to negotiate Game Boy rights for Spectrum Holobyte.
● In February 1989, Rogers meets with Nikolai Belikov of the official Soviet software trade organization (Electronorgtechnica) and Alexey Pajitnov. He discovers that the console rights were never licensed to anybody. "I said to myself, 'I got rights from Tengen, which is Atari. This is going to turn into a major lawsuit!'"
● The Russians send a fax to England, giving Kevin Maxwell 48 hours to respond. Ironically, he is in Moscow and doesn't receive the fax. The Russians agree to license the rights to Rogers.
● Rogers returns to Nintendo and explains the situation. They promise to back him up against Atari, whom they are about to sue over Tengen's unauthorized distribution of NES cartridges. They grant Rogers continued publishing rights in Japan in exchange for assistance in getting rights to consoles worldwide.
● In March 1989, Rogers, Arakawa, and Nintendo vice president Howard Lincoln all fly to Moscow to complete negotiations for console and handheld rights.
● Tetris for Game Boy sells well over 30 million units since its release on all platforms in 1989. More than 70 million Tetris units have been sold worldwide at the time this was written.
● In 1996 all rights to Tetris were placed in The Tetris Company; Blue Planet Software becomes the exclusive agent and all Tetris players play happily ever after.

The Games Group: Early History of Games at LucasArts

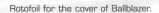

L ike Industrial Light & Magic and Pixar, the Games Group spun out of the vast creative empire of George Lucas. And like those other companies, it has been a consistent leader in its field. Now known as LucasArts Entertainment Company, the original Games Group was a small cadre of talented people looking for ways to make better games.

They started with a million-dollar investment from Atari. Ed Catmull, who was running an advanced technology group at Lucasfilm (the Computer Division), hired Peter Langston, who had designed several games in the 70s, including one of the earliest versions of Empire (see page 225) and an intriguing program called the Internet Oracle. (More information about this amusing program is available at http://livinginternet.com/l/la_known_oracle.htm.)

Langston, in turn, hired David Fox, who had written a book about computer animation and dreamed of working for Lucasfilm. He also hired programmers David Levine, Charlie Kellner (one of the first Apple employees), and Chip Morningstar, as well as artist Gary Winnick. Also present at the inception was David Riordan, who was a consultant at the time and had completed a research project on cable television opportunities for Lucasfilm.

"Everybody contributed game ideas," says Langston, "and the two from David Fox and David Levine were our favorites." The two ideas Langston refers to are Levine's Ballblazer and Fox's Rescue on Fractalus!,

though the original names were Ballblaster and Rescue Mission (or Behind Jaggi Lines as an alternate title).

A number of interesting stories surround these first games. They were somehow pirated before release and put out on the Internet. The various vehicles depicted on the game covers were actual models made just for the game covers by Industrial Light & Magic technicians. David Fox is the guy in the helmet on Rescue on Fractalus!, which was originally inspired by Loren Carpenter's early work with fractals. "I asked Loren, 'Do you think it's possible to do fractals on Atari computers?'" remembers Fox. "He said, 'Well, maybe.' After a few days he took an Atari 800 home,

Rotofoil for the cover of Ballblazer.

Original Games Group members: David Levine, Charlie Kellner, Peter Langston, David Fox, Loren Carpenter, and Gary Winnick.

Before 3D computer modeling, the Games Group had ILM actually create scale models of the type they had made for the *Star Wars* movies, including a detailed saucer and landing craft for Rescue on Fractalus!, and a rotofoil for the cover of Ballblazer.

Before becoming a publisher, Lucasfilm Games produced two excellent war simulations for Electronic Arts. Producers on these titles were Rich Hilleman (still at EA) and Randy Breen, now running LucasArts Entertainment Company.

learned 6502 assembly code, and came back with the first pass of a fractal landscape. Meanwhile, I had started designing Rescue on Fractalus!" (Ed Catmul, Carpenter, and Alvy Ray Smith went on to form Pixar with substantial early investment from Steve Jobs, who bought Lucasfilm's Computer Division.)

David Levine created accurate physics algorithms for Ballblazer, and there was even a tricky maneuver called the "Back Wall Charlie" named after Charlie Kellner. The music on Ballblazer was interactive and was modified by the player's controller movements. A musician himself, Langston got both Pat Metheny and Lyle Mays (among others) to contribute riffs for Ballblazer. Longtime *Newsweek* technology editor Michael Rogers wrote the original Ballblazer manual (although it's possible that Riordan and his partner, Garry Hare, also

wrote a manual, or contributed to one).

At the time they were ready to release these early games, Atari had changed hands and was now owned by Jack Tramiel. Unwilling to accept Tramiel's terms, the Games Group looked elsewhere, ultimately making a deal with Epyx. According to former Epyx president Michael Katz, "Their games were pretty esoteric, though great graphically. Hell, we couldn't even pronounce some of their early titles. But we wanted a relationship with Lucasfilm." Epyx wanted disk games, not cartridges, so that further delayed the release of the products, which finally came out in 1985.

The next two games, also published by Epyx, were Kellner's The Eidolon and Koronis Rift by Sinistar designer Noah Falstein, who had joined the team from Williams. "In some ways, Koronis Rift was a forerunner to first-person shooter games," says Falstein. "You traveled around a 3D sort of landscape with weak weapons and shield, and you'd find burnt-out tanks and integrate their capabilities."

The Games Group, which by this time was known as Lucasfilm Games, published several titles for other publishers. David Fox worked on Labyrinth (published by Activision), and comments, "It was in some ways a better game than a film." Falstein, inspired by Sid Meier's Hellcats and F-15 Strike Eagle, began to research military themes, ultimately featuring the hydrofoil in PHM Pegasus for Electronic Arts and inspiring David Levine to write an antiwar poem called "Blood on the Water" in protest. Levine's protest did cause the group to consider their treatment of war games, and according to Falstein, "Starting with Battlehawks: 1942, we made it a policy to show both sides of the war."

During these years, several changes of personnel occurred.

Steve Arnold came from Atari to help manage the division. Shortly thereafter, Levine left the company, as did Langston, who was lured away to "a job I couldn't refuse" at Bell Labs, and several notable programmers came on the scene. Graeme Devine (who later cofounded Trilobyte) did a conversion of Ballblazer and spent some time at the Skywalker Ranch (where Lucasfilm Games was located from 1985-1989); Larry Holland did an Apple 2 conversion of PHM Pegasus; and Ron Gilbert did a C64 conversion of Koronis Rift.

Falstein next worked with Larry Holland on Strike Fleet, an innovative naval warfare game that allowed the player to control fleets as an admiral or to captain individual ships. Strike Fleet, published by Electronic Arts, was the last game the group developed for an outside publisher.

The Two-Fold Path

The next phase of Lucasfilm Games' development was led by Ron Gilbert and Larry Holland, two former programmers for a short-lived company called Human Engineered Software (or HESware).

SCUMM Is Born

Up to this point, Lucasfilm's games had been innovative and technically excellent, but their impact on the art of computer game design had only just begun. The new era began in 1987, when they released their first game as a publisher, Maniac Mansion. The idea for the game originated from discussions between Ron Gilbert and artist Gary Winnick. In order to make it easier to develop, Gilbert developed a scripting language he called Script Creation Utility for Maniac Mansion, which was later shortened to SCUMM, and it was the SCUMM system that was used to create all the subsequent adventure games the company produced for years afterward. (David Fox offers the following comment:

"Knowing Ron, he came up with the name SCUMM first, and then figured out what to call it... just like another tool was called MMUCUS, Earwax, and another SPUTM—do you see a trend here?")

Gilbert, who had played text adventure games such as the original Adventure and Zork, wanted something different, so he developed a game with no typing. All possible verbs were listed on the screen, and the player simply clicked on the verb and then clicked on the object on the screen.

The script, written by Gilbert and David Fox, was notably irreverent and humorous, a trademark of later Lucasfilm adventure games. In part, this was a way to avoid the obvious absurdities involved in adventure games. Gilbert cites a theoretical example of a game where you are in Los Angeles and you need a pencil to solve a problem, but in the game, the pencil is in New York. "It's kind of silly to think that there are no pencils in L.A., but in many adventure games, that is how the world seems to be. Using humor lets you turn a weakness into an advantage. You can use crazy ideas to solve puzzles, and when the situation makes no sense, people don't grumble about it. If they are laughing, they are much less likely to groan and say, 'What was that all about?'"

Maniac Mansion was one of the landmark products in LucasArts' history. Its wacky humor combined with its innovative interface and story development set the stage for many amazing games to come, such as Zak McKracken and the Alien MindBenders, The Secret of Monkey Island, and several others.

About the time that Gilbert was getting started on The

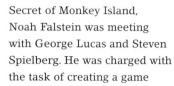

Secret of Monkey Island, Noah Falstein was meeting with George Lucas and Steven Spielberg. He was charged with the task of creating a game based on the upcoming movie, *Indiana Jones and the Last Crusade*. This was late 1988. The movie was due out in May 1989. There was no way to do a good game alone in that short time, but possibly with a team and SCUMM…

Steve Arnold assigned his best team—Falstein, Fox, and Gilbert—to work together and produce the game. The team produced the game in record time, according to Falstein, but they had different opinions about the game's ending. Falstein favored a serious ending, and Gilbert favored humor. Fox suggested that they use both versions and have them come up randomly. According to Falstein, Gilbert created a random number generator that presented different combinations of ending scenes, so that players would get different combinations of serious and comic endings. "I went over Ron's code to be sure he didn't bias it," adds Falstein

with a smile. (Fox adds that he remembers writing the ending code using Gilbert's random number generator.)

Steven Spielberg was a great fan of computer games and made frequent visits to the Ranch, where the game division was located. Noah Falstein relates a story about Spielberg playing Battle of Britain while the ILM crew waited to show him the first dinosaurs for *Jurassic Park*. So, when he wanted to do a game based on "The Dig," an original story he had penned for his Amazing Stories TV series, he turned to Lucasfilm. "Working with both George Lucas and Steven Spielberg was one of the high points of my career," says Noah Falstein, who was tapped originally to lead the project. Unfortunately, Lucas's management changed teams more than once on the project, which ultimately took six years to complete from initial meetings to shipping the game. In the end, although it had beautiful artwork, The Dig was one of the very few disappointing games put out by the Lucasfilm crew, and remains notable primarily because of Spielberg's involvement.

In 1990, Lucasfilm Games released one of its most evocative games—Brian Moriarty's Loom. This unusual game featured an intriguing storyline, innovative game play, and beautiful graphics. Unlike most of the early SCUMM games, Loom was a more serious game, with a deeper and more thought-provoking fantasy involving a mythical world of magic. Loom had no inventory, and all the puzzles were solved with the use of musical sequences, which the player learned while exploring the world. Loom was closer to a modern fairy tale, with timeless imagery and a hero's quest that evokes ancient myth.

Also in 1990, Ron Gilbert completed one of the funniest games of all time, The Secret of Monkey Island. Monkey Island was a pirate adventure full of wisecracks and jokes, and it featured several dialogue puzzles. "My favorite dialogue," says Gilbert, "was between Guybrush (Monkey's protagonist) and Stan the Used Ship Salesman. Stan is

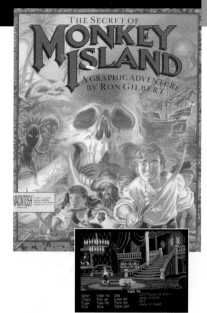

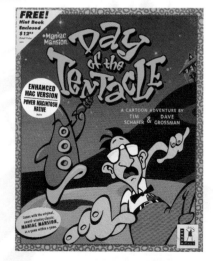

trying to convince Guybrush that he needs all these extra options. It's the classic used car salesman encounter. You have to leave and come back a couple of times. We wanted it to be slightly frustrating and a little irritating, but not too much so. We were treading that thin line where the player would be amused at the parody, the satire, with a tinge of frustration, but not so much as to be angry with the game."

After The Secret of Monkey Island, there was no stopping them. Adventure games became one of the mainstays of Lucasfilm Games, which ultimately changed its name to LucasArts Entertainment Company in the early 90s. An impressive list of titles followed, including LeChuck's Revenge (Monkey Island II), Indiana Jones and the Fate of Atlantis, Maniac Mansion II: Day of the Tentacle, Sam & Max Hit the Road, Zombies Ate My Neighbors, Full Throttle, The Curse of Monkey Island, Escape from Monkey Island, and the hilarious Grim Fandango.

LucasArts also entered the console market with several successful games, starting in 1991 with Star Wars for the NES and following the next year with the Empire Strikes Back and Defenders of Dynatron City. Also in 1992, they released Super Star Wars for the Super NES, following with several additional Super NES titles over the next two years. In 1997, they even released Ballblazer as Ballblazer Champions for the Sony PlayStation.

Taking Flight

After Strike Fleet in 1986, Larry Holland and Noah Falstein were thinking about the next step. "We got quite ambitious and grandiose and wanted to create entire theaters of operation," says Holland. Stuck doing a hi-res Apple 2 version of Zak McKracken, Holland was anxious to go back to military combat. In his readings, he became fascinated with the Battle of Midway in World War II. "I wanted to base the game on what really happened, on moments in history. Reading about tales of Midway really crystallized it—it still gives me chills. It was the most important five or ten minutes in the last 50 years. In minutes, three Japanese carriers were sunk; it was the moment the war changed. I wanted to capture that kind of impact and show how a small number of people can change everything, the moment when things were in the balance." The game he and Falstein produced was Battlehawks: 1942, which released in 1988 and was the first of three great World War II air combat games.

Holland was just getting warmed up, and by the next year he had produced Their Finest Hour: The Battle of Britain, in which he continued to improve technically while expanding the realism and human connection of his games. Depicting both sides of the air war, and with missions based in history, Their Finest Hour let players engage in one of the most dramatic conflicts of the war. "There were great heroes on both sides of the conflict," says Holland, "and our task was to let players experience even the German pilots without lionizing or demonizing them." Holland also came up with an innovative replay mechanism that allowed players to reenter a battle during the replay at any time.

In 1991 Holland completed his final WWII product, Secret Weapons of the Luftwaffe (SWOTL), a huge project that incorporated not only individual flight missions, but a vast overall campaign mode, great graphics, and huge fleets of B-17s. But there were lessons for Holland in doing the game, which was many months late. "I fell into the common trap of the overly ambitious and threw the kitchen sink into this game. I learned that even incremental elements can make a game far more complex. There are stories about the security guard coming by at 3:00 a.m. and finding me asleep on the couch. I think I lived at Lucasfilm for about a year. But what I loved about that game was the message—what war means to technological innovation, and strange turns it can take."

Ironically, Lucasfilm had licensed *Star Wars* game rights to Brøderbund, and it wasn't until 1992 that the rights reverted to the company that made the films. At that time, following SWOTL, Holland was ready to move on. Brian Moriarty made a comment to him that if Larry didn't do an X-wing game, he would. "When Brian said that, I thought 'I have to do it now!'" And so Holland took all his experience with WWII games and applied it to the first *Star Wars* game, *Star Wars* X-Wing.

"We recognized early on that, although we wanted to tell both sides, as we had in the previous flight games, we also wanted to tell the David and Goliath story. We didn't want to do the movie over again, though, but put in the familiar elements in a similar story."

X-Wing succeeded phenomenally, and gave rise to a series of great games, each of which expanded the genre and became more graphically rich, with ever deeper stories and mission threads. *Star Wars* TIE Fighter took the Empire's side. But playing the evil Empire created its challenges. "In most great works, the villain or evil side has a lot of intrigue, and we wanted to design with that in mind. We gave the Empire shades of gray, and gave the player a chance to achieve some nobility."

In *Star Wars* X-Wing vs. TIE Fighter, which came out in 1997, Holland and his team

offhandedly agreed to incorporate Internet play. "We got into it and said, 'Oh, my god...' We discovered how difficult it was to put in real-time action on the Internet. I remember testing into the predawn hours, and we'd think we had finally fixed a problem. Then, later in the day the 'fixed' version would not be any better than before. This happened several times until we finally understood that the problem was bottlenecks in the Internet itself." Ironically, most players only played the death match mode. "We put in a lot of cooperative missions, story, and cool military engagements, but people mostly played the death matches. In the end, I felt that only about five percent of the game was actually played."

Finally, with *Star Wars* X-Wing Alliance, Holland was able to expand the game genre even further. "X-Wing Alliance was an opportunity to bring together a lot of what we had learned over the past five years. The design allowed us to do things we had wanted to do, like fly the Millennium Falcon and be a gunner, do the Battle of Endor in grand scope. It was a nice wrap-up of the series." Of course, LucasArts produced many more *Star Wars* games for both the first series of movies and for Episode I.

TIE Fighter screen.

THE OLD MAN FROM HOLLYWOOD

"When I was a kid, I was always designing games, but in those days computers were something the size of a blue whale run by men in white lab coats," says Hal Barwood, veteran designer at LucasArts. "So I followed my other passion and went to film school." One of Barwood's film school buddies was George Lucas, which turns out to be significant.

To make a long story short, Barwood did teach himself to program, and even made a couple of games. One unreleased game of his from the early 80s was an epic action adventure on the Apple II he called Space Snatchers. "I fully intend to take that game one day and release it on the Internet," he says. In the meantime, here's a screenshot.

Barwood was successful in Hollywood, with credits ranging from "extensive, but uncredited" writing on *Close Encounters of the Third Kind* to producing *Dragonslayer*, which also happened to be the first non-Lucas film that Lucas' great special effects house, Industrial Light & Magic, worked on.

In time, Barwood returned to his passion for games. His first

game at Lucas was Indiana Jones and the Fate of Atlantis. He has continued to work as a writer, designer, and production manager at LucasArts ever since. Among his projects were the SNES title Big Sky Trooper published by JVC ("too long in

Screen from Hal Barwood's unreleased early 80s epic, Space Snatchers.

development—a great game but an 8-bit title in a 32-bit world"), Desktop Adventures ("the concept of developing modular games using similar elements, the way the chessboard squares and pieces are always the same, but no two games are alike"), Indiana Jones and the Infernal Machine ("some of the best level design I've ever seen, an absolutely wonderful game trapped in a defective 3D engine"), and Rebel Assault II: The Hidden Empire ("returning to my roots, I helped with the video and directed the shoot").

Barwood credits his movie experience very little in his game design work. However, he admits that it has influenced him in various ways. "In movies, narrative runs everything. It's the same with adventure games. People still come to me saying that movies are linear and games are nonlinear, and therefore can't tell a story. But of course they can, although there are subtleties and pitfalls you have to look out for."

Barwood then referred to an interesting bit of dialogue from the movie, *The War of the Worlds.*

Dr. Clayton Forrester (Gene Barry), a physicist, is in an army bunker watching the Martian invaders. General Mann (Les Tremayne) joins him.

General Mann: "From the data, from that picture the Air Force took tonight, what we've got out there is the original pilot ship. On the basis of its observations, the others were guided down. Patternwise, one lands, then two, making groups of three, joined magnetically. Is that possible?"

Dr. Forrester: "If they do it, it is."

Point made...

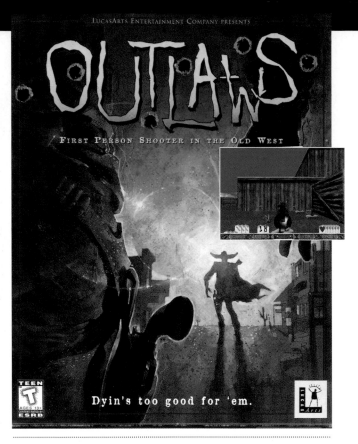

LucasArts has produced so many great games that it's hard to decide which ones to include here. We wish we could feature them all. Certainly two great games were Outlaws (a first-person shooter set in the old West) and Grim Fandango (set in a strange, modern world of the dead and one of the most twisted and hysterical of the modern adventure games). Also, there were the *Star Wars* Dark Forces games, which truly added the Force to the first-person shooter genre.

STAR WARS®
REBEL ASSAULT

AN ORIGINAL ACTION ARCADE
GAME FOR CD-ROM

NEW
FOR
MACINTOSH
CD·ROM

BY VINCENT LEE

X WING : RED D

75

Rookie One,
Welcome to Kolaador.

STRENGTH   PILOTS   SCORE

Star Wars Rebel Assault featured
some great graphics and intense
flying and shooting. In many ways,
it was the modern equivalent of
Rescue on Fractalus!

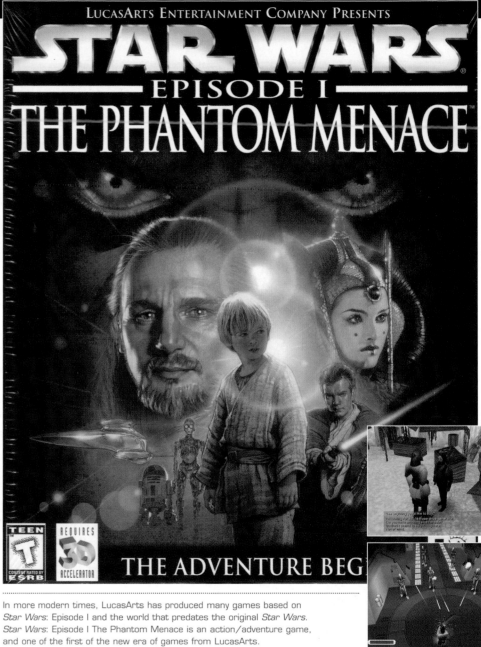

STAR WARS®
EPISODE I
THE PHANTOM MENACE™

TEEN
T
CONTENT RATED BY
ESRB

REQUIRES
3D
ACCELERATOR

THE ADVENTURE BEG

In more modern times, LucasArts has produced many games based on
Star Wars: Episode I and the world that predates the original *Star Wars*.
Star Wars: Episode I The Phantom Menace is an action/adventure game,
and one of the first of the new era of games from LucasArts.

Chris Roberts:
Wing Commander

T here was a time when Origin Systems was known almost exclusively for the Ultima series of role-playing games. That was before Chris Roberts joined the company. Roberts grew up in England, and his exposure to games started in the arcades. "When I was a young kid I was an artist, and I guess I was fascinated by storytelling and movies. At the same time, I went to arcades and played games like Space Wars, Galaxian, and Galaga... I was fascinated by the ability of computers to animate images on screen. So I taught myself to program on a Sinclair ZX81 with 1k of memory and tried to merge my two passions—storytelling and games."

He created his first games as a teenager on the BBC Micro computer. His first published game was called Wizadore and was published by Imagine (a subsidiary of Ocean Software) in 1984. It spent 8 weeks as number one on the English charts. His next game, a soccer game called Match Day, spent 12 weeks at number one. He followed that with Stryker's Run. "It was a sideways scrolling game set on a futuristic war-torn planet. You had to get a message across no-man's-land to your HQ. You could get into aircraft and fly them."

At that point, before going to university, Roberts decided

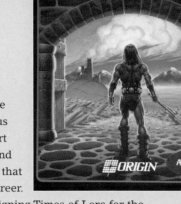

to take a year off to write games. Like other famous designers, such as Robert Woodhead (Wizardry) and Damon Slye (Dynamix), that year off turned into a career.

In 1987, he began designing Times of Lore for the Commodore 64, creating his own development system on an IBM PC, using a cross-assembler and his own download software to port it to a Commodore 64. About that time, his father moved to Austin, Texas, and Roberts decided he liked the weather and all the movie theaters, so he moved, too.

While visiting a local D&D gaming spot, he noticed some cool graphics on the walls depicting various characters. He asked the artist if he'd like to work on his game with him. Two weeks later, that same artist, Dennis Loubet, went to work at Origin Systems. Soon after, Roberts worked out a deal to have Origin publish Times of Lore.

Roberts' next game was a post-apocalyptic role-playing game called Bad Blood, also for Origin; but he was already thinking about a space epic he wanted to create. "I had grown up with *Star Wars* and *Battlestar Galactica*, and I read tons of science fiction. I remembered the game Elite, which I thought was pretty cool," says Roberts. "I was originally going to call my space game Squadron and create a fleet combat game from a top-down perspective. I started buying books and doing research. About that time, I had a chance to

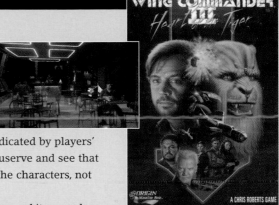

see Sid Meier's F-19 Stealth Fighter. It wasn't out yet, but it was running at 10 frames per second on a 386 25 MHz machine—at the time a $10,000 system. It was beautiful, but I thought, who would buy this game? You needed the best machine for it to perform with any reasonable frame rate. Of course, it went on to become one of the biggest hits that year. I was also inspired by Larry Holland's Battlehawks: 1942, and I liked his technique of using bitmaps to represent 3D images." In fact, there was some talk of locating the game in the Star Wars universe, but at Lucasfilm, the idea of doing their own Star Wars games was gaining strength.

In creating his own outer space fantasy world, Roberts was inspired by the themes of the Pacific theater in World War II. "The Pacific Ocean is analogous to the vastness of space, with islands and atolls being the equivalent of planets." Roberts then created the two warring sides—the Kilrathi and the Confederation, modeled roughly on the Japanese and the Americans in WWII.

In Times of Lore, Roberts had done a remarkable job of condensing code, "squeezing as much code and data as I could into the Commodore's meager memory. The whole game fit in 64K, a necessity for the European market, which was still tape driven, but irrelevant in the U.S. where everyone had floppy drives," he says. "But did anyone notice?" he asks. The answer would appear to be no. "After the success of F-19 Stealth Fighter, I decided that people just wanted to have the best, coolest game possible, period, and it was irrelevant if it ran really well on their particular machine. So for Wing Commander, I went 'balls to the wall' and really pushed the technology." No more squeezing. Roberts also tapped his fascination with movies to create more story and atmosphere. "All the elements of character, details in the ship, and action sort of came together and created something that was more than just a game. It was like a departure into another world."

Roberts knew he was on the right track when, while it was still in development, most of Origin was playing the game. Later, after the game's release, Roberts was further vindicated by players' responses to the game. "I'd go on Compuserve and see that they were talking about the world and the characters, not just what their high score was."

Of course, the original Wing Commander and its sequels were created by ever larger teams of people, including some of Origin's most creative talents, like Loubet, Warren Spector, Steve Beeman, Ellen Guon, and many others. Each succeeding game became ever more movielike, with animated cut scenes, lots of characters, and lots of environmental details. They were more than simple flight combat games. They were true adventures with a taste of role-playing that captured players' imaginations. Roberts created four Wing Commander games, each more ambitious than the last.

Also in 1991, a spin-off of the Wing Commander series, Privateer, debuted to a warm reception, and a sequel, Privateer—Righteous Fire, followed.

By 1993, Roberts was involved in creating the ambitious and ground-breaking game Strike Commander, which featured amazing 3D technology and required game fans to purchase state-of-the-art hardware even to run it. The technology for Strike Commander was ready in 1991, though the game didn't release until '93. But even in '93, it was at the top of the technology curve, pre-CD-ROM.

Wing Commander III was even more ambitious, evolving the Strike Commander technology and incorporating full live-action sequences with actors set against digital sets. Roberts went for an all-star cast, including Mark Hamill, John Rhys-Davies, Tim Curry, and Malcolm McDowell in the

Chris Roberts with Mark Hamill and Malcolm McDowell at Planet Hollywood, dedicating WC IV costumes.

filming. It was a very expensive project, and benefited by the 1994 sale of Origin to Electronic Arts, who provided much-needed financial resources.

Coming out in December 1994, WC III did so well for EA that they wanted another game from Roberts by the next Christmas. Wing Commander IV released in February 1996, again with a big cast of actors. "We didn't have time to retool the technology, so we spent our time and money on the story and content, shooting film and creating the missions."

After finishing Wing Commander IV, Roberts decided to strike out on his own, formed the company Digital Anvil, and ultimately went on to make movies. Origin continued to create Wing Commander products, including Wing Commander Prophecy (known as WC V), Wing Commander Armada, and Wing Commander Academy.

Interplay

"**I** was a big *Lord of the Rings* fan—comic books, movies… I read a lot of fiction. Everything pointed me toward games," says Interplay's founder Brian Fargo. In the

The earliest press photograph of Brian Fargo at Boone Software in 1983. From left to right: Mike Boone, Bill "Burger" Heineman, Brad Davis, Troy Worrell, Brian Fargo, and Dave Shore.

Left: Brian Fargo. Right: Brian Fargo and Bill Heineman demonstrating Dragon Wars to coauthor Johnny Wilson.

The Demon's Forge
By Brian Fargo

mid-70s, Fargo got a Magnavox Odyssey, followed by the Atari VCS. Fascinated by how these games were being made, at 16 years old he started calling publishers and asking them questions. "They were no help at all," he recalls. "One guy said something to the effect that 'if you don't know now, you'll never know.' Then, around 1979 or so, I got an Apple II computer, and that's when a light went on above my head. It had 48K of memory, and there was a 16K add-on. I thought,

'What a waste. What would you do with all that memory?'"

Fargo's first game on the Apple was an adventure game called Demon's Forge, which he published under the label Saber Software. He would call computer stores and ask if they had it and refer them to the ad in *Softalk*, which he had spent half his business budget on. Later, he'd get a call from those same stores ordering his game. (This is pretty much the same trick Bill Stealey used in the early days of MicroProse.)

Then some Stanford graduates approached Fargo to form a company called Boone Software. After about a year, Fargo decided to go off on his own again. Dick Lehrberg, formerly executive vice president of Interplay, relates, "At one of the Boone board meetings, all the other executives broke into a fistfight. That's when Brian left to form Interplay Productions." That was October 1983. The company began with conversions and other odd software projects. "When you start a company, there's what you want to do and what you have to do," says Fargo. And this included conversions of products for a division of K-Tel Records and even some military work for Loral. Finally, Interplay landed a three-product contract with Activision. "They had an incredibly sophisticated 3D engine for a golf game, some graphic adventures, and also a fantasy role-playing game with three-frame animations in this giant window—which you look at now and say, 'Oh my god, it's so small,'" remembers Lehrberg, who was at Activision then. "But I thought it would be right up our alley. However, when I mentioned it to Jim Levy, he said role-playing games were 'nicheware for nerds' and passed on the RPG." Eventually, Interplay did strike a deal with Activision. For $100,000, they agreed to create Mind Shadow (based loosely on Robert Ludlum's *Bourne Identity*), Tracer Sanction, and Borrowed Time (with Arnie Katz) for three different machines—essentially a nine-product deal. Later, a golf game developed by—in Fargo's words—"Steven Hawkings–smart" Stanford graduates was added to the mix and became the first 3D Gold game

sold under Activision's GameStar line.

The role-playing game Activision passed up was written by Brian Fargo's high school buddy, Michael Cranford, although Fargo did contribute some scenario design. Electronic Arts' Joe Ybarra liked the game and signed up Interplay to do it. It was called Tales of the Unknown Volume 1: The Bard's Tale, but it ultimately became known simply as The Bard's Tale.

Bard's Tale was a great success, selling around 300,000 copies. Interplay followed with a pair of sequels and Wasteland (see page 226), a more modern RPG using the Bard's Tale engine. However, Fargo was aware that, as developers, they were missing out on the real money. "We had solid products, but we weren't really making that much money. Individual designers like Eric Hammond, who did the One-on-One series, did really well."

After some "big hairy negotiations," as Fargo put it, Interplay became an affiliate label of Activision, which meant that Interplay would take more of the risk, but would also make more of the profit. In any case, Electronic Arts was not too excited about the first game that Interplay was about to publish and become its next big hit—Battle Chess. The game was at least partially inspired by the great chess scene in *Star Wars*.

William Gibson's Neuromancer was one of Interplay's next games, notable in part because they worked with Timothy Leary in developing the story and used the rock group Devo for the music.

By this time, Interplay had broken off from EA and was distributing through Activision, but by 1990, Fargo once again decided it was time to make a change and turn Interplay into a full publisher. Unfortunately,

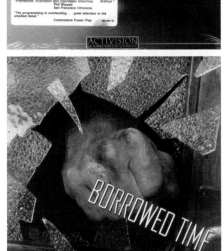

ADVICE TO BLIZZARD

Allen [Adham] came to me when he was starting Blizzard, talking about doing a strategy game. But Davidson had offered him $4 million for the company. I told him not to sell, that he had too much potential. Davidson only wanted them to do ports of other products. Then he came back later and said they'd offered him $7 million. This time I said, "Sell." But what Davidson got wasn't ports, they got Warcraft.

—*Brian Fargo*

Activision was in trouble at that time, and there was a lot of unsold inventory. Fargo hired veteran Phil Adam to head up his marketing and sales. "I had wanted to create a marketing and sales company to work with Origin, Interplay, and Dynamix," Adam remembers, "but Brian said, 'Why not just do that for Interplay.' So I joined in late 1990, but with Activision having problems, I told Brian we might have to go six months without revenue while we cleaned up the mess."

Fortunately for Interplay, their next product was Castles, a wonderful game of medieval building and warfare. "We sold 50,000 Castles in one day," says Adam. Fargo adds, "The idea came to me when I was watching a BBC miniseries on castles, and they said that castles weren't really homes, but were military machines. But I never quite got it to where I wanted it to be. I had a real-time strategy game in mind.

When I see Ensemble's Age of Empires, I think, 'That's what I wanted. They just nailed it.'"

Shortly after releasing Castles, Interplay hit it big with Star Trek: 25th Anniversary, which was the first really successful Star Trek game. In fact, Fargo remembers, "When we got the rights to Trek, people thought it would be a slam-dunk seller, but retailers were pretty much down on the concept due to the poor versions that came before it." Later, Interplay released a CD-ROM version of the game with actual voice-overs from the cast and crew of the original Enterprise. It was at the recording sessions for this product that William Shatner saw the complex interactive script and commented that it was more like three movies.

Interplay also created some cartridge games for the NES, including Swords and Serpents for Acclaim, Rad Gravity for

Activision, and a game called Rock and Roll Racing by Allen Adham, one of the founders of Blizzard, who also did Lost Vikings and Blackthorne for Interplay.

Interplay created some great games in the 90s, including Descent, which took the first-person shooter concept popularized by Doom and gave it new dimensions. They also began working with some outside studios—Bioware and Shiny Entertainment. Bioware's first product, Shattered Steel, didn't do very well, but Interplay stayed with them and was rewarded by the critically acclaimed Baldur's Gate series of role-playing games. Meanwhile, they purchased Dave Perry's Shiny Entertainment (see page 276) to have a strong cartridge development house, only to find Perry more interested in doing primarily computer games like MDK, Messiah, and Sacrifice. (Fargo relates that in their final negotiation phase, they played a game of pool to settle a particular issue involving who paid taxes. Fargo claims to have won approximately $20,000 by sinking the eight ball. "My previous biggest gamble was five dollars," he adds.)

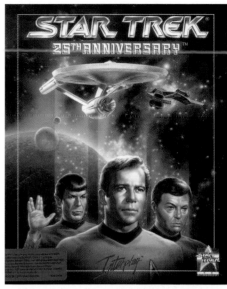

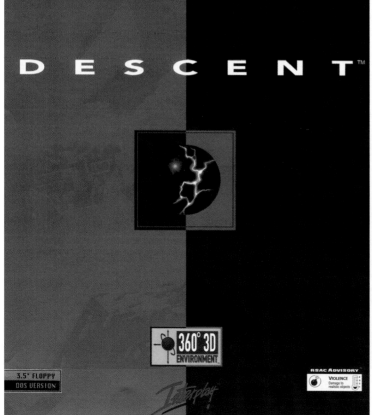

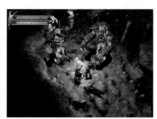

Screen from Baldur's Gate for the PlayStation 2.

New World Computing

In 1983, Jon Van Caneghem began work on a game inspired by Ultima, Wizardry, and his D&D experience. In 1986 he completed the game, started New World Computing, and released Might and Magic Book 1: The Secret of the Inner Sanctum. "It was such an awesome feeling to complete Might and Magic," Van Caneghem tells us. "This was my first creation, and it combined the best of other games I liked with the kinds of features I wanted." Might and Magic was the first RPG to feature really well-drawn indoor and outdoor locations, and to allow full exploration of both.

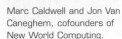

Marc Caldwell and Jon Van Caneghem, cofounders of New World Computing.

FIRST IMPRESSIONS

In 1986, I was asked by my editor at A+ Magazine if I wanted to review a new program called Might and Magic Book 1: The Secret of the Inner Sanctum. I remember chuckling over the name, which pretty much summed up the role-playing game genre nicely. I also remember calling up the guy who created the game on the telephone to ask him some questions about the game, wondering who the heck he was and where he came from. I wondered at the time how such a great game had come seemingly out of nowhere. Might and Magic was a great RPG, the packaging was bold and original; yet, I had never heard of New World Computing or Jon Van Caneghem before. I considered Might and Magic one of those gems you discover every once in a while, and continue to enjoy New World's games to this day. (RDM)

"In 1988, with Might and Magic II, we tried to push the envelope on the Apple II, doing things with color and resolution that nobody had done to that point," says Van Caneghem. "Our efforts were somewhat eclipsed by the introduction of VGA graphics on the PC, though.

"Might and Magic III came out in 1992, and it marked several exciting milestones," continues Van Caneghem. "It was the first time I had other programmers to help me. It was our first PC title. We also pioneered an item concatenation system, where, for instance, a sword might be the 'flaming sword of mayhem' or something. Some say it was our best Might and Magic, and certainly it won

many awards and was translated into a staggering number of languages."

Might and Magic IV and V (1992 and 1993) were pure genius. No one has quite duplicated this design in the history of computer games. If you owned M&M IV and M&M V and had them installed on the same hard drive, M&M V would open up a bridge, a dimension door, between the two games and the locations represented therein. Since the universe represented in 4 was the flipside of the universe represented in 5, this meant that you could go from one type of gaming experience to another. *But*, that's not all. *If* the two games were connected, there was not only a dimension door between the games, *but* there was an addition that amounted to approximately one third of the game—an extra quest, a new endgame, and additional dungeons that opened up if you had both games on your hard drive.

Might and Magic VI came out in 1998 and represented New World's first 3D graphic RPG. The team faced many unexpected challenges. "Working in 3D for the first time, we had to guess about the size of the game, the map size. It was very new and, in retrospect, several times we were inches away from guessing way wrong."

Might and Magic VII was based on the M&M VI engine, and therefore didn't require a lot of technical development. The design team concentrated on story and game play, with the result that VII was four times the size of VI. Might and Magic VIII is one of Van Caneghem's least favorites. It was based on the same engine again, which by this time was quite obsolete, and it was released in what he considers an "unfinished" state—ironically, it suffered the same fate as Ultima VIII.

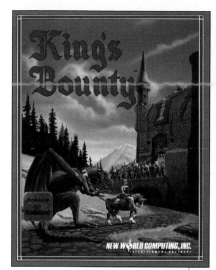

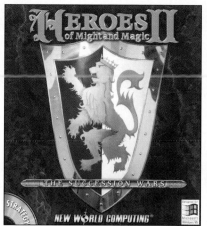

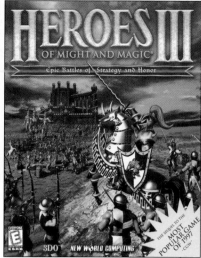

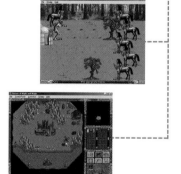

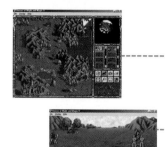

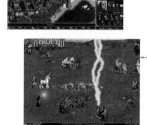

"I love role-playing and I love strategy, and I wanted a game in which I could control armies of creatures," says Van Caneghem about King's Bounty. This small, turn-based RPG adventure game came out in 1990 and was a very pleasant surprise. It was, by comparison with the Might and Magic games, quite small, and games were short in duration. And that was part of its appeal.

Years later, New World revised the King's Bounty games with the Heroes of Might and Magic series. "My wife, Debbie,

loved King's Bounty and so she pressured me to do more. So I finally gave in and made Heroes," relates Van Caneghem. "A good thing I listened."

SOMETHING DIFFERENT

Nuclear War was somewhat of a departure for New World, with a sort of tongue-in-cheek look at the world's political situation in 1989. It was basically a game that illustrated the principle of Mutual Assured Destruction. It was funny and sad at the same time.

Cinemaware: Made for CD

Master Designer Software Presents
A CINEMAWARE™ Production DEFENDER OF THE CROWN
Directed by KELLYN BEECK Computography and Art Direction by JAMES SACHS
Editing by Sculptured Software Inc. Special Effects by BRYAN BRANDENBURG
Original Score Composed by JIM CUOMO Unit publicist: MARC HALBERSTADT
Executive Producers: ROBERT & PHYLLIS JACOB
© 1986 Master Designer Software Inc. all rights reserved.

One of the most intriguing companies to come and go (and recently come back again) in computer game history, Cinemaware had a profound effect on a lot of us. Many of the alumni of this company are well-known developers who have continued long careers, including RJ Mical, John Cutter, Pat Cook, David Riordan, David Todd, and Doug Barnett.

Started in 1986 by Bob and Phyllis Jacobs, Cinemaware's initial mission was to produce games for the CD-ROM. Ironically, the CD didn't really catch on until after Cinemaware had closed its doors. But for glitz and glamour, nobody did it better. The box covers alone were worth the price, and the games were often offbeat, funny, and great to play.

Most of the games were originally created on the Commodore Amiga, much to the regret of those of us who were primarily using Apples and PCs.

Cinemaware's first release in 1986 was Kellyn Beck's

Defender of the Crown, a game set in England during the heyday of knights and fair maidens. It even included jousting, as well as castle raids and assaults.

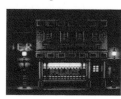

John Cutter likes to use S.D.I. as an example of the power of graphics in games. Cutter remembers, "We had already completed a version of S.D.I., but after seeing the graphics Jim Sachs did in Defender of the Crown, we realized we wanted better art. We hired professional artists and redid all the graphics. A month later, we got a new version back from Sculptured Software, who was programming the game. We were convinced that they had made all kinds of changes to the game play, but it turned out that they had not. It was just the improved graphics and some sound additions that made the game much, much better."

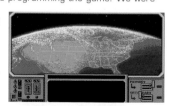

Sinbad and the Throne of the Falcon was another of Cinemaware's experiments in interactive cinema. "It was the first game I had seen where there was an active zoom feature triggered by the mouse. As the cursor moved across the map, you would click with the mouse to open up a window magnifying sections of the map. It had the effect of looking like you were peering at the map through a magnifying glass." (JLW)

In King of Chicago, you played a character named Pinky Callahan, and the object was to rise in the mob in post-Capone Chicago, "I remember the original Macintosh version of King of Chicago. It was downright weird. It featured clay-molded characters in a wicked, back-stabbing gangster adventure. This was definitely a 'do unto others before they do it to you' sort of game, and I loved it!" (RDM)

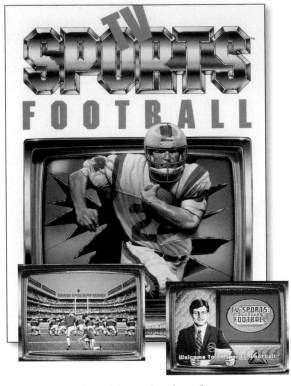

"When I'm talking to people about interface, the first example I give is S.D.I. The other example I give is Rocket Ranger," says Cinemaware producer John Cutter. "We had a fistfighting sequence against the Nazis in Rocket Ranger. When we first put the sequence together, it was missing something. For sound effects, we were using white noise, which was a common programmer's shortcut. But the Amiga could do real digitized sound effects, so we contacted Bill Williams, who had done everything for S.D.I. He actually went out and got a John Wayne movie and recorded a fistfight and used that sound as a punching sound. All of a sudden the fight became so much fun, in part, I suppose, because it really subconsciously sounded like a John Wayne movie. It's an example of how our emotions are affected, even when we don't know why or where it's coming from."

The TV Sports line of games that Cinemaware released attempted to create the same sort of atmosphere as sports on television, except, of course, that you got to control play of the game. But they had announcers, cheerleaders, and even funny commercials. The games themselves were pretty fun to play, too.

Producer John Cutter told us, "My favorite of the TV Sports games was TV Sports Football. Our passing interface was great. It required you to lead the receiver to complete the pass. One of my personal high points was when I beat Pat Cook in the finals of our tournament. Pat was a great game player, and to this day he swears I had the programmer tweak the game." Says Cook, "He's still telling that story? Of course he fixed it."

Designed by Doug Barnett, who did all the graphics and sounds for the game as well, and programmed by David Todd, Lords of the Rising Sun was possibly the most ambitious of Cinemaware's games. Barnett says, "I really got into it, reading books and buying swords—I couldn't eat sushi for a year after finishing the game." And David Todd adds, "Doug's original design had everything in it. A book an inch and a half thick. We had to trim it some."

Lords of the Rising Sun featured a stylized map of Japan set in the year 1180, during a famous period called the Gempi War. It featured two brothers, one more skilled in military matters and the other a superior politician. During the game, you had a first-person point-of-view (POV) in the ninja attack sequence, clever real-time battle formations, castle sieges, and various cut scenes. Barnett remembers, "This period of history had a lot of game play jumping out of it and saying 'Do me!' And in the end, one brother turns on the other, so you had to gauge when you were close to victory. That's when you'd lose half your forces."

During the development of the game, they flew Barnett to Dallas so he and Todd could work together more closely. "Every morning, the Dallas Cowboys cheerleaders would practice across the street. It was a good way to start the day," says Barnett. "David was married. He probably didn't even notice," he adds.

CINEMAWARE
PRESENTS

LORDS OF THE RISING SUN

David Riordan began in the music business, went to making films, and ultimately helped start Lucasfilm's game division at the request of George Lucas. Still, by the time he came to Cinemaware, he hadn't yet designed a game. It Came from the Desert was his debut as a designer. "I first came to Cinemaware at a time when I was considering quitting games and going back to films," says Riordan. "Then I saw my first Amiga, and the game on it was Defender of the Crown. I wrote Bob Jacobs a fan letter. Before I knew it, I was working for him. So then the time came to create a game for Cinemaware. I was thinking what kind of game I'd do. Something cinematic. I'm a big fan of the movie *Them*. So I asked Bob, 'What about a bug movie?' And he answered, 'Why not?' My original design was way too big. David Todd said to me, 'This is at least 10 disks. Hell, maybe it's 100.' So I asked myself, 'How do you do it all, keep it to a reasonable size and have it be fun without huge holes. How do you plot what we called a 'real-time environment?' I wanted the feeling that the ants were coming and things were happening where you were not. We thought we were heading to a time when we could really make movies."

CINEMAWARE® PRESENTS

BUY ONE GET ONE FREE SEE DETAILS INSIDE

IT CAME FROM THE DESERT™

SEE DECENT AMERICANS TERRORIZED!

HEAR TEENAGE GIRLS SQUEAL!

PRESENTED IN THRILL-O-VISION!

MAKE THEM ANTS CRY UNCLE!

M PC, Tandy and 100% Compatibles
GA, EGA, Tandy 16-color
OK Ram required
pports Ad lib, Soundblaster and
land Sound Cards
rd drive installable/recommended
ystick optional

" This was the first time I'd ever been put in a game. My first and last names were part of the random pool of pilot names, and once I even played as Jules DeMaria. (RDM)"

" What I liked most about Wings was the diary, which would continue with the story even if your pilot got killed. There was nothing to stop you from finishing the game, and lots of people commented that this was one of the first games they had been able to complete. We tried to give a good feeling for what it was like to be a pilot in World War I. When Bob first approached me to do the design, I wasn't very interested. But after an hour in the library reading about aviation in WWI, I was hooked. It was amazing, these young kids—often 18 or 19 years old—flying around and shooting at each other at a time when airplanes were so new."

—JOHN CUTTER, CINEMAWARE PRODUCER

For Cinemaware fans, old and new, there's exciting news. Go to www.cinemaware.com. See how the old company is being reborn!

Three-Sixty Pacific

I'D RATHER DO IT MYSELF!
Tom Frisina told *Computer Gaming World's* editorial staff that he planned to leave Accolade and start his own company, Three-Sixty Pacific. Ironically, when news of this was printed in the "Rumor Bag" column with Frisina's permission, Frisina called up all his investors and demanded to know where the leak came from. Later, reminded that he had given the story himself, he was astonished. "I was my own leak," he said, laughing.

In mid-1987, Tom Frisina left Accolade, which he had been running for about two years, and decided to start a company of his own. Tom had a vision of building a company around products that would appeal to a wider audience than the core computer game audience. At the beginning, however, he drew inspiration from Tom Clancy's novels. MicroProse had released Red Storm Rising, and Frisina was thinking about how to go even further with a submarine game. He knew that Clancy had used Larry Bond's Harpoon board game to work out some of his naval scenarios, so Frisina went directly to Bond, a former NATO referee for naval exercises.

Going for depth first and celebrity second, Three-Sixty Pacific not only published Bond's classic war game Harpoon, but also Dale Brown's Megafortress (a brilliant game version of Brown's best-selling thriller, *Flight of the Old Dog*); Jim Dunnigan's Victory at Sea (a campaign game set in the South Pacific theater of World War II using data compiled by Dunnigan, who was known among board gamers as the dean of war game designers); and Patriot (a game based on the Gulf War using the research compiled by veteran war game designer Frank Chadwick).

Frisina was savvy enough not to tie his future to military strategy games alone (although they became Three-Sixty's bread and butter). He had a vision of publishing software that would make even more of a difference. Working with former NASA psychologist Taibi Kahler (author of *The*

Mastery of Management), he published a software product called Bridges that tested for elements of six personality types using the prototyping developed by Kahler at NASA. Unfortunately, the buyers at the software chains simply wouldn't take seriously a psychological product developed by a "mere" game company.

Three-Sixty Pacific's biggest problem, however, was the fact that they sank too much money into products that didn't fully satisfy their customer base in between the innovative titles. For instance, Artech (the Canadian group that had worked with Frisina since Accolade) talked Three-Sixty into publishing an abstract puzzle game called Theatre of War. It was to war games what sophisticated jazz is to popular music and proved unsatisfying to the company's usual customer base. In addition, buggy initial versions made Patriot and Victory at Sea unplayable at launch, and Three-Sixty started to develop a negative cash flow. Barely finishing Harpoon II after a "shotgun wedding" with Intracorp, who also funded Capstone, Three-Sixty Pacific became one of those "coulda' been a contender" companies that faded into history.

More Favorite Games of the 80s

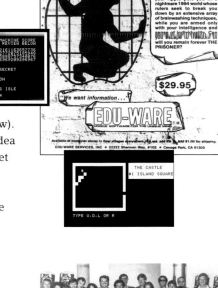

In addition to major companies who had a huge impact on the computer game industry, many small companies produced amazing game classics. There were also some games that came from major publishers that we wanted to acknowledge on their own—games such as Wasteland, Alter Ego, Shanghai, and Little Computer People. In the following section, we'll look at some of our favorite games of the 80s, starting with one of the least graphical, and yet most mental, of games—David Mullich's The Prisoner.

The Prisoner

David Mullich worked for Edu-Ware while still in college, later joining the company and becoming vice president of product development. Sherwin Steffin and Steve Pederson started Edu-Ware in 1978 for the purpose of creating educational software, but, according to Mullich, "they got more publicity out of their entertainment software."

Edu-Ware published several games, including Space, a port of the popular board game Traveler, as well as Terrorist and Windfall, which was an economic simulation about the oil crisis. They also did Network, in which they cast the player in the role of a TV network programmer trying for the highest ratings.

By far their most noteworthy game, however, was The Prisoner, which was inspired both by the TV show of the same name and by an experiment Mullich had learned about in a psychology class (see Rules of the Game below).

"I was so enthusiastic about the show and the whole idea of this community that was all geared toward trying to get information out of a spy by tricking him...playing mind games on him. I wanted to create a computer game that would play mind games on players, lead them down false alleys, change the rules on the fly, trick them into doing something they shouldn't do."

Muse Software—Castle Wolfenstein and RobotWar

At approximately the same time that The Avalon Hill Game Company was making its first venture into the world of computer games, another Baltimore company made its appearance. Muse Software appeared on the entertainment software horizon after they recruited a programmer named Silas Warner. Warner had worked for Commercial Credit Corporation, supervising their PLATO accounts and writing a sales call simulator as part of the company's training program. The simulator was programmed in two weeks after the company had undergone a role-playing experience as part of its training.

Early Edu-Ware

RULES OF THE GAME

The subject was placed in a room with strings tied to opposite walls. There was a pair of scissors in the room. The object was to tie the strings together, but the strings were too short. The solution was to use the scissors as clamps—the opposite of their normal use. I wanted to do a game where you would have to do the complete opposite of what you thought the rules would dictate.

—David Mullich

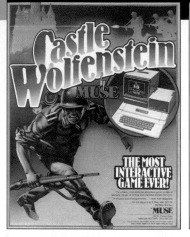

Magazine ads for Castle
Wolfenstein and RobotWar.

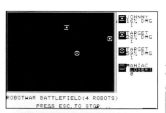

RobotWar and Castle
Wolfenstein screens.

When Warner arrived at Muse Software, he designed two games that defined the early era of computing, Castle Wolfenstein and RobotWar. The former was an action-adventure game that inspired id Software's Wolfenstein 3D. The latter was a programmer's dream, where players would use a special pseudocode to program robotic behavior. Then, much like the BattleBots of today, they would be placed in an arena and allowed to fight it out. The last robot standing was the winner. Although the game fostered numerous tournaments in regional user groups and a play-by-mail tournament for *Computer Gaming World* magazine (where competitors saved their source code to disk and then mailed it to the magazine so that editors could place their robots into tournament matches), it was more of a cult classic than a best-selling blockbuster. Tributes to RobotWar include Origin's OMEGA game and the shareware version of C-ROBOTS, available online.

Although best known for Castle Wolfenstein and RobotWar, Muse also published action games like ABM (similar to Missile Command), Frazzle (similar to Asteroids but with a spatial twist), and Firebug (a reverse Pac-Man where the player is destroying the maze of a building instead of avoiding ghosts). Firebug was later changed to Firefly because the publisher didn't want to be accused of promoting arson. Perhaps the most interesting thing about Firebug was its delightful pun whenever you lost the game. The screen would go dark and then display, "You made an ash of yourself!" Talk about adding insult to injury!

Muse Software quit publishing in the mid-80s, but

Silas Warner went on to become the conversion guru for MicroProse Software. At MicroProse, he converted Sid Meier's Pirates! to the Apple IIGS, Red Storm Rising to the C-64, Silent Service to the Atari ST, and Gunship to the Amiga.

The Perfect General

One of the finest tactical war games ever produced on the computer was the result of 12 years of play testing. Bruce Williams Zaccagnino, who had built what the Smithsonian called the World's Largest Model Railroad, also had a passion for military miniatures. His local war game club had developed rules for playing with miniature tanks and soldiers played on scale-model terrains.

Zaccagnino started Quantum Quality Productions (QQP) with the idea of bringing his war game experience to the home computer. He drafted Mark Baldwin and Bob Rakosky of Empire—and later, Empire Deluxe—fame, to design the interface and artificial intelligence for two games: The Perfect General and The Lost Admiral, both of which were released in 1991.

The Perfect General offered an easy point-and-click interface for movement and targeting, as well as three levels of difficulty for the AI. Using the tabletop miniatures

When we first got The Perfect General at **Computer Gaming World,** *one of our editors, Allan Emrich, lost five out of the next seven workdays to the game. I, being a responsible editor, only lost two out of the next three. (JLW)*

model, all QQP games allowed players to purchase units for points. The Perfect General was also one of the early point-to-point modem games, and for years it was one of the most-played games on the Web. Perfect General II still has quite a following, with new scenarios available free. Check http://www.members.tripod.com/~tpg2/index.htm.

Empire: Wargame of the Century

Like many other computer games, the history of Empire begins in the analog world of tabletop gaming. Peter S. Langston and friends were playing an abstract war game at Reed College in the early 70s. Langston wondered about using a computer to run the game and simulate the "fog of war" effect, which would prevent players from seeing the whole battlefield—something very difficult to accomplish with tabletop games.

Langston's Empire, begun in 1971, was a text-only multiplayer game. The world was updated once per day (usually at midnight). However, attacks were handled instantaneously, which led to some interesting ploys by avid players.

After Langston, Walter Bright continued to advance and popularize the game, drawing inspiration from the British war room in the film *Battle of Britain* and from Risk, the board game. Bright made refinements to the multiplayer game, and in the mid-80s, he developed a single-player game for personal computers. Bright's version was turned down by many of the major game publishers, however, largely for its out-of-date graphics and interface.

Independently, Mark Baldwin did a version of Empire for Interstel, and his version looked terrific on both the Atari ST and Commodore

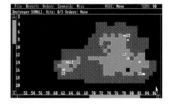

Amiga. He brought the game to current interface standards, offering point-and-click movement and pop-up menus. For the first time, players could escort transports with destroyers and group task forces efficiently. This Baldwin and Bright version of Empire: Wargame of the Century was to be converted to a half-dozen different computer platforms and was one of Interstel's best titles ever. It was also released with a Play-by-Mail feature so that players could trade disks via snail mail (and later files via email).

After Interstel's collapse, Baldwin joined with a frequent collaborator named Bob Rakosky to create Empire Deluxe, a Windows-based program for New World Computing, complete with a versatile construction set and, to make it more accessible, three different levels of game play (Basic, Standard, and Advanced). Empire Deluxe was successful enough that the team dipped into the well again and released Empire II, a tactical war game construction set using the expertise in AI design and interface development created for Empire Deluxe.

Peter Langston's favorite story about Empire is the one about the vice president of a large corporation who was so agitated by an attack on his country that he allegedly walked into the computer room and flipped the main circuit breaker to abort the attack. Then there's the Harvard student who refused to go to bed until everyone logged out of Empire. So the other players took turns staying up late in order to foil his dedicated plan for "national security."

Walter Bright tells a story about the sysops at Cal Tech who didn't want gamers tying up the PDP-10 with games, so they severely restricted the hours that people could play Empire. Bright simply switched the name of the game to "test" and played anytime he wanted for months before the sysops caught on.

Walter Bright's original version of Empire required a lot of command input and waiting while the computer thought, but still featured addictive play.

Mark Baldwin's refinement of Bright's design in Empire: Wargame of the Century significantly improved the interface.

Wasteland

Wasteland was created at Interplay and distributed by Electronic Arts. Although its interface bore a great resemblance to Interplay's The Bard's Tale, the game itself was quite different and featured plenty of innovation. Many players still consider it to be among the greatest role-playing games ever written. Wasteland differed from other games by being based, not in some medieval fantasy world, but on the modern science fiction tabletop role-playing game called Mercenaries, Spies and Private Eyes. The game demanded the use of modern weapons, and Wasteland was the first CRPG to feature an encounter with an armored vehicle. This, in turn, required the use of armor-piercing shells and some additional programming to modify the damage calculations. Wasteland also offered a robust skill-based system that allowed characters to improve without engaging in combat.

Wasteland's excellent design team included best-selling novelist Michael A. Stackpole, the creator of Mercenaries, Spies and Private Eyes. The game was set in a post-apocalyptic desert world. Stackpole also designed some of the game maps himself, and farmed out maps to others, including Ken St. Andre (designer of Tunnels & Trolls) and fantasy artist Liz Danforth. Danforth is the wicked designer who created the rabid dog dilemma. You needed to kill the rabid dog to get out of a cave on her map. If you killed the dog, a little boy followed you and complained, "You killed my dog, you dirty Rangers!" Some players ended up avoiding the town where Bobby was just to avoid the nuisance of his constant accusation. Others heartlessly killed Bobby to remove the annoyance factor. Vince DeNardo, *Computer Gaming World*'s art director at the time, restarted the game and kept saving and resaving the game until he could escape from the cave without killing the dog. As a result of such encounters, Wasteland became similar to Ultima IV as one of the few computer role-playing games that forced you to ask questions before you shot anything.

Shanghai

If the basic solitaire and Free Cell solitaire games that are bundled with Microsoft Windows are the most-played games in the personal computer world, Shanghai must be a close second. It has been converted to dozens of operating systems, from PCs to consoles and handhelds, including an amazing number of versions in Japan that ran on what were formerly "dedicated" word processors.

It is a simple concept. Take the beautiful tiles from a Mahjong set and assemble them on screen in the formation known for centuries as "The Turtle." Then, dismantle "The Turtle" by matching pairs until no tiles remain. The result is a simple and compelling solitaire game perfectly suited to the computer, where it takes mere seconds to set up, as opposed to the much more laborious task of setting up the real tiles.

Bill Swartz, longtime president of Activision Japan, remembers that no matter how many times Activision licensed the game in the Asia-Pacific region, no one would believe that the computer game was designed by a Westerner. Still less could anyone believe that every tile was painted and every line was coded by a brilliant man who could not move from the neck down.

Brodie Lockard was a Stanford University gymnast who suffered a terrible accident. After the accident, his body was confined to a wheelchair, but his mind and spirit could not be confined. Lockard accepted a job at Stanford, but continued to program educational projects on his own time. Fascinated with "The Turtle" Mahjong variation, he programmed it as an online game for one of the early communications services that antedated the World Wide

Shanghai screen.

Web. It quickly became the most-played game on the service, despite the fact that the meter was always running when people played. When the color Macintosh appeared, Lockard painted elaborate tiles, holding a special stylus in his mouth.

Activision producer Brad Fregger (who also produced the first computer solitaire game, Spectrum Holobyte's Solitaire Royale) saw the game on Christmas Eve of 1985. Borrowing a copy from Lockard, he took it home. Everybody who played it got instantly hooked. And, as they say, the rest is history.

Alter Ego

Electronic Arts often used "celebrity designers" for their games, picking their brains concerning their field of expertise. When EA published a psychological game (Mind Mirror), they consulted with Dr. Timothy Leary, the foremost advocate in the U.S. for mind expansion via mind-altering drugs.

When Activision published its psychological game, the emphasis was on fun. Designed by Peter J. Favaro, the adolescent and child psychologist who wrote *Smart Parenting*, Alter Ego had different versions for male or female characters. The game functioned as a role-playing game that pulled back the veil on psychological development. On screen, the game looked like a graphic flowchart. Players would choose from various options on the decision tree based on a family crest

for family matters, a heart for emotional decisions, a fluoroscope for physical decisions, and faces for social decisions. Often, the situations were humorous (particularly when players did the wrong thing on purpose), and sometimes, they were sexual (particularly during the adolescent phase of the game). Usually, the situations presented a dilemma to which the player would respond by choosing a mood and an action. Then, just as in a role-playing game, players would see their characters improve in physical characteristics, mental discipline, social skills, and occupational potential. Other icons represent opportunities for relationships, jobs, scholarship, and recreation. Alter Ego was an interesting experiment in nonviolent games that related to real life. It didn't sell enough to suit Activision's goals, but it is certainly one of the more interesting and fun-to-play games of its era.

Little Computer People

Little Computer People was a relatively obscure game, but one that created a lasting impact on the people who played it. Perhaps the first example of a commercial "artificial life" product, a decade before Tamagotchi (see page 313), this game was seminal. Here are some comments from designer David Crane (see page 64): "If it is little known that I was the author of Activision's Little Computer People, then it is even less known that this product began life as something else.

"An independent, creative guy in L.A. by the name of Rich Gold had an idea to bring the 'Pet Rock' concept to video games. He got some funding and developed a noninteractive product he called 'Pet Person' containing much of the animation and sound effects of the ultimate LCP product. It was his intention that the product would be used like a fishbowl. You

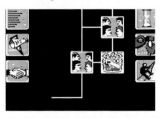

In Alter Ego, you could start at any of life's stages...

...then use the on-screen decision points to play the game. The screen shows part of the high school section. As characters matured, additional options like High School, Relationships, Job, and Recreation were added to the options at the side of the flowchart.

Screen from Little Computer People.

Screen from Tycoon.

turn it on and just watch it all day without any interactivity. He was unable to get it published in that form, but we got a look at it, saw its potential, and bought his early work.

"The graphics and animations were superb, and I kept them pretty much intact, adding sounds, music, and additional capabilities. I then put almost a year into it, turning the character into an interactive, semiintelligent, and responsive simulation. We came up with a way to customize every diskette so that each Computer Person would be unique in every way—appearance, personality, etc. Added to the technical effort was some great creative support from marketing. They developed the concept of invisible people living in your computer, the research publication, and all of the support materials that made the game something special. In spite of all that, the product was never a big success. That was unfortunate because we had all sorts of plans for follow-up products if it had been successful.

"Not that it was a failure; everybody's development costs got covered with a little profit. But we were all prepared to make an apartment building with dozens of Computer People, all interacting with one another and trading equipment and furnishings, etc. We had hopes to create disks full of new stuff and/or new houses that you could buy to customize your Computer Person's environment. But you don't do sequels unless the market demands it, and that demand never materialized. Oh well.

"Some users would write to us in a panic when a Commodore crash damaged their diskette. They would beg us to fix 'their Aaron' (or whatever the name). So I created a 'LCP hospital' computer so that our customer service people could make a fresh diskette that incorporated the 2048-bit personality parameter from the old one. We were able to 'save' hundreds of Little Computer People in our hospital.

"All in all, it was a fun project. I may yet do another product along those lines if the right deal comes along."

Blue Chip Software

In 1982, after learning some hard lessons in the stock market, Jim Zuber founded Blue Chip Software and published Millionaire, a stock market simulation that tracked earnings, volume, general trends, and specific industry trends. As in real life, stock performance tended to reflect overall market performance (bullish uptrends, bearish downturns, and mixed markets), industry group strength, corporate strength, and news.

The game (and its sequels) presented general market trends, industry sector trends, and individual stock performance in chart form. Less sophisticated than charts used by technical investors, they taught you a lot, nonetheless. Also, in what became a tradition for Blue Chip Software games, players could leverage their investments into more risky portfolios as they earned money up to certain thresholds. You started with $10,000 and could improve your investment power with several techniques, such as margin buying, puts and calls, and selling short. Each technique required higher earning thresholds.

Zuber followed up Millionaire's positive reception with his most interesting game, Tycoon. Using the same system, virtual investors could play the commodities market. Tycoon was faster moving than the stock market game and offered enough historical data so that players could invest as fundamentalists (following basic inferences on potential supply/demand for each commodity) or technicians (creating a strategy based on past performance charted against current trends).

Less successful were Blue Chip's games Baron, a real estate simulation, and Squire, an investment game that included such things as art and collectibles. They did come out with one more game with the quality and precision of Millionaire and Tycoon—American Dream, an IBM game in which you managed your own business.

Blue Chip was ultimately acquired by Britannica Software, but their only interesting release after that was a more detailed $99 version of Millionaire called American Investor, created for serious investors with assistance from the American Stock Exchange (Amex). When Britannica Software became Compton's New Media (the company who claimed a patent on multimedia products in the early 90s), the company faded to the backlist and off the shelf.

Rocky's Boots

In 1979, when Warren Robinett left Atari, after creating the first video game Easter Egg in his VCS Adventure (see page 39), he backpacked around Europe for a while and thought about what he'd do next. "I wanted to do another adventure game, and I wanted it to be one where you had to build machines to defeat monsters. I thought up two classes of machines—sensors and actuators. Sensors would put out signals that would go to the actuators. For instance, a monster sensor would activate a bomb."

When he got back from his travels, he was introduced to three women who were proposing to do games. These women, Anne Piestrup (now McCormick), Leslie Grim, and Teri Perl, were all highly educated academics. Working with money from a grant from the National Science Foundation, they started The Learning Company. Their first product was called Logic Tools, which was the precursor to the group's first game, and one of the true classics of computer gaming, Rocky's Boots.

Rocky's Boots was a construction set, ultimately, that allowed you to wire together machines that would use logic circuits (AND gates, OR gates, NOT gates, flip-flops) to trigger a big boot, which would sense and eliminate target items, such as red triangles or anything but green circles, as they passed by. The game was innovative and fascinating to play, and was, in some ways, a precursor to later construction games like The Incredible Machine.

The Learning Company went on to become the most successful educational game company in the history of electronic games, distributing many classic educational game series, including Reader Rabbit and Oregon Trail. And it all started with the boot. At the time of this writing, Robinett is working on the game he started out to create—an adventure game where you build machines to defeat the monsters. To keep up with his progress, check out www.warrenrobinett.com.

Flight Simulator

Bruce Artwick's 1975 thesis at the University of Illinois was entitled "A Versatile Computer-Generated Dynamic Flight Display." From this thesis evolved one of the all-time classic products, Flight Simulator. Originally published by SubLOGIC in 1979 for Apple II and TRS-80 computers, Flight Simulator came to the attention of Bill Gates and Microsoft, which Artwick thought of as a "nice small company." Microsoft obtained the license and released its first version of Flight Simulator in 1982. The rest is history.

Flight Simulator was known for its accuracy and realism, and subsequent versions became ever more accurate and detailed, with continued improvements in the graphics. Scenery disks ultimately became available so you could fly over your favorite city or landscape. Flight Simulator has been a perennial software leader, and Microsoft continues to produce new versions.

Warren Robinett testing Rocky's Boots at a Palo Alto, California, elementary school in 1982.

Some believe that Bruce Artwick was influenced by a game called Airfight on the PLATO system. This may or may not be the case, but it is plausible.

Home Systems of the Late 80s

A fter almost two decades of growth, the video game industry faced a meltdown in the mid-80s. The home computer game business was expanding, but the audience was too small to save the industry. Worse, the majority of the world just viewed computers as business utilities. Let's face it. Games were considered frivolous.

Radarscope flyer.

However, some bold players from Japan went against conventional wisdom. Because of their willingness to take risks, the video game business bounced back—ultimately stronger than before. Pole position in this new campaign was taken, not by Atari, whose credibility by this time was at an all-time low, but by Nintendo, whose previous successes had all been in the coin-operated arena.

Nintendo

Today Nintendo is a household name throughout the world, virtually synonymous with video games, but its march to dominance began over 100 years ago. In 1889, Fusajiro Yamauchi founded Nintendo as a playing card company. Over the next 50 years Nintendo grew to prominence. By 1959, they printed and

sold cards with Disney characters on them, opening up the market for children's playing cards.

In the 60s, Nintendo branched out and began to manufacture games. Their new game division was led by the legendary Gunpei Yokoi, whose first game product was a mechanical hand called the Ultrahand that sold more than a million units. Yokoi followed the hand with the Ultra Machine, an indoor baseball pitching

Nintendo's early cards: Japanese Hanafuda playing cards and Disney playing cards.

machine, a periscope toy called the Ultra Scope, and a very popular "love tester" that actually measured electric current flowing between two people. In 1970, Yokoi hired Masayuki Uemoura, who was selling solar cells for Sharp Electronics at the time. The two teamed up to create Nintendo's Beam Gun, a game that used optics and electronics together. People shot the guns, and the targets would fall over. The Beam Gun marked Nintendo's entry into the world of electronic games.

During the 70s, Nintendo created a number of electronic toys, including a video recording (EVR) player in conjunction with Mitsubishi Electric. They also licensed the Magnavox Odyssey for sale in Japan and began to create coin-operated video games. Then, in 1980 Nintendo introduced Yokoi's next brainchild—the fantastically popular and much-imitated

Game & Watch series. These small, highly addictive handheld games also featured a digital watch and alarm.

As the 70s drew to a close, Nintendo released their first coin-operated arcade game, Radarscope, which was second in popularity only to Galaxian in Japan. However, Radarscope didn't sell well in the U.S. Heading the U.S. operations, initially from New Jersey, was Minoru Arakawa, son-in-law to Nintendo's president, Hiroshi Yamauchi.

Arakawa remembers the early days. "We brought all the Radarscope machines from Japan via Panama to New Jersey. By the time they reached us, the game's market opportunity was already half dead. We asked Japan to come up with the next great game, but all the R&D heads were busy and didn't want to do anything for us. So they appointed a young guy who had just joined Nintendo to develop a game for us." The game was Donkey Kong. The young employee was Shigeru Miyamoto.

But Donkey Kong wasn't an instant hit with the employees at Nintendo of America. "Donkey Kong was really different from the existing shoot-'em-up games," Arakawa recalls. "All the employees at NOA were disappointed and started looking for new jobs. They saw no future with us. So we put it in a local tavern and the next day there was $30 in the cash box. The day after it was $35. That was really good back then. By the third day we thought, 'This is not a joke. It's a really good game!'"

At the time, Ron Judy, Nintendo's U.S. distributor, had just taken a bath trying unsuccessfully to distribute Radarscope machines, but he took Arakawa to meet a lawyer friend named Howard Lincoln in spring 1981. Lincoln vividly recalls his first meeting with Judy and Arakawa.

Nintendo's VS. arcade system.

"Arakawa wanted help trademarking a game. I remember Ron's face when he said the name Donkey Kong. It's a name that's incomprehensible to English-speaking people. I had to get the spelling first. But then they released the game, and it took off like wildfire. I didn't see Ron again until September, when he came to me to incorporate because he was making so much money."

In 1983, Yamauchi incorporated the U.S. subsidiary. Nintendo of America was started with Arakawa at its head. The same year, Howard Lincoln joined Nintendo of America, first as senior vice president and, the next year, as chairman. He now is chairman of the Seattle Mariners.

Donkey Kong figured heavily in the launch of both ColecoVision and the Adam computer, and it was during that time that Universal brought suit against Nintendo and Coleco over the similarity between Donkey Kong and their property, King Kong. Lincoln recalls, "It was very risky for NOA, which was still relatively small. And when somebody like Sid Scheinberg sends you a *cease and desist*, it gets your attention. The litigation was protracted, but in hindsight it turned out the right way." And, in the end, Nintendo was able to continue marketing Donkey Kong.

In the early 80s, Nintendo began work on a next-generation home game machine, introducing the Family Computer (or FamiCom) in Japan in 1983, where it was very successful. However, the collapse of the video industry made the timing bad for a U.S. release. Nintendo began negotiations with a disintegrating Atari to OEM the system. Nintendo's Arakawa remembers, "During the negotiations quite a few people at Atari were fired or laid off between meetings, and every meeting was attended by different people." Needless to say, the negotiations did not go

Nintendo's Family Computer (FamiCom) (above). Original Nintendo Entertainment System and Robot Operated Buddy (ROB) (below).

Sega cofounder Dave Rosen with some of Sega's early games.

well. "It was the best thing that happened to Nintendo," says Arakawa. "If Atari had taken the product, it's doubtful that Nintendo of America would exist today."

Unable to introduce the Family Computer in the U.S., Nintendo created a series of coin-operated games for the arcades called the VS. System, based on the FamiCom hardware and featuring many of the early FamiCom games. "We found from our testing in certain locations that the systems made lots of cash, and we knew our quality was good. We were confident by 1985 that people would like our system, but the retailers were a different story," says Arakawa.

To get past the once-burned-twice-shy retailers, Nintendo came up with the idea of bundling the FamiCom, now renamed the Nintendo Entertainment System (NES), with a toy robot called R.O.B. or Robot Operating Buddy. The system also included a light pistol (the Zapper) and the games Duck Hunt and Super Mario Bros.

It worked. The NES grew in popularity as consumers, once jaded by the early 80s machines, flocked to purchase the NES and play Super Mario Bros. and the other great games that began to appear on the new console. Arakawa once again: "The players were not tired of games. They were just tired of average games."

Sega

In 1952, two Americans, Dick Stewart and Ray Lemaire, went to Japan and started a company to place jukeboxes on U.S. military bases. Service Games eventually expanded to 5,000 locations all over Japan. In 1953, Dave Rosen went to Japan and formed an art and general import business, Rosen Enterprises, Ltd.

By 1956 or so, the Japanese economy was starting to revive, and there was more disposable income and time for entertainment. Rosen decided to import mechanical games

from the States. "At that time," recalls Rosen, "such licenses were only granted for necessities, and they didn't classify this as a necessity."

Rosen's idea to import mechanical games to Japan worked splendidly, and within a short time he had established arcades in virtually every town and city in Japan. "These

Some of Sega's pre-video games, including Punching Bag (1962), Rifleman, the first mechanical game they made (1967), Periscope (1968), and their last mechanical game (other than pinball), Jet Rocket (1970).

arcades were not like the arcades in the U.S.," he says. "It wasn't just a matter of placing the machines in a location. There were backdrops, and the machines were built into the scenery." Among the most successful games were the rifle shooting games. The Japanese were not allowed to own guns, and they flocked to these games.

Rosen remembers becoming more and more dissatisfied with the quality of games he was importing, many of which were older models. "By the mid-60s," he says, "it became apparent that the Chicago game manufacturers, such as Bally, Midway, Williams, Chicago Coin, and Gottlieb, were not really manufacturing games that were novel and new, but were satisfying themselves with cosmetic changes on the same games. So in 1965, I merged Rosen Enterprises with Service Games, which had since shortened its name to Sega. The new company was Sega Enterprises, Ltd. One of our main purposes was to begin to develop and manufacture our own games for the arcade locations we had."

Sega began developing new games, as many as ten a year at one point, and by 1967 had begun exporting them to the States. "The first game we built was Rifleman. Our first big success was Periscope," says Rosen. "From 1967 through 1979 we manufactured 140 different games, but soon afterward the Chicago companies began copying our games. In fact, our last game, and one of the finest mechanicals ever built, was Jet Rocket, and somehow a bunch of other companies had learned about it. Bally, Williams, and Chicago Coin each had a version of it when we brought it out."

In the late 70s, Sega began to build arcade video games, and in 1980, they acquired Gremlin, a San Diego–based company with a large manufacturing plant. Ironically, according to Rosen, Sega was the first distributor for Nintendo's Beam Gun product in the U.S.

In addition to arcade systems, Sega began producing and licensing games for the home systems. At about this same time, Sega was made part of Gulf & Western's Paramount group, best known for their movie business. Rosen joined the board of Paramount, and movie moguls Mike Heisner and Barry Diller joined Sega's board.

Although he had seen it coming, Rosen could do nothing to prevent the effects of the video game collapse of the early 80s, and consequently Gulf & Western decided to sell off Sega. Rosen, along with the head of the Japanese operation, H. Nakayama, and an investor, Mr. Ohkawa, bought it. Nakayama became president, and Ohkawa became chairman in Japan, while Rosen agreed to run the U.S. operation, but only for a few years.

The Master System

"Everybody was looking to produce a better product back in the Coleco days," says Rosen, "and we had developed a machine, but we were not really very aggressive in pushing it. We were more interested in attempting to sell software." Then, after the game market collapse, he adds, "The industry was fairly well written off. We had product in the pipeline, but we had put it on the shelf. We took it off the shelf when we started to see what was happening with Nintendo. But we were a year behind Nintendo, and that was a very difficult hurdle to overcome. Nintendo had a very deep foothold in the Japanese market and very strong alliances with third-party developers. We found ourselves in the position of having to scramble in the U.S., so we made a distribution deal with Tonka Toys."

In addition to being late, the Master System also suffered from having very little original software at the beginning. Nintendo had locked up most of the third-party Japanese developers with exclusive contracts. Sega drew from its well of popular arcade games, but remakes of arcade games couldn't compete with the original fare provided by Nintendo and its third-party developers.

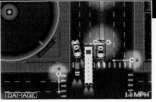

Midnight Club and Madden 2002 for Game Boy Advance.

Sega did ultimately come out with more original games. "But by that time it was becoming obvious to us that we would be, at best, a poor second," laments Rosen. Among the best of the Master System's games was Phantasy Star, the first in Sega's excellent RPG series.

While the Master System struggled to gain a foothold in the States, Sega was already working on their next machine—a true 16-bit home game console. "There was a difference of opinion in Japan about how to distribute the new machine. Some wanted to find a partner and do a joint venture, but I thought that would be difficult. The margins on the hardware were not great. The true profits were in the software. Still, we did approach several toy companies and others, including Atari, to distribute the new machine. But it all came to naught," says Rosen, "and we were left with the option of going out and doing it on our own."

Handheld Games

Handheld games had enjoyed considerable popularity in the late 70s and during the 80s, but the idea of a complete handheld game system really came into its own in the late 80s. Initially, there were four main contenders, each with its strengths and weaknesses. In the end, there was one clear winner.

Nintendo's Game Boy

In 1989, Gunpei Yokoi, who had designed Nintendo's popular Game & Watch hardware, produced a cartridge-based hand-held device, which Nintendo called Game Boy. The system was compact and well built, but it only featured graphics in four shades of gray. Compared with other handheld systems of the time, it seemed quite crude and unimpressive. But Nintendo's genius for marketing and for controlling their markets once again shined, and in the end, none of the other

handheld game systems survived long, while the Game Boy went on to sell more than 500 million units, more than any other console system in history. Of course, having Tetris bundled with the system in the U.S. was a brilliant stroke. It was the perfect game for the system.

Ironically, Game Boy was the only major handheld game system that was monochrome, but Nintendo eventually rectified this situation, first in 1994 by introducing the Super Game Boy, which was an attachment to the Super NES that allowed Game Boy games to be played in color on a TV. Later, in 1998, they released Game Boy Color; then, in 2001, they released the long-anticipated Game Boy Advance, with superior color graphics and far more sophisticated game play.

TurboExpress

NEC's TurboExpress was in some ways the premier handheld system. It was a full TurboGrafx-16 system and used the exact same HuCard games. Of course, it couldn't play the CD games, but its library of available games was much greater than any other system. Its color LCD screen gave a crisp, clean image. TurboExpress was even the first handheld game system to offer an optional TV tuner peripheral so you could watch your favorite shows

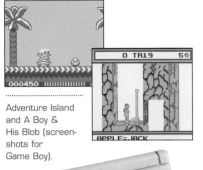

Adventure Island and A Boy & His Blob (screenshots for Game Boy).

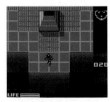

Metal Gear Solid for Game Boy Color.

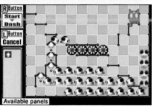

Available panels

Castlevania and Chu Chu Rocket for Game Boy Advance.

between games. However, the system was costly ($299.95 vs. $109 for Game Boy—even the TurboGrafx-16 system was only $189), and despite a large game library, its primary audience was players who already had the TurboGrafx-16, and therefore already had the games. Buying an even more expensive system to play the same games, even an ultracool handheld device, was probably not in most players' budgets.

Game Gear

The Game Gear was Sega's entry into the handheld market, but it did not fare well against the competition. It featured a color display and some good games, but it was a battery hog and was neither as crisp or advanced as the TurboExpress, and, although it did have a couple of exclusive Sonic the Hedgehog titles, it lacked the third-party support or marketing of its main competition, Nintendo's Game Boy.

TENGEN

Atari Games formed a new division called Tengen to create games primarily for the NES. Originally a legitimate Nintendo licensee, they didn't like the hefty cut of profits that Nintendo took. At the time, Nintendo kept strict control over all games produced for the NES, manufacturing the cartridges themselves and including a special microprocessor called the "lockout chip," which prevented any but those carts produced by Nintendo from working in the machine. Tengen reverse-engineered the lockout chip and announced that they were going to produce games independently, bypassing Nintendo altogether.

Nintendo took them to court for copyright infringement. One of the first Tengen titles was Tetris, but it ended up that they had bought the rights from Mirrorsoft, who, in the end, did not own them. Tengen was able to stay in the NES business for a while, but, by 1991, the courts upheld Nintendo's case against them, and they were forced to stop. Nintendo also purchased the legitimate Tetris rights and released their own versions of the product. For more about Tetris, see page 196.

THE ATARI LYNX

Originally called the Handy Game, the Lynx was an advanced system, but suffered from Atari's reputation and competition from Nintendo. Here's the story, as told by codesigner RJ Mical:

"There were three guys—Dave Morse, Dave Needle and me. Dave Morse's son said one day, 'Dad, you should take that Amiga idea and do something small that you can hold in your hand.' So we went to a restaurant and did some drawings on napkins to see what it would look like. We stole the napkins. We decided we should start a company, but then we found Epyx, which was a cool company and decided to throw our lot in with them. We became part of Epyx and completed the design. But due to reasons out of our control Epyx had spent too much money on other things and dipped into our project. They didn't have enough money to market it. The Lynx was done. It was in a phase where the hardware and tools were done and people were developing software for it. But it would die without marketing. Then we found out that Atari wanted to acquire it, but Needle and I had a bad impression of Atari at the time. If the stories we'd heard were true, they were not pleasant people to do business with. So when Epyx announced that they were making a deal with Atari, we didn't want to have anything to do with it. We said we'd quit if they went with Atari. And they said they were going with Atari. So we quit.

"The next time we were free to meet, we went to another restaurant and began drawing the 3DO system on napkins. We stole those napkins, too." (See also page 254.)

The Lynx was a good color handheld system, and probably deserved to do better than it did, but, like all the other handhelds other than Game Boy, it had a short life.

Cyberball, Ninja Gaiden, and Shanghai for Lynx.

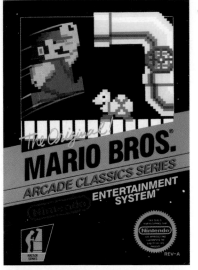

Mario & Zelda

It's amazing to remember that it all started with Donkey Kong, but the career of Shigeru Miyamoto began with the rampaging ape, and his genius for game character development and design has continued to delight and entertain millions ever since. These pages celebrate two of Miyamoto's most significant series: Mario and Zelda.

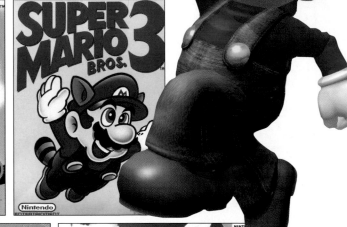

The first home Mario games were on the Nintendo Entertainment System, and they evolved in complexity and depth over several versions.

Mario leaped into our homes again as the launch title for the Super NES.

The first 3D version of Super Mario, for the Nintendo 64, was a marvel of game design and perspective.

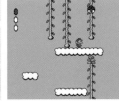

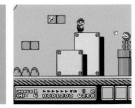

Screens from NES versions of Mario: Mario Bros., Super Mario Bros., Super Mario 2, and Super Mario 3.

Mario inspired many products, among the best being Super Mario Kart and Super Smash Bros.

Super Smash Bros.

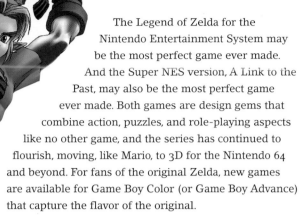

The Legend of Zelda for the Nintendo Entertainment System may be the most perfect game ever made. And the Super NES version, A Link to the Past, may also be the most perfect game ever made. Both games are design gems that combine action, puzzles, and role-playing aspects like no other game, and the series has continued to flourish, moving, like Mario, to 3D for the Nintendo 64 and beyond. For fans of the original Zelda, new games are available for Game Boy Color (or Game Boy Advance) that capture the flavor of the original.

Original Legend of Zelda screens.

Includes invaluable maps and strategic playing tips.

Link takes a swing at 3D on the Nintendo 64.

Shigeru Miyamoto with SimCity
designer Will Wright, around 1989.

Miyamoto Speaks!

S higeru Miyamoto is one of the most influential and successful designers in the history of electronic games. His importance to the success of Nintendo cannot be overstated. Today, he is a super-producer, designing games and also overseeing Nintendo's many development groups. "He is a fantastic tutor for new producers," says Minoru Arakawa, founder and president of Nintendo of America. On these pages, Miyamoto-san comments on various aspects of his games and career.

On the Origins of Mario

The Donkey Kong arcade game hit the market in 1981. Before that time, I had been designing posters to be affixed onto arcade game consoles or supporting others who were making video games. When the idea of this "new game to replace an old one" was proposed to teams of game designers in the form of an internal Nintendo company competition, I submitted several different ideas for Donkey Kong. As for the name, I just wanted to create an English name meaning "silly gorilla." As I consulted with my dictionary, there was the word "donkey" for "silly." Since apes were often called "kong" in Japan back then, I mixed them together.

On the Evolution of Mario's Identity

One of the new fun things I really wanted to realize on Donkey Kong was that players could move the character around and jump all over the screen for the very first time

in the history of arcade games. However, due to the technical restrictions of those days, I could not depict the movement of hair when Mario jumps, so I had to put a cap on him. Likewise, to make the movement of arms more visible for the players, I had to put a shirt on him with overalls, etc. In other words, in order to evade the technical restraints, I came up with a very rational design for the original Mario character. Nintendo internally decided to name and promote each character for Donkey Kong. Because I wanted Mario to appear in many of the later games with a variety of different roles, I just made a vague set of characteristics for him as "a middle-aged man with a strong sense of justice who is not handsome." When we made Mario Brothers, because the setting was an underground world, Mario's image as a plumber was set, which is still alive now.

When we were making Super Mario Brothers, I wanted players to control a Mario character who was bigger than ever. When we made the prototype of the big Mario, we did not feel he was big enough. So, we came up with the idea of showing the smaller Mario first, who could be made bigger later in the game ("super"); then players could see and feel that he was bigger.

When we were making Donkey Kong, we did not incorporate all the ideas I had initially conceived; so when we developed Donkey Kong Jr., we included some of the unused ideas from Donkey Kong. I originally wanted to make "Donkey Kong's revenge" as the main theme for this sequel, but Donkey Kong was too big a character for players to manipulate back then, so I made the story based upon Donkey Kong Jr. As for the Donkey Kong 3, because the game was designed with another game called "Green House" for Game & Watch (Nintendo's early 80s handheld game series) in mind, we decided not to use Mario.

On Easter Eggs and Secrets in the Early Mario Games

The first experiment we did for the game was to control big Mario. Because the development of Disk System was already under way at that time, we tried to pull out the best of NES's ability with Super Mario Brothers, which might have become the very last NES game. I recall the basic game design was completed about three months after we started the experiment, when we were satisfied with the control of big Mario and when we had completed the designing of small Mario and of such items as mushrooms. It is true that we had incorporated some of the programming errors and unexpected reproductions during the course of development as the official "secrets." However, the majority of them were intentionally designed by us. To name some of the unintentional secrets, "serial coin appearance block" and Mario's "walking on the ceiling" had originally been programming errors that we later employed as the official secrets, while the "Zero World" was the error that we found only after the game hit the market.

On Other Games He Plays

When I am working, I hardly play video games, but I do not get inspiration by playing others' video games. When I am asked of my most favorite video game ever made by someone else, I make it a point of answering, "Pac-Man."

On His Greatest Moment as a Designer

Because I am always trying to realize the best possible

unique entertainment in each day and age, I find the utmost joy whenever a new game is completed. Among the best moments is the time when I saw Nintendo employees enjoying themselves with the Donkey Kong arcade game that we had just completed. It was an especially delightful moment for me. Another time I recall is when I received the Hall of Fame Award at the E3 show a few years ago. When I received the applause of the audience, it was really something special for me.

On the Trade-offs Between 2D and 3D Game Design

I think a great advantage of 3D is that players can feel that they are inside the game. Also, we are able to create a greater number of character animations within a much shorter time. On the other hand, it is true that the number of difficult-to-play games has increased because, for example, we have to let players get accustomed to the way the camera works, and creators themselves have to understand the best possible way to use the camera.

On the Rumor That Pikmin Was Set in His Personal Garden

No, No! The fact of the matter is that one of the reasons why I hit upon the Pikmin idea was because I was intrigued by the movements of a group of ants and the ecology of plants when I was gardening. There's got to be some mix here. Come to think about it, however, it may be an interesting idea to place Pikmin dolls in my garden. I would have to put hundreds of them in order for people to see that such small figurines are actually there, since the real-size Pikmin is just about two centimeters high, though.

On Future Challenges in Game Design

I know people think Pikmin is a fairly unique game. On the other hand, I think it is not unique enough. Because my job is to surprise people all around the world, I must continue to

239

create more unique and fresh entertainment all the time.

On the Games He Wants to Make in the Future

There are too many such ideas to identify one. There are just fractions of comprehensive ideas. Integrating them together may need new technologies to develop them.

On the Evolution of the Original Legend of Zelda

The first Legend of Zelda was created based upon the original concept of "miniature garden that you can put inside your drawer," inside of which the player can freely explore. As you can see it in the recent Pikmin game too, I make it a point of making games where the player becomes more creative by playing the game. The Legend of Zelda was the first game which has successfully incorporated such a concept. I tried to make a game where the next move the player is supposed to take is not already determined. Each player has to decide the route he or she thinks is best and take the best possible action, and by doing so, players can encounter a variety of wonders. Another big element is that players themselves can grow. In the game you see and feel that Link actually grows. At the same time, players can become better game players. I believe that this is the most definitive difference with RPG games that make use of parameters to show such a growth. In 2002, we will introduce you to the new Zelda game on Nintendo GameCube. This one is also going to be a unique, unprecedented game full of fresh surprises. Please look forward to it!

More NES Games

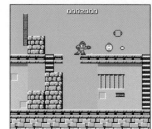
Mega Man *(Capcom)*

Operation Wolf *(Taito)*

Ghosts 'n' Goblins *(Capcom)*

Kid Icarus *(Nintendo)*

Metal Gear *(Konami)*

Metal Gear 2: Snake's Revenge *(Konami)*

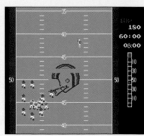
10 Yard Fight *(Irem)*

Battleroads *(Rare)*

A Boy and His Blob *(Absolute)*

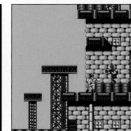
Bionic Commando *(Capcom)*

Bases Loaded *(Jaleco)*

Ballblazer *(Lucasfilm Games)*

Batman *(Sunsoft)*

Blades of Steel *(Konami)*

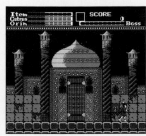
8 Eyes *(Taxan)*

Castlevania *(Konami)*

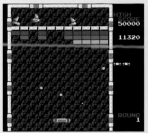
Arkanoid *(Taito)*

Blaster Master *(Sunsoft)*

Bomberman *(Hudsonsoft)*

Crystalis *(SNK)*

Duck Hunt *(Nintendo)*

Mike Tyson's Punch-Out!! *(Nintendo)*

The Lone Ranger *(Konami)*

Dragon Warrior *(Enyx)*

Attack of the Killer Tomatoes *(TH*Q)*

Double Dribble *(Konami)*

Little Nemo: The Dream Master *(Capcom)*

Metroid *(Nintendo)*

R.C. Pro-Am *(Rare/Nintendo)*

Smash TV *(Acclaim)*

Street Fighter 2010 *(Capcom)*

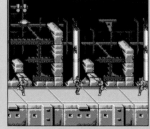
Super C *(Konami)*

Tetris *(Nintendo)*

Teenage Mutant Ninja Turtles *(Konami)*

Black Onyx *(BPS)*

Techmo Bowl *(Techmo)*

Wild Gunman *(Nintendo)*

Wizards & Warriors *(Acclaim)*

Ys *(Falcom)*

The New Console Wars

By 1989, the NES was unquestionably dominant in the U.S., but in Japan a different story was unfolding. In 1987, electronics giant NEC introduced a next-generation machine. The PC Engine was touted as the first 16-bit system, although its CPU was actually an 8-bit chip. The system did feature an upgraded graphics processor, however, and ran games both on credit card–sized "HuCards" and on CD. Yes, the PC Engine was the first home system to feature the CD-ROM.

The PC Engine was immensely popular in Japan, and by 1989, there were hundreds of titles available for it. A little after the PC Engine, Sega introduced its 16-bit Mega Drive system, but they were unable to push the PC Engine out of its position.

The stage was set for the ultimate launch of both the PC Engine, which was renamed TurboGrafx-16, and the Mega Drive, which became the Sega Genesis, into the U.S. market. And although both systems were released late in 1989, they are very much a part of the story of the 90s, when console games came of age.

Hudsonsoft's most popular NES game was Princess Tomato and the Salad Kingdom, which was created because one of the founders' daughter didn't like vegetables.

THE 90s

If the 70s were characterized by innovation and the 80s were about expansion, the 90s were a time of maturation. The CD-ROM, in particular, opened a virtual Pandora's box of good and evil. Like the CD, and in some even more significant ways, 3D technology radically changed the face of game design and development. Some designers decried it as the bane of good design, while others saw it as the path toward ultra-realism and games with movie quality worlds.

Because of these changes, games grew in size and technical quality, and even new types of games became possible; but all this growth was not without its costs. Game budgets skyrocketed, and development cycles often expanded from months to years. It was no longer possible for a game developer to be a one-man show. To succeed, games required teams of specialists and huge marketing machines. By the late 90s, with thousands of games coming out, the retail shelf life of a computer or video game could be measured in weeks if it didn't do well out of the gate. Just as the movie industry grew from silent beginnings, passed through the Golden Age of the studio system, and emerged into today's wide-open market of technological and storytelling innovation; so the business of electronic games has gone through its own evolution, which still continues.

Because of all these changes, telling the stories of the 90s is often very different from telling the stories of earlier decades. There were still a few wild and woolly events, like the rivalry between Nintendo and Sega, and the emergence of companies like Blizzard, id Software, and Eidos. However, once electronic games moved from being seen as a fluke or a passing fad and began to mature into a legitimate industry for which annual revenues total in the billions of dollars, the personal stories often give way to products that are developed in highly corporate environments. That is not to say that the passion and excitement are necessarily missing from the development process, but it does become ever harder to find the source of the product or to track the story in the same personal terms possible in the earlier, less structured environment of the 70s and 80s. By the end of the 90s, a few companies, such as Electronic Arts, Infogrames, and UbiSoft, owned most of the computer game companies and their trademarks, even if many of those companies technically no longer existed.

243

1990

Another Three-Way Race

The phenomenal success of the Nintendo Entertainment System (NES) in the U.S. paved the way for other companies to consider the lucrative American market; however, Nintendo's commanding market share made the prospect somewhat daunting. At Sega, after trying unsuccessfully to find a partner for the release of the Mega Drive, the decision was made to bite the bullet and introduce their 16-bit console to the U.S. market. This was what the Sega of America team had wanted all along.

After considering several new names for the machine, including Cyclone and "something with a fox logo," according to Al Nilsen, who became head of marketing for the new product, they decided to call it Genesis. "It had positive biblical connotations," says Nilsen, "a new beginning. Also it had a Star Trek connotation from the Genesis Project movie."

The American team had their orders from Nakayama in Japan. "Haku mandai!" became their slogan. It meant, "Sell a million units!" That was the goal to reach by the end of 1990. Of course, this was easier said than done. Not only did Nintendo have 90 percent of the market at the time, but NEC was also getting ready to introduce their PC Engine to the U.S. market. Nilsen remembers the prelaunch sales meeting, held in Monterey, California. "I remember one of the retailers telling us, 'You guys are really nice guys, and I like you, but NEC is going to blow you out of the water. Be prepared that on December 26th, I'm going to return it all to you.' What mattered to us, however, was that we had sell-in." Sega launched Genesis a day early, beating NEC to

the punch, shipping seven titles (two more than promised), including arcade hits Altered Beast and Golden Axe, as well as Tommy Lasorda Baseball, Arnold Palmer Tournament Golf, and three others. "After a week, we had 65 percent of the market, and by Christmas, we had over a 90 percent market share," remembers Nilsen. "We had done our research. We realized that the initial NES players had gotten older and entered their teens. Their systems ended up in closets. They discovered girls. So we positioned Genesis as the product you graduated to. Once you put away your toys, you got Sega. And we gave them arcade games and sports."

Meanwhile, Nintendo was not terribly concerned, having just completed their best year ever. "Being first to market is not of prime concern," says Peter Main, Nintendo's executive vice president of sales and marketing. "In any product, it's the third through the fifth year when the software to hardware ratio goes through the roof. Our business plan said that our new software releases would carry the NES through 1991, and that we'd introduce the Super NES at that time."

TurboGrafx-16

The PC Engine, which in the States was called TurboGrafx-16, was originally designed by Hudsonsoft, a Japanese game company started by two brothers. According to Ken Wirt, vice president and general manager of NEC's Home Division for TurboGrafx-16, the Kudo brothers grew up on the island of Hakkaido, *very* poor, next to the railroad tracks." They started a little electronics shop and got into citizen band radios. Their technician, Nakamoto, was programming some computer games, and ported them to Nintendo's FamiCom when it came out. "They made a ton of money," says Wirt. "And they were real characters. One of the brothers wore cowboy boots and drove around Japan in a Dodge Ram pickup. They also spent about a million dollars restoring the old steam engine

This is the first Keith Courage in the Alpha Zones chip. Keith Courage was named after Keith Schaefer, and this chip was given to him to commemorate the fact.

that used to run by their house when they were children. There's a number on the Hudson logo, which is the number on the steam engine they restored."

Hudsonsoft tried to get Nintendo interested in the machine they had developed, but were turned down, so they tried elsewhere, ultimately striking a deal with consumer electronics giant NEC, who brought out the PC Engine in 1987.

In Japan, NEC's PC Engine was powerful and successful, and, having been released earlier, was far more popular than Sega's Mega Drive. So, when NEC decided to bring the system to the U.S. and European markets, they were sure they would succeed. According to Keith Schaefer, executive vice president of NEC Technologies, "We had a better system, with a bigger, faster 16-bit graphics chip. Our marketing dollars were the same, we were in all the key distribution locations, and our price point was competitive."

However, in the all-important Christmas season of 1990, Sega emerged the clear winner. What happened? Again, according to Schaefer, "Sega Genesis came to market with what I consider to be inferior hardware, but a superior selection of software that was Americanized for the American consumer. TurboGrafx-16 came out with exactly the same

software that was popular on the PC Engine in Japan. These games were not the right games for the American audience."

Part of the problem was that all the software came from Japanese developers through Hudsonsoft, who had an exclusive deal with NEC to produce all the software for the system. The titles were mostly unknown in the U.S., while Sega launched with a combination of familiar arcade titles and sports games. "We saw the problem coming," says Schaefer, "but there was nothing we could do about it." So, despite having a huge number of games already made for the system in Japan, they turned out to be the wrong games.

Another problem with the launch of the TurboGrafx-16 traces its roots to the Japanese sense of honor. "We initially had orders for a million units over the first 12 months," says Schaefer, "so NEC went ahead and ordered production of 600,000 from their Taiwanese manufacturers. But the orders dwindled, and we ended up only selling through 250,000 units. When we saw the orders shrinking, we wanted to cut back on manufacturing; but for NEC it was a matter of honor, and they would not go back on their order with the Taiwanese. It's a very laudable quality of Japanese companies—their sense of honor— though if we had been able to cancel the excess manufacturing, we might have continued the product for a second or even third year."

NEC attempted to make their caveman, Bonk, into a character like Mario or Sonic, but without much luck. J.J. & Jeff, on the other hand, most resembled Beavis & Butthead.

Neo-Geo

In 1990, Nintendo licensee SNK (creators of the games Ikari Warriors and Crystalis) came out with the ultimate gamer's system, the 24-bit Neo-Geo. Unfortunately, its ultimate price of $399 was beyond the reach of most gamers in 1990. Neo-Geo was so close to arcade quality that it was actually used in many arcades, and the games that came out for the system tended to be action/fighting games. There wasn't much in the way of deep game development, but it was the console to have if you were an ultra-extreme hard-core gamer. It remained a fringe product, however, and never achieved the level of sales of the major systems.

1991

Hedgehog vs. Plumber

After its launch in the U.S., Genesis sales were good but not great. Nintendo remained the leader, and they were preparing to launch their own 16-bit system, the Super NES. And Nintendo had something that Sega did not— Mario! So Sega enlisted their employees in Japan and held a competition to see who could come up with the best character. One of the women had been reading a book about animals and thought hedgehogs were cool. Hers was one of two winners. The other was a very young preschool-type animal done in pastels. Al Nilsen remembers going into a conference room with Shinobu Toyoda, one of Sega's longtime top executives, and seeing the two winning drawings. "Here, pick one," he was told.

"Here was this image of Sonic the Hedgehog in a rock band with his blonde, human girlfriend, Madonna. There was no game design or story. Just this image, but it was the less objectionable of the two. So I said, 'Do Sonic but get rid of Madonna,' and we sent it back to Japan."

Super Baseball, Double Dragon, Fatal Fury, Art of Fighting.

Six months later, Nilsen was in Japan, having long since forgotten about the hedgehog, when the R&D group showed a nonplayable demo of the first Sonic game. Nilsen was blown away. Two months later, they had the first playable level ready. "It was just incredible," says Nilsen.

The designers were justifiably proud and wanted to show the game at an upcoming Tokyo game show, but the marketing team said no. They knew that Nintendo was planning the U.S. launch of the Super NES at the June 1991 Consumer Electronics Show (CES) in Chicago. "We immediately decided not to tell anyone about this thing," says Nilsen. "This could be our secret weapon."

Tom Kalinske

To help run the company, Sega hired former Mattel president Tom Kalinske. "I was on vacation in Hawaii. I had left Mattel and helped bring Matchbox Toys out of bankruptcy, buying it for $21 million and selling it three years later to Tyco for $120 million. I was on vacation when Nakayama found me. He and Rosen ganged up on me and convinced me to fly to Tokyo to see the Genesis and the product that became the Game Gear. Some months later, I got excited enough about it to go in and take on Nintendo."

By the time Kalinske joined Sega, the Genesis had launched; but after only a few weeks, he began to make some changes. He wanted to lower the price from $189 to $129, take out Altered Beast, which he said "looked like devil worship in the Midwest," and take on Nintendo in aggressive, competitive advertising. He also wanted to move some of the developers to the States. "My deal with Nakayama was that I made the decisions, so I went to Japan and announced my plan. At the end of a long discourse, all the Japanese executives began buzzing in Japanese, and I didn't have a clue what they were saying. At the end of about an hour of this, Nakayama said finally that nobody in the room agreed

with me. They thought bundling Sonic would weaken profits. You didn't mention your competition, especially if you were in a weaker position They couldn't afford establishing a development group in the States. And on and on. Nakayama began to leave the room, and I thought this was the shortest career on record. Then, at the door, he turned and said, 'When I hired you, I told you I wouldn't interfere. So do what you set out to do, and we'll support you.'"

"Sega Is Nothing"

Sega played a chess game, publicly expressing concern about the launch of Super Mario, saying they hoped it didn't get bundled with the Super NES (SNES), but secretly hoping it did. In head-to-head tests, Sonic had done better than Mario. They knew what they had. Nilsen adds, "It was a competitive business, but they were both great games. I've never denied that I played Nintendo games. But at the time, you looked at Sonic and you said, 'This is next generation.' Mario was maybe 50 percent toward the next generation at the time."

Nintendo's Arakawa comments further on the head games being played: "Tom Kalinske is a brilliant marketer, and the first thing he did was to pick up on a newspaper quote from Mr. Yamauchi in which he

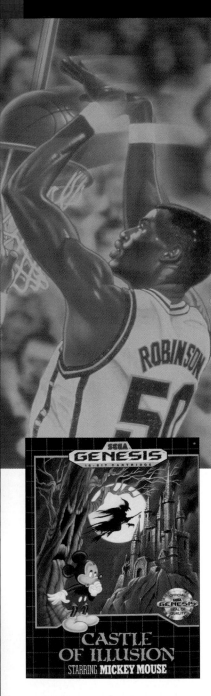

said, 'Sega is nothing.' Kalinske put it on every door in the Sega offices."

Sonic did make great waves at CES and stole some of Nintendo's thunder that year, but despite Sega's marketing spin, SNES did very well, and their launch title, Super Mario World, turned out to be a great game. With TurboGrafx-16 still hanging in, it became a legitimate three-way race... for a while. Ultimately it came down to Sega and Nintendo.

Electronic Arts and Sega

Another boost to Genesis occurred when Trip Hawkins decided that Electronic Arts would reverse-engineer the Genesis cartridges and start making their own Genesis games. This was a market departure for EA, which had stayed with computer software almost exclusively until then. "It happened right when I joined Sega," remembers Kalinske. "Trip had informed Sega that he intended to publish Genesis games without a license. The situation grew heated, and there were threats of lawsuits. We wanted to resolve it, and we needed publishers. At the time, Nintendo would threaten their third-party publishers with reprisals if they published Genesis games. I never revealed the deal, but in the end we granted EA a favorable arrangement relative to everyone else. That was fine. They got a good deal and we got a strong third-party publisher. You have to understand that no platform was ever really successful without third-party support."

The successful introduction of the SNES as well as the resurgence of the Genesis with Sonic the Hedgehog and third-party support from Electronic Arts helped to galvanize the industry. They were playing hardball, but they also gave each other mutual respect. Nintendo's Arakawa comments, "It was good for competition. It was good for the industry, too."

Indeed, the specter of the Atari collapse was beginning to fade, and video games enjoyed another age of expansion.

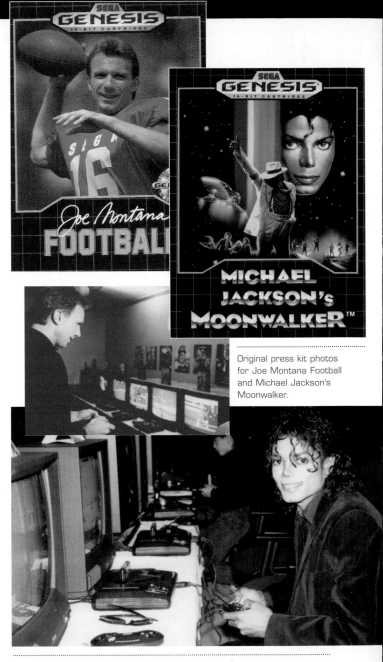

Original press kit photos for Joe Montana Football and Michael Jackson's Moonwalker.

In addition to their success with Sonic the Hedgehog, Sega created many successful games with celebrity endorsements from Joe Montana, Michael Jackson, Mickey Mouse, David Robinson, and others. In general, Sega's celebrity games were of high quality and fun to play.

YO! WHA'S UP?
THE STORY OF
TOEJAM & EARL

ToeJam & Earl was certainly one of the funniest and wackiest games ever released. And, in addition to its originality, it featured excellent game design. It was definitely a romp on the side of hipness. Codesigner Greg Johnson relates the background on one of our all-time favorite Sega Genesis games.

"This game was born out of a release from stress. Both Starflight I and II were huge, weighty projects that were very demanding. ToeJam was an opportunity to kick back and do something silly and just for the hell of it. I remember the genesis of the idea happened at about 4 in the morning when I stumbled out of bed and scribbled a bit of a dialogue onto a scrap of paper. It went like...

'Yo. Greetings and various apropos felicitations. My name is ToeJam and this is my homeboy, Big Rappin' Earl. Say Wha's up, Earl.'

'Wha's up.'

'Earl and myself are highly funky aliens from the planet Funkotron.'

"Well, that's where it started, with the characters. I love the hipness of black street culture (I'm half black) and old school R&B music, and I also have always loved aliens (at least all the ones I've met).

"Making ToeJam and Earl, more than anything else, was a way to have some fun. That's why it was such a great two-player game... so my business partner Mark Voorsanger and I could play all the time. The reason it was a random world was so we could keep playing it without getting tired of it.

"When I was in college I was totally addicted to Rogue—that was a truly great game. I would stay up till 3 and 4 a.m. watching the little C get chased around the screen by the little V on the mainframe computer, trying to get deeper than I'd been before in the dungeon. Structurally ToeJam and Earl is Rogue. It has all of the same elements, right down to the potions that do unidentified things."

Sega Genesis

Of the many popular Genesis games, we've included a few more screens to inspire memories of games gone by.

Sonic the Hedgehog *(Sega)*

Sonic the Hedgehog 2 *(Sega)*

Sonic the Hedgehog 3 *(Sega)*

Sonic the Hedgehog 4 *(Sega)*

Sonic & Knuckles *(Sega)*

Sonic 3D Blast *(Sega)*

Michael Jackson's Moonwalker *(Sega)*

Castle of Illusion Starring Mickey Mouse *(Sega)*

Revenge of Shinobi *(Sega)*

Alex Kidd in the Enchanted Castle *(Sega)*

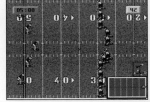
Joe Montana II Sports Talk Football *(Sega)*

Virtua Fighter *(Sega)*

Shining Force *(Sega)*

Alisia Dragoon *(Game Arts)*

Mario Lemieux Hockey *(Sega)*

Phantasy Star 2 *(Sega)*

David Crane's Amazing Tennis *(Absolute)*

David Robinson's Supreme Court *(Sega)*

Dick Tracy *(Sega)*

Decap Attack *(Sega)*

Ecco the Dolphin *(Sega)*

Strider *(Capcom)*

Revolution X *(Midway/Acclaim)*

Ninja Gaiden *(Tecmo)*

NBA Jam *(Acclaim)*

Flashback *(Delphine/U.S. Gold)*

Altered Beasts *(Sega)*

Golden Axe *(Sega)*

Gunstar Heroes *(Sega)*

Herzog Zwei *(Sega)*

Landstalker *(Sega)*

Kid Chameleon *(Sega)*

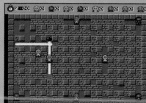
Mega Bomberman *(Hudsonsoft)*

Mega Turrican *(Data East)*

Cyberball *(Tengen)*

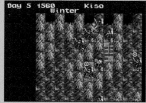
Nobunaga's Ambition *(Koei)*

Pit Fighter *(Tengen)*

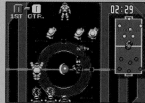
Powerball *(Namco)*

Primal Rage *(Time-Warner)*

Rings of Power *(Electronic Arts)*

Cadash *(Taito)*

Shining in the Darkness
(Sega—Japanese version)

Smash TV *(Acclaim)*

Sokoban *(Thinking Rabbit)*

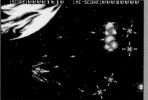
Sol Deace *(Sega)*

Space Harrier II *(Sega)*

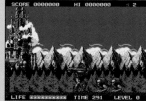
Rastan Saga *(Taito)*

Steel Talons *(Tengen)*

The Addams Family
(Ocean/Acclaim)

The Terminator *(Bethesda)*

Tin Tin au Tibet *(Infogrames)*

Ms. Pac-Man *(Namco)*

Lunar: The Silver Star
(Working Designs)

Lunar: Eternal Blue
(Working Designs)

Batman *(Sunsoft)*

Burning Force *(Namco)*

James Buster Douglas
Knockout Boxing *(Sega)*

Chuck Rock *(Core Designs)*

251

Super NES

There were hundreds of games made for the Super NES. Here are screens from a few of the best-remembered titles.

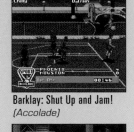
Parodius *(Konami)*

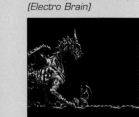
Batman Forever *(Acclaim)*

Barklay: Shut Up and Jam! *(Accolade)*

Boxing Legends of the Ring *(Electro Brain)*

California Games II *(Epyx)*

Castlevania V *(Konami)*

Contra III *(Konami)*

Darius Twin *(Taito)*

The Death and Return of Superman *(Sunsoft)*

Demon's Crest *(Capcom)*

Pocky & Rocky 2 *(Natsume)*

Return of Double Dragon *(Tradewest)*

Dr. Mario *(Nintendo)*

ActRaiser *(Enix)*

Addams Family *(Ocean)*

Dragon: The Bruce Lee Story *(Virgin)*

Drakkhen *(Kemco/Infogrames)*

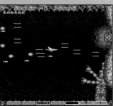
Dungeon Master *(JVC Musical)*

Earth Bound *(Nintendo)*

ESPN Baseball Tonight *(Sony Imagesoft)*

Final Flight 2 *(Capcom)*

Extra Innings *(Sony Music Entertainment)*

F-Zero *(Nintendo)*

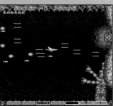
Gradius III *(Konami)*

Illusion of Gaia *(Nintendo)*

Kirby's Dream Course *(Nintendo)*

Lufia and the Fortress of Doom *(Taito)*

Micro Machines *(Ocean)*

Mickey Mania
(Sony Electronic/Disney)

Madden 97 *(Electronic Arts)*

Mario Excite Bike
(Nintendo—Japanese version)

Mega Man X *(Capcom)*

Mechwarrior *(Activision)*

NBA Jam *(Acclaim)*

NBA Live *(Electronic Arts)*

NHL 95 *(Electronic Arts)*

Ninja Gaiden Trilogy *(Tecmo)*

Star Fox *(Nintendo)*

R-Type 3 *(Irem)*

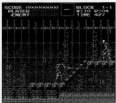
Street Fighter II Turbo
(Capcom)

Skuljagger
(American Softworks)

Sonic Blast Man *(Taito)*

Soul Blazer *(Enix)*

Space Ace *(Absolute Entertainment/Seika)*

Super Bases Loaded *(Jaleco)*

Super Castelvania IV
(Konami)

Super Star Wars *(LucasArts)*

Super Empire Strikes Back
(LucasArts)

Super Return of the Jedi
(LucasArts)

Super Off-Road *(Tradewest)*

Super Metroid *(Nintendo)*

Super Turrican 2 *(Seika)*

Super Virgin Girl *(TGL)*

Ys IV *(Falcom)*

Super Godzilla *(Toho)*

Total Carnage *(Malibu)*

Wizardry *(Sir-Tech/ASCII—Japanese version)*

Super Adventure Island
(Hudsonsoft)

Twisted
The Game Show™

FOR
USE
WITH

3DO

By Studio 3DO

1992

3DO

Electronic Arts' founder Trip Hawkins, having guided EA into the video game world, now left the company to start a bold new venture. Once a critic of video games and a hard-core computer game supporter, Hawkins had seen the light (so to speak) and was ready to go head-to-head against Nintendo and Sega, with support from (among others) Time-Warner, Matsushita, and MCA.

The 3DO Company was originally incorporated in 1991 as SMSG, Inc. and in that same year it entered into a development agreement with NTG Engineering, which included Amiga/Lynx designers RJ Mical and Dave Needle. "Trip had a vision, but needed a machine to do the vision," says Mical. "We had a machine, but nobody knew about us. We were in stealth mode. Ultimately, we were introduced to each other through a mutual friend, who couldn't talk to either of us due to conflicting nondisclosures."

NTG was a different sort of company from the beginning. Employees didn't work for the normal stock options, but for a percentage of profits based on what they contributed to each project. "It was almost a utopian socialist idea," says Mical, "and it might have worked, but the 3DO was too good. We were working on

several projects, but within a year and a half, all we were doing was 3DO. Then Trip bought us and we were employees. Certainly 3DO was one of the most remarkable places I've ever worked because of the density of really smart people who worked there."

Trip's eloquent evangelism of 3DO swayed many in the industry, who came to believe that the 3DO machine would become a ubiquitous appliance like the telephone or the TV. Says codesigner RJ Mical, "In our wildest dreams, we imagined getting into home-of-the-future trials where the 3DO was built into the wall, not only to do entertainment but to allow interactive video content to be received in the home as well."

Though 3DO got plenty of press, and had an impressive public offering even before they had a product, 3DO ultimately suffered from too high a price tag ($699.99 at launch) and some rushed titles, including the highly anticipated but disappointing Jurassic Park. Although the 3DO system couldn't boast the number of third-party developers that Nintendo had, they did have a couple of notable ones. On one side was a company called Rocket Science, one of the most impressive collections of talent ever assembled to do games—and one of the biggest disappointments. Despite the presence of some amazing designers, programmers, and artists, the company took a wrong turn from the beginning, concentrating on "rail games" that were ultimately not that interesting. On the other side of the coin was Crystal Dynamics, whose game The Horde was certainly one of the best games to come out for the 3DO. Crystal Dynamics has continued to create great games, while Rocket Science folded up and disappeared.

Trip Hawkins at the 3DO launch.

Electronic Arts published Twisted, a game show in a game, one of the more interesting 3DO titles. The wacky spoof of TV game shows featured full-motion video and some amusing games.

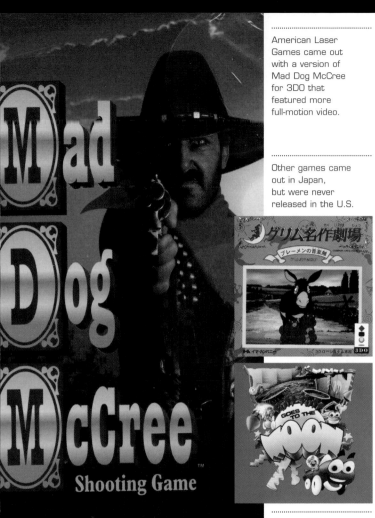

Mad Dog McCree
Shooting Game

The Arcade Smash Hit
by AMERICAN LASER GAMES, INC.

American Laser Games came out with a version of Mad Dog McCree for 3DO that featured more full-motion video.

....

Other games came out in Japan, but were never released in the U.S.

....

Also on 3DO was Humongous Entertainment's excellent and highly entertaining (even for some of us adults) Putt Putt series of games for children.

THE HORDE

After creating Star Control 2, Paul Reiche was playing around with a "crazy gardening game featuring a fat guy in lederhosen," which ultimately, through some creative metamorphosis, became The Horde. The game was first pitched to Madeline Canepa and Scott Steinberg at Sega, but somehow never got contracted. "Then, Madeline popped up at Crystal Dynamics and signed us up to do a 3DO and PC version of the game," says Reiche. "At the time, there were only three of us—Fred Ford, artist Mike Provenza, and me. When I asked Fred if he knew any other hot programmers, he said, 'My brother,' and that's how Ken Ford joined us."

At the time, Hollywood mogul and former 20th Century Fox CEO Strauss Zelnick was heading Crystal Dynamics, and new opportunities presented themselves. The idea of using some live actors for cut scenes of The Horde was one of those opportunities. On the short list to play Chauncy, the leading character, were Jim Carrey and Michael Richards (later of Seinfeld). According to Reiche, "Carrey fell through because he got a big movie deal, and Richards was an animal rights activist and didn't want to be involved with anything that showed the killing of cows." Finally, the part was played by Curt Cameron. "He was great," says Reiche. "He approached it as a serious job, not condescending at all.

"We almost killed one of the actors," adds Reiche. "The villain was played by another actor named Michael Richards, and at one point he was supposed to eat a big metal key, showing for the first time that he wasn't really human. The prop people created a giant key made of chocolate covered with cinnamon. It looked like a big, rusted iron key. But just before he bit into it, he asked, 'This isn't chocolate, is it?' It turned out that on all his personal information it stated clearly that he was deathly allergic to chocolate. They quickly made a carob key, and he was able to complete the scene."

Trilobyte

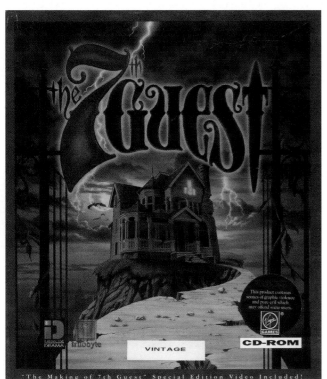

raeme Devine and Rob Landeros were both industry veterans by the time they joined forces in 1989. Devine had begun programming in the late 70s on TRS-80 computers and ultimately worked on porting games, including

Ballblazer, for Atarisoft's British offices. In time, he ended up on Lucas's Skywalker Ranch, working with the Games Group there, but returned to England to form IC&D Software. IC&D stood for Ice Cream and Donuts, which Devine says, "was a fine name for a game company."

The company did some original games, such as an adventure game called Metropolis; and they did ports for a company called Arcadia, which became Virgin/Mastertronic. "We were doing really well at making money," Devine recalls. Then Mastertronic asked if he'd be interested in coming to America again to help start their U.S. office. "I said I could do that for a while. Then, 14 years later... I was still there. I was employee number seven."

That's where he met Rob Landeros, who had moved to

Virgin/Mastertronic after a couple of years as Cinemaware's art director. "I didn't start with computers young. I had done some scrimshaw and, for a while, some political cartooning. When I saw the Amiga, I knew I had to have one. I was down in Redlands, California, and I happened to meet Jim Sachs, who was giving a demonstration of the art he was doing for Cinemaware's Defender of the Crown. I was blown away and went home to try to emulate the quality of what he had done. Ultimately, we got to know each other, and when Cinemaware was looking for an art director, he said, 'Why don't you go for it?' So I did get the job, and it was trial by fire. I learned how to be an art director by the seat of my pants."

Ultimately, Landeros left to take a job at Virgin, where he met Devine. For a while, he was happy there, but Virgin wasn't focused primarily on A titles, and they began doing a lot of licensed products. Most of these products were forgettable, but one game they did was Spot, their first NES game, which used the 7-Up Spot character. Landeros recalls, "We worked from Japanese documents to create the NES cartridge—four months of intense work, culminating in a mad over-night drive to make CES in Las Vegas with the first working carts, which Dan Chang and I had made by converting old Legend of Zelda cartridges." Spot was actually a very fun game, well put together, and it did well. However, both Landeros and Devine were getting itchy feet. Says Landeros, "They were moving in a different direction. They asked me, do I want to work on a McDonald's license, and I said, 'McNo.'"

Actually, the two had already begun brainstorming at a New York airport for a new game, right after attending a show dedicated to new CD-ROM multimedia technology. "We first thought about the board game Clue, because Virgin had that license," says Devine. "But we were also big fans of Twin Peaks. We even thought about having a Twin Peaks product that just let you wander around the town, but *that* ultimately evolved into a game we called 'Guest.' When we got back, we showed our proposal to Martin Alber, who was the head of Virgin/Mastertronic, and he took us out to lunch and fired us. He said, 'I can't produce this in-house, but I can give you a contract to do it as an independent developer. Just promise us a floppy disk version, because we probably can't sell enough CDs, and don't move more than 50 miles away.'"

Grateful for the opportunity, Devine and Landeros formed Trilobyte Software, set up offices in Jacksonville, Oregon (more than 800 miles away), and produced the first huge mega-hit CD-ROM game, The 7th Guest. There was no floppy version. There was also no complaint from Virgin, in the end, because the product sold more than a million copies.

The development of The 7th Guest was an adventure in itself. Working for the first time with CD technology and rendering some of the first 3D animation sequences and complex morphing, Devine and Landeros had many technical hurdles to overcome. First Devine backward-engineered a hi-res animation format called SLC and made an animation player, which he released as shareware. Autodesk's Gary Yost saw it and ended up providing the young company with several copies of Autodesk's 3D Studio software.

The rendered sequences were huge by current storage

standards: the sequence going up the stairway was more than 20 megabytes. They ended up having to get a huge $10,000 hard disk to store the material. Another problem they encountered turned into a feature in the game. They shot all the actors against blue screens, but apparently, they either used the wrong shade of blue or should have used a green screen. Whatever the problem, every image had a ghostly aura around it, and it was prohibitively expensive and time consuming to remove all those pixels, so they turned the actors into ghosts, and adapted the game to fit the graphics.

Ultimately, they added a lot of complex brain-teasing puzzles, without which the game would have been more of an interactive movie than a game. Landeros and scriptwriter Matthew Costello did a lot of puzzle research. One of the hardest puzzles, the infamous Microscope Puzzle, was actually a game of Spot set on the highest level. (Going back to the cluebook in the Library actually lowered the difficulty level of the puzzle each time, though it wasn't much help solving the puzzle, otherwise.)

After the amazing success of The 7th Guest, Trilobyte started working on a real-time strategy game called Cyber War. Devine describes it as "SimCity with a war going on." But they were also contractually obligated to do a sequel to The 7th Guest, and so they began work on The 11th Hour, which was a technical nightmare. The story of The 11th Hour was similar to that of The 7th Guest and easier to follow, but the game wasn't nearly as successful. By this time, CD-ROMs were less of a novelty, and another game called Myst had taken the world by storm.

In time, Trilobyte closed its doors, and Devine and Landeros went their separate ways. But they will always retain their place in the history of electronic games with The 7th Guest.

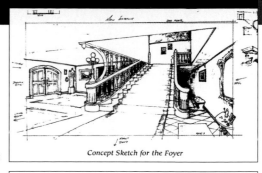
Concept Sketch for the Foyer

Concept sketch for the Music Room

Cyan: Tales from Two Brothers

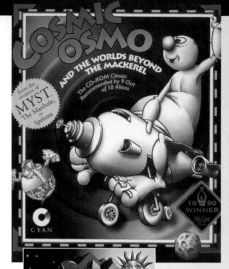

T his is the story of two brothers who made worlds. They began with the intention of creating an interactive children's book, but somehow, along the way, Rand and Robin Miller made the one game that *everyone* had to have in the early 90s.

Their first product, The Manhole, was completed in 1987. The Miller brothers also started their company, which they orignally named Prolog, in the same year, soon after changing the company name to Cyan. "We started with the idea of mapping the book medium to interactive, but the first page was so intriguing that we discovered we could go deeper instead of linear," says Rand Miller. "You click on the manhole and the cover slides open, a beanstalk grows out of the hole. There's a little door on the fire hydrant. At that point, our plans didn't matter. It was draw what's here, then draw a door. We didn't know what was behind it." Miller adds, "Honestly, when we created it, we had no plan. It came on five floppy disks, and you had to have a hard disk to play it. If we had examined the market, we'd have been cancelled." However, when they showed the product at a Hypercard convention, the brothers sold all their copies and ultimately made a publishing deal with Activision. "They offered maybe $20,000. It was serious money for something we'd enjoyed doing for six months."

The Manhole was a delightful, surreal, and fully interactive journey in which everything you clicked on caused some event to occur. It wasn't truly a game, but an exploration of a

world so malleable that a straw could become a tunnel and a tunnel could be the inside of a creature, and you might end up floating in a whirlpool in a glass of iced tea being drunk by a giant walrus. Or something like that. Originally created with rich black-and-white images on the Macintosh, The Manhole was a fascinating experience for young and old alike. (Ironically, it wasn't until 1992 that Brøderbund brought out the first of the Living Books series, which was very much what the Millers had originally conceived, though by then they were already working on Myst.)

The Miller brothers followed with Cosmic Osmo and the Worlds Beyond the Mackerel. Also published by Activision in 1990, Osmo was bigger and even more interactive than The Manhole, and it had a story and a main character. "It's amazing to us how much Myst evolved out of our earlier products. Osmo gave us the opportunity to have an unlimited universe. Osmo was also the first game where we began to put bits of story in it." Osmo was

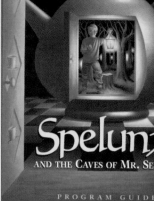

also the first game they did for CD-ROM, which opened their eyes to some expansive vistas to come.

Unfortunately, at the time Cosmic Osmo released, Activision was going bankrupt. Undaunted, the Millers created Spelunx and the Caves of Mr. Seudo, an educational game. "We wanted to motivate more than educate. Force-feeding information is never as effective as having someone want to suck you dry because they're so interested in what they're looking at," says Miller.

But it was their next product that made history. It was 1993 and the CD-ROM was becoming a de facto part of every new home computer. Two products really pushed the envelope and demonstrated the power and potential of the new storage medium—The 7th Guest and Myst.

It started with a call from Sunsoft, a Japanese company that had been trying to contact the Millers for a year to ask them to create a game for adults. "We had already created a concept called A Grey Summons. It was designed to be a fantastic world that adults would lose themselves in. Completely different from Myst in many ways, but the publishers we saw said no to it," says Miller. "So, when Sunsoft asked for a proposal, we sent them four pages— basically a map with a top-down view of some islands with a one-page description of these brothers and these books and how you'd get to go to these islands and explore them and go to different ages." They estimated their budget at around $400,000. "We ended up spending double that, and paid for the extra on our own."

In a great piece of irony, Sunsoft only wanted the console rights, anticipating a CD-ROM add-on from Nintendo that ultimately never came out.

The Millers kept the PC rights.

They took the PC rights and showed the early version of
the game to several publishers. For instance, at Maxis they
showed it to founders Will Wright and Jeff Braun (see page
262). "Will seemed to love it, and Jeff said, 'I'm not sure I get
it, but if Will likes it, I love it.'" They didn't publish with
Maxis, however, but struck a publishing deal with Brøderbund,
where the response was overwhelmingly positive.

Myst first released on the Macintosh in the fall of 1993,
with the PC version following shortly after. And very soon,
it became the product everybody had to have. Not a
traditional game, its incredibly beautiful scenes set in a
stark world simply compelled you to see more. Nothing
like it had been seen on home computers before.

"In Myst, you can't separate the graphics from the game
play. It was the visuals that pulled people forward. It was
the carrot that pulled people around the corner," adds
Miller. "It sounds like marketing drivel, but if you're sitting
in a room with the lights low and the sound turned up, we
want you to think you're really in that place. The box said,
'A surrealistic adventure that will become your world.'
That's what we wanted."

With the unprecedented success of Myst, the Millers had
the money to get the best equipment and the luxury to take
their time. In the sequel, Riven, they were able to complete
the Myst story—at least to their satisfaction. "We didn't
worry about making it a real-time game but took the Myst
concept and went as far as we could with that world. Riven
wrapped it up for us, and we weren't interested in doing
more sequels. We'd told this story. We were interested in
creating a larger, online world, something that goes back to
what we've always done." However, admits Miller, Myst fans
did want more. In 2000, they released realMyst, a more
dynamic version of the original game, and they licensed
Ubisoft to create the third game, Myst III: Exile.

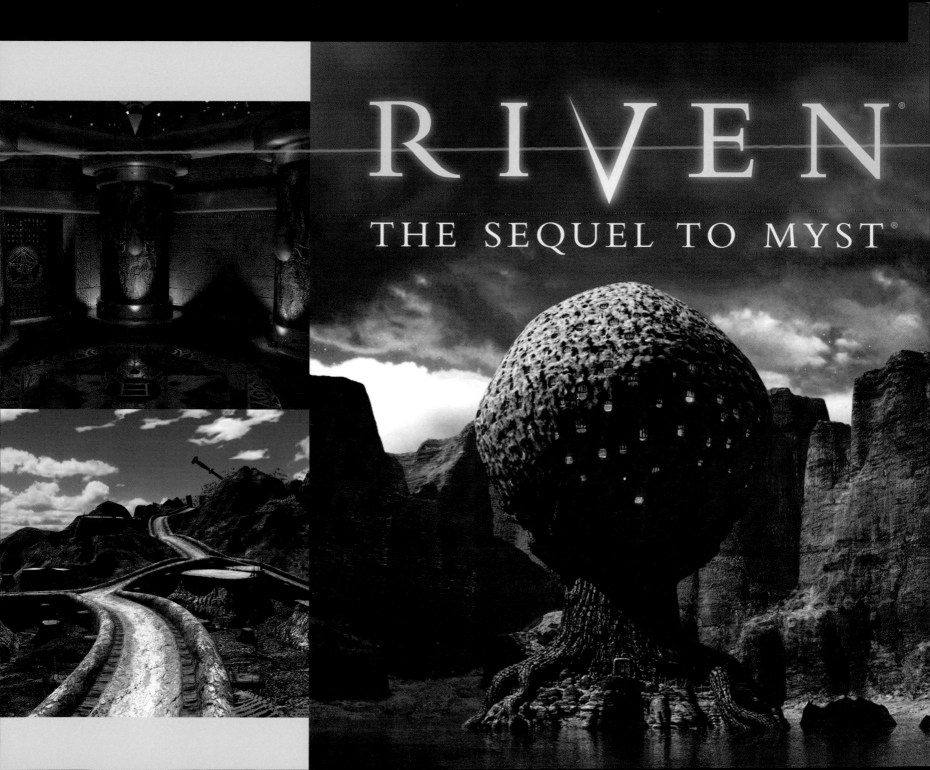

RIVEN

THE SEQUEL TO MYST

Maxis

Jeff Braun, referring to the original SimCity cover: "We got sued by Toho and had to pay them big bucks for infringing on Godzilla. We never used the word 'Godzilla,' honest, just a doll that wasn't Godzilla but was confused as Godzilla in a number of magazine reviews."

W ill Wright's first game was Raid on Bungeling Bay, which was published by Brøderbund (see page 124) in 1984. After that, he began working on two more games. One was a "weird strategy game" called Probot, and the other was called Micropolis. Probot was never released, but Micropolis was another story.

The concept for Micropolis came, in part, from the game editor Wright had written for Bungeling Bay and also from two books he read, *Urban Dynamics* and *System Dynamics*, by Jay Forester. Drawing also from John Conway's work with cellular automata and the game of Life, in 1985 Wright ultimately completed the game for the Commodore 64. He had no luck, however, in finding a publisher.

Meanwhile, Jeff Braun and Ed Kilham had gotten together to "form a game company for adults," as Braun described it, and were soon to be joined by A. J. Redmer.* Braun remembers how he met Will Wright: "I asked a friend in the game industry how to meet game programmers; he said, 'It's simple... beer and pizza.' So I threw a few game programmer pizza/beer parties, and Will showed up at one. Once I saw Will's 'city

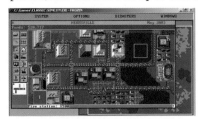

builder' (pre-Micropolis) on the C-64, I knew this was what Maxis should be doing."

Working out of Braun's apartment,

the small company began to revise the original game. Along the way, they found out that there was a disk drive manufacturer called Micropolis, so they searched for a new name for the product. "I think it was our writer Michael Bremer who came up with the name," remembers Wright. "Bremer was also the first to call the city's inhabitants 'sims'. He saved us much pointless work over the ensuing years coming up with titles for our games."

The original Micropolis game was rewritten for the Macintosh and Amiga. Then, going against convention, the small company released SimCity in February 1989, well after the traditional Christmas selling season. Brøderbund distributed it. Ironically, remembers Wright, "A lot of our later games also came out around that same time of year...

Kilham later went on to create an intriguing battle game, Robosport, for Maxis, then moved on to join Larry Holland's team on X-Wing and TIE Fighter. Eventually, he formed his own company, Ronin Entertainment, with Lucas veteran Kalani Striecher. Redmer also moved over to Lucasfilm and has continued to work with various companies in the industry.

SimCity 2000 and 3000, even The Sims." Whatever they did, it worked. Shortly after the release of the game, a reporter from *Newsweek* called and ultimately wrote a full-page article on the game and the fledgling company. "We made a lot of mistakes in developing the company," says Wright, "but SimCity was successful enough to pay for those mistakes, and then some." This is a classic understatement from Wright.

If you haven't already figured it out, Will Wright is an avid reader and is always fascinated by new ideas. His next game, which he thought should be on a grander scale, was based on the work of James Lovelock, to whom he was introduced by Whole Earth's Stuart Brand. SimEarth was far less popular than SimCity, but Wright enjoyed the research into geology, climatology, evolution, ecology, and so forth. With SimCity, Maxis had begun a tradition of writing very detailed manuals and contracting out to experts to write scholarly sections. In SimEarth, says Wright, "the best thing, for me, was the manual, which contained the best 30 pages on earth science ever written." One of the little known facts about SimEarth was its ability to play music based on particular layers of the simulation. For instance, you could set up the music to correspond to the air temperature or the mixture of atmospheric gasses.

Instead of moving logically to SimGalaxy or some other

even larger topic, Wright went small for his next game and wrote SimAnt with high school friend Justin McCormick. SimAnt was based largely on Wright's fascination with ants and on the work of E. O. Wilson, who wrote the Pulitzer Prize–winning book *The Ants*. "It was much more playful than SimEarth—a much more approachable game. I was hoping to show grown-ups how cool ants were, but we had our biggest following with younger kids."

It was at about this time that Wright began his fascination with a game that for years went by the name Project X and eventually became The Sims. But he had to put aside this game many times.

MAXIS

SimEarth™

FOR WINDOWS

The Living Planet

The early Maxis team:
Left photo (left to right):
Jeff Braun, Daniel Goldman, Will Wright, Michael Bremer, unknown, David Cagiano, Tim Johnson.

Right photo: (front) Steve Hales, Jeff Braun, Will Wright; (back) Ed Kilham (Maxis' first employee), Brett Durett, A. J. Redmer, Brian Witt, Rob Stroebel.

WHERE'S THE LLAMA?

Will Wright could quite legitimately be called an eccentric genius. He has a quirky sense of humor, a mild manner, and some strange obsessions with unlikely subjects such as Elvis and llamas. When I was writing my SimEarth strategy guide, I had my artist, Ocean Quigley, sneak a llama into the book. We told Will there was a llama in the book, and he looked for it in vain. It was peeking from behind the lunar landing pod in a photo of the moon landing we had obtained from NASA. Ironically, Ocean later became Maxis' Art Director. Small world.

—RDM

He worked first with Fred Hasslam to complete SimCity 2000. "We actually took the code I'd developed for Project X, and that became the code base for 2000. All the references in the code are like 'draw house' and 'draw yard,' and so forth." SimCity 2000 added new perspectives and layers to the game. "We got to add in a lot of stuff we'd had to leave out of SimCity, and I personally went through hundreds of letters to see what players wanted."

SimCopter was an ambitious project. The idea was to let players actually go into a 3D model of the cities they had built in SimCity. Still with one part of his mind on Project X, Wright tackled the challenge of producing a 3D game in which the world would be created based on an unpredictable set of criteria—a player's own SimCity. "We had to look at the buildings, the crime, and population density at that spot, and many other factors. Really, it was probably too ambitious for the size of the development team we had. Recently I saw the concept done really well in Rockstar's Grand Theft Auto III. Many of the same elements were there, but done much better."

In 1995, Maxis went public, just before Netscape. At their peak they hit a market cap of over $500 million. Then, in 1997 they were sold to Electronic Arts.

The Sims

Over the years, Maxis published a number of other Sim games that Wright did not create, such as SimLife, SimTower, and SimFarm. But ultimately, after nine years of working on it, and after overcoming all sorts of corporate roadblocks, Wright finally completed Project X, which by now had been named, quite simply, The Sims.

Inspiration for The Sims began with another pair of books—one on architecture called *A Pattern Language*, by Chris Alexander, and *Understanding Comics*, by Scott

McCloud. Wright first came across *A Pattern Language*, which he describes as the Western equivalent of the Chinese art of feng shui, back around the time he was writing SimCity. "My original concept was to do a game based around architecture the way SimCity was about cities. There were several home design packages on the market at the time, but none of these were fun to use." From *Understanding Comics*, Wright came across the concept of levels of abstraction. "The book shows a range of faces, from photographic to a simple smiley face. It becomes clear that the photographic image leaves little room for interpretation, whereas a more abstract image is easier for someone else to read in what they want to see— themselves, for instance, or a friend or neighbor. We used the concept of abstraction quite a bit in The Sims, especially in the visual language they speak."

Maxis published many other games in addition to those designed by Will Wright, and many very talented people have contributed to all their products. Still, Will Wright can be considered the soul and inspiration of Maxis.

Sim behavior was modeled, to some degree, on the ant behavior he had worked with in SimAnt. "Some of the elements of The Sims were in SimAnt… the guy with his house and the ants' responses to their environment. How The Sims react to objects in their world is modeled roughly on ant behavior, what I call a 'proximity pheromone' model. What this means is that the people in The Sims will generally respond to objects that are close to them. So, if the urge for some entertainment is strong and they are near a TV, they might switch it on and watch. But if they are nearer to the fish tank, then that is where they might go. This depends on specifics of the Sim's personality, of course. They seek out whatever will increase their happiness the most, which depends on all their needs and personality traits. Of course, if there is something very compelling like a hot tub or someone they love around, they'll go all the way across the house."

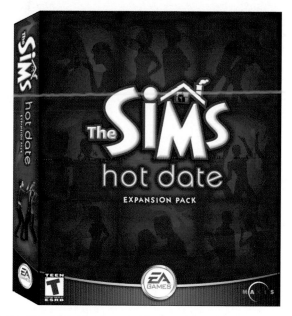

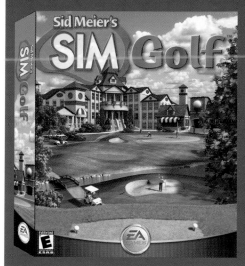

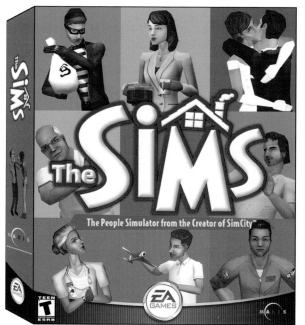

Several Sims expansion packs have come out since the original debuted, including The Sims: Livin' Large, House Party, Hot Date, and Vacation. These images are from the original Sims, except above right, which is from House Party.

The incomparable Sid Meier (see page 186) has turned his attention to the links and produced SimGolf for Maxis/Electronic Arts.

God Gamer

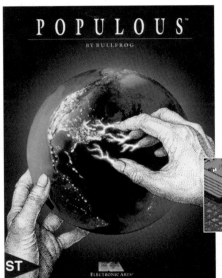

Often credited with being the inventor of the "god game" category, Peter Molyneux started producing software in the mid-80s. His first company was Taurus, which he founded with his partner Les Edgar. They intended to produce business database software, but the company wasn't going anywhere fast. Then one day they were invited to a meeting with Commodore. "They started saying how much they loved our product and how they really wanted to see it on the Amiga," says Molyneux. "I felt extremely flattered and then delighted when they offered to supply us with ten free machines. Slowly the realization dawned on me that they thought they were dealing with another company called Torus, who were doing something with networking, but times were hard so I kept quiet and in time took delivery of our free machines."

Molyneux quickly realized that the Amiga could be a great game machine, "so, as ardent gamers, we happily switched to developing games." They started out with a port of Druid 2 from the Atari ST and used the money to begin their own project.

They changed the name of the company to Bullfrog. "We were both Taureans," recalls Molyneux, "which is where the Bull comes from. We chose frog because at the time we were both big fans of the game Frogger."

Bullfrog's debut product was called Populous, and in it the player got to be a god looking down on his or her world and doing various godlike things while worshipers act out their dramas on the surface. "The idea of being all-powerful is something that has always fascinated me since I was a kid," says Molyneux. "Much later I can remember going up in one of those scenic lifts and looking down at all the little people below going about their lives, and this also made me think about using little people, to convey this feeling of power. Then Glenn Corpes, one of the original Bullfrog team, showed me a landscape engine that he had been working on, and I suddenly knew that this engine would give me the most perfect view for the game I had in mind."

Populous was a huge hit, and one of those rare games that spawns a genre of its own. It featured a great isometric view, humor, and intriguing game play. It was similar to SimCity, which came out around the same time, in that you affected a world full of simulated people but didn't interact with them directly. It also had something in common with real-time strategy games in that your followers would build up villages

A "QUIRKY IDEA"

Populous was my first ever game and, in some ways, after Black & White, it is still the game I am most proud of. Never in my wildest dreams did I imagine it would sell over 4 million copies. I thought maybe a few people would appreciate this rather quirky idea we had come up with. Populous was essentially a simple game. It had no story or goal, so that ultimately the game play was extremely repetitive.

—*Peter Molyneux*

and would war on the followers of rival gods.

Bullfrog followed Populous with a game of territory and resource management called Power Monger. Power Monger was not as popular as Populous, but it was also a very clever game that involved building armies as well as villages and technologies. It consisted of a large map divided into segments, and each segment represented a different scenario. The goal was to conquer the map segments to take over the world. Molyneux, ever his own worst critic, says Power Monger "was a good world simulation, but it had an overly complex interface and no story."

Bullfrog came out with a succession of clever games, including several sequels to Populous—Syndicate, Theme Park, Magic Carpet, and Dungeon Keeper. Each was unique and interesting in its own right, though not always commercially successful. In particular, Theme Park did very well in Europe and Japan, but poorly in the States. Molyneux comments that the graphics might have been "too childish" for the U.S. market and, "Theme Park could have been improved with more disasters and more kinds of challenges."

Dungeon Keeper was really enjoyable in many ways. The ultimate antihero, you played the demonic keeper of a dungeon,

building up your troops of nasties to take on the invading heroes. Although the game was great fun to play, its interface was unnecessarily complex.

Black & White

Molyneux's most recent work, created for his new company, Lionhead Studios, is also his most ambitious work at the time this was written. The inspiration came in part from an episode of *Outer Limits* called "Sand Kings," in which a scientist discovers a new species that comes to worship him as a god. The other inspiration came from an electronic pet Molyneux obtained during the final weeks of the Dungeon Keeper project. "I managed to keep my Tamagotchi fed and watered despite being totally exhausted, but we were cooped up in a very small office, and its beeping was driving everyone else mad. Finally, Andy Robson, who is now head of testing at Lionhead, snapped and drowned it in a cup of coffee. I was stunned at how upset I felt at the 'death' of my helpless pet, but then it occurred to me that if I had become so attached to an egg-shaped piece of plastic, how much more attached might I and other people become to a unique computer creature."

Black & White not only allows you to play god in a much more direct way with your worshipful populous, but it also introduces the concept of an artificially intelligent, unique, and often quirky creature who becomes your pet and develops a personality based on its experiences and your training methods.

Black & White also allows players to create their own kind of world. You can be a dark, cruel god or a good and beneficent deity—or anything in between— and the world shapes itself in the image of its master.

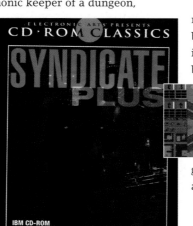

Blizzard

When Allen Adham got a couple of friends—Mike Morhaime and Frank Pearce—together to form a company called Silicon and Synapse in 1991, none of them had any idea what lay ahead. To start the new company, Adham and Morhaime each put up $10,000. Their loftiest goal at the time was to make great games and have fun.

Adham had done some play testing for Brian Fargo at Interplay and had been involved in Fargo's Demon's Forge project, and so it was natural that the new company started out doing conversions of existing games to different platforms for Interplay and, after a couple of years, began creating original console games such as Rock & Roll Racing and Lost Vikings for Interplay. Adham comments on those early years: "We got to see how games were made. We were just sponges, absorbing information."

Although their games were moderately successful, the young company was living on the edge. "We were living from paycheck to paycheck," says Morhaime. "One late check from a publisher would have put us in the red." Living in debt, both Morhaime and Adham often used their credit cards to make payroll.

In 1994, it all changed. Silicon and Synapse (which had by now become Chaos Studios) changed its name to Blizzard Entertainment. Adham and Morhaime sold the company to "edutainment" giant Davidson & Associates for several million dollars (see page 209), and completed the fantasy game Blackthorne for Interplay and the Death

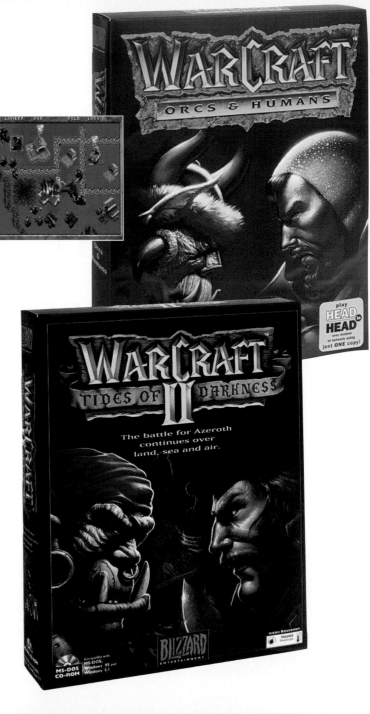

OUT OF NOWHERE

I remember seeing Warcraft for the first time when Blizzard attended their first Consumer Electronics Show. Never having heard of Blizzard, I found myself wondering who these people were. What I noticed most was how infectious their enthusiasm was and how friendly everybody was. I wasn't immediately aware of what Warcraft would mean to the industry, but I definitely made a note to watch Blizzard in the future.

—RDM

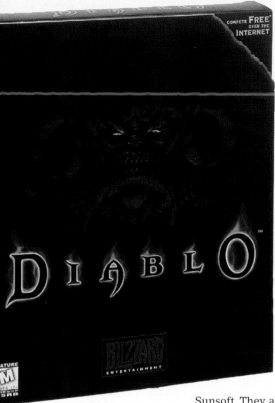

down. The game was called Diablo.

Ultimately, Blizzard decided to contract with Condor to do the game, though it was somewhat different in its original conception. "Originally, we modeled our world and look after X-Com," says Max Schaefer. "Then, late in the spring, someone from Blizzard proposed that the game be real-time. We fought heavily against it. We said it would ruin the strategy of the turn-based action." However, codesigner Brevik agreed to prototype the real-time implementation. Within three hours, he had a mockup. When he clicked on the monster, his character started swinging and the monster went down. It was clear to them then that real-time was the way to go.

and Return of Superman for Sunsoft. They also introduced their first Blizzard product and their first big computer game hit, Warcraft: Orcs and Humans. Along with Westwood's Command & Conquer, Warcraft helped to usher in a new genre: real-time strategy (RTS).

Meanwhile a small development group called Condor was looking for an opportunity, shopping a proposal for a game around CES, but getting no takers. People at both Condor and Blizzard had worked on ports of Justice League Task Force for Sunsoft, and so they knew each other. When Condor cofounder David Brevik called his friend Allen Adham to ask for a copy of Warcraft, the conversation eventually got around to what Condor was doing. Brevik mentioned the proposal that had been universally turned

Shipping in late 1995, Warcraft II included far better graphics, a map editor, and some added character development and humor. Its success was astronomical, far beyond the developers' expectations. Whereas the original game had sold an amazing 100,000 copies in the first year, the sequel exceeded that number ten times over. All of a sudden Blizzard wasn't making hits, they were making blockbusters. In early 1996, Blizzard acquired Condor, which became Blizzard North.

With the merger of the companies, the designers of Diablo experienced a new sense of freedom. "Now we could make the best Diablo we could, instead of basically building toward milestones," says Max Schaefer. At that time, they began to consider the possibility of playing over the Internet, and Blizzard's Battle.net was born. Diablo was finally released in late December 1996, too late to catch any

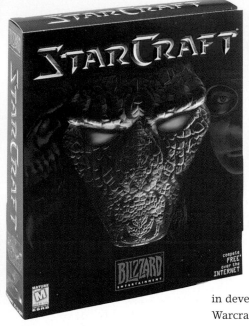

Above: Starcraft screens.
Far right: Brood War screen.

Christmas sales. They were worried that they had blown it. However, Diablo exploded off the shelves and was a runaway hit.

Blizzard was far from finished. While the Diablo team got started on the sequel, another game was in development. Originally, StarCraft was meant to be like Warcraft but in space. An early preview at the Electronic Entertainment Expo in 1996 convinced the team that it needed work, though. They redesigned the Warcraft II engine to allow the graphic effects they wanted for the game and revamped the design. By August 1997, they had entered the crunch mode of the project. Programmer/ designer Bob Fitch remembers how the project consumed him, going from 50 hours a week ultimately to 80 hours a week and basically living at Blizzard. "People would bring me food. I was sleeping on the couch, and despite all of that, I still wanted to play the game. I thought, if it is this bad—if I want to play the game when I am sleeping here, showering here, and people are bringing me my food—then this game is going to be great."

Fitch was right. The game shipped in April 1998 and within three months had already sold a million copies. The expansion pack, Brood War, was even better according to

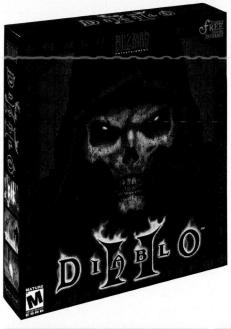

Fitch. "People call Brood War an expansion, but really, Brood War is the game that Starcraft should have been."

Starcraft's amazing speed out the door was later eclipsed by Blizzard's long-awaited Diablo II, which sold its first million copies in 18 days. By Blizzard's tenth anniversary, Diablo II had sold more than 2.5 million copies worldwide, and Battle.net had nearly 9 million active accounts, with more than a million games played a day.

In 2001, Sierra, Blizzard, and Universal Interactive all combined to become Vivendi Universal Interactive.

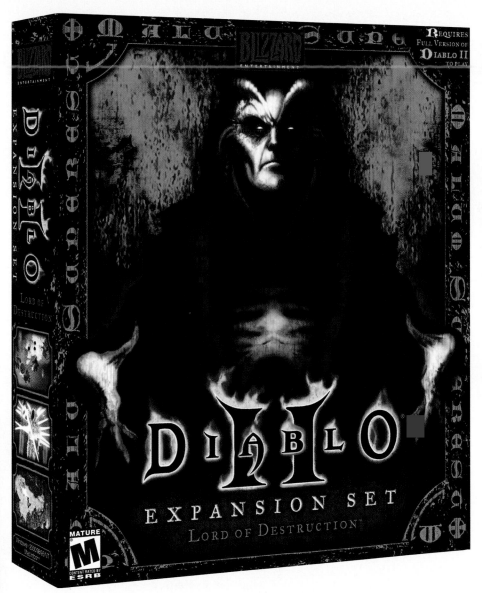

id Software

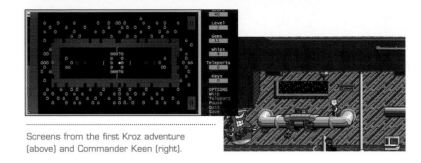

Screens from the first Kroz adventure
(above) and Commander Keen (right).

John Romero (top) and
John Carmack (bottom)
at their computers.

Romero's early business card,
before id.

T hey've rocked the world of computer games since 1991, but the story of id Software began much earlier. For John Romero, it began in 1979 when he learned to program on an HP 9000 mainframe at Sierra College in Rocklin, California. A year later, he discovered the Apple II, and he was off and coding. Romero, who is today a walking encyclopedia of Apple II game information, eventually taught himself assembly language programming—without a computer. "We had moved to England, and my Apple was on the boat for six months. I had to teach myself assembly language in my head. Amazingly, I wrote down the code for my first assembly game, and when I got my computer, I input it and it worked!"

After graduating from high school, Romero moved back to California. He wanted to work for a game company, and ultimately he landed a job as a programmer at Origin Systems' New Hampshire offices. He was also publishing games in magazines such as *A+* and *Nibble* (where he received the prestigious December cover three years in a row). He left Origin to start up Inside Out Software, a company dedicated to porting games to different systems. But the company didn't do well, and he moved on to Softdisk, a monthly magazine-on-disk company located in Shreveport, Louisiana. There he caused the formation of a game division within the company. He also met Tom Hall, Jay Wilbur, and artist Kevin Cloud (all of whom became part of the original id Software) and worked with another experienced programmer, Lane Roathe.

One of the contractors who contributed to Softdisk was a kid who worked in a pizza parlor in Kansas. His name was John Carmack, and he also started programming early on the Radio Shack TRS-80 and the Apple II. Impressed by Carmack's work, Romero invited him to join them at Softdisk. Carmack had twice refused to join Softdisk, but when Romero invited him he said yes and went to Shreveport. "It was pretty cool for me," says Carmack. "I got to meet really good programmers like John Romero and Lane Roathe. I had never known any other good programmers. I learned a lot in my first six months at Softdisk." Carmack's first project at Softdisk was Catacomb for the Apple II.

In short order, Carmack came up with a technique for creating smoothly scrolling graphics on the PC, something that hadn't been done previously. As a prank, he and Tom Hall re-created the first level of Super Mario 3, pixel by pixel, replacing Mario with one of Romero's characters, Dangerous Dave. Working all night, they completed it at 5:00 a.m. and showed it to Romero, calling it "Dangerous Dave in Copyright Infringement." Their results were just short of miraculous. "I was thunderstruck by Carmack's smooth-scrolling code," says Romero, "and made a big deal about it to the other guys, saying, 'This is it, guys. We're outta here.' Very seriously. Jay was laughing, but I looked at him seriously and said, 'Dude, I'm not joking.' Then he slowly closed the door so we could talk..." When a full version (with Mario, not Dave) was presented to Nintendo, however, the console company said they weren't interested. Dangerous Dave went on to have more adventures, but not in Marioland.

A Real Get-Rich-Quick Scheme

"Back in 1985," says Apogee's Scott Miller, "I was making games and releasing them into shareware, but they weren't making any money. I spoke with other shareware authors, such as Nels Anderson, who did EGA Trek, and Mike Denio, who did Captain Comic, and they weren't making any money either. There were good games out in shareware, but they weren't making money." In 1987, Miller came up with a stroke of genius. He split his latest game, Kroz, into three parts and released only the first part for free. Players who wanted the rest would have to pay for it. (Spell Kroz backwards to see one of Miller's favorite games, along with Rogue, M.U.L.E., Archon, and Spelunker.)

Miller's scheme was immensely successful, and he started Apogee with the idea of finding other shareware game authors and marketing their games according to this lucrative plan. Among the authors he contacted was John Romero. (See the sidebar "Fan Letters" to learn how he made contact.)

Miller tried to convince Romero to create a game for him, but Romero was unconvinced. Miller tells it this way: "He had a pyramid game for Softdisk, and I said it would be perfect for shareware, but John thought it was bullshit. But when I told him how much money Kroz was making, he finally said, 'Are you willing to put your money where your mouth is?' I said I'd send him a $3,000 advance. I had $5,000 in my bank account."

Romero agreed and got his friends at Softdisk to work with him. Tom Hall came up with the idea for their first shareware game—Commander Keen—in about 15 minutes. (The full proposal is reproduced in the sidebar "The Commander Keen Proposal.)

Meanwhile, Romero had spotted Adrian Carmack (no relation to John) in what he calls the "five buck an hour art farm" at Softdisk. According to Adrian, "I was told by my college art professor that an internship position was open at Softdisk. The job was to create artwork for monthly computer games. I worked in the computer art department, but Romero and Carmack wanted me to be in their group. Romero went to the owner with his complaint and after a meeting between the two groups I was switched over to the game department. Shortly after that Carmack asked me if I wanted to work with them on a side project, which was Commander Keen." The team was complete. Three months later, Commander Keen: Invasion of the Vorticons was ready to ship, and a month after that, they received their first royalty check for $10,500. Immediately they realized that staying at Softdisk, working on salary, was a dead end. Other than Jay Wilbur and Kevin Cloud, the whole group resigned but agreed to produce games for six more bimonthly Softdisk installments. They formed id Software on February 1, 1991.

id Software Goes 3D

Carmack wasn't finished innovating. After creating his smooth-scrolling technology, he went to work creating a 3D game engine. The first games using that engine—Hovertank One and Catacombs 3D—were published by Softdisk between April and November 1991. They were also the first first-person 3D shooters ever made. However, it was id's third 3D game that blew the lid off.

Scott Miller, anxious to get the id team to work on a 3D game for shareware release, actually had his Apogee team create one of the games (Scubaventure) to complete id's Softdisk contract. Miller remembers, "I guaranteed that they would make at least $100,000 on a 3D game."

Meanwhile, in September 1991, id moved its offices from Shreveport to Madison, Wisconsin, because Tom Hall had told them it was a cool place. According to Jay Wilbur, "No one realized that when Tom said 'cool,' he meant 'cold!'"

Wolfenstein 3D screenshot.

VOTED THE BEST GAME OF
1994! AMAZING 3D GRAPHICS
WITH DIGITAL MUSIC AND
SOUND EFFECTS! PLUS 2 MORE
GUT WRENCHING GAMES!

Preferring warmer climates, the company moved again on April 1, 1992, to Dallas, Texas. They hired Jay Wilbur to run the business side, and they hired artist Kevin Cloud, both of whom had remained at Softdisk.

Shortly after completing their obligations to Softdisk, the id team also completed their second set of Commander Keen episodes for Apogee (in December 1991) and turned their attention to the 3D game Scott Miller wanted so badly. Their first idea was to do a game involving a bio-lab mutant, for which Tom Hall had coined the name, "It's Green and Pissed"; but in the end they decided that was trite. (Jay Wilbur swears that the name somehow was also used during the early development of DOOM.) Then Romero suggested doing a game inspired by Silas Warner's classic Castle Wolfenstein (see page 223). The original design for Wolfenstein 3D included some strategy elements, where you could search corpses for items and drag the dead Nazis out of sight to escape detection, but they eventually dropped those elements and made the game a pure shooter.

Wolfenstein 3D was a smash hit, and true to his promise, Miller was able to deliver the id team the promised $100,000—the first month! The team followed up with a commercial release called Spear of Destiny.

id's brief stay in Wisconsin did have one significant result. They met and befriended another small game development group called Raven Software. Romero had read an ad they placed in the newspaper, seeking programmers. Carmack wrote a new engine for Raven, somewhere between the Wolfenstein engine and the DOOM engine, which Raven used to create Shadowcaster for Electronic Arts. This was the basis for a lasting relationship between the two companies.

THE COMMANDER KEEN PROPOSAL

Billy Blaze, eight-year-old genius, working diligently in his backyard clubhouse, has created an interstellar starship from old soup cans, rubber cement, and plastic tubing. While his folks are out on the town and the babysitter has fallen asleep, Billy sneaks into his backyard workshop, dons

his brother's football helmet, and transforms into...

COMMANDER KEEN— defender of Earth!

In his ship, the Bean-with-Bacon Megarocket, Keen dispenses galactic justice with an iron hand!

Breaking the Mold

After the release of Wolfenstein 3D, id realized they could go it alone, and decided to stop publishing through Apogee. (The breakup between id and Apogee is a story in itself. This is the short version.) "They had lots of money and had learned how to make money with shareware," says Miller. And, according to Jay Wilbur, "Basically, all we needed was someone to answer phones and lick stamps."

According to Wilbur, "Carmack was working on his next-generation game engine. One day he came out of his office and said, 'I have a perfect name for the game. DOOM.' We *all* thought it was perfect."

The conceptual inspiration, according to Romero, was to somehow combine elements of two movies—*Aliens* with *Evil Dead*—demons and monsters in space. But they had to rethink their philosophy of design because Carmack's DOOM engine was way more powerful than the previous one. "Now we had ceilings of any height, walls with angles, lighting, and floors. We had to break out of our Wolfenstein design mold and push the engine. I came up with a design motto—that we don't want anything we do to look like you could have made it with our previous technology."

With superior level design, multiple artifacts, weapons, and monsters, superbly moody music, and fast 35-frames-per-second 3D set in a world full of danger, DOOM was the perfect game for its time. Where Wolfenstein 3D had been a huge success, DOOM was a revelation, a phenomenon, and practically an industry unto itself. It was the basis for much of what has come from the game industry in the years since. Ironically, according to Romero, "DOOM was released in December 1993, the day after Senator Lieberman did his big speech at the violence hearings." Talk about timing!

Once again, the first few levels of DOOM were offered as shareware, and anybody could sell that version. "There were

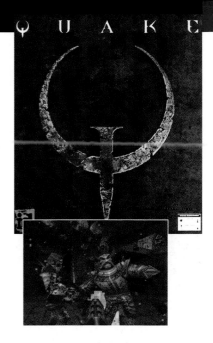

as many as ten different boxes of the product. You walked up to the counter and took your pick. They were all the same, except for the packaging," says Romero.

Another of the innovations that DOOM offered was peer-to-peer play over the modem or LAN. There was a cooperative mode in which up to four players could hunt the enemy together. This required id to rewire the game so that the monsters would randomly target a different player each frame. And then there was the death match mode. DOOM introduced the death match to multiplayer gaming and started something that can only be thought of as a new sporting event still popular today. (Romero claims credit for first using the term "death match.")

The relationship with Raven Software then bore new fruit as id and Raven teamed up to create both Heretic and Hexen using the DOOM engine. id also created DOOM II, an impressive expansion of the original product that released in October 1994.

Quake

How do you top DOOM? Carmack was up to his usual tricks, and he created an engine that was as much a step forward as DOOM had been from Wolfenstein. However, developing groundbreaking technology has its challenges, and Carmack created many versions of the engine before it was complete. Meanwhile, they brought in programmer Michael Abrash (who had written a book called *Power Graphics Programming*) from Microsoft ("Bill Gates tried to talk him out of it, but it didn't work," says Romero).

The original concept was to have the player go through the game with a big hammer. No DOOM-like weapons here. And, although the exploration would be in the now-familiar first-person view, the fighting would be in a perspective, "like Tekken 3," according to Romero. But, according to Kevin

Cloud, "Although there were some good elements in the earlier Quake design, the id team was never comfortable with it. It wasn't working out for a number of reasons. So, about halfway through the development process, id decided to change directions and focus on further developing the fast action game play that made Wolfenstein and DOOM so popular."

After Quake shipped, id and Romero parted ways, and Romero went on to form Ion Storm. Quake was a huge hit, as DOOM had been before it. And, like DOOM before it, but to an even greater degree, it inspired the evolution of the "mod" community—allowing players to create their own levels and modifications by releasing the source code. Although they were no longer alone in the market, and other engines such as Apogee's Build engine, Bethesda's X engine, and the Unreal engine from Epic Megagames were competing, id continued to produce great games, such as Quake II and Quake III, each of which further improved on the speed and depth of the Quake engine, as well as substantially improving online death match play. Versions of the Quake engine have been licensed to produce a staggering legacy of games: Heretic, Hexen, Hexen II, Heretic II, Soldier of Fortune, Kingpin, Half-Life, Half-Life: Opposing Force, Half-Life: Counter-Strike, Daikatana, Sin, Heavy Metal: F.A.K.K. 2, Star Trek: Elite Force, Anachronox, American McGee's Alice, Return to Castle Wolfenstein, Medal of Honor Allied Assault, Team Fortress II, James Bond 007: The World is not Enough, Soldier of Fortune II: Double Helix, and Jedi Knight II: Jedi Outcast.

Although a few of the founders are no longer at id, Kevin Cloud, Adrian Carmack, and John Carmack are still there, still working magic.

Both Carmack and Romero were famous for their matching Ferarri Testarosas.

JOHN CARMACK ON 3D

If you look at our 3D games, they were basically like 2D overhead games, but with a fresh perspective. We took the same game design concepts, but it became much more exciting when, instead of a 16-pixel blob on the screen, we put you in it. We created a brand-new generation of games—the first-person shooter—but it's really an overhead action shooter game with a new perspective.

Shiny Entertainment

A fter years of creating games in England and the United States, Dave Perry started Shiny Entertainment in October 1993. He had just gotten his green card.

Perry had done several games for the UK company Virgin Interactive, including one based on a McDonald's license, called Global Gladiators. "I remember working my ass off—sleeping in the parking lot at Virgin," says Perry. "But the game won Game of the Year on the Genesis." He also developed Cool Spot, based on the 7-Up license and using the Global Gladiators engine, as well as Disney's Aladdin, where he and his team developed sophisticated paper-to-digital animation techniques called Animotion™.

Earthworm Jim

When he started Shiny, Perry took with him many of Virgin's best designers and artists, including longtime associates Nick Bruty, Mike Deitz, Ed Schofield, and Steve Crow. Later they were joined by Andy Astor, Nick Jones, and Tom Tanaka. At about this time, yet another Virgin Interactive employee, animator and cartoonist Doug TenNapel, decided it was time to move on. He applied to Shiny for a job.

According to TenNapel, "Mike Deitz told me to come up with a character and maybe animate a walk cycle.

Original cover art and screen-shots for Earthworm Jim.

Storyboard for Earthworm Jim TV show.

Original early drawings of Jim and of Queen Pulsating Bloated Slug for a Butt.

Mithra

'We'll see if you're Shiny material,' he told me. So I went home and put on a Fleetwood Mac album. By the time the album finished, I had designed Earthworm Jim, Peter Puppy, the Queen—every major character in the Earthworm Jim world."

With Perry's background in doing licensed games, and with investment from Playmates and Interactive Entertainment backing the company, the concept of Earthworm Jim was planned from the start as a multifaceted attack—toys, TV, comic books, and video games. The result was one of the oddest heroes of all time and several truly great games.

TenNapel, who later went on to create The Neverhood for Dreamworks (see page 294), deserves a lot of the credit for the original concept, but he also spreads the credit around. "We worked round the clock—animated our asses off—but we all brought a lot of experience with us. Nick Bruty added a lot. He's probably the best game designer I've ever worked with. Mike Deitz is an old-school animator, while I'm like wild lightning; and he had a lot of influence on the game. Combined, we had all done hundreds of games. We finished it in a year."

After EWJ

After the phenomenal success of Earthworm Jim and its sequel, Shiny continued to make great games; but they were faced with a changing industry. "After we did EWJ 2, 3D technology had become the standard," says Perry, " and it caused a division at Shiny. Many of our team didn't want to move from 2D traditional animation to 3D. And it was expensive. I was funding the company out of my own

Above: Doug TenNapel at work.
Right: Model sheet for Psy-Crow.

pockets—buying Silicon Graphics systems and motion capture... It was very expensive."

Ultimately, Shiny did move into 3D. But in the middle of developing their next game (a 3D shooter called MDK), they accepted an offer to become part of Interplay "We acquired Shiny because of their strength in the console market," says Interplay's Brian Fargo (see page 206). "Dave's a great visionary, and they had great technology. Ironically, their next projects were for high-end PC products, not the mass market console products we were anticipating."

Despite Fargo's comment, MDK sold more than 500,000 copies and was successful on both PC and PlayStation platforms. They followed with another wacky PlayStation game, Wild 9, and Messiah, a highly innovative PC title. There was considerable hubbub about some of the content of Messiah, which includes such features as the ability of the player's angel character to possess the bodies of other beings, including prostitutes. After Messiah, Shiny created Sacrifice, an ambitious story-based game of strategy, action, and magic set in a 3D world. Shiny's games are consistently imaginative, ground-breaking, and critically acclaimed. In 2003, they plan to release The Matrix, based on the hit movie.

Earthworm Jim©
Shiny Entertainment,
All Rights Reserved.

Sacrifice was actually based on the old-style Wizards games. However, its state-of-the-art engine really gave it a special look and made the experience a lot more immersive. There is still life in the games where you play as a wizard, collect incredibly powerful spells, build an army, and then go and sacrifice the bodies of your enemies to your god.

—*DAVE PERRY, FOUNDER OF SHINY ENTERTAINMENT*

277

1993

Jaguar

In the early 90s, Atari attempted to come back to the console business one more time. The company was simultaneously developing a 32-bit system called the Panther—which was scheduled to release in 1991 at the same time as the Super NES—and an even more advanced system called the Jaguar. Touted as the first 64-bit system (which was astounding when compared with the 16-bit Genesis), Jaguar was impressive on paper, and Atari was able to line up several third-party publishers. At launch in 1993, the system sold well, although at a price tag of $250—far higher than Atari had originally announced.

The Jaguar was a sleek and powerful machine, but its initial software did little to convince consumers that the machine could live up to its hype. The development system proved to be difficult to work with, and many third-party titles either released very late or were never completed. Ultimately, however, some fine games were released for the Jaguar, including Tempest 2000 and versions of Doom, Wolfenstein 3D, and Alien vs. Predator; but the initial reaction held the system back. Most of these games were available on other systems, anyway. Jaguar really had no "killer app" and too small a list of titles to keep growing.

In a weak selling year in general, hobbled by a lack of good titles, and with Sega's Saturn on the horizon, Jaguar did poorly. With the release of PlayStation in late 1995, its fate was sealed. Despite its claims to be a superior 64-bit system, the new 32-bit consoles, Saturn and PlayStation, both produced superior products. Although Atari continued to support the system, introduced a CD add-on, and even had a more powerful Jaguar II in production, their support lasted only a matter of months. Jaguar was discontinued in 1996.

Top to bottom: Atari Karts, Alien vs. Predator, Battlemorph.

A brand new Jaguar game from JDK, StarAlliance: Battle for Earth, screen courtesy of Lars Hannig.

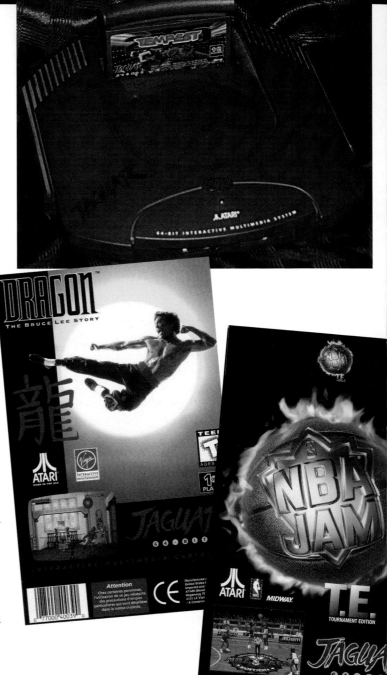

Marketing shot of Sega CD, the most successful enhancement to the Genesis.

1994

The Entertainment Software Rating Board

In 1993, games like Mortal Kombat and Night Trap came to the attention of U.S. Senators Joseph Lieberman and Herb Kohl, who launched a campaign against video game violence and the "culture of carnage" rampant throughout the entertainment industry. There were valid arguments on both sides, but certainly the game industry wasn't about to succumb to outright censorship and the possible loss of revenues. Violence was a part of gaming, and the increasing technology allowed increasing realism. Ultimately the game industry offered a compromise—the Entertainment Software Rating Board (ESRB), which created a rating system for video games in 1994. This ratings system alerts parents to possibly offensive material but does not necessarily prevent young kids from gaining access to violent games or other games deemed unsuitable for young minds.

Peripheral Madness

At the time of Nintendo's SNES introduction, Sega was on the rise. The competition between Nintendo and Sega grew ever tighter as they shared the market, and NEC ultimately faded. For the first time, there were two nearly evenly successful console systems. According to Nintendo's numbers, they ultimately sold 18.5 million of the SNES to 16.4 million of Sega's Genesis.

However, Sega may have leaned a little too hard on Sonic. Although many other great games did come out for the Genesis, including Phantasy Star 2, Revenge of Shinobi, Virtua

Fighter, and Shining Force (which in many ways was the forerunner to Square's Final Fantasy Tactics), Sonic was the only real franchise character Sega had. He was featured in comic books and cartoons and was definitely a big hit, but Sega came out with more Sonic games than you could shake a stick at. Even the introduction of the popular character Tails in Sonic the Hedgehog 2 wasn't enough to carry the company.

An even greater problem stemmed from Sega's various attempts to expand the Genesis. They tried different peripheral devices, including the Sega CD unit, but none were immensely successful, and their 32x add-on for the Genesis—a hybrid CD enhancement with its own games—simply diluted their market and left a bad taste in the mouths of both consumers and retailers. If you had Sega CD and Sega 32 attached to your Genesis, the sleekly designed console was transformed into an ungainly jumble of badly fitting parts. In the end, Nintendo's franchise games and its immense third-party support kept them strong, while Sega began to stumble amid increasing competition from new console makers.

279

Street Fighter II

In 1991, when Capcom's Street Fighter II hit the arcades, it looked like the cavalry coming to the rescue in some B western. Instead of the sound of bugles, however, it announced itself with a resounding "Ryuken!"

Street Fighter II was far from the first fighting game. The history of fighting games goes back at least to the 80s, and there were several types of games that featured punches and kicks. Many early games involved the "walk and fight" theme, such as Double Dragon and Final Fight. The Teenage Mutant Ninja Turtle games were popular fighters in both the arcades and on home systems. A few early games attempted to provide one-on-one excitement, such as Data East's 1984 Karate Champ and Kung Fu Master. In 1987, Capcom came out with Street Fighter, their first attempt to make a one-on-one fighting game. However, technology of the time was really not

sufficient to realize the designers' visions. Although they tried creating a sophisticated control system and smooth animations, the technology was not able to keep up with what they intended.

Street Fighter II, on the other hand, introduced the smoothest animation and the fastest, most complex controls ever seen, and when it came out, the arcades suddenly breathed new life, and one-on-one fighters rapidly became the new "killer app." Street Fighter II also provided a truly imaginative assortment of fighters, each with his or her own basic and secret moves, and strengths and weaknesses. It was cartoons come to life, and it was a game in which mastery mattered. Over the next few years, Capcom came out with several revisions of the game, though each represented primarily incremental improvements and no giant leaps ahead.

Imitators abounded. On both arcade and home systems, fighting games were everywhere following the release of Street Fighter II. It's safe to say that games inspired by Street Fighter II dominated the scene until Doom and the first-person shooter took over around 1994.

ORIGINAL STREET FIGHTER II ART COURTESY OF CAPCOM.

Mortal Kombat

One of the most significant of the games to enter the market in the wake of Street Fighter II was Midway's blockbuster 1992 release, Mortal Kombat.

In game play, it rivaled Street Fighter II, with secret moves, death moves, and something that even Street Fighter II did not have—real actors digitized into the game. Instead of cartoon characters, you were fighting with and against more or less realistic depictions of people.

The so-called realism of Mortal Kombat was part of its appeal, and part of its controversy. While fighting, blood spurted from every hit, and the finishing moves, once an opponent was sufficiently beaten down, were gory to the point of absurdity—like ripping the unfortunate loser's heart out of their chest or yanking their whole spinal column out.

Mortal Kombat had more than just a lot of gory graphics and an intense fighting game, however. It also had an ongoing story—one that grew increasingly complex for some fans as Midway continued the game series, released movies and other ancillary products, and furthered the story in other ways. Most of all, Mortal Kombat is remembered for its innovation, intensity, and great effects. Toward the end of 2002, Midway will relaunch the Mortal Kombat franchise with Mortal Kombat: Deadly Alliance.

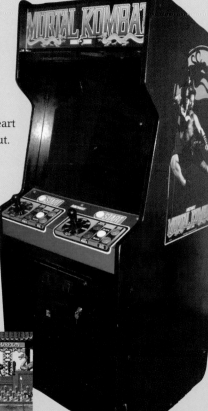

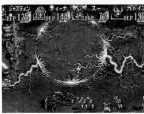

Top to bottom: Sega's Panzer Dragoon Saga and Shining Force III, and Game Arts' Grandia.

1995

Saturn

In 1995, Sega introduced the Saturn, but the system sold initially in limited markets. Sega's reputation had been tarnished as a result of several poorly received add-on products for the Genesis, and the few initial games available for Saturn at launch were uninspired. On top of that, they were going up against a newcomer to the race, but one powerhouse of a newcomer—Sony. Although Saturn's limited introduction was some months before Sony's, both Saturn and Sony's new 32-bit PlayStation were competing for 1995 Christmas sales, with Saturn selling for $399 and PlayStation a hundred dollars less.

Saturn did claim to be the first fully Internet-ready system, and indeed it allowed gaming, and even email, using its built-in modem. But that wasn't enough to save the system. Between 1995 and 1998, only a little more than a million units were sold, though its sales in Japan were much better than in the States. Their flagship title at launch was Nights, by Sonic and Phantasy Star designer Yuki Naka. Nights was an intriguing game, with many Sonic-like aspects (although it did not feature Sonic). However, Nights was not popular enough to drive sales of the system. Despite poor launch titles, many excellent games ultimately appeared on Saturn, including Panzer Dragoon Saga, a huge action RPG that deserved a much bigger audience. Virtua Fighter 2 and 3 and Sega Rally headed up a strong arcade conversion list. It was too little too late, however, and some of the best Saturn games from Japanese developers such as Capcom and SNK were never released outside Japan.

Left to right, top to bottom: Albert Odyssey, Dragon Force, and Capcom's Vampire Savior and D&D Tower of Doom.

PlayStation

Back in 1991, the consumer electronics giant Sony had contracted with Nintendo to create a CD add-on for the Super NES, but the project ended when Nintendo jumped ship to work with Philips and their CD-i technology. However, Sony had gained a good deal of knowledge working with Nintendo and they turned it to good use, developing their own 32-bit CD-based system. They called it PlayStation.

PlayStation turned out to be the perfect system for playing the popular 3D games of the day, such as the ground-breaking Tomb Raider (see page 286). Game makers found the system easy to work with, and Sony was able to line up many third-party developers.

Sony's marketing effort was massive and broad. They advertised on TV and in magazines aimed at older audiences. Using Sony's strength and experience as a leader in consumer electronics as well as a strong and ever-growing number of titles, PlayStation came out of the gate blazing. With Sega's weakened position, strong titles, and Nintendo's N64 still a year away, PlayStation established itself as a premier console system, and Sony became a major player in the console wars.

On the next few pages, we've included some of the many great PlayStation games.

Original
PlayStation
sellsheet.

PlayStation™

Prepare yourself for a blast of ultimate game system power. Sony's breakthrough 32-bit processor, CD-ROM architecture delivers real-time experience with ever-changing 3-D perspectives and stereo CD-quality sound. Custom multiple processors including a dedicated 32-bit RISC CPU pulse at the heart of the system. Result? Gameplay will never be the same.

Features

- Custom multiple processors for the most realistic 3-D graphics rendered in real-time and the most responsive gameplay ever.
- 360-degree movement provides ever changing 3-D perspectives to enhance realism.
- Full frame video at 30 frames per second for the highest quality images.
- 360,000 polygons per second giving a smoother, more realistic look to the graphics and movement of the games.
- 16.8 million simultaneous colors.
- 2MB of RAM, 1MB VRAM. Players can download an entire game into RAM memory.
- Custom ports for two controllers and two memory cards.
- Includes custom controller, AC power cord and stereo AV cable.

Marketing

Support within the PlayStation's unprecedented marketing campaign includes:
- National TV
- National Print
- Full PR and Editorial Coverage
- Retail Promotions and Merchandising
- Sony Home Page Web Site Coverage

Product Profile

Available: September 9, 1995
Part No: SCPH-1001/94000

SONY
COMPUTER

Left to right, top to bottom: Tomb Raider (Eidos), Doom (id Software), Spyro the Dragon (Sony), Gran Tourismo (Sony), Tony Hawk Pro Skater 3 (Activision), Twisted Metal 2 (Sony).

Dark Stalkers: The Night Warriors
(Capcom)

Bloody Roar *(Hudsonsoft)*

Street Fighter 3 Alpha *(Capcom)*

Tekken *(Namco)*

Breath of Fire *(Capcom)*

007 Racing *(EA)*

007: Tomorrow Never Dies *(EA)*

007: The World is Not Enough *(EA)*

Soul Caliber *(Namco)*

Marvel Super Heroes *(Capcom)*

Dragon Warrior *(Enix)*

Dragon Warrior VII *(Enix)*

Madden 2002 *(EA)*

NCAA Final Four 2002 *(EA)*

Tiger Wood Golf *(EA)*

Triple Play Baseball *(EA)*

Legend of Dragoon *(Sony)*

Soul of the Samurai *(Konami)*

Castlevania: Symphony of the Night
(Konami)

Nightmare Creatures II *(Konami)*

Metal Gear Solid *(Konami)*

Tenchu 2 *(Activision)*

Azure Dreams *(Konami)*

Dance, Dance Revolution *(Konami)*

Jumping Flash 2 *(Sony)*

Ridge Racer *(Namco)*

WWF Smackdown: Know Your Role
*(TH*Q)*

MLB 2001 *(Sony)*

Working Design's
Arc the Lad collection.

Alunda *(Working Designs)*

Lunar 2: Eternal Blue Complete
(Working Designs)

Lunar: Silver Star Story Complete
(Working Designs)

Arc the Lad *(Working Designs)*

Noticeably missing from these pages are images from Square's amazing games, such as all the Final Fantasy games, Chrono Cross, and so many more. We respect Square's request not to be included.

Eidos

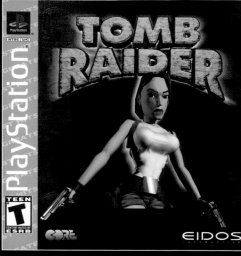

Lara Croft has become the first electronic gaming sex symbol, with the possible exception of Ms. Pac-Man.

In 1990, Eidos was a brand-new company specializing in video compression technology. By 1996, they were right at the top of the game charts with Tomb Raider. Who would have guessed that by purchasing two relatively average companies—Domark in 1995 and U.S. Gold in 1996—they would suddenly transform into a gaming giant? Of course, they also got Core Design along with the U.S. Gold deal, which turned out to be a fortuitous twist of fate. It was Core Design that came up with Lara Croft and Tomb Raider, a game that first released in 1996 for the PC and PlayStation.

Tomb Raider was a huge hit. It helped establish the PlayStation as the leading console system, and it made significant waves throughout the PC game community. Moreover, Tomb Raider somehow proved the ultimate value of 3D action worlds, incorporating exploration and acrobatics reminiscent of the classic Prince of Persia games with a dynamite new character, Lara Croft.

Originally, the design emphasis was on creating the environment for the game, but during brainstorming sessions, it became clear that the game's lead character should be something different from the usual buffed battering-ram male protagonist. The role called for someone with physical skills combined with flexibility, and with flexibility, the designers reasoned, came an element of gracefulness.

The more they considered it, the more they leaned toward a female protagonist. The first character was Lara Cruz, a buffed and Amazonian sort—still too close to the male stereotype. Cruz soon gave way to Croft, however, and Lara was born, complete with her own story—a well-educated young woman from a wealthy background, more the female James Bond than Rambo.

Lara Croft has become an icon over the years. Once there was a question of whether male game audiences would be interested in playing a female lead character. That question has been answered definitively.

Eidos has made its fortune largely on the strength of the Tomb Raider series, but they have also made distribution deals with various companies, including Ion Storm—the company John Romero founded after leaving id Software—and have acquired or invested in several other successful development companies, including Crystal Dynamics (Gex, Soul Reaver series), Michael Crichton's Timeline Studios, Elixir Studios (Theme Park),

Poster for the Tomb Raider movie.
Inset: The "real" Lara Croft and
Angelina Jolie as Lara in the
Tomb Radier movie.

Soul Reaver 2 screenshots.

Artwork from Soul Reaver 2.

Rare Ltd. spinoff Free Radical Design (Time Splitters 2), and others.

In 2001, Tomb Raider became one of the few electronic games to make it to the silver screen, with Angelina Jolie in the leading role. Although not an across-the-board critical success, financially the movie did extremely well, grossing $300 million worldwide, and it spurred even more sales of games in the already popular series.

More recently, Eidos licensed the 2002 Winter Olympics, and they have released the controversial Hitman and Hitman 2 from Norwegian developers IO Interactive. They are also continuing to develop more games in Crystal Dynamics' Soul Reaver series and from Ion Storm with Deus Ex 2.

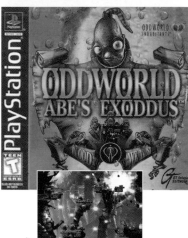

Oddworld cofounders Sherry McKenna and Lorne Lanning.

Slog and Slig: Two of Abe's main meanies.

Story of an Odd World

When Lorne Lanning saw his first example of computer graphics, he knew.

"I knew that was the future, and it was my future," he tells us.

Perhaps that recognition was due in part to the influence of his father, who was in the navy and worked on nuclear submarines. "We were still drooling in Pampers," says Lanning, "when he'd come home with a transistor and tell us how this little thing used to take rooms full of vacuum tubes, and we'd say, 'What?'" When Lanning was in his teens, his father went to work at Coleco. Meanwhile, Lanning was sneaking into bars and drinking in order to play arcade games like Asteroids and Missile Command.

Many years later, as a painter and student at the School of Visual Arts, he became dissatisfied with photo-realistic paintings and illustrations. "They were like Polaroids—no sound, no movement. I wanted to create living fantasy worlds that looked believable." He packed his bags and moved from New York City to Los Angeles and enrolled at Cal Arts to study visual effects and traditional animation techniques.

In 1987, after completing his studies, he found that there was very little work for a computer graphics artist. He did, however, land a job at TRW, working on the Strategic Defense Initiative (SDI) program, sometimes referred to by the press as "Star Wars." Lanning reveals, "Working on space visualization graphics allowed me to get a glimpse of what was happening on the super high end of simulations as well as real-time databases the military was using to simulate F-14s, for instance. It was mind-blowing. I was aware of how the military blazed the trail for technology, so I could see that these big expensive simulations were going to become your average consumer video game experience in time. I saw virtual reality, the ancestors of today's multiplayer worlds—the military was doing that long ago with tanks, planes, ships, and submarines all in the same database."

Lanning eventually went to work at Los Angeles–based effects house Rhythm & Hues (the creators of the famous Coca Cola Bears, among many other projects). At first, he was told he should play the role of art director, but he wanted to be a technical director. "Only computer programmers were in that role." Ultimately breaking the mold, Lanning spent a couple of years honing his CG chops in animation, choreography, texture mapping, and other techniques that he would eventually employ in making games. He was learning while waiting for the right time.

That time came with the advent of the CD-ROM and

32-bit graphics. Lanning finally started on what he really wanted to do, to make storytelling—Storydwelling®—worlds. He approached Sherry McKenna, an award-winning film, commercial, and location-based special effects producer, and proposed forming a game company. Her response? "Why do I care?" McKenna was not into computer games, which she considered incapable of producing the results she was used to in film and location-based entertainment.

Lanning, however, is nothing if not impassioned. He presented a plan to McKenna that involved story, characters you care about, and graphics that were close to movie quality. It was 1994, and Oddworld Inhabitants was born. Lanning and McKenna have run a successful company, based in San Luis Obispo, California, ever since.

Oddworld: Abe's Oddysee® was the company's first product, a highly imaginative story and game with, of all things, a character who didn't fight or wield a weapon. It's one thing to have a great technology and superior art and animation, which Abe did, but it's another to have brilliant and original game design. And Abe had that, too. The game played like a series of logic puzzles that could only be solved by precise movements and appropriate use of Abe's unusual abilities, which included sneaking in shadows and chanting to possess the minds of some enemies. Abe could also run, jump, and climb—much in the mold of Prince of Persia— and the game made great use of his abilities.

Oddworld: Abe's Exoddus® was a worthy sequel to the first game, and added a few new wrinkles. It was much bigger and in some ways trickier, although the main character was more or less the same and the basic game play remained.

Another feature, which began in the first game and has evolved in later products, was the concept of GameSpeak®, the ability of Oddworld's characters to communicate with each other and to work cooperatively. Many of the puzzles in Abe's Oddysee, and to an even greater extent in Oddworld's later games, required the player to find ways to communicate with other characters in the game, and to control them purely by the use of cleverly designed word commands.

In Oddworld: Munch's Oddysee™, Oddworld introduced a new character, Munch, and their first fully 3D world for the Xbox. Munch is a far more ambitious project than the original Abe's Oddysee, and still retains Lanning's vision of storytelling and the highest production values. But is Lanning content? No way. His standards are high, and he has yet to hit his own ultimate mark. More to come from Oddworld…

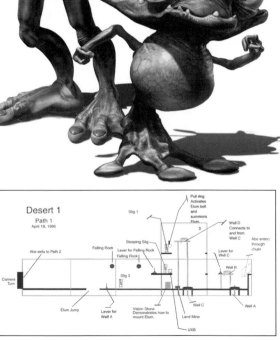

Abe & Munch

Production sketch and final game screen from Oddworld: Munch's Oddysee™.

Desert 1
Path 1
April 19, 1996

Level design for Oddworld: Abe's Oddysee®.

1996

Nintendo 64

Nintendo made a rare false move with their 1994 release of the 3D game system Virtual Boy. However, they released the Silicon Graphics–powered Ultra 64 console in Japan that same year, following with the 1996 release of the same system, now renamed Nintendo 64 (or N64 for short), world-wide and sold unprecedented quantities in their first months after release. Mario made the move from 2D to 3D in Super Mario 64, and in the process blew everyone away (including many computer game designers), paving the way for a succession of 3D games from Nintendo. At the top of the list was the first 3D Legend of Zelda title, the Ocarina of Time. Nintendo also released several games from one of their premier developers, Rare, Ltd., including Killer Instinct Gold, Goldeneye, Banjo-Kazooie, and Donkey Kong Country.

Nintendo continued to support a cartridge-only machine—no CD, no Internet—and did it very well. Meanwhile Sony reduced the price of the PlayStation to $199, and Sega, already in trouble, was forced to follow suit. Over the next few years, both N64 and PlayStation continued to sell well, but PlayStation proved the stronger system. "At the end of our twelfth month, N64 had a bigger installed base than PlayStation," says Nintendo's Peter Main, "but in our second year, their third, they smoked right by us. At the time we launched the GameCube, we had sold about 18 million N64s to about 27 million PlayStations. It happened in the second or third year and had to do with who had the most compelling software story to tell. We didn't have a broad enough array."

The Nintendo 64 continued to be a very popular system for years, however, and was Nintendo's flagship console until the release of the GameCube in 2001. Many great games came out for N64, some of which we've memorialized on these pages.

Super Mario 64

Top to bottom: Mario Party, Paper Mario, Mario Tennis.

Legend of Zelda: Ocarina of Time

Legend of Zelda: Majora's Mask

EXPANSION PAK INCLUDED!

DONKEY KONG 64

REQUIRES N64 Expansion Pak™

Designed For N64 Rumble Pak™

1-4 Players Simultaneous

COLLECTOR'S EDITION YELLOW GAME PAK

DOLBY SURROUND

EVERYONE E CONTENT RATED BY ESRB

RAREWARE

Donkey Kong 64

N64 GAMES BY RARE, LTD.

Rareware, as they're called, are games from one of Nintendo's finest developers. Based in the UK, Rare, Ltd. has produced consistently great games for Nintendo consoles, going all the way back to Battletoads for NES.

Donkey Kong Country

007 Goldeneye, Bad Fur Day, Killer Instinct Gold, and Perfect Dark.

Screen shots of Yoshi's Story, Wave Race 64, and Pilot Wings.

POWER UP!

THE NEW TETRIS

NINTENDO.64

Only For

Designed For N64 Controller Pak™

1-4 Players Simultaneous

4-Player Frenzy!

EVERYONE E CONTENT RATED BY ESRB

STAR WARS ROGUE SQUADRON™

Designed for N64 Expansion Pak™

Designed For N64 Rumble Pak™

Official Nintendo Seal of Quality

TEEN T CONTENT RATED BY ESRB

The picture on the far right is an archival photograph of an Orient Express car. On the near right is the game scene.

More Games of the 90s

60 MINUTES LEFT

Out of hundreds of games that made an impact on our lives in the 90s, here are a few we just had to include.

Jordan Mechner: Prince of Persia and The Last Express

Jordan Mechner (see also page 128) published his first game, Karateka, while attending Yale University in 1984. Interested in filmmaking techniques, he experimented with rotoscoping, which takes actual film, then colors in the images in cartoon-like fashion. The result is very smooth and realistic animation. Mechner first experimented with rotoscoping in Karateka.

In 1989, Mechner completed his next game, which was

to become a classic. Prince of Persia, like Karateka, was published by Brøderbund (see page 124), and again used rotoscoping techniques. Mechner used his younger brother as a model for the title character, who could run, leap, and climb with exceptionally smooth animation. Of course, the Prince needed all his skills to avoid the numerous, and quite devious, traps that Mechner built into his game. Prince of Persia and its sequel, The Shadow & The Flame, are among the most inspirational games of all time and influenced game makers for years to come. Fans of the games wrote many letters praising them. One such letter came from Saudi Arabia, and among the comments, the writer said, "…you are truly the Prince of America… You frighten me a lot, You excite me a lot, You Enjoy me a lot." Amen.

Mechner's next major epoch began during the height of the multimedia craze. New companies

were springing up to dazzle the industry with digitized video or CDs crammed to bursting with images. Companies were funded by New York publishing giants and by Hollywood's famous studios, and it was at this time that Mechner started Smoking Car Productions with the idea of creating a different sort of game, a mystery based around the last journey of the famous Orient Express.

In The Last Express (1997), Mechner returned to rotoscoping on a grand scale. He and his colleagues at Smoking Car did meticulous research, finding and accurately modeling surviving cars from the Orient Express, poring over transportation records discovered by a bit of sleuthing in Paris, and creating a story of international intrigue and murder in a historical setting.

The project turned out to be horrendously difficult— a labor of love and dedication for Mechner and his staff.

An example of the rotoscoping technique used to put actors in the scene.

Each scene was filmed with real actors over a blue screen backdrop; then each image was meticulously redrawn using special software to create the rotoscoping effect. The postproduction took far longer than anticipated, and the project went way over budget.

But The Last Express was a pure gem, a remarkable game that creates an exceptionally rich atmosphere all its own. The characters are strongly written, and the use of people speaking in their native languages further enhances the realism and compelling sense of detail in the game. A lush musical score from film and television composer Elia Cmiral (*Somebody Is Waiting* and *Nash Bridges*) further enhances the international flavor of the story, providing aural counterpoint to the colorful and accurate graphic presentation. In some ways, The Last Express is reminiscent of one of those murder mystery train excursions where you have to eavesdrop and observe everything in order to piece together the entire story.

Unfortunately, in an era when first-person shooters and fast-paced action was the rule of the day, The Last Express offered too slow a pace for many gamers, and the open-ended flow of play was too confusing for others. On top of that, The Last Express was overbudget and undermarketed. The result was a commercial failure that still offers an aesthetic and cerebral treat to anyone who plays the game to this day.

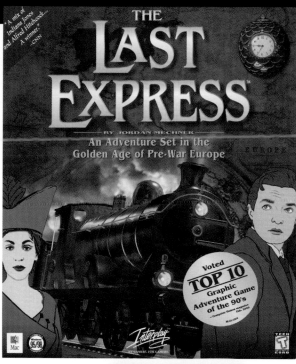

Three of the developers, testing the rotoscoping process: Jordan Mechner, Nicole Tostevin (art director), and Robert Cook (technical director).

Here's an entire sequence showing how the scenes were produced, from sketches to final rotoscoped images in the game.

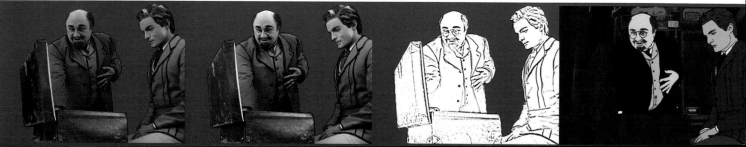

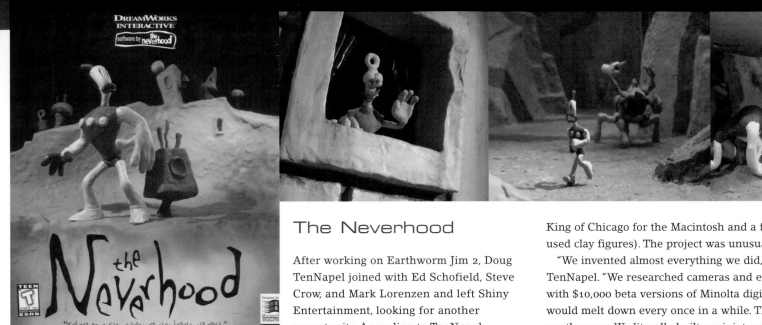

The creation of The Neverhood involved a clay-covered set and cameras on rails. Here are images of Doug TenNapel repositioning figures in the set. Below: Two animation poses in front of a green screen.

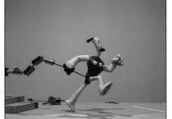

The Neverhood

After working on Earthworm Jim 2, Doug TenNapel joined with Ed Schofield, Steve Crow, and Mark Lorenzen and left Shiny Entertainment, looking for another opportunity. According to TenNapel, "Steven Spielberg was a huge Earthworm Jim fan. And Jeffery Katzenberg had wanted it for Disney, but Shiny went with Universal. So, when they formed Dreamworks, they invited me to pitch a game." The game they pitched was called The Neverhood, a game done all in claymation and inspired by a series of paintings TenNapel had done in the late 80s called "A Beautiful Day in the Neverhood." The deal to produce this unusual game was struck at a meeting at Spielberg's house. According to TenNapel, "Steven is probably the only executive who would have the balls to make that kind of decision."

Nobody had ever tried a fully animated game using all claymation before (although the original King of Chicago for the Macintosh and a few others had used clay figures). The project was unusual and risky.

"We invented almost everything we did," remembers TenNapel. "We researched cameras and ended up working with $10,000 beta versions of Minolta digital cameras, which would melt down every once in a while. They'd send us another one. We literally built a miniature world coated in clay in a 60-by-60-foot warehouse. We set it off the ground and built a hub and rail camera system through it."

Since all of the animators on the project were traditional cel animators, they did all the first drawings on paper and then applied the animation directly to the clay figures.

The game was completed in a year, though it took three months just to build the set. However, The Neverhood was not a commercial success. Like many experimental and artistic games, it failed to reach a significant audience, although, according to TenNapel, "We got letters from old men and little children—people who had never touched a PC before—telling us how much fun they'd had wandering around in our world, and thanking us for creating it."

And, although The Neverhood contained interesting puzzles and some very funny animation, even TenNapel admits that it was not exactly a game. "It's a fine artwork that ten people made and Dreamworks funded," he says. Game or not, The Neverhood, like Jordan Mechner's The Last Express, was a notable and creative attempt to do something different. One of a kind.

100 Brand New Lemmings™ Adventures!

Lemmings

You've probably heard of lemmings—those little rodents reputed to flock en masse over cliffs and into raging rivers, committing mass suicide when societal urges push them to their population limit. It's a myth, but did you ever figure this as the premise of a game? Dave Jones of DMA Design did. And in the process, he produced one of the greatest puzzle games in computer game history.

Psygnosis' Lemmings might have gotten the "cute" award for games of the 90s, except that it was not only cute, but also devious, humorous, cruel, and brilliant. Those little critters would just keep on going, heedless of all perils, and it was up to you to save their furry little butts, often by judiciously sacrificing one or two of the horde for the common good. In the end, if you saved the required number, you advanced to the next, probably even more devious, level. Lemmings seemed to have endless permutations, and the characters, though tiny on the screen, became endearing figures in several sequels and on a staggering variety of ancillary products ranging from mouse pads to lunch pails. Coming a long way from Lemmings, DMA Design has more recently produced games such as Grand Theft Auto 3 and State of Emergency.

A Lemmings mouse pad.

System Shock

One of our favorite producer/designers is Warren Spector, who has worked variously at Steve Jackson Games, TSR, Origin Systems, Blue Sky Software, and Ion Storm. He worked often as a producer and designer, with multiple credits, including several Ultima and Ultima Underworld games and several Wing Commander games. He was the producer on the ground-breaking game, System Shock, which set the stage for 3D first-person adventure games. System Shock was developed by Looking Glass, the same great team who brought us the Ultima Underworld games, with Doug Church as the project leader.

"I think Doug Church, Looking Glass studio head Paul Neurath, and I were so tired of fantasy games," says Spector. "We just wanted to move into a different genre entirely. The science fiction setting had a strong appeal. But mostly, I think, it was an attempt to bring even more depth—of story, of simulation, of player experience—to gaming."

Spector comments on the collaborative nature of the project: "Doug Church was clearly a guy with a vision, and I kibitzed mightily, but the design work was spread around as much as I've ever experienced. Programmers came up with

SYSTEM SHOCK

ORIGIN.

IT'S ALL IN THE DETAILS

Warren Spector comments on the special attention that went into the details in System Shock: "I just remember being blown away (and, I admit, terrified) at the team's audacity. They'd do stuff like take time out from actually finishing the game to implement little minigames you could download in cyberspace, or make a starfield outside the station windows appear to move, or start security cameras rotating the day before we signed off. Drove the poor producer crazy, but it's stuff like that that takes a game from really good to great... That's what I keep telling myself anyway."

system designs...writers came up with story elements... designers built levels...but there were some incredible team meetings where high-level conceptual stuff got hammered out, as well as a lot of details, in an atmosphere of total respect and commitment to quality. That was a cohesive team, I can tell you..."

Like many games, System Shock nearly didn't make it out the door. "On Shock, the biggest challenge from my perspective as out-of-house producer, was communicating what the game was all about to a management group that didn't always get what the team was trying to do," said Spector. "You don't want to know how many times the game came *this* close to getting killed (or how late in the project)."

Deus Ex

Later, Spector got the opportunity of a lifetime when John Romero offered him the chance to make "the game he's always wanted to make" for Romero's newly established company, Ion Storm. The game Spector made, Deus Ex, has been hailed by players and press as one of the most innovative action adventure games ever made. In a time when so many games were plotless firefests, Deus Ex offered deep stories, characters, real dilemmas, and alternative methods of play.

Again, Spector comments: "I was really feeling like I had to prove something to execs, journalists, and fans who had pounded into me the idea that the kind of games I loved were doomed to be nichey and appealing only to the hard core.

I wanted so badly to prove them all wrong. I think we did OK on that score!

"Deus Ex was the next logical step, at least in my mind, along an evolutionary path that started with the Underworlds and then Shock and then Thief. I spent a year working with the Thief team and found myself a little frustrated at how narrowly focused that game was shaping up to be. That's not a bad thing, but I just kept arguing that we could allow players more freedom of action than Thief allowed. We could let them fight their way through problems as well as sneak... We could allow them to interact directly with NPCs as well as overhear them and avoid them... None of those ideas had any place in Thief, so I knew I had to find a way to make a game that allowed a broader range of player choices than any other game ever had.

"On Deus Ex, the biggest challenge, in terms of process, was dealing with a game that was, by design, unfocused. We didn't want it to be a shooter or an RPG or an adventure game or a strategy game. We wanted it to incorporate elements of *all* of those game types. And I (perhaps foolishly) assembled a team of people who, well, let's just say they didn't always agree on what made a good game, a bad game, and so on. Merging disparate opinions and differing design and implementation styles into a reasonably coherent end product was tough! In terms of design and implementation, the biggest challenge was probably making sure that a wide enough variety of play style choices was supported at the macro level *and* at the micro level. Every problem had to have multiple solutions. Every character development choice—every augmentation, every skill, every item—had to be useful in enough circumstances to be worthy of inclusion in the game. And the emergent game play possibilities were so broad we couldn't always predict what circumstances players would find themselves in! Balancing DX was the toughest challenge I've experienced."

STRANGER THAN FICTION?

"On DX, the 'coolest' thing would have to be the way various plot elements keep coming true. Seems like every time we turn around something we thought we were making up ends up being true. I mean, we started out with the idea that we'd use reality as our starting point for as much stuff as possible, but some of the more outlandish stuff is already coming true—be afraid... be very afraid..."
—Warren Spector

Age of Empires

An Epic Game of Empire-Building and Conquest

Age of Empires
composite screen.

adding the little touches to make each civilization in the game have different strengths, weaknesses, and styles.

At the same time, the artists involved with the project went to extraordinary lengths to develop a grittier and more realistic look, as opposed to the sterile, tiled effects seen in many of the other real-time strategy games of that era. Ensemble Studios, as the brothers were to name their development house, probably had more pictures of dirt and grass as reference photos than a forensic laboratory. Their artists overlaid their work onto these reference images, and if the art didn't look right against the realistic terrain, they went back to the drawing board.

The result of all the attention to detail was that Age of Empires rose above the noise of its competition.

Age of Mythology
(prerelease screen).

Age of Empires

Age of Empires appeared on the scene in the midst of the real-time strategy game glut. Nearly 50 new real-time strategy game titles clogged the channel during that era, and most of them were "more of the same" mediocre efforts where the player who could click the fastest would win. Rick Goodman (who later went on to create the massive Empire Earth for Sierra) and his brother Tony had a broader vision. Noticing how most other real-time strategy games tended to be extremely repetitive and didn't offer a great deal of variety in terms of their style of play, the Goodman brothers started working in 1995 on a game that would evolve with the players.

Since they envisioned the game as something of a faster-paced Sid Meier's Civilization and they knew Sid was working on his own new game, they recruited Sid's codesigner from Civilization and Railroad Tycoon, Bruce Shelley. Shelley joined the team and immediately began

Hitting in late 1997, it managed to ransack a number of Game of the Year awards, and the designers achieved the ultimate accolade from their peers—the knowledge that the playing of Age of Empires caused slippage on competitive products. Today, Ensemble Studios is still supporting releases of products like Age of Empires II: Age of Kings and the expansion pack, Age of Empires II: The Conquerors. The AOE engine was also used in Star Wars: Galactic Battlegrounds from LucasArts. In September 2002 Ensemble will release Age of Mythology, which uses a new 3D engine.

Age of Wonders

To some, Age of Wonders was a throwback to the ancient days of turn-based gaming, an aberration in the age of real-time strategy games. A fantasy game with the best elements of a Sid

Age of Wonders

Johnny's car sits atop a grassy knoll after a spinout during practice at Nurburgring.

Not only could cars go airborne in Grand Prix Legends, but they could flip upside down.

Meier's Civilization-style game (a global map that you gradually uncover by discovery and conquest), Master of Magic (a research tree for magical spells), and Fantasy General (tactical turn-based combat), Age of Wonders was a superb example of the "Just one more move, honey!" syndrome.

With two full campaigns, one for the good guys and one for the bad guys, players would usually end up playing all of the races in the game during the course of the campaigns. Another interesting feature of Age of Wonders was the idea of having a new population migrate into a conquered city. Migrations reduced the necessity of keeping large garrisons in the city to keep the conquered citizens in line.

Age of Wonders was one of those games that went through many hands and publishing relationships before it came to market, a symptom of the 90s. The developer was Triumph Studios, a group associated with Epic Megagames (makers of Unreal). The publisher was Mars Publishing, who in turn had a distribution deal with Gathering of Developers. By the time the game was being distributed, Gathering of Developers had been acquired by Take 2. So, in a very real sense, Age of Wonders was the quintessential end-of-the-decade game, a product that was touched by many hands and felt somewhat dated by the time it was released. Fortunately, it will spawn an Age of Wonders II by the time this book is printed, and the sequel looks as up-to-date as they come.

Grand Prix Legends

There is simply no automobile racing simulation in the history of computer games that is as faithful to its subject as Grand Prix Legends. Not only was GPL a dream come true for Dave Kaemmer, the genius behind it, but it was the apex of reality-based automobile simulations. Although the game was released in the latter part of the decade, Kaemmer opted for the nostalgia of 60s-era Formula I Grand Prix. He chose that era because the sophisticated technology and aerodynamics of the current period hadn't come into play. Cars could still become airborne, and more than one engine and chassis were competitive.

In addition to the bells and whistles of the VCR replays, the joy of seeing lost logos from a bygone era, the seven great models (Lotus, Brabham, Eagle, BRM, and three fantasy V-12s), and the sheer beauty of the graphics (perfectly modeled cars and lovingly re-created tracks), the entire driving experience of Grand Prix Legends was authentic. Kaemmer didn't just consider tire damage and how it affected the car. He figured in fuel consumption, individual tire pressure and damage, steering linearity and ratio, static ride height, as well as transmission and drive ratios. No matter what chassis you selected in GPL, you had all of these options and more to play with. Want to up the realism? GPL was the first simulation to truly simulate a clutch, using optional wheel and peddle controllers.

For many, it was so realistic and so difficult to drive that the sim didn't put up the kind of numbers in sales that Kaemmer and the Papyrus team had seen in multiple releases of IndyCar Racing and NASCAR Racing. For many of us, however, it was the high-water mark of racing simulations.

Jane's Combat Simulations

Look over the annual awards in the latter half of the 90s and you'll notice that, most of the time, the winners in the Simulation category are titles in the Jane's Combat

An F/A-18 pilot looks to his left to spot an approaching Mig 23 in Jane's F/A-18 Simulator.

In Jane's Fleet Command, carrier-based Hornets are intercepted on their way to bomb a secret Iraqi chemical plant.

Simulation series. There is a very good reason for this. Electronic Arts already dominated the Sports category and had experienced great success with the Chuck Yeager series of air combat games. In the early 90s, EA made a commitment to dominate in the Simulation category. In addition to Paul Grace, their in-house veteran designer and producer who had been working in this category since the earliest Yeager releases, EA went after Andy Hollis, the veteran designer and programmer from the MicroProse stable.

Not satisfied with celebrity designers, EA also went after celebrity specialists—the world's foremost research group for military information, Jane's Information Group, Ltd.

Andy Hollis had created his own simulation, Mig Alley Ace, contemporaneous with Sid Meier's Hellcat Ace in the formative years of MicroProse. In addition, Hollis had collaborated with Meier on a couple of versions of F-15 Strike Eagle and on F-19 Stealth Fighter. When Meier moved on to other interests, Hollis stuck with aviation. In 1993, he started work on an AH-64D Longbow simulation. In 1996, this became Jane's AH-64D Longbow, the first in an award-winning series. The beauty of the simulation, in addition to the awesome graphic presentation, was that a beginner could get in and experience instant action without the frustration of having to learn every possible system, while experts could spend hours upon hours mastering tactics and systems.

As the series expanded into Advanced Tactical Fighters, F-15, Longbow 2, Israeli Air Force, World War II Fighters, USAF, 688i Sub Hunter/Killer, and F/A-18 Simulator, this hallmark of easy entry mixed with a challenging growth path continued. One title, Jane's Fleet Command, offered such a realistic view of the modern world situation that its screens adorned network newscasts during more than one Middle Eastern crisis. Of all the titles in the series, Fleet Command was the only one that was more of a strategy game than a simulator; it was Harpoon taken up a notch.

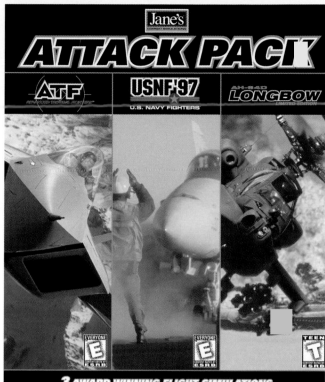

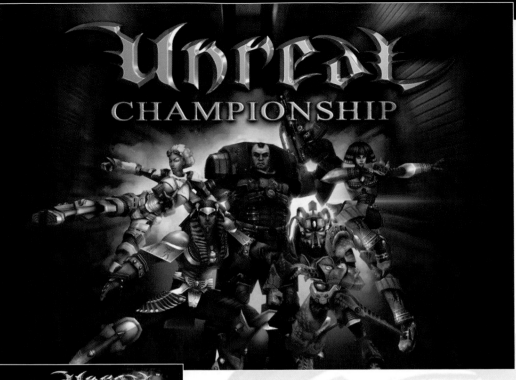

Canada, where they began working insane hours. Unable to come up with a name that satisfied the whole team, they ultimately called the game—and the underlying technology—Unreal. And, in many ways, it was.

When it was released by GT Interactive in 1998, Unreal had the hottest technology around and some of the best level design of any game to date. Its integrated engine and level editor (which was architected by Tim Sweeney and contributed to the great level design) were considered the best. The artificial intelligence, including Steve Polge's AI bots that let people practice death matches offline, further set the game apart. Unreal garnered a lot of attention from the press and quickly gained fans all over the world. Ultimately, several sequels, including Unreal II, Unreal Championship, and Unreal Tournament, continued to expand and improve the Unreal product line, and the Unreal engine has been licensed to other publishers to power their games as well.

Unreal®

In the early 90s, Epic Megagames (now known as Epic Games, Inc.) was a small company known for their Jazz Jackrabbit platform games and Extreme Pinball. No one would have suspected that they were only a few years away from creating a ground-breaking game technology.

The concept began with James Schmalz; he had an idea for something he thought of as a magic carpet game with robots. He showed the prototype to fellow designer Cliff Blezinski and Epic founder Tim Sweeney. There wasn't much to it, but everyone agreed it had promise.

Years went by, and the small group of developers literally spread all over the world, forming a virtual team of talented programmers, artists, and designers. For the last year of the project, they closeted themselves together in Waterloo,

Short Takes

Ishido

Next to Archon, Ishido is one of the finest original adaptations of a board game concept to the computer. This game of stones featured an innovative rule

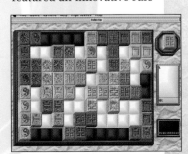

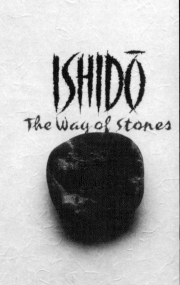

set, addictive play, and wonderful stone sets by Brodie Lockard (of Shanghai fame).

Duke Nukem 3D

When id Software released Doom, they not only started the first-person shooter phenomenon, but also were the acknowledged kings of the genre. However, Apogee's Duke Nukem 3D added some elements, especially a really cool character and lots of humor. Duke Nukem's world full of strippers, nightclubs, and weird aliens offered plenty of opportunities for interactive fun, and clearly distinguished itself from the moody quality of id's games. Not just an imitator, Duke blasted his own path, and a damn good path it was. Not to mention the jiggle factor.

Detroit

Impressions Software was a strategy game company that began with a business simulation where players could run their own software company. It was a crude effort that loaded from a cassette tape into a Spectrum or Amstrad, but it was successful enough to give David Lester (creator of Lords of the Realm I and II and Caesar I–III) his start in the PC games business. In spite of their best-selling historical games, Impressions never lost sight of the fact that it was a

PC Impressions' Detroit allowed you to play Henry Ford or Lee Iacocca as you tried to balance workers, tasks, costs, and opportunities. Most screens were combinations of graphics and pop-up menus like this.

real-life business simulation that got the company going. Air Bucks let you set everything about the airline business, from route through planes flown to seat configuration and on to marketing and fare calculations. Detroit accomplished the same thing for automobile manufacturing. Players tried to balance marketing, manufacturing, research, and safety needs against the dreaded monster called profitability.

Battlecruiser 3000 AD

Derek A. Smart had a vision for Battlecruiser 3000 AD. He wanted its entire universe to become so real that it would become more interesting than real life. He had such a clear vision that he fought his way through relationships with multiple publishers and is still supporting and selling the latest versions of his game on the Web. Players assume the role of commander of a starship that has a huge crew, each programmed with AI to have their own skills and individual agendas based on their crew assignment.

Hollywood Mogul

When Carey DeVuono sold his first script over the transom, he thought his dream had come true. After a few months of script meetings and a period in which his script went into the

When previewing the game, Johnny was privileged to have a working copy in which DeVuono had used the names of real actors and actresses. The game you can purchase doesn't have real people in it.

never-never land of "turn around," he decided to transform his hard-earned lessons about Hollywood into a marvelous strategy game. Although the game is written in simple Visual Basic with crude graphics and no on-screen action beyond text over blocky buildings and theaters, this is a marvelous little game that can still be purchased on the Web. Players become the head of a studio. They buy ready-made original scripts, rights to make scripts from literary blockbusters, or they order scripts to be written from their ideas. Would-be

moguls get to set budgets, film locations, and select everyone from producer to supporting actress, not to mention test-screening the films and determining the size and scale of the opening weekends. In short, everything you could want in a movie-making strategy game is here except a toolkit to make your own movies.

The 90s and Consolidation

Mergers and acquisitions are an inexorable fact of life in the business world. Entrepreneurial companies get gobbled up by big, diversified corporations after the original company outgrows the skills of the management team; small companies fall upon hard times during economic downturns and are purchased by companies with deep pockets to acquire their intellectual property, or a start-up company has to be sold in order for the venture capitalists to reap the harvest of the investments they seeded.

During the 80s, companies sprang up everywhere, like homesteaders staking their claim. But by the end of the 90s, many of these pioneers were gone, absorbed into much larger entities.

To be sure, big acquisitions had taken place before. For instance, in the 80s, Activision picked up Infocom and Gamestar for a song, and Sierra took over Dynamix and Cocktiel; but by 1996 Sierra itself had been sold to Cendant Corporation. In 1991, Electronic Arts picked up Distinctive Software and turned it into its money-making sports game machine called EA Canada, and in 1992 they acquired Origin Systems. Since then they have acquired Bullfrog Productions, Maxis, Westwood (from Virgin), Dreamworks (the game division), and Kesmai (the first online game provider in the U.S.). They distribute many other lines as well.

EA's acquisitions have been pretty straightforward compared to some. Take the story of Mindscape, which acquired Strategic

Simulations, Inc., then became Software Toolworks, which was ultimately purchased, along with Brøderbund, by The Learning Company. The Learning Company was then sold to Mattel, but massive losses ultimately caused Mattel to bail out, and the whole bundle went to French publisher Ubisoft.

In another complex series of transactions, Spectrum Holobyte bought MicroProse, but was then purchased by Hasbro, who already owned Avalon Hill. But Hasbro was unable to achieve the kinds of profits they expected, and they ultimately sold their game companies, along with the classic Atari license, to another French publisher, Infogrames.

Elsewhere, Sony acquired Psygnosis, and Sierra locked up deals to buy Blizzard Entertainment, Papyrus Software, and Impressions. 3DO acquired New World Computing. Microsoft acquired Access Software (the publisher of Links, the classic golf program that became Microsoft Golf). Then Microsoft turned to the online world and purchased VR-1 (Fighter Ace), before snapping up FASA (the paper game company who published Battletech, Shadowrun, and Crimson Skies) as soon as it hit the market. By the end of the decade, Microsoft had also purchased Ensemble (Age of Empires), Bungie (Myth), part of Oddworld (Munch's Oddysee), and Chris "Wing Commander" Roberts' Digital Anvil.

On the East Coast, GT Interactive (from the people who brought us Good Times Video and Good Times Food) decided that computer games could be marketed as easily as food and home video. They started on a profitable note with distribution of id Software's products (prior to being usurped by Activision), but ultimately their quest for the mass market was their undoing as the public tired of cheap versions of legacy software and multiple retreads of Deer Hunter. At first, the company tried to fill in the gaps by signing a deal with Epic Software for Unreal and purchasing Humongous Entertainment in order to get the Putt-Putt and Blue's Clues business. Humongous used the GT funds to fuel their Cavedog division and published a best-selling real-time strategy game called Total Annihilation. TA was an impressive hit for GT, but its sequel, TA: Kingdoms, was less successful, and GT eventually pulled the plug.

One more tale to tell—Take 2 Interactive. Founded by the son of a Manhattan real estate wheeler-dealer, Take 2 Interactive began with the acquisition of a small Pennsylvania developer/publisher called Paragon Software. Paragon had published a number of games in the 80s and served as an affiliate label for Electronic Arts before moving to MicroProse as their second-tier developer/publisher. Take 2 purchased Paragon and went on to publish some of the worst games ever. Hell: A Cyberpunk Thriller featured a cast of well-known actors but no play value whatsoever. Yet, the company eventually pulled itself together and created some interesting products, including Star Crusader, Ripper, and Black Dahlia, before purchasing war game specialty shop Talonsoft and the action specialists at GodGames and Rockstar.

With all this industry consolidation came a more businesslike approach to game development overall, but often at the cost of innovation. Companies with fresh perspectives and approaches had difficulty cracking the monolithic retail barrier established between huge corporate publishers and the retail chains, and it became tougher than ever for clever designers to get support for their projects. A new relationship in retail channels had arrived, in which MDF (Marketing Development Funds), end caps, shelving/stocking fees, and other costs became the established way of doing business. Shelf space diminished, and large retailers even got away with requiring game companies to reduce the size of their boxes to accommodate their shelf sizes. By the beginning of the new millennium, the face of game development and marketing had changed radically from its wild and wooly beginnings, and nobody can truly predict what it will become.

A Very Brief History of Online Gaming

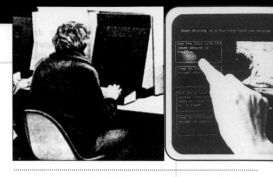

Images from the 1976 PLATO System Overview showing a typical PLATO workstation and touchscreen details.

Empire and Avatar on PLATO, much as they used to look.

Y ou could say it started with Sputnik and the Space Race of the 50s and 60s. The launch of the Soviet satellite in 1957 spurred the U.S. to create ARPA (Advanced Research Projects Agency). One ARPA agency, the Information Processing Techniques Office (IPTO), eventually created something called an Interface Messenger Processor. ARPAnet, the ancestor to the Internet, began with four IMP nodes at UCLA, UC Santa Barbara, Stanford Research Institute, and the University of Utah.

PLATO

The first real online community emerged from a system first conceived in 1960 by Don Bitzer, a professor and electrical engineer at the University of Illinois. Bitzer was trying to answer a question posed by one of his professors, who wondered about using computers for education. What evolved ultimately was a system called PLATO, which several years later was turned into the acronym "Programmed Logic for Automatic Teaching Operations" to satisfy journalists who wanted to know what it stood for.

The PLATO system, which eventually migrated to college campuses all over the country, was a true model of things to come. It included email, newsgroups, split screen chat, and, of course, online games. PLATO had a profound impact on the future history not only of games but of the Internet and the World Wide Web, as most of the early structures of online communities were first developed on PLATO systems.

Game designers such as Silas Warner (RobotWar, Castle Wolfenstein), Robert Woodhead and Andrew Greenberg (Wizardry), and Peter Langston (a non-PLATO version of Empire, early Lucasfilm Games) fondly remember the PLATO communities and the early inspirations they got from PLATO. The creative atmosphere of PLATO was wide open in all aspects. "We were craftsmen," says Silas Warner.

Another notable inspiration includes the game Airfight, which may have been the progenitor of what eventually became Microsoft Flight Simulator. "One of the central games on PLATO," remembers Warner, "was a huge space war simulation called Empire." But, according to David Woolley, one of the designers of the PLATO system, "The most popular game was called Avatar, which logged even more hours than Empire." He continues, "I think the very first PLATO game was written by Rick Blomme in the 1960s. It was Spacewar, a copy of the MIT game, and very simple graphically. As I recall, the spaceships were represented just by X and O characters that moved around the

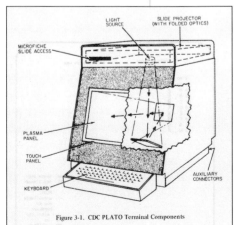

Figure 3-1. CDC PLATO Terminal Components

(Frame 5)

screen." Woolley wrote the second PLATO game, a horse racing game. "There would be three horses, represented by letters, which would race around an oval racetrack."

Originally run on funding from ARPA and the National Science Foundation, PLATO was ultimately sold to Control Data, but failed to remain prominent under their guidance.

If you want to learn more about this fascinating chapter in the history of online computing, check out Brian Dear's Web site at http://www.platopeople.com for information about his upcoming book—15 years in the making—on PLATO.

MUD

The first Multi-User Dungeon was created by Roy Trubshaw and Richard Bartle on the DEC-10 mainframe at Essex University in the U.K. By freely sharing their code, Trubshaw and Bartle ensured the proliferation of MUDs all across academia, and inspired another generation of game players and designers. The format of the MUD, which involves intense role-playing in a text environment, ultimately became the inspiration for later graphical online role-playing games such as Meridian 59 and Ultima Online. MUD itself (and its successor MUD II) is still around as the oldest, continuous running multiplayer game. You can play it at www.mud2.com.

Early Pay and Play

The early 80s marked a new era in online gaming when large companies realized they could charge money for users to access their mainframe computers during slack times at night. Such early systems included The Source (Dow-Jones), Compuserve (H&R Block), and Delphi (General Videotex). Users on these systems paid a premium during work hours, but a much reduced fee during the evening hours, plus each system also required a sign-up fee to join the service. Hourly

pricing ranged from $5 in the nonpeak hours to as high as $22.50 an hour.

All of the services offered an array of text-based games that had been bouncing around university and corporate systems for a while: Adventure, Blackjack, Football, Hangman, Lunar Lander, Maze, and Star Trek, among others. In addition, Compuserve and The Source offered Civil War, Hammurabi, and Wumpus, while Delphi offered Empire and Geowar. Compuserve, however, proved to be the more aggressive game provider. In 1982, John Taylor and Kelton Flinn started programming the MUD that would become Dungeons of Kesmai and Island of Kesmai and named their company Kesmai. In addition, Compuserve purchased a multiplayer space combat simulator (using ASCII characters only) called DECwars that Kesmai overhauled and relaunched as MegaWars I. Since this program was one of Compuserve's big money generators for years, it's interesting to note that Compuserve purchased full rights to the program for $50, an amount that would have been recouped as soon as the original maximum of 10 players played even one off-peak hour at the game.

BBSs

Gamers were willing to pony up fees that were exorbitant by today's standards, just for the experience of playing with other gamers all over the country. Of course, in a free market economy, other options soon appeared. The BBS, or Bulletin Board System, phenomenon was beginning to take shape. Individuals would run their own bulletin boards and invite others to play games by email, trade software (piracy was

Every week our subscribers take cheap shots at each other.

The GEnie™ service lets you take your best shots without shooting your budget. That's because our non-prime time rates are good and low. In fact, it's just $6 an hour for 1200 baud access.*

And that means more time for more fun and games. Exciting multi-player games like Air Warrior, Stellar Emperor, Orb Wars and Gemstone. Where you can test your skills against some of the best in the world.

Plus enjoy classics like chess, checkers, backgammon, black jack and Reversi. At rates so good you're sure to come out a winner.

And with GEnie signing up is as easy as one, two, three.

(1) Set your modem for local echo (half duplex), 300 or 1200 baud.

(2) Dial 1-800-638-8369. When you're connected, just enter HHH.

(3) At the U#= prompt simply enter XTX99637, GEnie thet RETURN.

And have a major credit card or your checking account number ready. For information in the U.S. or Canada, call 1-800-638-9636. Or write GE Information Services, 401 North Washington St., Rockville, MD 20850.

We bring good things to life.

*applies to A.E.I. Hrs. Fri. 6:00 A.M. and prime time all day Sat., Sun. and national holidays. Subject to service availability. Some services may be subject to a surcharge. Prices effective May 1, 1989.

Screens from Air Warrior.

rampant), or swap hints and reviews about commercial games. Usually, a BBS only cost the user the price of a telephone call, but some had membership fees. The trick was to find one near you.

Many of these bulletin board systems offered play-by-email or play-by–bulletin board versions of tabletop role-playing games like Traveller and Dungeons & Dragons. Others offered games like those on Compuserve, Delphi, and The Source. Dragon's Lair (in California) offered Nukewar and Lunar Lander; Big-Top Games (Wisconsin) had Civil War and Blackjack; Signature Software (California) offered Star Trek, Blackjack, and Othello; A.R.C.A.D.E. (Michigan) provided Civil War, Island Jumper, and Horse Race for its users; ARK-NET (Arkansas) had Centipede and Rubik's Cube on its boards; and Lethbridge (Canada) had B-1 Bomber to go along with Wumpus. Many systems had text versions of adventure games to add to their selection. Nessy (in Illinois) published a version of Adventure in Time and Queen of Phobos; Drucom (Pennsylvania) had King Tut and Atlantis; and Commnet-80 (Ohio) offered Isle, Dogstar, and CIA.

In addition, some BBS operators turned their hobbies into businesses. One entrepreneur was Harlow Stevens, Jr., who established The Mansion in Evanston, Illinois, to provide Medieval Conquest, 18 Wheeler, Cargo Master, GM Air Freight, Nuke Strike, Destination Midway, and Oil Baron. These multiplayer games stood alongside the standard play-by-email Diplomacy games appearing on virtually every system, and the email role-playing games.

Of lasting significance was the experience of Mark Jacobs. He established a system in 1984 that was dedicated to playing one game—a text-based role-playing game called

Aradath. Jacobs would eventually form AUSI and then Mythic Entertainment, creating almost a dozen online games over the years, including Online Diplomacy, Galaxy II, Godzilla Online, Independence Day Online, Silent Death, and his masterpiece, the critically acclaimed Dark Age of Camelot. Aradath began with eight phone lines and charged gamers a flat rate of $40 per month to stay in the game before it evolved into the popular Dragon's Gate MUD that is still played on the Internet.

1985: New Players

Bill Louden, the man who built the games business for Compuserve, found himself out of a job in 1985. He still loved games and was reputed to be addicted to Compuserve's Kesmai MUD, but he wanted more, while Compuserve's management seemed willing to settle for the status quo. Louden began to look for another opportunity and found the excess bandwidth waiting for him at the General Electric Information Service (GEIS), the corporate backbone of GE's worldwide interests.

The GEnie (General Electric Network for Information Exchange) system launched in October 1985. GEnie quickly became the serious venue for gamers, primarily because it offered free support accounts to any software company and to a plethora of celebrity designers and authors. GEnie also added programs over the years including MUDs like Simutronics' Gemstone (which still exists as Gemstone III), Alan Lenton's Federation (which still exists as Federation II), and Mark Jacobs' Dragon's Gate (still available on the Web via the Mythic Entertainment site). It added graphic simulation programs like Kesmai's Air Warrior (eventually to become Air Warrior III), Kesmai's Multi-Player BattleTech, and Simutronics' Cyberstrike (still available as Cyberstrike 2); and multiplayer play-by-email like Jim Dunnigan's Hundred Years

War (www.hyw.com) and AUSI's Diplomacy, among others.

Little did observers realize in 1985 that the "big dog" was coming. One month after the launch of GEnie, Quantum Computer Services launched the first of its services, QuantumLink. Q-Link supported only Commodore 64/128 computers and had a pricing structure that could net slightly more than the existing services. It cost $9.95 per month and $5.00 per hour. Q-Link was notable for two things: Habitat and its eventual identity as America OnLine (AOL), which has continued to provide online games ever since, although games form only a part of AOL's overall service.

Habitat

Habitat was a graphical MUD created by Lucasfilm Games. You could create graphical Avatars to represent your characters and input commands via the joystick (Go, Get, Put, Do, and Talk). New objects were constantly being brought into the environment, and the first graphic cyburb still exists in Japan via the Fujitsu network. For more information, see http://salesgroup.fujitsu.com/journal/232e/e32inter.html. Unfortunately, an attempt to bring it back to the U.S. in the late 90s was doomed to failure.

Despite the failure to bring Habitat to commercial success in the U.S., the legacy of Habitat is far-reaching. It was studied closely by other game designers and by academicians. The lessons it taught served as models for later attempts at online multiplayer gaming. For a seminal article on Habitat, check out this link, which is where we found the original screen image: http://www.stanford.edu/class/history34q/readings/Virtual_Worlds/LucasfilmHabitat.html.

Along with the original MUDs, Habitat can legitimately be regarded as one of the chief influences on later, more successful online role-playing games such as Ultima Online and EverQuest.

Big Blue Blues

If you've noticed a pattern in online opportunities to this point, it would have to be that companies with large amounts of unused bandwidth on their mainframes decided to put their assets to work. In 1984, two giants of the commercial world formed a joint venture. IBM and Sears Roebuck and Company created the Prodigy Network. Prodigy was originally designed with the mass market in mind and was based on the thinking—somewhat prematurely—that online advertising and online shopping were keys to the future. Like failed dotcomers on the Internet, the originators of Prodigy thought they could become the biggest thing since television by providing mass market audiences with short bursts of information (for some reason, every time we open a PowerPoint presentation, we think of Prodigy) and using banner ads to drive commerce.

Unfortunately for Prodigy, once you assumed that your audience had a computer and a modem, you were no longer talking about a mass market. Worse yet, the rigid manner in which information had to be presented on Prodigy worked against doing games with graphic front ends and simultaneous users.

Despite its inherent problems and nongaming direction, some interesting games appeared on the system. Rebel Space was a brilliant play-by-email space conquest game with minimal decorative graphics. It was designed by Beyond Software (Tony La Russa Baseball) and had two female system operators who kept the story interesting and matters lively. Business Simulator from Reality Technologies was designed by a Wall Street firm that understood serious business. It offered numerous decision points and spreadsheet presentations so you could compete against other virtual entrepreneurs as the CEO of your own fictitious company. Mad Maze was largely the creation of Greg

Original Habitat screen.

Screen from Fujitsu's Habitat II. (Courtesy of Fujitsu Limited).

The map/menu of TSN,
Sierra's early online service.

Scenes from Shadows of Yserbius.

Costiykan of board game design fame (The Creature Who
Ate Sheboygan, Paranoia). Mad Maze tried to present the
dungeon exploration experience in snapshots of action
and puzzles. Next President involved tens of thousands of
players in choosing fictitious candidates for president and
running detailed simulated campaigns. Although it was a
poll/survey-driven game, it was fascinating enough to run
successfully during two different presidential elections.
Baseball Manager was a classic fantasy sports league with
a twist. If you set a lineup, there was a statistical engine that
figured out how your game would evolve, even if a given
manager didn't play a member of your roster on a given day.
It was part simulation, part fantasy league.

The Jack Nicklaus Golf Tour was one of the boldest
experiments by Prodigy. You could download a unique golf
course and play one round offline. Then, you would upload a
check file on your results and the service would post the
"tour" results. Two great ideas never actually came to pass.
Stymied by Lucasfilm with regard to doing a campaign game
in the Star Wars universe where players would fight their
TIE fighters offline and upload the results with a check file,
Prodigy attempted to do the same thing with Secret Weapons
of the Luftwaffe. Unfortunately, both games ended up
grounded by dueling legal departments.

Peaks and Valleys

In the early 90s, two dedicated online game networks
appeared, neither of them tied to the excess bandwidth
of a major corporation. The Multi-Player Game Network
(MPGN) was a tremendously graphical network built around
a fantasy role-playing game called Drakkar (the first online
game to allow players the right to create guilds and have
guild clubhouses, hideouts, and so on) and the idea that
board game players would like to play board games online.

MPGN had some marvelous implementations of board
games, many overseen by Marc Miller (designer of the
Traveller role-playing game for Game Designers Workshop):
Operation Market-Garden (a two-player WWII game),
Empire Builder (one of the finest railroad strategy board
games ever made), Imperium (space conquest), and Minion
Hunter (brilliant implementation of a monster hunt game
that used the racetrack board à la Monopoly and simple
player statistics as in role-playing).

MPGN was something of a victim of its own success.
Financed by a wealthy financial angel, the company never
felt the pressure to make money until it was too late.
Further, Drakkar was so successful that it was difficult to
pull regulars out of Drakkar long enough to fill a game of
Junta (the multiplayer game of back-stabbing and intrigue
in a fictional banana republic) or any of the other strategy
games. Great games were overlooked on MPGN.

The Sierra Network (TSN) was the brainchild of Sierra
founder Ken Williams, who realized that the future of the
interactive entertainment business would be online. Rather
than purchasing huge mainframes, Sierra built their network
around a patchwork quilt of PCs. TSN was a real network, not
a time-sharing service. It started with a graphical interface
that allowed you to create a Habitat-style avatar, divided the
games up into "lands," as though the network were a theme
park, and offered a mixture of common games (backgammon,
card and gambling games), a children's area, and premium
games (a golf game for four players, but missing a chat
feature), a popular area called Larryland (after Leisure Suit
Larry), and Shadows of Yserbius. Yserbius was TSN's big game.

Shadows of Yserbius was overseen by a fellow named Joe
Ybarra, and it was the first graphical online fantasy role-playing game to allow multiple players to join together in parties.
The game was compelling, both because of its interesting
quest-based design and because of the new experience of

adventuring with other players in a graphical world. Although MUD players might have seen it as nothing new, its graphical environment introduced many new fans to online multiplayer gaming, and many TSN subscribers joined the service strictly to play Yserbius and never went anywhere else.

TSN ultimately became the ImagiNation Network (INN), was sold to AT&T, and closed up shop when AT&T decided not to continue with an ambitious cyberworld project under way at the time.

Changes and Experiments

In the mid-90s, the online world changed radically. The main online services, such as AOL, Compuserve, and Prodigy, were still the main destinations for online gamers, but their dominance was about to end. First, the World Wide Web was born, and subsequently Netscape made it available to just about anyone with a modem and a mouse. Then id Software came out with Doom and made it possible to play on direct modem and LAN connections. The clamor for Web-based death matches was deafening, and it was only a matter of time before "death match" became the home user's arcade game of choice. Meanwhile, Blizzard was inventing Battle.net and introducing players to online games. Soon, Quake was creating an online obsession at home and in workplaces all over the world.

Taking another direction, experiments in graphical role-playing games started to appear. Sierra's Oakhurst Studios began to beta-test The Realm, which replaced INN as their online endeavor of the future. Elsewhere, in their parents' garage, Andrew and Christopher Kirmse were assembling a virtual team of developers to create their online brainchild, Meridian 59, which was ultimately purchased and released by 3DO. Both games were similar in many ways to games that came later, such as Asheron's Call and EverQuest, and

featured lots of hack 'n' slash role-playing combined with social interaction. In many ways, The Realm and Meridian 59 were both early attempts at making graphical MUDs. But they were just a little before their time. More than one developer has lamented the role of pioneer: "They're the ones who get all the arrows in the back." Although The Realm never made it out of beta, Meridian 59 did release publicly, and attracted many initial fans. But Meridian 59's intense player versus player gaming did not appeal to the mass market, and, in any case, the game suffered from the "arrows in the back" syndrome. Ultimately, 3DO closed down the servers. (However, the game is being revived. For more information, check out http://meridian59.neardeathstudios.com.)

Ultima Online booth at E3.

Ultima Online

Around the time that Meridian 59 was in its inception phase, Starr Long was working with Richard Garriott on Ultima IX. But around the end of 1994 or so, his attention was pulled toward a new idea inspired by the emergence of the World Wide Web. "We looked at every online game we could find — INN, Air Warrior. We realized that we had to get in right now… this is the next thing," says Long. Garriott agreed, and told Long and his group to make a prototype. Two weeks later, they had a game, which could support up to 50 players. There wasn't much action, only a sort of scavenger game based on Ultima V graphics. But the seed was there.

Origin's budget didn't have room for another project at the time, so they approached Larry Probst, who was the head of Electronic Arts at the time, and Probst granted them $250,000 to begin work on the project.

Ultima Online was a different sort of game than any others that had been seen. It was based around Richard Garriott's desire to create complete worlds, and included a

Screens from the original UO and Ultima Online: The Third Dawn.

Asheron's Call: Dark Majesty

Asheron's Call—original version.

EverQuest: Scars of Velious

lot of noncombat skills. "It's all in the details," says Long. "A lot of our inspiration came from the infamous 'baking bread' in Ultima VII."

In the end, Ultima Online was the first of several commercially successful massive multiplayer online games. With its deep skill system and detailed world, based on the Ultima series, it has created a dedicated group of players.

Asheron's Call

By the time Ultima Online was released, other groups around the country were already working on massive multiplayer games, each with unique ideas. One group was originally called Second Nature, then Turbine Entertainment. This group, some of whom had never created a commercial game before, began work back in 1995 on a game called Asheron's Call, which was finally released in 1999, just after the debut of Sony's EverQuest.

Among the key features in Asheron's Call was a method of sharing experience and encouraging group cooperative play. Previous games, such as Ultima Online and Meridian 59, had been notorious for the predominance of player killing, which many game players found too adversarial, and which sometimes created frustration for new players. Asheron's Call attempted to change the focus from player killing to monster killing and group social dynamics. During the game's development, Microsoft became the publisher and released Asheron's Call successfully as a premium service on the Microsoft Gaming Zone.

EverQuest

At nearly the same time that Microsoft released Asheron's Call, Sony Online Entertainment came out with EverQuest, another massive multiplayer role-playing game, set in a

D&D-like fantasy world. EverQuest was instantly successful and quickly rose to the top of the heap, featuring excellent graphics and imaginative play.

Dark Age of Camelot

Late in 2001, Mythic Entertainment, which had been running text-based online games for more than 15 years and had also done a couple of graphic multiplayer games, came out with their most ambitious game to date. Set in three

Dark Age of Camelot screen.

"realms"—an Arthurian Albion, the Norse-inspired Midgard, and the Celtic-based Hibernia—DAoC has introduced another rich online experience, and has further refined the concepts of player versus player by setting up areas where players from different realms may engage in combat. Although conceptually similar to Asheron's Call and EverQuest, DAoC introduces some new ideas and well-conceived game design to the genre.

Electronic Arts Motor City Online is dedicated to the virtual driver in all of us.

THE FUTURE OF ONLINE GAMING

Myst fans are looking forward to the 2003 release of Parable, Cyan's massive multiplayer world. And millions are expected to flock to Star Wars Galaxies, which is being produced for LucasArts by Verant, the creators of EverQuest. Here are a couple of screen images to whet your imagination.

Background and below: Star Wars Galaxies (prerelease screens).

Cyan's Parable (pre-release screen).

1999

Dreamcast

In 1999, Sega introduced certainly their finest machine of all—the Dreamcast. Although Sega of America had been working on a different machine (code-named Black Belt), Dreamcast was designed by Sega of Japan (originally code-named Dural, later Katana). This excellent 128-bit machine was far superior technically to the PlayStation and N64. It could render 3D graphics at amazing speeds, and it boasted a built-in 56K modem, optional keyboard and mouse, and quite a few innovative features. To support the online capabilities of the system, Sega launched SegaNet, an online gaming network.

At first, Sega's strategy seemed to work, and they quickly sold a million units in their launch. However, despite Dreamcast's technical superiority, and the excellence of its games, it was still up against the PlayStation and N64.

Sega's reputation was working against them. Many potential Dreamcast owners had written Sega off by this time, having endured several failures. Sega had slipped from the second spot to the unhealthy third spot. Even their Sonic Adventure, a direct answer to Nintendo's 3D Mario64, wasn't a strong enough title, though it had many fascinating features, including the use of the Tamagotchi-like memory card to incubate eggs for little pet creatures. Despite some good action segments, Sonic Adventure seemed not to catch on with players in nearly the way that Mario64 had done. Even their strong arcade conversions and their strong support of online gaming, with games like NFL2K and Phantasy Star Online (not to mention an excellent lineup of third-party games like Quake III), couldn't unseat PlayStation.

Sonic Adventure *(Sega)*

Sonic Adventure 2 *(Sega)*

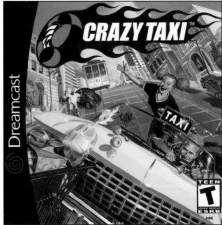

History will tell if this was Sega's last console system, but for the moment, it would seem so.

Also in 1999, Sony released specifications for its upcoming PlayStation 2 product, while Nintendo kept mostly mum about a system code-named Dolphin, and Microsoft, the 800-pound gorilla of the office software market, announced its intention to enter the home console market with something called Xbox. For gamers, the 21st century promised a whole new round of technological improvements and gaming mayhem.

Skies of Arcadia *(Sega)*

Crazy Taxi 2 *(Sega)*

Deadly Skies *(Konami)*

Capcom vs. SNK *(Capcom)*

Crazy Taxi *(Sega)*

Mr. Diller *(Namco)*

Phantasy Star Online *(Sega)*

Chu Chu Rocket *(Sega)*

Jet Grind Radio *(Sega)*

Power Stone *(Capcom)*

Gunbird 2 *(Capcom)*

Grandia *(Game Arts)*

Resident Evil *(Capcom)*

Soul Caliber *(Namco)*

Virtua Tennis *(Sega)*

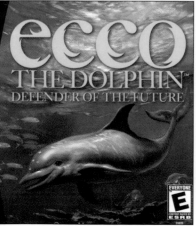

TAMAGOTCHI

Invented in 1996 by Japanese housewife Aki Maita (who was seeking a pet that was easy to care for), the Tamagotchi virtual pet was originally distributed in Japan by Bandai. This little egg-shaped electronic device quickly became an obsession, and when released throughout the rest of the world, it launched a whole new era of electronic toys, as well as many imitators (including Tiger Electronics' Giga Pets).

The concept behind Tamagotchi was that within the egg-shaped container there resided a cute little alien creature that required your care. It required food, cleaning, play, and sleep. If neglected, the creature would become cranky or ill, and if totally neglected, it would die. Amazingly, millions of Tamagotchis were sold, and people took them quite seriously. It wasn't uncommon for people to bring them to work to be sure to take good care of them. Ironically, at about the time that Tamagotchi hit, Sega and Bandai were discussing a merger, but that fell through, possibly because with the success of their cyberpets, Bandai no longer needed Sega.

Jak & Daxter

2000

PlayStation 2

The sequel to Sony's PlayStation was well worth the wait. This powerful system set the standard for console makers to match, and its ability to play DVD movies added to its mass market appeal. On these pages are screens from just a few of the many phenomenal PlayStation 2 games.

Maximo *(Capcom)*

Spy Hunter *(Midway)*

Grand Theft Auto 3 *(Rockstar)*

Metal Gear Solid 2 *(Konami)*

Silent Hill 2 *(Konami)*

Star Wars Starfighter
(LucasArts)

Madden Football 2002 *(EA)*

March Madness 2002 *(EA)*

ICO *(Sony)*

Jak and Daxter
(Sony/Naughty Dog)

Gran Turismo 3 *(Sony)*

NBA Street *(EA)*

Quake III Revolution *(EA)*

007 Agent Under Fire *(EA)*

Wizardry *(Atlus)*

Knockout Kings *(EA)*

Dead to Rights *(Namco)*

Midnight Club *(Rockstar)*

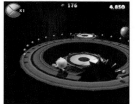
Pac-Man World 2 *(Namco)*

Unreal Tournament
(Epic Games)

Heroes of Might & Magic *(3DO)*

Super Bust-A-Move
(Taito/Acclaim)

Mortal Kombat *(Acclaim)*

Ready to Rumble

Dead or Alive: Hardcore
(Tecmo)

State of Emergency *(Rockstar)*

Street Fighter 3 Ex *(Capcom)*

Tekken Tag Tournament
(Namco)

Ridge Racer *(Namco)*

2001

Game Boy Advance and GameCube

As far back as 1996, Nintendo had plans for a new generation color handheld device code-named "Atlantis." However, development of the system was on again, off again. Several generations of Game Boy did come out, including Game Boy Pocket, Game Boy Light (a backlit Game Boy available in Japan), and Game Boy Color, which, ten years after the product's original introduction, finally brought color to the system. However, it wasn't until 2001 that Atlantis, now called Game Boy Advance, was released.

GameCube

First announced in 1999 and code-named "Dolphin," Nintendo finally released GameCube in time for Christmas 2001, almost simultaneous with the release of Xbox. Despite many rumors and products that were never released, GameCube is the first disk-based system from Nintendo, but it does not use the customary CD-ROM disks, or even the up-and-coming DVD format. Nintendo's disks are small optical minidisks. The system's quality and power are demonstrated by the screenshots from early GameCube releases shown on these pages.

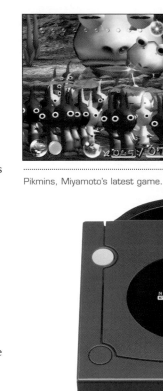

Pikmins, Miyamoto's latest game.

Game Boy Advance games

Mario Kart Advance *(Nintendo)*

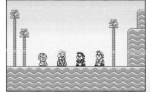

Super Mario Advance *(Nintendo)*

Breath of Fire *(Capcom)*

Frogger's Adventure GBA *(Konami)*

Madden 2002 GBA *(EA)*

GameCube games

Super Smash Bros *(Nintendo)*

SSX Tricky *(EA)*

Madden 2002 *(EA)*

Crazy Taxi *(Acclaim)*

Spy Hunter *(Midway)*

Xg3 Extreme G Racing *(Acclaim)*

Smashing Drive *(Namco)*

Xbox

Microsoft has had a hand in gaming since the early 80s, when they began publishing Microsoft Flight Simulator. However, they were not a major force in games for most of the intervening years. In the late 90s, they began to get serious about games, and released several strong titles, including Age of Empires and Asheron's Call on the Microsoft Gaming Zone.

In 2001, they released Xbox, and instantly became a serious player in the electronic game industry. When released, Xbox was a technologically advanced system that used Microsoft's proprietary Windows technologies, and, unlike any other game system, included a built-in hard drive.

On these pages are screens from some of the first Xbox titles.

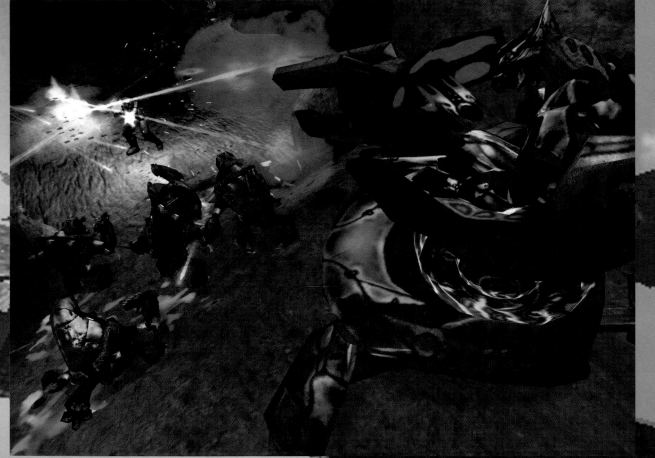

Halo *(Bungie/Microsoft)*

Blood Wake
(Stormfront Studios/Microsoft)

Fuzion Frenzy
(Blitz Games/Microsoft)

Azurik: Rise of Perathia
(Adrenium Games/Microsoft)

Project Gotham Racing
(Bizarre Creations/Microsoft)

NBA Inside Drive 2002
(High Voltage/Microsoft)

Madden NFL 2002 *(Electronic Arts)*

NFL Fever 2002 *(Microsoft)*

Amped: Freestyle Snowboarding *(Microsoft)*

BONELESS + MUTE BACKFLIP
4750 x2

Tony Hawk's Pro Skater 2x *(Activision)*

Final Word

Is this the end? Hardly. With a great three-way race between Sony, Nintendo, and Microsoft in the console market just heating up, and with amazing PC simulations, adventures, sports, and action games like you've never seen before just hitting the street, the future promises to be spectacular. The story of electronic games is just beginning.

And so we look toward the future. What amazing new technologies will arise, creating ever greater realism? What new directions will games take that we never dreamed of before? Who will take the lead as the game developers of tomorrow? What will online and wireless gaming, which are still in their infancies, eventually evolve into? More and more, we are eliminating technology as a barrier to game creation. If you can imagine it, you can probably do it. If not today, then soon.

But the barrier to entry is high, and getting higher. What once cost a few hundred or a few thousand dollars to create now costs in the millions. What once could be done by one person working alone in a garage or spare bedroom now requires teams of highly skilled experts. The era of the lone visionary designing hit games at his or her kitchen table is probably gone forever. The new generation of visionaries has to be able to attract funding, guide teams of developers, and market their product successfully to the major retail chains.

You can riffle the pages of this book and see the astounding evolution of electronic games play out before your eyes. From the crudest images of the earliest games to today's movielike immersive adventures, one thing remains true: Games are all about fun. Whether the protagonist is a blip on the screen, a slice of dot-eating pizza, or a fantastic fantasy hero or heroine whose every muscle is rendered with 3D technology and inverse kinematics, the common factor is the imagination of the person behind the controls.

Without you, it doesn't work.

Credits

All products and characters mentioned in this book are trademarks of their respective owners. The use of images in this book does not imply ownership or any other claim by The McGraw-Hill Companies.

3DO: Box cover artwork and in-game images from the Might and Magic® and Heroes of Might and Magic® product series, and other New World Computing products, are provided courtesy of The 3DO Company. New World Computing is a division of The 3DO Company. All Rights Reserved.

Activision® games and images are the property of Activision, Inc. Photos of the Activision organization, party pictures, Family Tree, Fortune picture, and newspaper ad provided courtesy of Jim Levy. Neither the text nor the materials presented in this book have been reviewed or approved by Activision.

Apple images provided courtesy of Apple Computer, Inc.

Archon™, Archon II: Adept™, Murder on the Zinderneuf™ are properties of Free Fall Games. Images from Archon™, Archon Ultra™, and Murder on the Zinderneuf™ provided courtesy of Free Fall Games. Original George Barr Archon Ultra art used with permission.

AT&T: Photographs of transistor developers and the first transistor provided by and property of AT&T Archives. Reprinted with permission of AT&T.

Blizzard Entertainment®: Box cover, cinematic, and in-game images from Diablo®, Diablo® II, Diablo® II: Lord of Destruction™, StarCraft Diablo®, StarCraft®: Brood War™, Warcraft®, Warcraft® II, and Warcraft® II: Beyond the Dark Portal™ courtesy of Blizzard Entertainment®.

Brian Moriarty photo courtesy of Brian Moriarty.

Brøderbund material and photos provided courtesy of the private archives of Doug Carlston. Software © Brøderbund Properties LLC, and its licensors. All rights reserved. Some product names are either trademarks or registered trademarks of Brøderbund Properties LLC.

All other trademarks or copyrights are the property of their respective owners.

CAPCOM and STREET FIGHTER II are registered trademarks of Capcom Company, Ltd.

Cinemaware: Copyright© 2002 Cinemaware, Inc. Cinemaware, the Cinemaware logo, Heroes Are Forever and Cinematech are trademarks of Cinemaware, Inc. Defender of the Crown, S.D.I., The King of Chicago, Sinbad and the Throne of the Falcon, Rocket Ranger, Lords of the Rising Sun, It Came From the Desert, Antheads: It Came From the Desert II, Wings, and TV Sports are trademarks of Cinemaware, Inc. All Rights Reserved.

Cyan® images of Myst, Riven, Cosmic Osmo, Manhole, Spelunx, and Parable provided courtesy of Cyan Worlds, Inc. Myst is a registered trademark of Cyan, Inc., under license to Ubi Soft Entertainment S.A.

Dragon's Lair art property of Bluth Group and Don Bluth, licensed to Dragon's Lair LLC. Used by permission. ©1983 Bluth Group, Ltd. Dirk the Daring and Singe are part of Dragon's Lair 3D action figure series one. The figure line was sculpted by Sculpt This, licensed and produced by AnJon Inc.

Eidos games and images are the property of Eidos Interactive Ltd. Tomb Raider/ Laura Croft cover image provided courtesy of Eidos Interactive. The Horde™, The Unholy War™, and Pandemonium™ are properties of Crystal Dynamics, Inc.

Electronic Arts games and images are the property of Electronic Arts. Electronic Arts, EA Sports, Origin, Bullfrog, Maxis, Westwood Studios, and all associated logos are trademarks, registered trademarks or service marks of Electronic Arts Inc. in the U.S. and/or other countries. Neither the text nor the materials presented in this book have been reviewed or approved by Electronic Arts. Photos supplied by Trip Hawkins, Richard Garriot, and Jeff Braun used with permission.

Epic Games: Unreal® images provided courtesy of Epic Games Inc. Unreal is a registered trademark of Epic Games Inc. Used with permission, all rights reserved.

Historical photographs provided by IBM Corporate Archives. Reprinted with permission of IBM.

Historical photographs provided by Intel Corporation. Reprinted with permission of Intel.

AUSTRALIA
McGraw-Hill Book Company Australia Pty. Ltd.
TEL +61-2-9417-9899
FAX +61-2-9417-5687
http://www.mcgraw-hill.com.au
books-it_sydney@mcgraw-hill.com

CANADA
McGraw-Hill Ryerson Ltd.
TEL +905-430-5000
FAX +905-430-5020
http://www.mcgrawhill.ca

GREECE, MIDDLE EAST, & AFRICA
(excluding South Africa)
McGraw-Hill Hellas
TEL +30-1-656-0990-3-4
FAX +30-1-654-5525

MEXICO (Also serving Latin America)
McGraw-Hill Interamericana Editores S.A. de C.V.
TEL +525-117-1583
FAX +525-117-1589
http://www.mcgraw-hill.com.mx
fernando_castellanos@mcgraw-hill.com

SINGAPORE (Serving Asia)
McGraw-Hill Book Company
TEL +65-863-1580
FAX +65-862-3354
http://www.mcgraw-hill.com.sg
mghasia@mcgraw-hill.com

SOUTH AFRICA
McGraw-Hill South Africa
TEL +27-11-622-7512
FAX +27-11-622-9045
robyn_swanepoel@mcgraw-hill.com

SPAIN
McGraw-Hill/Interamericana de España, S.A.U.
TEL +34-91-180-3000
FAX +34-91-372-8513
http://www.mcgraw-hill.es
professional@mcgraw-hill.es

UNITED KINGDOM, NORTHERN, EASTERN,
& CENTRAL EUROPE
McGraw-Hill Publishing Company
TEL +44-1-628-502500
FAX +44-1-628-770224
http://www.mcgraw-hill.co.uk
computing_neurope@mcgraw-hill.com

ALL OTHER INQUIRIES Contact:
Osborne/McGraw-Hill
TEL +1-510-549-6600
FAX +1-510-883-7600
http://www.osborne.com
omg_international@mcgraw-hill.com